The Prose Writings of Robert Louis Stevenson

The Prose Writings of Robert Louis Stevenson

A Guide

by

Roger G. Swearingen

First published in the USA 1980
First published in the UK 1980

Published by
THE MACMILLAN PRESS LTD
London and Basingstoke
Associated companies in Delhi
Dublin Hong Kong Johannesburg Lagos
Melbourne New York Singapore Tokyo

Printed in the USA
by Cushing-Malloy, Inc., Ann Arbor, MI.

British Library Cataloguing in Publication Data

Swearingen, Roger G.
The prose writings of Robert Louis Stevenson
1. Stevenson, Robert Louis — Bibliography
I. Title
016.828'8'08 Z8843

ISBN 0-333-27652-3

CONTENTS

1850s

1860-65

1866

1860s

1870

1871

1872

1873

1874

1875

1876

1877

1878

1879

1880

1881

1882

1883

1884

1885

1886

1887

1888

1889

1890

1891

1892

1893

1894

ADDITIONAL WORKS

PREFACE

This work offers a complete chronological list of the writings of Robert Louis Stevenson, excluding only his poems. It derives in part from my doctoral dissertation for Yale University, "The Early Literary Career of Robert Louis Stevenson, 1850-1881: A Bibliographical Study" (1970), and the corrected condensation of that work published in *Studies in Scottish Literature* (January-April 1974). But this is mostly a new compilation, covering as it now does Stevenson's entire literary career and presenting this earlier material in newly revised and, in some instances, newly corrected form. It is based primarily but by no means exclusively upon materials in the Edwin J. Beinecke Robert Louis Stevenson Collection at Yale University.

Entered below in chronological order of their composition are the more than three hundred and fifty prose works which Stevenson can be shown to have written, dictated, contemplated, or planned from earliest childhood through his death in 1894. The entries are not limited to works which were actually completed or even published during Stevenson's lifetime, nor are they segregated according to the form—book, periodical, pamphlet—in which a work appeared originally, if it was published. My aim has been to give the most complete picture possible of Stevenson's actual literary activity as his career progressed—not, or not only, a list of his publications in order of their appearance. Readers interested only in bibliographical information of this sort should consult, besides the present compilation, W.F. Prideaux, *A Bibliography of the Works of Robert Louis Stevenson*, 2nd ed. (1917), and the published catalogues of the Beinecke Collection at Yale (6 vols., 1951-64), of the

Widener Collection at Harvard (1913), and of the Stevenson materials now in the Princeton University Library (1971).

Each entry below supplies, insofar as is known or is applicable, the following information: (1) the title of the work, all titles except those in square brackets being Stevenson's own; (2) the date of its composition; (3) the location of all manuscripts of the work, including outlines, drafts, notes, proofs, and source materials; (4) the place and date of its first publication, if published; (5) the details of its first appearance in book form if it appeared in this form during Stevenson's lifetime; (6) the volume in the Tusitala Edition of Stevenson's works (35 vols., 1924) in which a text of the work may be found if it is available; and (7) additional notes, sometimes extensive ones, giving the history of the work's composition, revision, publication, and sources.

All titles except those in square brackets are Stevenson's own, and all works appear under their original titles even when, as sometimes occurred, they were given new titles when they were collected. "The Suicide Club" and "The Rajah's Diamond," for example, first appeared under the general title "Latter-Day Arabian Nights," and they are so entered here. Not until they were republished did they become the *New Arabian Nights*. Stevenson's essay on San Francisco, "A Modern Cosmopolis," never reprinted during his lifetime, first appeared together with his essay on Monterey in the Edinburgh Edition (1895), where for the first time the two essays were titled jointly "The Old and New Pacific Captials." Both are entered under their original titles here. But in these and all other such instances works appear under *all* of their various titles in the general index at the end of this volume.

The dates given for each work represent as precisely as possible the date of the actual composition of the work or, if it was never written or left unfinished, the date when Stevenson's attention appears first to have been significantly engaged by it. When Stevenson worked, as he often did, on several pieces at the same time, the entries are arranged chronologically according to the date on which Stevenson appears actually to have begun working on each piece even though it may have taken him some time to complete it or other works were written in the meantime. "The Pavilion on the Links" thus appears under the date of November 1878, when Stevenson began it, even though it was not finished until a year later and was not published until almost another year after that. *The Ebb-Tide*, in the same manner, appears under the date of its final writing by Stevenson, February to early June 1893, even though it was begun by Lloyd Osbourne in Honolulu in 1889 and even as a serial was not published until the very end of 1893. Cross-reference is made within the main body of the compilation whenever Stevenson did significant work on a piece entered elsewhere. And, of course, all works are listed in the general index.

Manuscripts and other materials in the Edwin J. Beinecke Robert Louis Stevenson Collection at Yale University are identified by location as "Yale"; in the Henry E. Huntington Library, San Marino, California, as "Huntington"; in the National Library of Scotland, Edinburgh, as "NLS." Manuscripts in other collections are identified more fully, at the point of citation. Untraced manuscripts which have appeared at auction are cited by the consignor's name, the year date of the auction, and the lot number, except for the large number of manuscripts and other materials consigned by Stevenson's stepdaughter Mrs. Isobel Field to the Anderson Auction Company, New York, for a three-part sale in 1914. These are identified as, for example, "Anderson 1914, II, 000," giving part and lot number but omitting Mrs. Field's name as consignor. Copies of all of the auction catalogues to which reference is made are in the Beinecke Collection and are listed in part 8 of the catalogue of that collection.

Letters refers to the collection of Stevenson's letters which comprises volumes 31-35 of the Tusitala Edition of his works (1924). *Baxter Letters* refers to *RLS: Stevenson's Letters to Charles Baxter*, ed. DeLancey Ferguson and Marshall Waingrow (1956). Balfour, *Life*, refers to the London edition of Graham Balfour's *The Life of Robert Louis Stevenson*, 2 vols. (1901). Beinecke 0000 identifies an item in the Edwin J. Beinecke Robert Louis Stevenson Collection, Yale University, described under that number in the catalogue, *A Stevenson Library: Catalogue of a Collection of Writings by and about Robert Louis Stevenson Formed by Edwin J. Beinecke*, compiled by George L. McKay, 6 vols. (1951-64). Stevenson materials in the Widener Collection, Harvard University, are described in the catalogue of that collection, *A Catalogue of Books and Manuscripts of Robert Louis Stevenson in the Library of the Late Harry Elkins Widener* (1913). Stevenson materials in the Princeton University Library are described in *Robert Louis Stevenson: A Catalogue*, compiled by Alexander D. Wainwright (1971).

At the end of the main body of the compilation appears a group of works, chiefly unpublished manuscripts, for which no date can be assigned with any great confidence. These appear together as "Additional Works," arranged in what would appear to be their actual chronological order. Information relevant to the date or contents of these works is given in each entry, but owing to the great uncertainty as to their actual dates they have been left out of the main chronological sequence.

My debts are many, but above all I must mention the inspired and intelligent collecting of the late Edwin J. Beinecke. His generosity brought into being the collection at Yale University which now bears his name—only one of his many benefactions to Yale—and without it this study, dependent as it so often is upon unpublished, scarce and little-known materials and sources of information, would hardly have been begun. George L. McKay's catalogue of the Beinecke Collection has been a constant source of information as well as of access to the materials themselves. Students and scholars by the thousands have reason to thank Marjorie G. Wynne and her staff at the Beinecke Rare Book and Manuscript Library, Yale University, and it is a pleasure to be among them. Professor A. Dwight Culler has looked after this work (and its author) continuously during the many years since it was begun as a dissertation at Yale under his direction.

Ernest and Joyce Mehew have personally contributed more than can readily be said to every entry in this compilation, sharing with patience and good humor their unparalleled knowledge of every aspect of Stevenson's life and career. Miss Ellen Shaffer and Mr. Norman H. Strouse have made the Silverado Museum, St. Helena, California, a home away from home for all Stevensonians, and not least for the present one.

I must also thank for their assistance and generosity all of the following persons and institutions: Alan Bell, Department of Manuscripts, National Library of Scotland; George Young and Robin Hill, City Museums Department, Edinburgh Corporation; C. S. Minto, City Librarian, and the staff of the Edinburgh Public Library; Robin Picton-Phillipps, Richard Burns, and their colleagues in the Speculative Society, University of Edinburgh; Professor Alastair Fowler, Peter Keating, Valerie Shaw, and Ian Campbell in the Department of English Literature, University of Edinburgh; F. W. Robertson, County Librarian, Caithness; Waverley B. Cameron, Edinburgh, for access to a letter by Stevenson in his own collection; J. H. Matthews, Dean and Son, publishers, London; and above all David Burns and Kathleen and John Macfie in Edinburgh. In the United States, I have been helped especially by Eleanor Nicholes and Marte Shaw, Houghton Library, Harvard University; Alexander D. Wainwright, Princeton University Library; Mrs. Evelyn Semler, Pierpont Morgan Library, New York; Frank Halpern, Free Library of Philadelphia; Virginia Renner, Huntington Library, San Marino, California; James T. Forrest, director, Bradford Brinton Memorial Ranch, Wyoming; by the staffs of the New York Public Library, the

Haverford College Library, the Bancroft Library, University of California, Berkeley, and the San Francisco Public Library; and by the curators of the Stevenson collections at Saranac Lake, New York, and Monterey, California. To Robert W. Reese in Monterey I am especially indebted for his making available a complete xerox copy of Stevenson's mother's scrapbooks now in the Stevenson House Collection. I must also thank Paul Fry, New Haven, Connecticut; Susan C. Fox, New York; Agnes Mitsunaga Tshua, Honolulu; Graham Good, University of British Columbia; and Professor James D. Hart, University of California, Berkeley. Professor G. Ross Roy, editor of *Studies in Scottish Literature*, first encouraged me by publishing an earlier version of part of this work. He has been a constant source of encouragement since, and I am grateful to him also for permission to make use of the earlier material published first in his journal. My wife, Sarah, has been a help at all times in the completion of this work, and there are no words adequate to describe her contribution.

Permission to quote from unpublished manuscripts and letters by Stevenson has been kindly granted by Alan Osbourne and the various libraries where these materials are now held: the Beinecke Rare Book and Manuscript Library, Yale University, the Huntington Library, the Pierpont Morgan Library, and the Silverado Museum, St. Helena, California. To the American Council of Learned Societies I am indebted for a Grant-in-Aid which materially aided my research during its closing stages.

Roger G. Swearingen
San Francisco
January 1980

1850s

[Stories dictated to Alison Cunningham.] Before 13 November 1854. MSS destroyed. Unpublished. See E. B. Simpson, *Robert Louis Stevenson's Edinburgh Days* (1913), p. 106.

THE HISTORY OF MOSES. November-December 1856. MS, Chrysler, 1952, 291: 23 pp. octavo in the hand of Stevenson's mother, signed by Stevenson at the end, R.L.B. Stevenson. Sold with 8 pp. of pencil sketches colored in water colors by Stevenson; a reproduction of one of these appears as frontispiece in the 1919 edition. *The History of Moses* (Daylesford, Pennsylvania: privately printed for A. Edward Newton, 1919); published from this source, Vailima Edition, 25 (1923), 5-13. Tusitala 28. Dictated by Stevenson to his mother, 23 November-21 December 1856, in competition with his cousins for a prize at Christmas; see her "Notes from his Mother's Diary," Vailima Edition, *26*, 293. Stevenson's prize was *The Happy Sunday Book of Painted Pictures with Verses to each for Good Children* (London: Dean and Son, [1856]). It was sold along with the manuscript in 1952, and in the 1919 edition the inscription is reproduced in facsimile: "R. Lewis Balfour Stevenson / A reward for his history of Moses with illustrations / From his affectionate Uncle David / Christmas 1856."

THE AMERICAN TRAVELLERS. Spring 1857. MS, Anderson 1914, I, 295. Unpublished. Beginning of an adventure tale in the style of Mayne Reid, dictated to his aunt Jane Whyte Balfour during a visit to Colinton Manse, 20 February-10 April 1857.

THE BOOK OF JOSEPH. Spring 1857. MS, Anderson 1914, I, 295, in the same notebook as "The American Travellers," above. Vailima Edition, 25 (1923), 14-23. Tusitala 28. Dictated to his mother during a visit to Colinton Manse, 20 February-10 April 1857.

TRAVELS IN PERTHSHIRE. Summer 1859. MS, Anderson 1914, I, 296. Unpublished. Describes, with drawings by Stevenson, a family trip to Bridge of

Allan, 14 June-6 July 1859, and part of their short trip after that to Perth, Dundee, and Crieff. Dictated to his mother, probably after their return to Edinburgh on 11 July 1859.

[Stories dictated at Colinton Manse.] Late 1850s. MSS untraced if extant. Unpublished. See Stevenson's "Reminiscences of Colinton Manse" (early 1870s; Beinecke 6788), partly quoted in Balfour, *Life, 1,* 45. "I would often get some one for amanuensis," Stevenson recalled, "and write divers pleasant and instructive narratives." One of these, "intended to be something very thrilling and spectral," was set in the Witches Walk at Colinton Manse and had for its heroine "a kitten." Another was called "The Adventures of Basil" and consisted, Stevenson wrote, "mainly of bungling adaptations from Mayne-Reid, to whom as you will see I was indebted even for my heros name; but I introduced the farther attraction of a storm at sea, where the captain cried out 'All hands to the pumps.'"

1860-65

THE ANTIQUITIES OF MIDLOTHIAN. March 1861. MS, Yale. Unpublished. Describes excursions to Craigmillar Castle and Corstorphine Church, both near Edinburgh; dictated to his mother.

[Dictations to Alison Cunningham.] 7 January, 25 February 1863. MS, Lady Stair's House Museum, Edinburgh, item 21. R. T. Skinner, ed., *Cummy's Diary* (1926), pp. 8, 79. Short accounts of seeing "Le Petit Prince" and Notre Dame Cathedral, and of scenery in the Alps and a Mentonese workman, dictated to his nurse in Europe in 1863.

THE SCHOOL BOYS MAGAZINE. October 1863. MS, Pierpont Morgan Library. Quoted with a summary of each story in Balfour, *Life, 1,* 65-66. Unpublished otherwise. Stevenson wrote "The School Boys Magazine" during the autumn term he spent at the Burlington Lodge Academy, Spring Grove, Isleworth, Middlesex, in 1863. It contains four stories, all but the second "to be continued." "The Adventures of Jan Van Steen" is set in Belgium in 1818 and tells of French soldiers overrunning a Belgian village: the boy hero hides in a ditch and seems likely later to become a spy. "A Ghost Story" takes place on "a cold and stormy night on the 11th of December 1842" in the far north of Norway. A traveler takes refuge in a hut which later proves to be used by robbers, whom he drives away by putting a sheet over his head and impersonating a ghost. "The Wreckers" is set in North Berwick "about the middle of the last century." Two men, picking over a wreck, spot a boy clinging to the mast and decide to kill him by pushing him off the cliff. "Creek Island or Adventures in the South Seas" begins with the sudden sinking of the line-of-battle ship *Shark* "on the 2d of August 1720" and the washing ashore of the two heroes Frank Morton and Harry Hall. Stevenson probably wrote these stories, and made them into this manuscript magazine, during the first month of his attendance at Burlington Lodge Academy—where no doubt he showed the magazine to his mother when she visited him there in late October and early November 1863. Although three of the stories are "to be continued" and the issue is called "No. I," there is no evidence that Stevenson ever wrote more than this one issue.

[The inhabitants of Peebles.] Summer 1864. MS untraced if extant. Unpublished. The only record of this work, written in the manner of Thackeray's *The Book of Snobs* (1846-47), is in Stevenson's essay "A College Magazine" (1887): "Even at the age of thirteen I had tried to do justice to the inhabitants of the famous city of Peebles in the style of the *Book of Snobs*" (Tusitala, *29*, 29-30). Stevenson stayed at Elibank Villa, Springhill, Peebles, during family vacations there, 2 June-3 October 1864 and 4 July-6 September 1865. This work dates from the first of these two summer visits.

THE PLAGUE-CELLAR. Summer 1864, possibly later. MS, Princeton University Library; photostat, Yale. Unpublished. See James Milne, "Memories," in Masson, ed., *I Can Remember Robert Louis Stevenson* (1922), pp. 5-6, and Stevenson's letter to his mother 18 July 1893, when he learned that his cousin Henrietta Traquair, later Mrs. Milne, had found this MS among her papers. "I would rather perish unmourned," Stevenson wrote, "than allow 'The Plague Seller' to appear under any form or under any pretense. You can break this to Henrietta tenderly as you can, but it must be final" (Beinecke 3433).

DEACON BRODIE (early draft). Late 1864. MS untraced, probably destroyed. Unpublished in this form. See H. B. Baildon, *Robert Louis Stevenson: A Life Study in Criticism* (1901), p. 22, for his account of Stevenson's reading him a play on this subject in 1864. In late 1878 the project was revived and the play rewritten collaboratively with William Ernest Henley. See the principal entry of *Deacon Brodie* under date of October 1878.

"THE TRIAL" MAGAZINE. Dated 5 June 1865. MS, Yale. Unpublished. Collaborative magazine with H. B. Baildon, in Baildon's hand, containing the beginnings of two serial tales by Stevenson, "The Counts Secret" and "The Convicts," and other contributions by Baildon.

[Hackston of Rathillet.] Before 13 November 1865. MSS presumably destroyed. Unpublished. See Stevenson's remarks about his many abortive novels on the Scottish Covenanter in "My First Book: *Treasure Island*" (Tusitala, *3*, xxiii), "Contributions to the History of Fife" (*30*, 14-15) and "The Education of an Engineer" (*30*, 20).

1866

THE SUNBEAM MAGAZINE. Issued January-March 1866. MSS, Yale. Unpublished. Two complete issues and one partial issue of this magazine, with additional drawings, in the hand of Stevenson's cousin Jessie Warden. Stevenson's contributions are: "The Banker's Ward: A Modern Tale" (serial), "Essays on Italy: San Remo" (travel), "Farewell to Mentone" (poem), "How to write a sensation tale" (satire), "The Power of Imagination" (humorous anecdote). An additional sheet, probably intended for a later issue, is lettered "The Pentland Rising."

THE PENTLAND RISING. Dated 28 November 1866. MS untraced. *The Pentland Rising* (Edinburgh: Andrew Elliott, 1866): a sixteen-page pamphlet of which one hundred copies were printed at Stevenson's father's expense in November 1866. Tusitala 28. See Stevenson's remarks on this work in "My First Book: *Treasure Island*" (Tusitala, *3*, xxiii) and his aunt Jane Whyte Balfour's recollections in Balfour, *Life, 1*, 67-68. On the reprinting of this work in the Edinburgh Edition see Stevenson's letters to Sidney Colvin and Charles Baxter, May-June 1894 (*Letters, 5*, 128, and *Baxter Letters*, pp. 354, 360).

Late 1860s

[Stylistic imitations and exercises.] Late 1860s and 1870s. MSS untraced and probably destroyed. See "A College Magazine" (1887) for Stevenson's comments on his various flights of poetry, prose, and drama, undertaken in his program of self-education in the art of writing. He mentions by title "Cain," an epic in imitation of Browning's *Sordello*; "Robin Hood," a verse tale indebted to Keats, Chaucer, and Morris; "Monmouth," a tragedy listed below and indebted to Swinburne; "The King's Pardon," a tragedy indebted first to Webster then to Congreve; and "The Vanity of Morals" and "The Vanity of Knowledge," essays indebted to Hazlitt, Ruskin, and Sir Thomas Browne. Stevenson also mentions what would appear to be another early version of *Deacon Brodie* and a tragedy, *Semiramis*, which he notes having seen "on bookstalls under the *alias* of *Prince Otto*" (Tusitala, *29*, 30). See the principal entries of these last two works under dates of October 1878 and April 1883, respectively. See also the next two entries.

[Plays.] 1867-68. MS notebook list, NLS. Unpublished. In a notebook kept for P. G. Tait's natural philosophy course at the University of Edinburgh during

1867-68, Stevenson lists by title, genre, and number of acts the following eleven plays: "Edward Ferren" (3-act tragedy), "Edward Bolton (the last will)" (5-act comedy), "Ananias Proudfoot, Baker and Elder" (3-act comedy), "The Witch" (5-act tragedy), "A Poor Heart; or the King's Pardon" (5-act tragedy), "The Brothers" (3-act comedy), "Charlie is my darling" (3-act tragedy), "Francis Nesham" (5-act tragedy), "The Point of Honour, or a partie quarée on the Bass" (3-act comedy), "The Duke's Jester" (5-act tragedy), "The Sweet Singer" (5-act tragedy). The notebook also contains seven pages of notes and speeches for "The Brothers," which shares characters with "Cosmo: A Novel" (1868-69, 1873) and may be a dramatic version of it. Stevenson comments briefly on "The King's Pardon" in "A College Magazine" (Tusitala, *29*, 29).

[Play inspired by Massinger.] Late 1860s. MS untraced. Unpublished. Edmund Gosse, *Biographical Notes on the Writings of Robert Louis Stevenson* (1908), p. 97, writes that during the late 1860s or early 1870s Stevenson began "a modern murder drama in the style of *A New Way to Pay Old Debts*. I remember him saying that he thought Charles Lamb, and most later critics, had been unjust to what he called 'the gentlemanlike plainness' of Massinger." Probably this play is among those listed in the previous entry.

MONMOUTH: A TRAGEDY. April-September 1868. MS, Yale. *Monmouth: A Tragedy*, ed. Charles Vale (New York: William Edwin Rudge, 1928). Unpublished except in this edition. Stevenson originally planned to collaborate with his cousin Bob, to whom he sent two one-paragraph sketches of possible plays, including this one, in early 1868 (Widener Collection, Harvard University; this letter is quoted in full in the Widener Collection *Catalogue*, 1913, pp. 236-38). On 17 April 1868 Stevenson sent his cousin a detailed outline of *Monmouth*, dividing the various scenes between them, but except for encouragement Bob Stevenson seems not to have written anything for the play (Beinecke 3550). On 6 September Stevenson wrote to his cousin, "Monmouth is finished," and commented at some length on his mixed feelings about it (item 3 in the 11 July 1922 sale at Christie's, quoted in the catalogue, Beinecke 1782). See also Stevenson to his cousin Bob, 2 October 1868 and 29 March 1870 (Beinecke 3552, 3555), and the various remarks quoted in Charles Vale's introduction to the 1928 edition.

[Essay on, or inspired by, Carlyle.] July 1868. MS untraced if written. Unpublished. "If I am to write the essay," Stevenson wrote to his mother in July 1868, "I require Carlyle's 'Heroes and Hero-Worship' and that shortly." Later in July he reminded her to send the "Essays," and still later in July he acknowledged receipt of "Carlyle." See Beinecke 3314, 3318, and *Letters, 1,* 14-15. Apparently Stevenson planned to write about Carlyle or draw on his works for an essay on some other subject. Possibly this work is related to the

"Rejection slip from Blackwoods, 1868" of which a transcript is among Graham Balfour's papers (NLS).

NIGHT OUTSIDE THE WICK MAIL. Before 17 November 1868. MS, Yale. Unpublished. 1500-word narrative sketch included in an unpublished letter from Stevenson to his cousin Bob, 17 November 1868, describing a journey made that October (Beinecke 3553).

PAINTING AND WORDS. 1868-69. MS, Yale. Unpublished. 340-word pencil draft comparing the descriptive powers of writing and painting, in Stevenson's "Modern Geometry" notebook, RLS/S, Yale.

COSMO: A NOVEL. 1868-69, 1873. MS lists of chapter titles and characters, in two notebooks Stevenson kept at the University of Edinburgh, Yale. Unpublished.

A COVENANTING STORY-BOOK. 1868-69. MS lists of titles: Yale, Haverford College Library. Unpublished. Two separate notebook lists of short stories, planned and completed, set in Scotland during the seventeenth century, both made early in Stevenson's attendance at the University of Edinburgh. Yale list, Beinecke 6642, gives "The Introduction" and then seven stories: "The Story of Houliston House"; "The adventures of William Spang, a prisoner after Bothwell, sent as a slave to the west Indies, shipwrecked on the Coast of Caithness and finally a companion of Mr Peden's"; "Hylsop and the Coals of Fire: being . . . a relation of the strange chances that befell the Reverend Mr Nehemiah Solway in the year 1687"; "Satan's power exemplified: the story of Bailie Grierson and Mrs Elspeth Montclieth"; "The Sweet Singers"; "The story about Corstorphine"; "The story about Grizell Baillie." Haverford list is titled as a whole "A Covenanting Story-Book" and lists ten stories by title, marking five with an (X) presumably to signify that they had been written: "The Curate of Anstruther's Bottle (X)"; "Strange Adventures of the Reverend Mr Solway (X)"; "The Devil of Crammond (X)"; "Meery [?] Story of the Curate of Colinton"; "Sir William Bannatyne's Papers"; "Advocate McMincha's Client (L. Moir)"; "The Story of Thrawn Janet"; "Some passages in the life of singular, worthy, pious, excellent Mr Ephraim Blethers, as communicated to that whited sepulchre, &c"; "Houliston House (X)"; "A story of James Renwicks College Days (X)." "The Story of Thrawn Janet" is the only one of these stories ever published; see the entry below under date of June 1881. Stevenson continued to list various of these stories in other lists during the 1870s and early 1880s. See *Letters. 1,* 213-14, and *2,* 89, 150-51, and the next two entries.

THE CURATE OF ANSTRUTHER'S BOTTLE. Late 1860s or early 1870s. MS untraced. Unpublished. Stevenson entered the title of this story, marking it as complete, in his list for "A Covenanting Story-Book." See the previous entry. On 20 December 1873 he asked Charles Baxter to send him the MS of "two stories: one (which you read a long while ago) called *The Curate of Anstruther's Bottle*; the other called *The Devil on Crammond Sands* . . . . They cover each about 30 leaves written on one side only" (*Baxter Letters*, pp. 39-40). In January 1874, at Mentone, Stevenson was busy revising the story, remarking to Sidney Colvin that "I find much in it that I still think excellent and much that I am doubtful about" and commenting on the difficulties he was having with his "convention" in the story: "The idea is not, of course, to put in nothing but what would naturally have been noted and remembered and handed down, but not to put in anything that would make a person stop and say—how could this be known?" (*Letters, 1,* 133). In November 1874 he listed this story with others for another projected collection, as he did again in June 1881 when he seems to have changed its title to "The Case Bottle." See *Letters, 1,* 213-14, and *2,* 150-1. Stevenson tells the historical anecdote upon which the story was probably based in "Contributions to the History of Fife" (1888), Tusitala, *30,* 16-17. But the story is otherwise unknown.

THE DEVIL ON CRAMMOND SANDS. Late 1860s or early 1870s. MS untraced. Unpublished. See the previous two entries. Stevenson entered the title of this story, marking it as complete, in his list for "A Covenanting Story-Book" (1868-69), and probably he revised it at Mentone in early 1874. He listed it among the stories for another collection in November 1874, wrote to Sidney Colvin in mid-November 1876 that he had recently rewritten it, and again listed it for collection in December 1879. See *Letters, 1,* 213-14 and *2,* 89, and Beinecke 3025. But the story is otherwise unknown.

[Journal written aboard the *Pharos*.] 18-22 June 1869. MS: Yale, Lady Stair's House Museum, Edinburgh. Published in Sidney Colvin, ed., "The Letters of Robert Louis Stevenson," *Scribner's Magazine*, 25 (January 1899), 41-48, but not subsequently published or collected. Account of a voyage with his father and the Commissioners of Northern Lights through the Shetland and Orkney Islands, written in dated segments and sent in two installments to his mother.

SKETCHES. Late 1860s and 1870s. MSS, including first drafts of two and part of a third of these essays, Yale. Edinburgh Edition, 21 (1896), 31-48. Tusitala 30. The individual sketches are: "The Satyrist," "Nuits Blanches," "The Wreath of Immortelles," "Nurses," "A Character." A very early draft of the first, and notes for the third essay, also appear in a notebook of 1868-69, "Modern Geometry," RLS/S, Yale.

1870

[Speculative Society Talks.] 8 March 1870-19 January 1875. MSS untraced except for "Law and Free Will: Notes on the Duke of Argyll" (11 February 1873) and Stevenson's "Valedictory Address" (25 March 1873). See the separate entries of these works below. Unpublished except for Stevenson's "Valedictory Address."

Stevenson was elected a member of the Speculative Society, University of Edinburgh, on 16 February 1869, and enrolled as member 992 on 2 March 1869. He served as one of the society's five presidents during the 1872-73 and 1873-74 sessions and continued to attend meetings through 1875. He contributed altogether seven papers and his "Valedictory Address" and participated actively in debates. Stevenson's seven papers were: "The Influence of the Covenanting Persecution on the Scottish Mind" (8 March 1870); "Notes on *Paradise Lost*" (14 March 1871); "Notes on the Nineteenth Century" (9 January 1872); "Two Questions on the Relation between Christ's Teaching and Modern Christianity" (12 November 1872); "Law and Free Will: Notes on the Duke of Argyll" (11 February 1873); "John Knox" (3 November 1874); "John Knox, and Women (No. 2)" (19 January 1875). On the Speculative Society and Stevenson's membership in it see William Kirk Dickson, *The History of the Speculative Society* (1905); Charles Baxter's "Introductory Notes" to "The Last Unpublished Robert Louis Stevenson," *The Outlook*, 19 February 1898, p. 71; and Balfour, *Life, 1,* 77-79.

THE RIGHT CONDUCT OF THE IMAGINATION. 29 March 1870. MS untraced. On 29 March 1870 Stevenson wrote to his cousin Bob that he had "two essays on 'the right conduct of the Imagination' simmering in my brain. One of them is in draught" (Beinecke 3555). Nothing else is known of this work or works.

[A Retrospect.] Early 1870s. MS, Yale. Edinburgh Edition, 21 (1896), 89-101; title supplied by Sidney Colvin, who edited and conflated the two MS versions. Tusitala 30. Based on a visit to Dunoon, Argyllshire, 26 April-3 May 1870.

OBERMANN. Early 1870s. MS, Yale. Unpublished. 165 words of the beginning of an essay so titled, written on one leaf of the MS of "A Retrospect."

[Children's games.] Early 1870s. MS untraced. Unpublished. Mentioned in "Notes of Childhood" (1873) and probably the germ of "Child's Play" (1878).

REMINISCENCES OF COLINTON MANSE. Early 1870s. MS, Yale. Balfour, *Life, 1,* 40-47 (abridged). Unpublished otherwise. As Balfour notes, Stevenson probably used this essay in writing "The Manse: A Fragment" (1887).

1871

Contributions to THE EDINBURGH UNIVERSITY MAGAZINE. January-April 1871. MSS untraced. *The Edinburgh University Magazine*, Nos. 1-4 (January-April 1871); six essays, two signed L. and the others unsigned. Only "An Old Scotch Gardener" (March 1871) was ever collected except posthumously, in *Memories and Portraits* (1887). The other five essays—"Edinburgh Students in 1824," "The Modern Student Considered Generally," "The Philosophy of Umbrellas," "Debating Societies," and "The Philosophy of Nomenclature"—appeared in the Edinburgh Edition, 21 (1896), 51-85. Tusitala 25, 29. See Stevenson's own remarks on this magazine and his work in it, "A College Magazine" (1887; Tusitala, *29*, 31-36), and his comments on "The Philosophy of Umbrellas" in letters to Sidney Colvin and Charles Baxter about the Edinburgh Edition (*Letters, 5*, 129, and *Baxter Letters*, p. 360). See also George W. T. Omond, "R.L.S. and *The Edinburgh University Magazine*," in Masson, ed., *I Can Remember Robert Louis Stevenson* (1922), pp. 76-79, and Sir Alexander Grant, *The Story of the University of Edinburgh*, 2 vols. (1884), *2*, 489-92.

NOTICE OF A NEW FORM OF INTERMITTENT LIGHT FOR LIGHTHOUSES. Delivered 27 March 1871. MS, NLS. *Transactions of the Royal Scottish Society of Arts*, 8, iii (1870-71), 271-75; also offprints distributed as a pamphlet. Tusitala 28. Stevenson read this essay before the Royal Scottish Society of Arts on 27 March 1871, and on his twenty-first birthday, 13 November 1871, received one of the society's five annual silver medals, value three sovereigns, for it. "No one can say that I give up engineering because I can't succeed in it," Stevenson remarked to his mother when he learned of the award, "as I leave the profession with flying colours" ("Notes from his Mother's Diary," Vailima Edition, *26*, 322). Graham Balfour, *Life, 1*, 85n.2, notes on the authority of Stevenson's cousin D. A. Stevenson, then head of the family engineering firm, that "the proposed light has never been constructed in consequence of several mechanical difficulties."

STUDENTS' MEETING AND CLASS EXCURSION. April 1871. MS, Anderson 1914, II, 319. Unpublished. Stevenson's narrative was probably based on the class supper and subsequent excursion to Glasgow made with Professor Fleeming Jenkin's engineering class, 5-6 April 1871.

Letter: PAROCHIAL WORK AND ORGANISATION. April 1871. MS untraced. *The Church of Scotland Home and Foreign Missionary Record*, 1 May 1871, pp. 349-50. Published anonymously but attested by Stevenson's mother's "Notes from his Mother's Diary," Vailima Edition, *26*, 321. Unpublished since its original appearance.

1872

IMAGINARY CONVERSATIONS. Winter 1871-72. MS, Yale: outline listing four conversations, of which the fourth follows in rough pencil draft. See G. L. McKay's entry of this work as Beinecke 6400 in the Beinecke Collection catalogue, *A Stevenson Library . . .*, p. 1841. Unpublished. The first page is headed "Imaginary Conversations Edinburgh. 1872." and is written in a notebook mostly occupied by notes taken in Professor James Muirhead's course in public law at the University of Edinburgh, 31 November 1871-21 March 1872.

INTELLECTUAL POWERS. Winter 1871-72. MS, Yale. Unpublished. One-page outline of an essay, written at the back of Stevenson's notebook on public law mentioned in the previous entry.

[Journal written as a law clerk.] 9 May-5 July 1872. MS, Arnold, 1924, 822. W. H. Arnold, "My Stevensons," *Scribner's Magazine*, 71 (January 1922), 54-55. See also Balfour, *Life, 1*, 105, where excerpts from this journal appear, and M. M. Black, *Robert Louis Stevenson* (1898), pp. 72-74.

THE NEW LIGHTHOUSE ON THE DHU HEARTACH ROCK, ARGYLLSHIRE. Summer 1872. MS, Huntington HM 2403: 8 leaves folio, 12 pp. of text, with corrections by Stevenson's father. Signed at the foot of p. 12 Robert Louis Stevenson. Stevenson's essay on the building of this lighthouse by his father's engineering firm seems written for a general rather than highly specialized audience. He spent three weeks observing the construction during its early stages, in August 1870, and wrote this account two years later when construction was nearly finished: "During the present summer," Stevenson writes, "the lantern and interval fittings have also been brought to completion. Before the end of 1872, the light will have been exhibited." This establishes the date certainly as 1872.

LAW AND FREE WILL: NOTES ON THE DUKE OF ARGYLL. Winter 1872-73; delivered 11 February 1873. MS, Anderson 1914, II, 347. Unpublished. On this critique of G. D. Campbell's *The Reign of Law* (1866), delivered before the Speculative Society on 11 February 1873, see *Baxter Letters*, p. 21, and Lord Dunedin, "Reminiscences," in Masson, ed., *I Can Remember Robert Louis Stevenson* (1922), p. 95. On 22 September 1873 Stevenson wrote to Mrs. Sitwell that he had read "some notes on the Duke of Argyll" to his father in hopes that this might clarify for him the nature of his religious views. This had only negative results, however, and only widened the breach between them (*Letters, 1,* 78).

THE INN OF ABERHUERN. Winter 1872-73. MS returned to Stevenson in Samoa in 1894 and probably destroyed by him. Unpublished. Stevenson's "little sketch, in essay form . . . poked fun at the young girls who were enlivening the dullness of mid-winter in the country by the ambitious project of editing an amateur magazine" and was sent by him to Margaret M. Black and her friends at Leven, Fife, in the winter of 1872-73. See her comments in *Robert Louis Stevenson* (1898), p. 50, and Vincent Starrett's lengthy discussion in *Bookman's Holiday* (1942), pp. 212-33. Stevenson acknowledged receipt of the manuscript in a letter to one of the magazine's editors, Louisa Middleton, in 1894 (*Letters, 5*, 158).

1873

[On spiritualism.] Begun 15 January 1873. MS untraced. Unpublished. See *Baxter Letters*, p. 21. On Stevenson's connection with the Psychological Society of Edinburgh, founded in 1872 and of which he was for a short time secretary (and his cousin Bob Stevenson a vice-president), see the remarks of David Gow quoted from the periodical *Light* in J. W. Herries, *I Came, I Saw* (1937), pp. 286-87. Though Stevenson's article was apparently never written, it would seem to have been based on his experiences in this society and may have been intended for presentation to the Speculative Society.

[Speculative Society Valedictory Address.] Delivered 25 March 1873. MS, Speculative Society, University of Edinburgh. "The Last Unpublished Robert Louis Stevenson," *The Outlook*, 19 February 1898, pp. 71-73. Read by Baxter in Stevenson's absence at the closing meeting of the Speculative Society during its 1872-73 session. An inaccurate and mistitled version of this speech, edited by Katharine D. Osbourne from a transcript by Stevenson's mother, was privately printed as *The Best Thing in Edinburgh* (1923).

ON THE THERMAL INFLUENCE OF FORESTS. Delivered 19 May 1873. MS untraced. *Proceedings of the Royal Society of Edinburgh*, 8 (November 1872-July 1875), 114-25; also fifty offprints published by Neill and Company, Edinburgh. On T. J. Wise's forgeries of this offprint issue see John Carter and Graham Pollard, *An Enquiry into the Nature of Certain Nineteenth Century Pamphlets* (1934), pp. 247-50. Tusitala 28.

[Notes of childhood.] 18 May 1873. MS, Yale. Partly published in Balfour, *Life, 1*, 31-34, 40. Autobiographical reminiscences dated at the end 18 May 1873; later drawn upon in "Memoirs of Himself" (1880) and "Rosa Quo Locorum" (1893).

LOCAL CONDITIONS INFLUENCING CLIMATE. Delivered 2 July 1873. MS untraced. Notice of Stevenson's delivery of this paper appears in the *Journal of the Scottish Meteorological Society*, 4 (July 1873), 59-60, and his authorship of it is further attested by his mother's "Notes from his Mother's Diary," Vailima Edition, *26*, 324. But no detailed record of the contents of this essay survives.

DESIDERATA. 5-6 July 1873. MS, Lloyd Osbourne, 1914, 590. Unpublished except for the facsimile in the catalogue of the sale at which the MS was offered. Stevenson also includes his list in a letter to Mrs. Sitwell; see *Baxter Letters*, p. vii, and *Letters, 1*, 185-86.

COCKERMOUTH AND KESWICK. Probably before August 1873. MS, Yale. Edinburgh Edition, 21 (1896), 101-14. Tusitala 30. The tour described took place in 1871 but the essay is written on paper watermarked 1873 identical with that Stevenson used for his "Notes of Childhood" (18 May 1873). Probably it was among the essays Stevenson had already on hand when he met Sidney Colvin for the first time in July 1873.

[Essays suggested by Alexander Macmillan.] September 1873. MSS untraced if written. Unpublished. Macmillan, with whom Sidney Colvin had put Stevenson in touch, suggested that he write on Savonarola and, later, on some other subject. See Colvin's remarks in Masson, ed., *I Can Remember Robert Louis Stevenson* (1922), pp. 90-93.

ROADS. Late August-14 September 1873. MS untraced. *The Portfolio*, 4 (December 1873), 185-88; signed L. S. Stoneven. Tusitala 25. Stevenson's first paid contribution to a periodical, for which he received £3.8.0. Of this essay Sidney Colvin notes that "it had been planned during walks at Cockfield; was offered to and rejected by the Saturday Review and ultimately accepted by Mr. Hamerton for the Portfolio" (*Letters, 1*, 67).

[Walt Whitman.] September 1873-summer 1874. MS and "a lot of notes" on Whitman lost by Stevenson in August 1874. Unpublished. According to Sidney Colvin (*Letters, 1,* 64) Stevenson had "already on hand" an essay on Walt Whitman when they first met in July 1873, an "earlier and more enthusiastic version" of the one eventually published in 1878. Stevenson began reworking this essay in late September and October 1873, and at intervals during that winter and in 1874. But he lost the MS and his notes after the month's cruise he took with Sir Walter Simpson in July and August 1874 and did not return to the subject until he wrote "The Gospel According to Walt Whitman." See the entry for this later essay under date of October 1878.

COVENANTERS. 22 September 1873. MS untraced. Unpublished. Apparently a projected essay or group of essays. See *Letters, 1*, 78, and the entry "Covenanting Profiles" (late 1878).

ORDERED SOUTH. Late November 1873-5 February 1874. MS untraced. *Macmillan's Magazine,* 30 (May 1874), 68-73; signed Robert Louis Stevenson. *Virginibus Puerisque* (1881). Tusitala 25. Stevenson received £5 for this essay.

GRAND HOTEL GODAM. Winter 1873-74. MS untraced. One of the two known printed copies is in the Widener Collection, Harvard University. Reprinted in full in E. V. Lucas, *The Colvins and Their Friends* (1928), pp. 84-85. Unpublished otherwise. Stevenson and Sidney Colvin wrote this bilingual parody of hotel advertising cards while Colvin was visiting Stevenson at Mentone during the winter of 1873-74.

[Herostratus.] Projected winter 1873-74. This projected "spectacle-play on that transcendent type of human vanity, Herostratus" was apparently never written. See Sidney Colvin's comments on his visits to Stevenson at Mentone during the winter of 1873-74 in his *Memories and Notes of Persons and Places* (1922), pp. 112-13.

1874

FOUR GREAT SCOTSMEN. Projected January 1874. See *Letters, 1*, 135-36. Although Stevenson soon abandoned this project, he did publish essays on Knox (1875) and Burns (1879) and comments at some length on Scott in "Victor Hugo's Romances" (1874).

VICTOR HUGO'S ROMANCES. Spring 1874-4 May 1874. MS, Yale. *Cornhill Magazine,* 30 (August 1874), 179-94; unsigned. *Familiar Studies of Men and Books* (1882). Tusitala 27.

On 20 March 1874 Leslie Stephen, declining a proposal from Sidney Colvin, suggested that Colvin give him instead "an article on V. Hugo's novels generally, for June" (Beinecke 5547). Stevenson may have been at work on such an essay already, for Colvin mentions that when he visited

Stevenson at Mentone in January and February 1874 Stevenson "was busy with the essay *Ordered South*, and with that on *Victor Hugo's Romances*" (*Letters, 1*, 64). Colvin no doubt suggested to Leslie Stephen that Stevenson write the essay instead, and by the third week of April Stevenson was asking Colvin "when Cornhill must see it" and remarking that he could send "some of it in a week easily." Stevenson sent the finished manuscript to Colvin on 4 May 1874, and on 15 May Leslie Stephen wrote to Stevenson a long, cordial letter accepting the essay (Beinecke 5549). (See *Letters, 1*, 149, 151, 158-59, 161-63; Stephen's letter is published in a note, *Letters, 1*, 161-63, and is reproduced in facsimile in the Beinecke Collection catalogue, *A Stevenson Library. . .* , facing p. 1590.) A week later, on 21 May, Stephen wrote to Stevenson again, calling his attention to Victor Hugo's comment on Scott's *Quentin Durward*. "That would almost do for a motto to your essay," Stephen wrote (Beinecke 5550), and in the essay as published this comment, lacking in Stevenson's manuscript, appears as an epigraph.

Stevenson lost the first set of proofs sent to him and so had to request a second set on 9 June 1874. Sometime before 25 June, correcting these proofs, Stevenson remarked to Mrs. Sitwell that the essay was "not nicely written, but the stuff is capital, I think" (*Letters, 1*, 167). He was paid £16.16 for it, and when the essay was published, an anonymous critic in the *Spectator*, 8 August 1874, p. 1013, attributed the unsigned article to Leslie Stephen and praised it lavishly as "masterly" and "full of thought and appreciation." Years later, Stevenson wrote to H. B. Baildon about the mistake: "Poor gentleman! all lost! Devil a bit of favour in Waterloo Place for all this monstrous quantity of praise" (Stevenson to Baildon, n.d., probably 1890s, Maggs Brothers Catalogue 607, 1935, 1126). Stevenson also told Graham Balfour in Samoa that the essay, in Balfour's words, "marked, in his own judgment, the beginning of his command of style . . . in this essay he had first found himself able to say several things in the way in which he felt they should be said" (*Life, 1*, 139).

LORD LYTTON'S FABLES IN SONG. 2—15 May 1874. MS draft, Yale. MS untraced. *Fortnightly Review*, n.s. 15 (June 1874), 817-23; signed Robert Louis Stevenson. Tusitala 28. Stevenson received £5 for this review of Edward Robert Bulwer-Lytton, Lord Lytton's *Fables in Song*, 2 vols. (Edinburgh and London: William Blackwood and Sons, 1874). Vol. 1 of Stevenson's review copy is in the Silverado Museum, St. Helena, California; passages are marked and underlined in pencil but the volume is not otherwise marked. Vol. 2 is among uncatalogued Stevenson materials in the Beinecke Collection.

[The function of art.] Projected early May 1874. MS untraced. Stevenson to Sidney Colvin: "I have an idea for a little page and a half or two pages in the Portfolio about the function of art: I think it will turn out rather jolly and pleasant, if not very deep" (Lady Stair's House Museum Collection, Edinburgh, item 179). No other record of this projected essay survives.

NOTES ON THE MOVEMENTS OF YOUNG CHILDREN. Late June-July 1874. MS untraced. *The Portfolio,* 5, (August 1874), 115-17; signed Robert Louis Stevenson. Tusitala 25. Stevenson received £2.12 for this essay. On the original incident upon which this essay was based see Sidney Colvin, "Some Personal Recollections, III. Robert Louis Stevenson," *Scribner's Magazine*, 67 (March 1920), 346-47, and at greater length in *The Hampstead Annual* (1902), pp. 144-54.

Review: THE BALLADS AND SONGS OF SCOTLAND. July 1874. MS untraced. *The Academy*, 8 August 1874, pp. 142-43; signed Robert Louis Stevenson. Tusitala 28. Stevenson probably finished this review of J. Clark Murray's *The Ballads and Songs of Scotland, in View of their Influence on the Character of the People* (London: Macmillan, 1874) before he left for a month's cruise in the west of Scotland with Sir Walter Simpson on 22 July 1874.

Review: SCOTTISH RIVERS. July 1874. MS untraced. *The Academy*, 15 August 1874, p. 173; signed Robert Louis Stevenson. Tusitala 28. Stevenson probably finished this review of Sir Thomas Dick Lauder's *Scottish Rivers* (Edinburgh: Edmonston and Douglas, 1874) in July 1874 at the same time as the review mentioned in the previous entry.

FABLES. Summer 1874. MSS untraced. Stevenson to Colvin: "I have done no more to my *Fables*. . . . I am constant to my schemes; but I must work at them fitfully as the humour moves" (*Letters, 1*, 175). Colvin suggests that among these early pieces are "The House of Eld," "Yellow Paint," and possibly "The Touchstone," "The Poor Thing," and "The Song of To-morrow." Tusitala 5. See the principal entry of Stevenson's "Fables" under date of 1893-94.

ON THE ENJOYMENT OF UNPLEASANT PLACES. Late August-11 September 1874. MS untraced. *The Portfolio*, 5 (November 1874), 173-76; signed Robert Louis Stevenson. Tusitala 25. Stevenson's remarks derive chiefly from his visit to Wick in September and October 1868.

ESSAYS ON THE ENJOYMENT OF THE WORLD. Late August-September 1874. MS untraced. See Stevenson's sketch of this uncompleted project, *Letters, 1*, 174-75.

AN APPEAL TO THE CLERGY OF THE CHURCH OF SCOTLAND. Late August and September 1874-February 1875. MS untraced. *An Appeal to the Clergy of the Church of Scotland With a Note for the Laity* (Edinburgh and London:

William Blackwood and Sons, 1875); unsigned twelve-page pamphlet dated at the end of the "Note for the Laity" 12 February 1875. A facsimile of the title page of this pamphlet appears in the Beinecke Collection catalogue, *A Stevenson Library* . . . , facing p. 6. Tusitala 26. See *Letters, 1*, 173-75 and "Notes from his Mother's Diary," Vailima Edition, *26*, 327. As Stevenson remarks at the beginning of his "Note for the Laity," the main text had been in type "since the beginning of last September [1874]." He wrote it in late August and early September 1874, had the work set in type, and then added his "Note for the Laity" in early 1875. According to his mother, a copy of Stevenson's pamphlet was given to "every member of the General Assembly [of the Church of Scotland] that year [1875]." But as J. A. MacCulloch notes, *Robert Louis Stevenson and the Bridge of Allan* (1927), p. 151, Stevenson's advice was "a piece of generous Quixotry . . . somewhat gratuitous, if not impertinent . . . and . . . it has never appeared that any minister followed the advice given."

JOHN KNOX AND HIS RELATIONS TO WOMEN. September-November 1874. MS untraced. MS notes: Anderson 1914, II, 344; W. M. Hill, 1916, 140; Vailima Edition, *25*, 56-58. Source books: Anderson 1914, II, 43, 274; Beinecke 2510, 2547; Stevenson Cottage collection, Saranac Lake, New York. *Macmillan's Magazine*, 32 (September 1875), 446-56, and 32 (October 1875), 520-31; both parts signed Robert Louis Stevenson. *Familiar Studies of Men and Books* (1882). Tusitala 27. Stevenson had a version of this essay "already on hand" in July 1873, having discovered Knox's *First Blast of the Trumpet against the Monstrous Regiment of Women* (1558) the year before. See the remarks of Stevenson's tutor in classics and philosophy during 1872, the Rev. Archibald Bisset, in Masson, ed., *I Can Remember Robert Louis Stevenson* (1922), p. 52, and Sidney Colvin's note, *Letters, 1*, 64. Stevenson's intention by 1874 was to write a biography of Knox as part of a work to be called "Four Great Scotsmen," on which see the entry under date of January 1874. But as he wrote to Sidney Colvin in early May 1874: "I am quite determined once more to write the article 'John Knox and Women' as there will not be any comfortable position for much of the stuff in the life" (Lady Stair's House Museum Collection, Edinburgh, item 179). He wrote the two parts of this essay during the late summer and early autumn of 1874. The first part was in proof by mid-October and the second, written in nine days, finished by the end of November 1874. Stevenson read the two parts before the Speculative Society on 3 November 1874 and 19 January 1875, and after some delay they were published in *Macmillan's Magazine* in September and October 1875. Seven years later, getting together the essays for *Familiar Studies of Men and Books* (1882), Stevenson found himself reluctant to reprint these essays on Knox and did so only on his father's particular request: "I tell you the Knoxes are an error," Stevenson wrote to this father in November 1881; "it would be far better to keep them back and work them into a life of Knox some day: there is no readable life of him; and these are as dull as McCrie. . . . I have, of course, written to Macmillan but I protest" (*Letters, 2,* 175).

COLLEGE FOR MEN AND WOMEN. Late September-October 1874. *The Academy*, 10 October 1874, p. 406; signed Robert Louis Stevenson. Tusitala 28. Probably written at the request of Mrs. Sitwell, who served for a time as secretary to the College for Working Women, Bloomsbury, London.

THE SEABOARD OF BOHEMIA. Late October-early November 1874. MS untraced. Stevenson to his cousin Bob, autumn 1874: "I am going to write two nice things as soon as I have time; one notes of real tour . . . the other notes of a sham tour, sham people, sham legends &c called 'The Seaboard of Bohemia'—Winter's Tale, you understand" (Beinecke 3560). Cf. Stevenson to his cousin Katharine DeMattos, November 1874: "I am trying my hand at a novel just now; it may interest you to know, I am bound to say I do not think it will be a success. However, it's an amusement for the moment" (*Letters, 2*, 19). The "real tour" Stevenson mentions is that described in "An Autumn Effect," entered below under date of December 1874. But of the novel nothing else is known.

Review: A QUIET CORNER OF ENGLAND. November 1874. MS draft, Yale. *The Academy*, 5 December 1874, pp. 602-3; signed Robert Louis Stevenson. Tusitala 28. For Stevenson's own comments on his review of Basil Champneys's *A Quiet Corner of England: Studies of Landscape and Architecture in Winchelsea, Rye, and the Romney Marsh* (London: Seeley, Jackson, and Halliday, 1874) see *Letters, 1*, 205.

A BOOK OF STORIES. Planned November 1874. In a letter to Sidney Colvin written in November 1874 (*Letters, 1*, 213-14, misdated January 1875) Stevenson listed twelve stories for collection under this title, most of them already written or in draft. The first four were Scottish stories, three of them having earlier been listed by Stevenson in the contents of "A Covenanting Story-Book" (1868-69): "The Curate of Anstruther's Bottle," "The Devil on Crammond Sands," and "The Strange Adventures of Mr. Nehemiah Solway." See the discussion of this collection and the first two of these stories above under date of 1868-69. The fourth, "The Two Falconers of Cairnstane," Stevenson was then writing and was complete except for "a few pages." He revised it for publication anonymously as "An Old Song" in *London*, 24 February-17 March 1877, under which dates it is entered below. Of the remaining eight, non-Scottish stories, three are described by Stevenson as "all ready." "King Matthias's Hunting Horn" was written in Edinburgh in November 1874. "The Barrel Organ" Stevenson seems to have read to Mrs Sitwell during his visit to London in September and October 1874 (*Letters, 1*, 213). Nothing is known of the third such story, "Life and Death." Of the remaining five stories, three are listed as "in gremio." "Autolycus in Court" Stevenson eventually wrote as a play: see the principal entry for this work under date of February 1879. The other two are otherwise unknown: "The Family of Love" and "Martin's Madonna."

Last, Stevenson listed "The Last Sinner," which then needed only recopying, and "Margery Bonthron," which "wants a few pages." The first is otherwise unknown. "Margery Bonthron" Stevenson mentioned again in a letter to Sidney Colvin in December 1879 discussing a possible volume of "carpentry stories," but even at that time it was still unfinished (Beinecke 3043). The idea of publishing "A Book of Stories" was soon dropped, however. Stevenson's first collection of stories was *New Arabian Nights* (1882), and all of the stories there collected were first published in periodicals. Except for "An Old Song," none of the stories listed for "A Book of Stories" in 1874 was ever published.

[On winter.] Winter 1874. MS untraced if written. Stevenson's only reference to this essay, which had been suggested by Sidney Colvin and may never have been written, appears in a letter to Mrs. Sitwell, December 1874, quoted in E. V. Lucas, *The Colvins and Their Friends* (1928), p. 89. Four years later Stevenson began sketching an essay "The Four Seasons," but there is no evidence that it is related to this earlier projected essay; see the entry of the later project under date of late 1878.

AN AUTUMN EFFECT. December 1874-January 1875. MS untraced. *The Portfolio,* 6 (April 1875), 53-58, and 6 (May 1875), 70-75; both parts signed Robert Louis Stevenson. Tusitala 30. Originally titled "In the Beechwoods" and based on Stevenson's walking tour of the Chiltern Hills, Buckinghamshire, in October 1874.

Review: THE WORKS OF EDGAR ALLAN POE. December 1874. MS untraced. *The Academy*, 2 January 1875, pp. 1-2; signed Robert Louis Stevenson. Tusitala 28. Stevenson's review copy of John H. Ingram's edition of *The Works of Edgar Allan Poe* (London and Edinburgh: Adam and Charles Black, 1874-75) was sold as Anderson 1914, I, 473, and contains many caustic marginal comments, some of which are quoted in the auction catalogue. Ingram wrote to Stevenson complaining of the review: see Stevenson's comments, *Letters, 1*, 202-3, 209, *Baxter Letters*, p. 46, and his letter to Ingram, mid-January 1875, New York Public Library. The article signed A. E. P., "Stevenson and Poe," *Notes and Queries*, 18 December 1943, pp. 367-68, consists only of quotations from this essay with a plea that it be included in popular editions of Stevenson's works.

[Selections from his notebook.] 1874-75. MS, Anderson 1914, I, 340: 73 pp. small quarto notebook. Vailima Edition, 25 (1923), 24-58, with such obvious misreadings of Stevenson's hand as "Tzlai's Prin Cult" for Stevenson's actual abbreviation for Edward Tylor's *Primitive Culture* (1871). Tusitala 29. Selections made by Lloyd Osbourne from this notebook of 1874-75 comprise remarks on politics, society, religion, poetry, logic, the theory of language, Walt Whitman, Milton, John Knox, and other subjects.

1875

WHEN THE DEVIL WAS WELL. January-February 1875. MS, Yale, with marginalia by Sidney Colvin and Leslie Stephen. *When the Devil Was Well* (Boston: Bibliophile Society, 1921), and from this source in the Vailima Edition, 26 (1923), 417-76. Tusitala 5. See *Letters, 1*, 210-11, 216.

[The French Parnassiens.] Projected January 1875. MS untraced if written. Unpublished. See *Letters, 1*, 211.

DIFFERENCES OF COUNTRY. Winter 1874-75. MS draft, Yale. Unpublished. Stevenson's unfinished five-hundred-word draft comments on the different physical appearance of different countries and praises Théophile Gautier's presentation of the differences between Spain and France in *Tra los Montes* (1843). Probably this is the beginning of the essay "Scotland and England" which Stevenson mentions as in prospect in a letter of January 1875 (*Letters, 1*, 211). He returned to this subject, in part, in "The Foreigner at Home" (winter 1881-82).

A COUNTRY DANCE. February 1875, begun earlier. MS untraced. Stevenson's only reference to this story is in a letter to Mrs. Sitwell written on 11 February 1875 in which he mentions having just finished "When the Devil Was Well." "And now I have taken up an old story, begun years ago; and I have now re-written all I had written of it then, and mean to finish it. . . . I have got a jolly new name for my old story. I am going to call it *A Country Dance*; the two heroes keep changing places, you know; and the chapter where the most of this changing goes on is to be called 'Up the middle, down the middle.' It will be in six or (perhaps) seven chapters" (*Letters, 1*, 215-16). Although the idea of two heroes changing places suggests that this story may be a version of "The Two Falconers of Cairnstane," written in November 1874 and eventually published in 1877 as "An Old Song," Stevenson's reference to it as "an old story" to which he was only then returning makes it clear that "A Country Dance" is in fact a separate story.

FOREST NOTES. Spring 1875-January 1876. MS notes, partial draft, and corrected page proofs, Yale. *Cornhill Magazine*, 33 (May 1876), 545-61; signed R.L.S. Tusitala 30. Based chiefly on Stevenson's visit to France and the Fontainebleau forest during March and April 1875 and written that summer; publication was delayed due to the length of the essay.

[Prose fragments: A French legend, A note at sea, A night in France.] Spring 1875. MSS, Yale. *Hitherto Unpublished Prose Writings* (Boston: Bibliophile Society, 1921), pp. 77-89, and from this source in the Vailima Edition, 24 (1923), 36-40. Tusitala 25, 30. Although printed separately, none of these prose pieces is a separate work. All are notes for the essay "Forest Notes" and appear in final form in that essay as published. The titles were supplied by G. S. Hellman, who cut these pieces from notebooks he had earlier acquired and had them mounted and bound for sale separately.

SPRINGTIME. Spring 1875. MS draft fragment, Yale. Unpublished. See Stevenson to Sidney Colvin, *Letters, 2*, 14-16. The MS fragment at Yale, Beinecke 6907, is probably a draft from which was taken the fair copy sent to Colvin and then lost.

[Prose poems.] May-June 1875. MSS of six of the fifteen or more prose poems which Stevenson wrote in late May and early June 1875 survive: "Sunday Thoughts" and "Good Content" (Yale), dated at the end, respectively, 2 June and 7 June 1875; "The Lighthouse: No. 1; On the Roof" and "The Lightroom" (Huntington), dated 29 and 30 May 1875; "The quiet waters by" (Anderson 1914, II, 374), dedicated to Mrs. Sitwell and dated 25 May 1875; and "A Summer Night" (British Red Cross, 1918, 2202), dedicated to Charles Baxter although the actual night in question had been spent by Stevenson with his cousin Bob, dated 26 May 1875. Stevenson mentions as already written on 28 May 1875 three other prose poems of which the MSS are untraced if indeed they are still extant: "In a Garden," "The drunkard and the Sea," and "A sermon by your leave." Three of Stevenson's prose poems have been published. "Sunday Thoughts" and "Good Content," *San Francisco Call*, 14 April 1895, p. 14, and later in A. H. Japp, *Robert Louis Stevenson . . .* (1905), pp. 166-69; "A Summer Night," *Scribner's Magazine*, 52 (November 1912), 593-94. Unpublished otherwise. Stevenson comments at some length on his prose poems in letters to Sidney Colvin and Mrs. Sitwell in the early summer and autumn of 1875 (*Letters, 1*, 233-35, and *2*, 14-15). His copy of Baudelaire's *Petite Poëmes en Prose* (1869), in which Stevenson wrote a one-word critical estimate of many of the pieces, is now held as Beinecke 2500.

[Advocate's thesis.] Early Summer 1875. MS, NLS. Unpublished. Stevenson's thesis for admission as advocate, signed by him at the end, consists of six pages commenting on Justinian's *Pandects*, book 41, title 9. Stevenson's subject is the distinction between "Pro Dote" and "Pro Suo" as these definitions apply to a person's state before and after marriage. On 14 July 1875 he passed his final examination, and two days later he was called to the Bar. On Stevenson's short legal career see his mother's "Notes from his Mother's Diary," Vailima Edition, *26*, 328-29; Balfour, *Life, 1*, 119; C. J.

Guthrie, *Robert Louis Stevenson: Some Personal Recollections* (1920), pp. 36-39; and Rosaline Masson, *The Life of Robert Louis Stevenson* (1923), pp. 132-39. Stevenson's petition to be admitted to candidacy for advocate, 31 October 1872, his certificate of admission to the Bar, 18 July 1875, and other documents were sold as Anderson 1914, I, 453.

PIERRE JEAN DE BÉRANGER. Summer 1875. MS notes and draft, Yale. MS untraced. *The Encyclopaedia Britannica*, 9th ed. (1875), *3*, 581-82; signed (R.L.S.). Tusitala 30.

[Dickens and Thackeray; other essays.] Summer 1875 (uncertain). On one page in his notebook 62, Yale, Stevenson listed three titles, apparently of essays projected during mid-1875: "Dickens and Thackeray," "Villon & Charles of Orleans," "Painters to Match." Stevenson actually wrote only on the second pair of authors.

CHARLES OF ORLEANS. Summer 1875-July 1876. MS notes and partial draft, Yale. MS untraced. *Cornhill Magazine*, 34 (December 1876), 695-717; signed R.L.S. *Familiar Studies of Men and Books* (1882). Tusitala 27.

[Three plays and a story.] June-July 1875. MSS untraced if written. Stevenson mentions these pending projects in a letter to Mrs. Sitwell, *Letters, 1*, 237-38. He may have been inspired to return to writing plays by William Ernest Henley, whom he met for the first time in Edinburgh on 12 February 1875.

ROBERT BURNS. Summer-autumn 1875. MS untraced. Rejected by the *Encyclopaedia Britannica,* 1875, though Stevenson was paid £5.5 for it nevertheless. The essay probably served as the basis for Stevenson's "Some Aspects of Robert Burns" (1879).

THE CHARITY BAZAAR. September-November 1875, possibly later. MS, Yale. *The Charity Bazaar: An Allegorical Dialogue*, privately printed four-page folder without place, publisher, or date. Edinburgh Edition, 28 (1898), 1-4. Tusitala 5. Although dated by Sidney Colvin in the Edinburgh Edition 1868, the manuscript of *The Charity Bazaar* is written on paper watermarked 1871 and the folder was distributed at a bazaar held by Stevenson's mother to benefit the Zenana Missions of the Church of Scotland and recorded in her diary 25 November 1875. A copy of *The Charity Bazaar* is pasted into the scrapbook of reviews and notices of Stevenson's work kept by his mother now in the Stevenson Cottage collection, Saranac Lake, New York. Its location in this scrapbook suggests that it was pasted in sometime during 1876.

THE MEASURE OF A MARQUIS. Published 25 November 1875. MS untraced. *Vanity Fair: A Weekly Show of Political, Social, and Literary Wares*, 25 November 1875, pp. 305-6; unsigned. Unpublished since its original appearance. Stevenson's authorship of this review of the Marquess of Lorne's *Guido and Lita: a Tale of the Riviera* (London: Macmillan and Company, 1875) is attested by his remarks in a letter to Mrs. Sitwell, November 1875 (NLS): "Figure to yourself, I wrote a review of Lord Lorne for Vanity Fair—a few pages of scurrility that I wrote laughingly in an hour or two—and I got—guess!—I got five pounds for it and the price of the book! That was jolly wasn't it? Long live Vanity Fair!"

MR. BROWNING AGAIN! Published 11 December 1875. MS draft of the first two paragraphs, Yale. *Vanity Fair: A Weekly Show of Political, Social, and Literary Wares*, 11 December 1875, pp. 332-33; unsigned. Unpublished since its original appearance except in abridged form, *Notes and Queries*, 12 February 1944, pp. 102-3. Stevenson's review of Browning's *The Inn Album* (London: Smith, Elder, and Company, 1875) is attested both by his draft and his remark in a letter to Mrs. Sitwell probably written in early December 1875: "I have done a rather amusing paragraph or two for *Vanity Fair* on *The Inn Album*. I have slated R. B. pretty handsomely!" (*Letters, 2*, 17-18). See also Stevenson's short poem on this review in Janet Adam Smith, ed., *Collected Poems*, 2nd ed. (1971), pp. 335, 540.

1876

[A history of the Union.] Projected ca. 1876. MS untraced if written. C. J. Guthrie, *Robert Louis Stevenson: Some Personal Recollections* (1920), pp. 47-48, recalls discussing at length with Stevenson "about the year 1876" a book "on the union of England and Scotland, which should discuss the success of that union as contrasted with the failure of the union of Great Britain and Ireland, although both were equally obnoxious to the majority of the lesser nations most directly concerned." Stevenson returned to historical writing on this subject during 1880. See the entry "Scotland and the Union" under date of late summer 1880.

A WINTER'S WALK IN CARRICK AND GALLOWAY. After 17 January 1876. MS untraced. MS notes expanded for the final draft, Yale. *The Illustrated London News*, summer 1896, pp. 13-15. *The Chap-Book* (Chicago), 15 June 1896, pp. 108-19. Tusitala 30. The essay was probably begun just after Stevenson's short walking tour in January 1876 (see *Letters, 2*, 20) but it remained unfinished and unpublished during his lifetime.

[Literary criticism.] Early 1876. MS outline, Yale. Unpublished. Stevenson sketches the opening of an essay on the function and present state of literary criticism.

WALKING TOURS. January-February 1876. MS untraced. Page proof, Princeton University Library. *Cornhill Magazine*, 33 (June 1876), 685-90; signed R.L.S. *Virginibus Puerisque* (1881). Tuistala 25. Accepted for publication by Leslie Stephen on 24 February 1876 (Beinecke 5555).

Review: THE POETS AND POETRY OF SCOTLAND. Published 12 February 1876. MS untraced. *The Academy*, 12 February 1876, pp. 138-39; signed Robert Louis Stevenson. Stevenson's copy of James Grant Wilson's *The Poets and Poetry of Scotland: From the Earliest to the Present Time. . . . Period: From Thomas the Rhymer to Richard Gall* (London: Blackie and Son, 1876) is now in the Silverado Museum, St. Helena, California. In it Stevenson has marked many passages, most of which he quotes in this review. His copy of the second volume of this anthology, which covers the years 1777 to 1876, was sold as Anderson 1914, I, 704.

SALVINI'S MACBETH. April 1876. MS untraced. *The Academy*, 15 April 1876, pp. 366-67; signed Robert Louis Stevenson. Tusitala 28. Mrs. Fleeming Jenkin discusses Stevenson's writing of his review of the Italian actor Tommasso Salvini's first performance of *Macbeth* in a letter to the *Edinburgh Academy Chronicle*, 2 (March 1895), 50-52. See also Stevenson's "Memoir of Fleeming Jenkin" (1887), chap. 6, part 2 (Tusitala, *19*, 120-21).

"VIRGINIBUS PUERISQUE." Before 18 May 1876. MS sold together with the MS of "On Falling in Love," British Red Cross, 1918, 2203; discussed in detail, *TLS*, 7 March 1918, p. 115. *Cornhill Magazine*, 34 (August 1876), 169-76; signed R.L.S. *Virginibus Puerisque* (1881), where this essay was made the first of four essays under the same general title used for the volume as a whole. Tusitala 25. According to the catalogue description of the annotated copy of *Virginibus Puerisque* which Stevenson gave to his father (C. Gerhardt and Company, 1915, 54), Stevenson marked this essay as having been written in Edinburgh and London.

JULES VERNE'S STORIES. May 1876. MS untraced. *The Academy*, 3 June 1876, p. 532; signed Robert Louis Stevenson. Tusitala 28. Stevenson wrote this review of eight novels by Jules Verne published by Sampson Low and Company in 1876, one of half a dozen English editions of Verne published during the 1870s, shortly before it was published.

AN APOLOGY FOR IDLERS. July 1876. MS untraced. *Cornhill Magazine*, 36 (July 1877), 80-86; signed R.L.S. *Virginibus Puerisque* (1881). Tuistala 25. According to the catalogue description of the annotated copy of *Virginibus Puerisque* which Stevenson gave to his father (C. Gerhardt and Company, 1915, 54), Stevenson marked this essay as having been written at Swanston and Queensferry. Publication was delayed while George Grove considered it for *Macmillan's Magazine*, where Stevenson had originally submitted it, and later because Stevenson considered saving it for initial publication in book form. See *Letters, 2*, 28, 31, and Beinecke 3021, 3025, 5560. Edward D. Snyder, "Another 'Apology for Idlers' in the Light of Some New Stevenson Discoveries," *Saturday Review of Literature*, 3 August 1935, pp. 12-13, calls attention to some interesting parallels between remarks in this essay and notes in one of Stevenson's notebooks from the University of Edinburgh now in the Haverford College Library.

Review: THE COMEDY OF THE NOCTES AMBROSIANAE. Published 22 July 1876. MS untraced. *The Academy,* 22 July 1876, p. 76; signed Robert Louis Stevenson. Tusitala 28. Stevenson probably wrote this review of John Skelton's edition and arrangement of the essays of John Wilson ("Christopher North") first collected as *Noctes Ambrosianae* (1822-35), *The Comedy of the Noctes Ambrosianae* (Edinburgh and London: William Blackwood and Sons, 1876), shortly before it was published. On 22 July 1876 W.E. Henley wrote to Stevenson that he found the essay "the first word of adequate description" of the essays. "How little did Christopher ever imagine that his appetites alone would immortalise him, as the best & only vital parts of his huge incoherent personality! How grateful I am to you for having dared to say as much!" (Beinecke 4708).

[A novel.] Begun summer 1876. MS untraced. Stevenson to Sidney Colvin, late August 1876: "I've written five or six chapters of a novel; but I think I'm written out for the moment and shall lay it aside." The following spring Stevenson wrote that the novel was then "at a standstill" (Beinecke 3021-22).

SOME PORTRAITS BY RAEBURN. October 1876. MS untraced. *Virginibus Puerisque* (1881). See the correspondence, Beinecke 5557, 4490, 5558, 3025. as too specialized for the *Cornhill Magazine*. Stephen then submitted it to the *Pall Mall Gazette* and later to *Blackwood's Magazine*, again without success, and the essay was laid by until first published in *Virginibus Puerisque* (1881). See the correspondence, Beinecke 5557, 4490, 5558, 3025.

ON FALLING IN LOVE. November 1876. MS sold together with the MS of "'Virginibus Puerisque,'" British Red Cross, 1918, 2203; discussed in detail, *TLS,* 7 March, 1918, p. 115. *Cornhill Magazine*, 35 (February 1877), 214-20;

signed R.L.S. *Virginibus Puerisque* (1881), where this essay was made the third of those published under the general title used also for the volume as a whole. Tusitala 25. According to the catalogue description of the annotated copy of *Virginibus Puerisque* which Stevenson gave to his father (C. Gerhardt and Company, 1915, 54), Stevenson marked this essay as having been written in Edinburgh.

[Autobiography.] November 1876. MS untraced. The only surviving record of this composition appears in Stevenson's passing remark, in a letter to Sidney Colvin in mid-November 1876, that he had recently begun an autobiography and then abandoned it as altogether unsatisfactory (Beinecke 3025).

EDIFYING LETTERS OF THE RUTHERFORD FAMILY. 1876-77 (uncertain). MS outline and incomplete draft, Yale. Unpublished. This semiautobiographical composition comprises three fictitious letters and part of a fourth, all apparently deriving from Stevenson's membership in the "L.J.R." during his years at the University of Edinburgh, on which see Balfour, *Life, 1*, 90, 113. Stevenson's outline appears in a notebook of 1876-77, but there is no other evidence for the date of this work.

1877

[Minor contributions to LONDON.] January-February 1877. MSS untraced. Four essays and two reviews by Stevenson appeared anonymously in the first four issues of the weekly *London* (114 issues, 3 February 1877-5 April 1879): "Our City Men. No. I.—A Salt-Water Financier" and "The Book of the Week. Mr. Tennyson's 'Harold,' " 3 February 1877, pp. 9-10, 18-19; "In the Latin Quarter. No. I.—A Ball at Mr. Elsinare's, " 10 February, pp. 41-42; "In the Latin Quarter. No. II.—A Studio of Ladies, " 17 February, p. 64; "The Paris Bourse" and "The Book of the Week. Wallace's Russia," 24 February, pp. 88, 92-93. Only the third and fifth of these have been reprinted, in *The Stevensonian: The Journal of the Robert Louis Stevenson Club, London*, No. 2 (August 1965), pp. 2-7, with a brief commentary by Ernest J. Mehew. On *London* and Stevenson's work in it see Balfour, *Life, 1*, 151-52; Fanny Stevenson's "Prefatory Note," Tusitala *1*, xxviii-xxix; *Letters, 2*, 45-46; *Baxter Letters*, p. 51; Beinecke 5760, 5625, 5501, 3363, and 4179; Stevenson's "Memoir of Fleeming Jenkin" (1887), chap. 6 part 4 (Tusitala, *19*, 129-30); Will H. Low, *A Chronicle of Friendships* (1908), p. 209; and the letters quoted in John Connell, *W. E. Henley* (1949), pp. 80-86. G. L. McKay's attribution of the review of Henry Irving's performance in *Richard III*, "At the Lyceum on Monday" (3 February 1877, pp. 13-14), is incorrect. The review was written by W. E. Henley. See Beinecke 5760, 5625. McKay also lists nine other contributions to *London* in 1877, Beinecke 7682-90, as possibly written by Stevenson, but there is no certainty that they were actually written by him. See the discussion in the Beinecke Collection catalogue, *A Stevenson Library. . .*, pp. 2347-50. Stevenson's contributions to *London* during 1878—"A Plea for Gas Lamps," "Pan's Pipes," and "El Dorado," the series of stories "Latter-Day Arabian Nights," and "Leon Berthilini's Guitar"—were all reprinted by him and are entered separately below. His only other known contribution in 1877, the story "An Old Song," is discussed in the next entry.

AN OLD SONG. Rewritten and published, February-March 1877; drafted November 1874. MS fragment, Yale (Beinecke 6106): 1 leaf, folio, numbered at the top, 23, containing the end of chap. 6 and the beginning of chap. 7 of this story; the paper is watermarked A. Pirie and Sons / 1874. "An Old Song," four weekly installments, *London*, 24 February-17 March 1877; unsigned. Unpublished since its original appearance.

Stevenson's first reference to the story eventually published as "An Old Song" is in a letter to Sidney Colvin written in November 1874. Having written and sent off his second essay on John Knox, Stevenson wrote, he had since finished one story and was then "engaged in finishing another called *The Two Falconers of Cairnstane.*" This story, which is "An Old Song" titled for its two main characters, John and Malcolm Falconer, was one of four Scottish stories which in the same letter to Sidney Colvin Stevenson listed along with eight non-Scottish stories as making the contents of a volume he was thinking of publishing, "A Book of Stories." At this time the story was complete "except for a few pages" (*Letters, 1,* 213-14, misdated January 1875). The idea of publishing "A Book of Stories" was dropped, however, and seemingly the story was laid aside altogether until *London* was founded two years later in early 1877.

One feature of *London* was its weekly "Feuilleton," installments of light fiction published serially. Stevenson's was the second such story, and like those which appeared before and after it during the first eight months of the journal's publication, it appeared anonymously. (Emile Gaboriau's *The Orcival Murder*, translated from the French, was the first signed "Feuilleton" in *London* and appeared from 22 September through 1 June 1878. It was followed, 8 June through 26 October, by Stevenson's "Latter-Day Arabian Nights," and in November by his "Leon Berthilini's Guitar." Both of these were signed, Stevenson's only signed contributions to *London* during the slightly more than two years of its existence.) As noted in the previous entry, Stevenson was a contributor to *London* from the beginning, and in mid-February 1877 he wrote to its editor Robert Glasgow Brown that he was rather annoyed with Brown's pressing demands for material. "I shall give you the Feuilleton as fast as I can with personal convenience," Stevenson wrote. "As for reading three volumes and writing an article in two days, I shall make an attempt this once without promising success; but I must ask you not to put me again in the same position." Moreover, as Brown was apparently not entirely pleased with the material which Stevenson had sent him for the earliest issues of *London*, Stevenson suggested that his connection with the magazine should perhaps cease as soon as possible.

"Mind you, I don't desert; I only say as soon as you are able to fill the place I have unworthily occupied, the better for your paper and my own comfort" (Stevenson to Brown, mid-February 1877, NLS). Probably as a result of this suggestion, Stevenson contributed little or nothing to *London* during the rest of 1877; and not until the spring of 1878, when his friend W. E. Henley was editing *London*, did Stevenson again become in any sense a regular contributor.

FRANÇOIS VILLON, STUDENT, POET, HOUSEBREAKER. Spring 1877. MS untraced. Beinecke 7086 is a draft of the concluding section of "Charles of Orleans," not of this essay as the catalogue indicates. *Cornhill Magazine*, 36 (August 1877), 215-34; signed R.L.S. *Familiar Studies of Men and Books* (1882). Tusitala 27. Stevenson contemplated writing an essay on Villon as early as the autumn of 1875 (*Letters, 2*, 11), but not until the appearance of August Lognon's *Étude biographique sur François Villon* (Paris: H. Menu, 1877) did he actually take up the subject. Leslie Stephen accepted his proposal of an essay on Villon for the *Cornhill Magazine* on 1 March 1877 (Beinecke 5560), and by late spring or early summer Stevenson had finished the essay. See Beinecke 3022-23 and *Letters, 2*, 32-33. Stevenson's copy of Lognon's *Étude biographique* was sold as Mrs. W. E. Safford, 1926, 19, and is now in the Rare Book Collection, State University of New York at Buffalo. In the Safford sale catalogue it is described as providing ample evidence of careful reading and as containing about forty words of marginal comment by Stevenson, whose remarks range from historical memoranda to such observations as "Sentimental bosh!" The review of Lognon's *Étude biographique* published in *London*, 3 March 1877, p. 116, was probably written by W. E. Henley.

A LODGING FOR THE NIGHT: A STORY OF FRANCIS VILLON. Spring and summer 1877. MS draft of roughly the first half of this story, Yale. *Temple Bar*, 51 (October 1877), 197-212; unsigned. *New Arabian Nights* (1882). Tusitala 1. See Beinecke 6626, 3023; *Letters, 2*, 31; and Stevenson to George Iles, 29 October 1887, *Bookman,* 7 (London, February 1895), 136.

THE HAIR TRUNK: OR, THE IDEAL COMMONWEALTH. Begun May 1877. MS: Huntington HM 2411 (145 pp.), Yale (8 pp.). Unpublished. See Stevenson's comments on this unfinished comic extravaganza, *Letters, 2*, 28.

IN THE WINDBOUND ARETHUSA. Begun May 1877. MS, Anderson 1914, I, 299: 82 pp. comprising part 2, chapters 2-9, of an unfinished novel. Unpublished. Balfour, *Life, 1*, 142, mentions this as "another attempt of the same date" as "The Hair Trunk" and that it "attained no better result."

[Privately circulated novel.] Middle or late 1870s. MS destroyed. Unpublished. See the remarks of E. B. Simpson, *Robert Louis Stevenson's Edinburgh Days* (1913), pp. 244-45, and "The Late Sir W. G. Simpson," *Bookman*, 14 (London, July 1898), 94; see also *Baxter Letters*, p. 215. Stevenson, Sir Walter Simpson, W. E. Henley, and either Charles Baxter or R.A.M. Stevenson, all wrote deliberately shocking novellas in competition sometime during the 1870s. In its "strength, its terribleness, its outrageous blackness of human depravity," Stevenson's apparently made the other versions "schoolgirl reading in comparison." The MS was bound as the *History of Mexico* and kept by Charles Baxter, who later destroyed all but a few passages at Stevenson's request.

SCHOOL FOR THE SONS OF GENTLEMEN. Summer 1877. MS untraced; typescript by Lloyd Osbourne, Yale. An outline of chapter titles together with a list of the projected membership, agreements, and profits of the "Barbizon Free-Trading Company, Unlimited." Unpublished. On the plan to outfit a barge and finance their travels by giving instruction in art see Will H. Low, *A Chronicle of Friendships* (1908), pp. 187-93, and Stevenson's dedication of *An Inland Voyage* (1878). Apparently Stevenson planned to write a story based on the idea.

WILL O' THE MILL. June-July 1877. MS untraced. *Cornhill Magazine*, 37 (January 1878), 41-60; signed R.L.S. *The Merry Men and Other Tales and Fables* (1887). Tusitala 8. Accepted, with reservations about the story's indeterminate hovering between realism and allegory, by Leslie Stephen, 29 September 1877 (Beinecke 5561). Stevenson received twenty pounds for this story. For Stevenson's later comments on "Will o' the Mill" see his draft preface to *The Merry Men* (Tusitala, *8*, 15-16), Balfour, *Life, 1*, 160, and especially Isobel Strong's "Vailima Table-Talk," *Memories of Vailima* (1902), pp. 45-46.

CRABBED AGE AND YOUTH. July-August 1877. MS untraced. *Cornhill Magazine*, 37 (March 1878), 351-59; signed R.L.S. *Virginibus Puerisque* (1881). Tusitala 25. Begun in response to Leslie Stephen's remark about "An Apology for Idlers" that "something more in that vein would be agreeable to his views" (*Letters, 2*, 31). Stevenson received £9.9.0 for this essay. According to the catalogue description of the annotated copy of *Virginibus Puerisque* which Stevenson gave to his father (C. Gerhardt and Company, 1915, 54), Stevenson marked this essay as having been written in Edinburgh and Penzance.

NEW NOVELS. July 1877. MS untraced. *The Academy,* 4 August 1877, pp. 108-9; signed Robert Louis Stevenson. The novels reviewed are James

Walter Ferrier's *Mottiscliffe: an Autumn Story* (Edinburgh and London: William Blackwood and Sons, 1877), Ernte Ariel Wolfe's *Shamrock and Rose* (London: Remington and Company, 1877), Mrs. Fetherstonhaugh's *Kilcorran* (London: R. Bentley and Son, 1877), and Annie L. Walker's *Against Her Will* (London: Samuel Tinsley, 1877). Two copies of Ferrier's *Mottiscliffe*, one presented to Stevenson's mother and the other probably Stevenson's review copy, are now in the Silverado Museum, St. Helena, California.

THE SIRE DE MALÉTROIT'S DOOR. August 1877. MS untraced. *Temple Bar*, 52 (January 1878), 53-69; unsigned. *New Arabian Nights* (1882). Tusitala 1. Stevenson received eight pounds for this story, originally titled "The Sire de Malétroit's Mousetrap." It is unknown whether Stevenson or someone else altered the title to its present form for publication. See *Letters, 1*, 241.

LA SALE AND PETIT JEHAN DE SAINTRÉ. Planned August 1877. MS untraced if written. Unpublished. See *Letters, 2*, 32. Stevenson's copy of J. M. Guichard's *L'Hystorye et plaisante cronicque du Petit Jehan de Saintré* (Paris, 1843) is now in the Rare Book Collection, State University of New York at Buffalo.

THE STEPFATHER'S STORY. Planned August 1877. MS untraced if written. Unpublished. In August 1877 Stevenson mentioned as in prospect "another story, in the clouds, *The Stepfather's Story*, most pathetic work of morality or immorality, according to point of view" (*Letters, 2,* 32). He listed it among various planned and completed "Fables and Tales" in his notebook for *An Inland Voyage* (Yale). But nothing seems to have come of this project.

THE TWO ST. MICHAEL'S MOUNTS. After August 1877. MS notes, Yale, from Fortescue Hitchins, *The History of Cornwall* (1824), and F. G. P. B. Manet, *État ancien et de l'état actuel de la baie du mont Saint-Michel* (1828). Unpublished. The essay itself appears never to have been written. See Stevenson to Mrs. Sitwell, *Letters, 2,* 32, in which he mentions possibly including the Bass Rock also and titling the whole essay "Three Sea Fortalices."

AN INLAND VOYAGE. Rewritten from Stevenson's journal of September 1876, November 1877-January 1878. MS journal, Yale. MS untraced. *An Inland Voyage* (London: C. Kegan Paul and Company, 1878); published 28 April 1878 in an edition of 750 copies. Second printing, 1881, called "SECOND EDITION" on the title page, is the first to include Stevenson's "Dedication" to Sir Walter Simpson. See the Beinecke Collection catalogue, *A Stevenson Library. . .*, pp. 7-10, on the publication of this work later by Chatto and Windus. First American edition (Boston: Roberts Brothers, 1883) published

June 1883. The first five pages of Stevenson's notebook appear in *Hitherto Unpublished Prose Writings* (Boston: Bibliophile Society, 1921), pp. 37-47. Tusitala 17. Stevenson rewrote his journal of the canoe trip which he had taken in Belgium and France with Sir Walter Simpson (September 1876) chiefly in Edinburgh during November and December 1877, finishing the book in early January 1878 at Dieppe. C. Kegan Paul accepted *An Inland Voyage* for publication on 8 January 1878; Stevenson was reading proofs in February; and after some delay in Walter Crane's preparing the frontispiece the work was published on 28 April. Stevenson was paid twenty pounds for *An Inland Voyage*, royalties of 1/- a copy to begin after 1,000 copies had been sold. But during its first year after publication only 485 copies were actually sold, and in 1884 C. Kegan Paul and Company still showed a net loss of £180 on Stevenson's first three books. In the C. Kegan Paul *Publication Account Books*, vol. 9, p. 45, the entry of *An Inland Voyage* is closed out by a payment of £47.14.0 apportioned from the sum of £101 or more paid to recover Stevenson's interest in the three books of his first published by C. Kegan Paul and Company. See *The Archives of Kegan Paul . . . 1853-1912*, ed. Brian Maidment, 27 microfilm reels (1973), reel 8.

THE ENGLISH ADMIRALS. Late 1877. MS untraced. *Cornhill Magazine*, 38 (July 1878), 36-43; signed R.L.S. *Virginibus Puerisque* (1881). Tusitala 25. Stevenson had submitted this essay to *Blackwood's Magazine* before the end of 1877, but when four letters written in late March, April, and early May 1878 failed to elicit a response, he recovered the manuscript and sent it instead to Leslie Stephen for the *Cornhill Magazine*. He received £8.8 for this essay. Stevenson's copy of Southey's *Life of Nelson* (London, 1830), originally owned by his father, was sold as Anderson 1914, II, 493. Stevenson was familiar with Southey's *Lives of the English Admirals* (1833-40) by September 1873 (*Letters, 1*, 80), and his remarks on names in this essay almost exactly reproduce those he made in 1871 in "The Philosophy of Nomenclature" (cf. Tusitala, *25*, 88 and 166).

A DIALOGUE ON MEN, WOMEN, AND *CLARISSA HARLOWE*. Late 1877-78. MS, Anderson 1914, II, 366: 5 pp. folio, comprising an imaginary dialogue between husband and wife chiefly about Richardson's novel. Unpublished. See *Letters, 2*, 37.

1878

LATTER-DAY ARABIAN NIGHTS: THE SUICIDE CLUB, THE RAJAH'S DIAMOND. March-September 1878. MS chapter outlines, including titles of stories never eventually written, Yale. "Latter-Day Arabian Nights," seventeen weekly installments, *London*, 8 June-26 October 1878, excepting the issues of 24 August, 21 September, and 5 October; each installment signed Robert

Louis Stevenson. Seven stories, each also titled individually, the first three under the collective subtitle "The Suicide Club," the last four similarly as "The Rajah's Diamond." *New Arabian Nights* (1882), in which the modified general title was adopted as the title of the whole collection, not only of these seven stories, and the original collective subtitles were thus promoted to stand as the only collective titles of the stories first published in *London* from 8 June through 27 July and 3 August through 26 October 1878, respectively. Tusitala 1. Stevenson received £44.12 for the serial publication of these stories, and according to Edmund Gosse, early in 1879 he proposed that C. Kegan Paul bring them out as a volume. "After much consideration," Gosse writes, "that publisher refused to do so on account of their preposterous character" (Introduction, Pentland Edition, *4*, 1906). Not until 1882 were these stories eventually collected, as the first volume of *New Arabian Nights*. See the entry of that collection below under date of spring 1882.

On the composition of these stories see Fanny Stevenson's "Prefatory Note," Tusitala, *1*, xxvii-xxix; Lloyd Osbourne, *An Intimate Portrait of R.L.S.* (1924), pp. 5, 10-12; Balfour, *Life, 1*, 152; Stevenson's mother's "Notes from his Mother's Diary, " Vailima Edition, *26*, 331-32; Stevenson to George Iles, 29 October 1887, *Bookman*, 7 (London, February 1895), 136; and Lloyd Osbourne's transcription, Beinecke 6626, of Stevenson's memorandum (Anderson 1914, I, 651) listing the stories in *New Arabian Nights* and where they were written. See also the excellent discussion of the biographical and other backgrounds of the stories, "The House of the President of the Suicide Club," *The Sketch*, 4 January 1899, p. 422. On the periodical *London* see the entries of Stevenson's contributions to it under dates of January-March 1877, above.

AES TRIPLEX. Published April 1878. MS untraced. *Cornhill Magazine*, 37 (April 1878), 432-37; signed R.L.S. *Virginibus Puerisque* (1881). Tusitala 25. Stevenson received £6.6.0 for this essay.

A PLEA FOR GAS LAMPS. Published 27 April 1878. MS untraced. *London*, 27 April 1878, pp. 304-5; unsigned. *Virginibus Puerisque* (1881). Tusitala 25. Stevenson received £1.11.6 for this essay.

PAN'S PIPES. Published 4 May 1878. MS untraced. *London*, 4 May 1878, p. 328; unsigned. *Virginibus Puerisque* (1881). Tusitala 25. Stevenson received £1.11.6 for this essay.

EL DORADO. Published 11 May 1878. MS untraced. *London*, 11 May 1878, p. 352; unsigned. *Virginibus Puerisque* (1881). Tusitala 25. Stevenson received £1.16 for this essay, a special favorite of W. E. Henley's. See Henley to Stevenson, April or May 1878, Beinecke 4714.

WHY AM I A BANKER?; BOHEMIA (CONSIDERATIONS ON); ON MONEY. Planned mid-1878. MSS untraced if written. Unpublished. Stevenson lists these titles among fourteen "Essays" (most of them eventually included in *Virginibus Puerisque*) in his notebook for *An Inland Voyage* (Yale). In subject, all appear to anticipate "Lay Morals," begun in April 1879.

[Novel solicited by Leslie Stephen.] June 1878-February 1879. MS untraced. Unpublished. Leslie Stephen to Stevenson, 7 June 1878: "I cannot help thinking that if you would seriously put your hand to such a piece of work you would be able—I will not say to rival the success of Waverley or Pickwick but—to write something really good & able to make a mark in the Cornhill. Of course you must have thought of this; but a little push from outside may help the thought to develope itself. . . . You might start a few chapters & then let me see whether I thought them available for Cornhill purposes" (Beinecke 5562). Stevenson appears to have responded favorably to Stephen's request, whether beginning a new novel or reworking an earlier effort is unknown, and their correspondence on the matter continues intermittently through the fall and winter. Nevertheless, it does not appear that Stevenson actually submitted any of the work he did on this project.

EDINBURGH: PICTURESQUE NOTES. June-September 1878. MS draft of "To the Pentland Hills" in Stevenson's notebook for *Travels with a Donkey*, Huntington; outline of chapters and a few notes in Stevenson's notebook for *An Inland Voyage*, Yale. MS untraced. Stevenson's draft of "To the Pentland Hills" appears partially in W. H. Arnold, "My Stevensons," *Scribner's Magazine*, 71 (January 1922), 60-61. "Notes on Edinburgh," *The Portfolio*, 9, seven monthly installments, June-December 1878; each installment signed Robert Louis Stevenson. *Edinburgh: Picturesque Notes* (London: Seeley, Jackson, and Halliday, 1879); published mid-December 1878. For publication in book form Stevenson added the chapters "The Parliament Close," "The Villa Quarters," and "To the Pentland Hills," made a few small changes in the text, and rearranged the order of chapters. Tusitala 26. Stevenson wrote these essays chiefly in Paris and London during the summer of 1878, finishing work in Le Monastier in mid-September (*Letters, 2*, 52; Beinecke 26 is a copy of this work with the place where each essay was written pencilled at the end). On 18 October, having finished his walking tour in the Cévennes, Stevenson wrote to his mother, "the Edinburgh book is about through the press," and on 30 October, from London, he wrote to her that he was "seeing Edinr through the press" and had been appealed to for another such series by Richmond Seeley, publisher of *The Portfolio* (letters, Bradford Brinton Memorial Ranch Collection, Wyoming).

CHILD'S PLAY. Summer 1878, published September. MS untraced. *Cornhill Magazine*, 38 (September 1878), 352-59; signed R.L.S. *Virginibus Puerisque*

(1881). Tusitala 25. This essay probably derives from an earlier one, "Children's Games" (early 1870s), which Stevenson mentions in his "Notes of Childhood" (18 May 1873). See also Balfour, *Life, 1*, 49, 104.

THE GOSPEL ACCORDING TO WALT WHITMAN. Summer 1878, published October. MS, Bradford Brinton Memorial Ranch Collection, Wyoming: 8 pp., evidently a fair copy of the MS in that a catchword appears at the foot of each page; further described as written in ink on unruled paper 8¼ inches by 13 inches and lacking pages from the middle of the essay. *New Quarterly Magazine*, 10 (October 1878), 461-81; signed Robert Louis Stevenson. *Familiar Studies of Men and Books* (1882). Tusitala 27. See also the entry of Stevenson's earlier essay on Walt Whitman under date of September 1873, above. Of the present essay John Addington Symonds wrote in his *Walt Whitman: A Study* (1893), p. 40: "My friend Mr. R.L. Stevenson once published a constrained and measured study of Walt Whitman which struck some of those who read it as frigidly appreciative. He subsequently told me that he had first opened upon the key-note of a glowing panegyric, but felt the pompous absurdity of its exaggeration. He began again, subduing the whole tone of the composition. When the essay was finished in this second style, he became conscious that it misrepresented his own enthusiasm for the teacher who at a crucial moment of his youthful life had helped him to discover the right line of conduct." Stevenson first became acquainted with Whitman's poetry in 1871, and his copies of *Leaves of Grass* and *Passage to India* (both Washington, 1871) were sold as Anderson 1914, I, 703 and II, 599. In a letter to his cousin Bob written in November 1872 Stevenson urged him to read Robert Buchanan's essay on Whitman in the current number of *The Broadway: A London Magazine of Society and Politics* (Christie's sale, 11 July 1922, 11). See also Stevenson's comments on Whitman in "Books Which Have Influenced Me" (1887), Tusitala, *28*, 64.

COVENANTING PROFILES. Summer 1878. MS outline, Yale. Unpublished. On a page in his notebook for *An Inland Voyage* Stevenson outlined a book of 185 pages to be titled "Covenanting Profiles" which would cover the careers of various Scottish Covenanters from Walter Pringle through Patrick Walker. The position of this outline in the notebook suggests that it was made before the end of 1878, possibly during the summer, when Stevenson's interest in the Covenanters may have been reawakened by his work on the essays collected as *Edinburgh: Picturesque Notes* at the end of the year. Beinecke 6128, 12 pp. of notes chiefly from the Rev. Robert Wodrow's *Analecta* (1842-43; Beinecke 2606), probably represents notes taken for this project. See also the entries of "A Covenanting Story-Book" (1868-69), "Covenanters" (22 September 1873), and "Colonel Jean Cavalier" (June 1881).

A MOUNTAIN TOWN IN FRANCE. September 1878. MSS: Arnold, 1924, 828 (2 leaves, folio, probably numbered 1-2); Yale (2 leaves, folio, numbered 3-4;

twenty-three pencil sketches); Silverado Museum, St. Helena, California (5 leaves, folio, headed "Travels with a donkey in the French Highlands. I. Le Monastier," sold as Arnold, 1924, 827); Huntington (11 leaves, folio and quarto, comprising the text eventually published). *The Studio*, Winter 1896-97, pp. 3-17, including four of Stevenson's pencil sketches. One additional sketch appears in the limited edition, *A Mountain Town in France* (New York and London: John Lane, The Bodley Head, 1897). Tusitala 17, where this material is published as the first chapter of *Travels with a Donkey*. Stevenson no doubt drafted this material on Le Monastier during his stay there in September 1878 and revised it in Edinburgh that winter, intending it for the first chapter of the book eventually published as *Travels with a Donkey*. But it was never so published during his lifetime. It is unknown whether Stevenson or someone else decided to drop this beginning from the published version.

TRAVELS WITH A DONKEY IN THE CÉVENNES. Rewritten December 1878-January 1879 from the journal Stevenson kept the previous autumn during the walking tour itself, 22 September-2 October 1878. MS journal, Huntington HM 2408 (74 leaves), Yale (4 additional leaves). MS untraced. As noted in the previous entry, "A Mountain Town in France" represents material originally intended as the beginning of this work but eventually discarded. *Travels with a Donkey in the Cevennes* (London: C. Kegan Paul and Company, 1879). Walter Crane's original drawing for the frontispiece of this edition is now in the Walter Crane Collection, Beinecke Rare Book and Manuscript Library, Yale University. Published 2 June 1879; on further printings of this edition see the Beinecke Collection catalogue, *A Stevenson Library . . .*, pp. 18-20. American edition (Boston: Roberts Brothers, 1879) listed in *The Publishers' Weekly*, 21 June 1879, printed from English sheets sent to Roberts Brothers on 22 May. Tusitala 27.

Selections from Stevenson's journal were published in *Hitherto Unpublished Prose Writings* (Boston: Bibliophile Society, 1921), pp. 92-94, and in W. H. Arnold, "My Stevensons," *Scribner's Magazine*, 71 (January 1922), 57-62. Published in its entirety as *The Cevennes Journal: Notes on a Journey through the French Highlands*, ed. Gordon Golding [and Robin Hill] (Edinburgh: Mainstream Publishing, 1978) and, translated into French by Jacques Blondel with an extensive French commentary and annotations by Jacques Poujol, as *Journal de Route en Cevennes* (Toulouse: Edouard Privat for the Club Cévenol, 1978).

Stevenson left for France almost immediately after Fanny Osbourne's departure for the United States on 15 August 1878. As Graham Balfour writes, *Life, 1*, 157: "All was dark before them . . . and for the present all idea of a union was impossible. . . . So there came the pain of parting without prospect of return, and he who was afterwards so long an exile from his friends, now suffered separation from his dearest by the breadth of a continent and an ocean." By early September Stevenson was in Le Monastier, south of Le Puy, finishing his "Latter-Day Arabian Nights" stories and the essays collected as *Edinburgh: Picturesque Notes*, walking in the vicinity of Le Monastier, and shortly planning another walking tour. "I shall soon go off on a voyage," Stevenson wrote to Charles Baxter on 17 September, "for which I think I shall buy a donkey, and out of which, if I do not make a book, may my right hand forget its cunning" (*Baxter Letters*, p. 56). Two days later he had purchased his donkey, Modestine, "costing 65 francs and a glass of brandy" (*Letters, 2*, 52), and on Saturday 22 September he left Le Monastier, arriving on 2 October at St. Jean du Gard. From St. Jean du Gard, the walking tour over, he made his way to Alés and Lyons, to Autun to visit P. G. Hamerton, and then to Paris. By late October or early November Stevenson was again in England.

Stevenson rewrote the journal of his walking tour chiefly in Edinburgh during December 1878 and early January 1879. W. E. Henley read the finished manuscript during the week which he spent with Stevenson at Swanston, 14-22 January (see Henley to Colvin, 26 January 1879, in E. V. Lucas, *The Colvins and Their Friends*, 1928, pp. 110-11), and on 14 January P. G. Hamerton wrote agreeing to Stevenson's request to act as his agent in London (Beinecke 4505). On 24 February 1879, other proposals having been rejected by the publisher, Hamerton wrote to Stevenson that he had accepted C. Kegan Paul's offer of thirty pounds down and a royalty of two shillings a copy (see Beinecke 4506-9 and the slightly different terms recorded by C. Kegan Paul and Company mentioned below). Stevenson accepted this offer, had proofs by the end of March or early in April, and the book was published on 2 June 1879 in an edition of 750 copies. Sales were good, Stevenson reported to his mother in July: "My new book sold 450-60 last week. The Ind. V. has sold 485 altogether. They hope to have a 2nd edition of the donkey. Trench (Paul's pardner) told me it was the only book of theirs that was selling at all" (Bradford Brinton Memorial Ranch Collection, Wyoming). An additional printing of 500 copies was ordered, identified as "SECOND EDITION" on the title page, and these seem to have appeared in London sometime during the autumn of 1879. See *Letters, 2*, 79, 89, 97.

According to the C. Kegan Paul and Company *Publication Books*, vol. 3, p. 256, Stevenson was to receive £30 on the day of publication and a royalty of 4 shillings a copy after the first 700 copies; and in the same place it is noted that £30 was paid to Stevenson on 30 May 1879. In the firm's *Publication Account Books*, vol. 9, p. 43, the entry for *Travels with a Donkey* is closed out with an entry showing a net income from sales of £5.10.2, debits of £8.14.0, and a payment of £19.1.1 apportioned from the sum of £101 or more paid in January 1884 to recover Stevenson's interest in the three books of his first published by C. Kegan Paul and Company so that he could put these works into the hands of Chatto and Windus. These records appear in *The Archives of Kegan Paul . . . 1853-1912*, ed. Brian Maidment, 27 microfilm reels (1973), reels 2 and 8.

Stevenson's most important source for the historical material he included in *Travels with a Donkey* was Napoléon Peyrat's *Histoire des Pasteurs de Désert* (1842). Although an English translation, *The Pastors in the*

Wilderness, appeared in 1852, Stevenson used the more inclusive French edition. In Edinburgh, using the collection of the Advocates' Library, he also drew upon the English edition of Jean Cavalier's memoirs, *Wars of the Cevennes* (2nd ed., 1727); *A Cry from the Desart; or Testimonials of the Miraculous Things Come to Pass in the Cevennes*, 2nd ed., trans. with a preface by John Lacy (1707), a translation of Francois M. Misson's *Le Théatre Sacré des Cevennes* (1707); Antoine Court's *Histoire des Troubles des Cevennes* (1760); and de Bruyes' *Histoire du Fanatisme* (1692). No doubt he consulted other books in the Advocates' Library. He also seems to have used, for information in the last chapter of *Travels with a Donkey*, Jean-Baptiste Louvreleuil's *Le Fanatisme Renouvellé, ou Histoire des sacrilèges . . . que les calvinistes revoltes ont commis dans les Cévennes* (1704–6; 3rd ed., 1868). Stevenson's copy of the first volume of Misson's *Histoire des Camisards* (London: Moise Chastel, 1744) is now in the Silverado Museum, St. Helena, California. Stevenson's markings indicate that he used this work chiefly for information on Rolland and Jean Cavalier. Stevenson's copies of Eugène Bonnèmere's *Histoire des Camisards* (Paris: Dècembre-Allonnier, 1869; Paris: E. Dentu, 1877) are now in the Rare Book Collection, State University of New York at Buffalo. Further on Stevenson's interest in the Cévennes see the entry "Colonel Jean Cavalier" under date of June 1881.

PROVIDENCE AND THE GUITAR. October-November 1878. MS untraced. "Leon Berthilini's Guitar," *London,* four weekly installments, 2-23 November 1878; each installment signed Robert Louis Stevenson. *New Arabian Nights* (1882), in which publication the story was given its present title. Tusitala 1. See Balfour, *Life, 1*, 152-53, for an account of the composition of this story.

DEACON BRODIE. October 1878-January 1880 and at other times through 1887. MS notes on scenery and characters, Yale. MSS untraced. Copyright edition: *Deacon Brodie, or, The Double Life: A Melodrama, Founded on Facts In Four Acts and Ten Tabeaux*. "Entered at Stationer's Hall . . . All rights reserved." Printed by T. and A. Contstable, Edinburgh, December 1879-January 1880. On 26 January 1880 Henley inscribed copies of this edition to Henry James (Rosenbach, 1933, 257) and Andrew Lang (Princeton University Library). Probably at the same time he sent copies to Sidney Colvin (McCutcheon, 1925, 536), to Professor Fleeming Jenkin (see Beinecke 4987), to the actor Charles Warner (Beinecke 7402; see also Beinecke 4733), to Stevenson himself (Rosenbach, 1947, 576), and no doubt to others. Corrected copies of this edition were used for the performances of *Deacon Brodie* in 1882, 1883, 1884, and 1887. Among such copies are those of E. J. Henley (Princeton) and Mrs. W. P. Byles (Silverado Museum, St. Helena, California). From a copy of this 1880 edition which Henley inscribed to J. Brander Matthews on 4 July 1883 (Widener Collection, Harvard University) was taken the text of *Deacon Brodie* published in the variously titled edition, *The Works of Robert Louis Stevenson*, ed. C. C. Bigelow and Temple Scott, 10 vols. (New York: Lamb Publishing Company, 1906), *8*, 249-322. The 1880 edition of *Deacon Brodie* is otherwise unpublished.

Revised edition, 1888: *Deacon Brodie or the Double Life A Melodrama in Five Acts and Eight Tableaux By William Ernest Henley and Robert Louis Stevenson* (Edinburgh: T. and A. Constable, Edinburgh University Press, 1888). Printed "For Private Circulation Only." From this revised text derives the first published edition of *Deacon Brodie*, in *Three Plays By W. E. Henley and R. L. Stevenson* (London: David Nutt, 1892). Tusitala 24.

Stevenson read "portions of a proposed drama on" Deacon Brodie to his friend H. B. Baildon in late 1864, and according to Edmund Gosse he had a complete draft of such a play by 1869. See Baildon's *Robert Louis Stevenson: A Life Study in Criticism* (1901), p. 22, and Gosse's *Biographical Notes on the Writings of Robert Louis Stevenson* (1908), p. 98. "When I was about nineteen years of age," Stevenson himself told an interviewer in 1887, "I wrote a sort of hugger-mugger melodrama, which lay in my coffer until it was fished out by my friend W. E. Henley." This was in the autumn of 1878 and Stevenson and Henley revised this work together during the next several months, from October 1878 to January 1879. The play was offered to Henry Irving, but by 6 February 1879, as Colvin wrote to Henley, it was clear that "nothing can be got out of . . . Irving" (Beinecke 4338; in E. V. Lucas, *The Colvins and Their Friends*, 1928, p. 113). Henley returned to the play and revised it himself in November and December 1879, Stevenson then being in the United States, and printed copies were ready in January 1880. On 2 March 1880, having still further revised the work, Henley wrote to Stevenson that he was about to offer the play through the actor Charles Warner to the manager of the Princess's Theatre, Walter Gooch. "I will send you a marked copy immediately with all the corrections & excisions," Henley wrote, describing the changes in detail (Beinecke 4734). By 20 April Gooch had definitely refused the play and Henley had sent it through Sidney Colvin to the playwright and actor John Clayton (Beinecke 4736). But Clayton, too, disliked the play (Beinecke 4737), and after this disappointment Henley seems to have left the play aside entirely until late 1882, when he was at last able to get it produced, by Haldane Critchon's company at Pullan's Theatre of Varieties, Bradford. Scheduled originally for 21 December, the play was first performed a week later on 28 December 1882.

Later performances were held at Her Majesty's Theatre, Aberdeen, in April 1883, and at the Prince's Theatre, London, in July 1884. See Colvin to Henley, July 1884, in Lucas, p. 158, and Stevenson's mother's scrapbook of notices and reviews of Stevenson's work now in the Monterey State Historical Monument Stevenson House Collection, California, vol. 2, pp. 35 and 66ff. (xerox, Yale). As Stevenson remarked in 1887: "after a desperate campaign we turned out the original drama of 'Deacon Brodie,' as performed in London, and recently, I believe, successfully in this city [New York]. We were both young men when we did that, and I think we had an idea that bad-heartedness was strength. Now the piece has been all overhauled, and although I have no idea whether it will please an audience, I don't think either Mr. Henley or I are ashamed of it. We take it now for good, honest melodrama not so very ill done" (New York *Herald,* 8 September 1887, rpt. in *The Critic,* 10 September 1887, and from this source in J. A. Hammerton, ed., *Stevensoniana*, 2nd ed., 1907, pp. 84-85). Stevenson refers to the production of *Deacon Brodie* then soon to be taken on tour in the United States and Canada by Henley's brother Teddy, on which see G. L. McKay's comments in the Beinecke Collection catalogue, *A Stevenson Library . . .* , p. 28, and the reviews in Stevenson's mother's scrapbook (Monterey), vol. 3, pp. 3, 4, 10, 27, 29-32, 56. The cabinet made by Brodie which was in Stevenson's bedroom during his childhood is now in the Lady Stair's House Museum Collection, Edinburgh, item 301.

THE LATE SAM BOUGH, R. S. A. Late November 1878. MS draft of the first half of this essay, Yale. *The Academy,* 30 November 1878, pp. 530-31; signed Robert Louis Stevenson.

THE PAVILION ON THE LINKS. November 1878-November 1879. MS untraced. *Cornhill Magazine*, 42 (September 1880), 307-27; and 42 (October 1880), 430-51; both installments signed R.L.S., the first containing the opening four chapters, the second the rest. *New Arabian Nights* (1882). Tusitala 1. In a paragraph later omitted from the end of his essay "The Education of an Engineer" (*Scribner's Magazine*, 4, November 1888, 640) Stevenson remarked of his experiences in Caithness in 1868: "Years after, I read in the papers that some defaulting banker had been picked up by a yacht upon the coast of Wales; the two vagabonds of Castleton (I know not why) rose up instantly before my fancy; and that same night I had made the framework of a blood-and-thunder tale, which perhaps the reader may have dipped into under the name of *The Pavilion on the Links.* But how much more picturesque is the plain fact!" He began this story shortly after he finished "Providence and the Guitar" in November 1878, intending it for the periodical *London (Baxter Letters*, p. 61). But it was still unfinished when he left for the United States on 7 August 1879 and was finished in November at Monterey. Somewhat to Stevenson's surprise, Leslie Stephen accepted it for the *Cornhill Magazine*, publication being delayed chiefly because of the story's length and Stephen's expectation of a novel from George Meredith requiring immediate serialization. See *Letters, 2*, 79, 97, 103-4, and Beinecke 4733, 5565. Stevenson recieved £22.1 for this story, paid to his account with Mitchell and Baxter on 1 September 1880 (Beinecke 7268).

On Stevenson's revisions between the serial and book-form versions, chiefly the dropping of the first paragraph and some four hundred words from chap. 6, see Arthur Conan Doyle, *Through the Magic Door* (1907), p. 117, and G. F. McCleary, "Stevenson's Early Writings," *Fortnightly,* n.s. 168 (November 1950), 343-2. On Doyle's high estimate of this story see also Doyle to Stevenson, 30 May 1893, and Barrie to Stevenson, 8 May 1891 (Beinecke 4455, 3955).

THE FOUR SEASONS. Late 1878. MS outline, Yale. MS untraced if written. Unpublished. On a page in his notebook for *An Inland Voyage* Stevenson outlined an essay titled "The Four Seasons," making a few notes under the headings "Prologue," "Spring," and "Summer," and writing down the next title, "Autumn." But he seems to have abandoned the project almost immediately. Stevenson's earlier essays, "On Winter" (winter 1874) and "Springtime" (spring 1875), do not appear to be related to this project.

1879

TRUTH OF INTERCOURSE. January 1879. MS untraced. *Cornhill Magazine*, 39 (May 1879), 585-90; signed R.L.S. *Virginibus Puerisque* (1881), where this essay was made the fourth of those published under the general title used also for the volume as a whole. Tusitala 25. Written at Swanston during Stevenson's stay there with W. E. Henley, 14-21 January 1879, and accepted for publication on 7 February. See the catalogue description of the annotated copy of *Virginibus Puerisque* which Stevenson gave to his father (C. Gerhardt and Company, 1915, 54) and Leslie Stephen to Stevenson, 7 February 1879 (Beinicke 5564).

ON THE CHOICE OF A PROFESSION. January 1879. MS, Huntington HM 401. MS draft of roughly the first third of this essay, Yale. *Scribner's Magazine*, 57 (January 1915), 66-69. Tusitala 28. Offered to Leslie Stephen in January 1879 (Beinecke 5564) but rejected and laid by until offered again to *Scribner's Magazine* in 1888, when it was again rejected in favor of "A Letter to a Young Gentlemen Who Proposes to Embrace the Career of Art." See the entry of this work below under date of March-April 1888 and Lloyd Osbourne's remarks with the reprinting of the earlier essay, Tusitala, *28*, 12.

HESTER NOBLE. January 1879; January-May 1880. MS outline, Princeton University Library: 3 leaves, folio, headed "Hester Noble's Mistake; or a word from Cromwell. Drama in four acts," giving as an alternate title "The Tragedy of H. N.," listing nine characters including Oliver Cromwell and Roger Denzil, "called Rogue D[enzil]," and outlining the action of the eight scenes of act 1 in detail. MS untraced. Unpublished.

Stevenson and Henley wrote a rough draft of this play, about whose title they were then uncertain, during their stay at Swanston in January 1879. "The second act of 'Rogue Denzil's Death' or a 'Word from Cromwell,' or whatever it is, was made yesterday afternoon," Henley wrote to Sidney Colvin on 20 January 1879. "It is the finest act in dramatic literature. 'Whaur's Wullie Shakespere noo?' as they say in Kirkcudbright. (*Entire and passionate concurrance of R.L.S.*)" (Beinecke 3060; quoted in E. V. Lucas, *The Colvins and Their Friends*, 1928, p. 109; see also Stevenson to Mrs. Sitwell, 19 January 1879, Sotheby sale, 4 December 1973, 246, now among uncatalogued letters in the Beinecke Collection). Other projects intervened during 1879, but by early 1880 the collaborators had turned again to the play. "I shall make a shot for *Hester*, as soon as I have finished the *Emigrant* and the *Vendetta* and perhaps my *Dialogue on Character and Destiny*," Stevenson wrote to Henley on 23 January 1880 (*Letters, 2*, 98). And on 23 March 1880 Henley wrote to Stevenson that he was hard at work on the opening, probably working from Stevenson's outline of the first act as well as their earlier draft, and wished "the rest (II, III, & IV) in detail" as soon as possible: "I don't want much," Henley wrote; "only the lie of the thing — that, however, I must have. Have no fear as to the results" (Beinecke 4375). Henley seems to have sent Stevenson a draft of some or all of the play later that spring, with which draft Stevenson then returned his own comments. But on 15 June 1880 a blast from Professor Fleeming Jenkin put an end to the project. "I went into a frenzy of wrath at your suggestions of changes in Esther or Hester etc—All tag ends of old stock incidents and not one single word about the only things which really matter in any play," Jenkin wrote to Stevenson. "Not a new idea or an old one of how Hester would feel just then—You give up every thought of ever writing a play—If you did not know theoretically what was right you might learn but you do know & yet your mind will harp away on the dropping of letters the sending of messengers etc. etc. — as if the handkerchief in Othello had anything to do with the play. . . . I am not sure that Henley could not write a play but if so you are hindering not helping him" (Beinecke 4988).

More than ten years later, commenting in June 1891 on his share in various collaborations with Henley, Stevenson wrote to Charles Baxter: "*Hester Noble*, being very largely mine and founded on an old play of mine, should come to me. . . . I have named *Hester Noble* because it was so very largely mine and I have been always tempted to make a story of it." In December 1891 Stevenson wrote, also to Baxter: "I have no intention of writing any of the plays; but of *Hester Noble* I wish to make a short story some one of these days for a collection. . . . He [Henley] has all the papers in a portfolio; if there ever was a sketch of *Hester*, I should be obliged if he would send it me" (*Baxter Letters*, pp. 281-82, 291).

AN APRIL DAY: OR, AUTOLYCUS IN SERVICE. February 1879; early 1883. MSS, Folger Library, Washington, D. C.: two complete drafts of this three-act farce with a third version of the first act. Unpublished except in the dissertation by Nancy Blonder Schiffman, "A Critical Edition of Robert Louis Stevenson's Unpublished Play Autolycus in Service" (Univ. of South Carolina, 1973; *DA*, 34 [1973], 1933-34A). Begun by Stevenson as a short story, "Autolycus at Court," in November 1874 (*Letters, 1*, 213), then revived as an idea for collaboration between Stevenson and Henley during their stay at Swanston in January 1879, and actually begun as a play in February 1879. See Henley's letters to Stevenson, Beinecke 4713, 4718-19. Early in 1883 Stevenson wrote to Henley that he was again at work on "Autolycus at Service," which he had now "rewritten with a literary, not a dramatic finish" and wished proposed to Chatto and Windus for inclusion with other stories in a volume to be ready by the autumn (Beinecke 3164, 4665). But the work seems to have been abandoned thereafter.

LAY MORALS. March 1879; October 1883. MS outline, Yale. MSS: Yale; Silverado Musuem, St. Helena, California. Stevenson's outline, Beinecke 6128, consists of a detailed paragraph outline of the first two chapters. It is unpublished. Yale MSS, Beinecke 6498-99, 37 leaves, folio, comprise the 1879 version: chaps. 1-4 and a second draft of chap. 4. First published in the Edinburgh Edition, 21 (1896), 313-77, where all but the last four paragraphs of chap. 4 are from Stevenson's full draft (Beinecke 6498). The concluding paragraphs are from his second draft of chap. 4 (Beinecke 6499). Tusitala, *26*, 5-49. One sentence and one page of summary ("And now, let us look back and see what we have reached upon this practical point of money," etc.), both from the second draft of chap 4, first appeared in *Hitherto Unpublished Prose Writings* (Boston: Bibliophile Society, 1921), pp. 59-61; Tusitala, *26*, 3-4. Silverado MS, 9 leaves, folio, comprises the 1883 version: pp. 1-2 are prefatory in nature and first appeared in *Hitherto Unpublished Prose Writings* (1921), pp. 55-59. Tusitala, *26*, 1-3. The remaining 7 pp. are unpublished and comprise three numbered sections and the beginning of a fourth. The first section derives clearly from the first six paragraphs of chap. 3 of the 1879 version but the others represent new material. Tusitala 26, which conflates the various versions as indicated above. On Stevenson's two separate efforts on this work see especially Balfour, *Life, 1*, 162, 209, and *2*, 215, and *Letters, 1*, 98, and *2*, 272-74. As Malcolm Elwin suggests, *The Strange Case of Robert Louis Stevenson* (1950), p. 62, many of the arguments in "Lay Morals" probably derive from Stevenson's essay for the Speculative Society, "Two Questions on the Relations Between Christ's Teaching and Modern Christianity" (12 November 1872). See also the entry of "Why Am I a Banker?" and other essays under date of mid-1878.

WHAT WAS ON THE SLATE. March-April 1879. MS untraced, probably destroyed. Unpublished. See *Letters, 2*, 59, 106, and Stevenson to Colvin, March 1879, Beinecke 3034. At work on "Lay Morals," then titled "Man and Money," Stevenson remarked to Sidney Colvin in March 1879 that he expected to finish that work "ere a month." He continued: "On about the same time, the sensation novel that F and I began should be finished. I have changed the denouement and it becomes a good, almost kindly story" (Beinecke 3034). Not long afterwards Stevenson wrote to Henley that James Walter Ferrier "likes my *What was on the Slate*, which, under a new title, yet unfound, and with a new and, on the whole, kindly *dênouement*, is going to shoot up and become a star" (*Letters, 2*, 59). But in February 1880 the project was abandoned, as Stevenson wrote to Henley: "The *Slate* both Fanny and I have damned utterly; it is too morbid, ugly, and unkind; better starvation" (*Letters, 2*, 106).

SOME ASPECTS OF ROBERT BURNS. May-August 1879. MS untraced. *Cornhill Magazine*, 40 (October 1879), 408-29; signed R.L.S. *Familiar Studies of Men and Books* (1882). Tusitala 27. On 8 May 1879, reading John Campbell

Shairp's study of Burns in the English Men of Letters series, Leslie Stephen asked Stevenson for an article on Burns for the *Cornhill Magazine* (Beinecke 5565). By 28 July 1879, as he wrote to Sidney Colvin, Stevenson had finished three of the four parts of this essay (*Letters, 2*, 64) and presumably he submitted it before he left for the United States on 7 August. Stevenson received twenty pounds for this essay. See also the entry of Stevenson's essay on Burns for the *Encyclopaedia Britannica* under date of summer-autumn 1875. On 27 November 1884 Stephen asked whether Stevenson would like to write on Burns for the *Dictionary of National Biography* (Beinecke 5770), but Stevenson apparently declined the offer. The entry was eventually written by Stephen himself.

THE STORY OF A LIE. July-August 1879. MS untraced. *New Quarterly Magazine*, 25 (October 1879), 307-55; signed Robert Louis Stevenson. The separately printed issue of this story (London: Hayley and Jackson, 1882) is probably a forgery by Thomas J. Wise. Tusitala 14. C. Kegan Paul apparently commissioned this story in May 1879, offering Stevenson fifty pounds for its publication in his *New Quarterly*. Stevenson worked on it over the next few months and finished it aboard the *Devonia* shortly before he arrived in New York on 17 August 1879. The fifty pounds Stevenson was to receive for this story was paid to his account with Mitchell and Baxter on 30 January 1880 (Beinecke 7268). See also *Letters, 2*, 64; *Baxter Letters*, p. 66; and Beinecke 3036, partly published in *Letters 2*, 72. On Thomas J. Wise's forgery of *The Story of a Lie* (Hayley and Jackson, 1882), see John Carter and Graham Pollard, *An Enquiry into the Nature of Certain Nineteenth Century Pamphlets* (1934) pp. 251-53; William B. Todd, "A Handlist of Thomas J. Wise," in Todd, ed., *Thomas J. Wise: Centenary Studies* (1959), pp. 104-5; and Todd's *Suppressed Commentaries on the Wisean Forgeries* (1969), pp. 39-42.

THE AMATEUR EMIGRANT. September 1879-June 1880. MS, Yale. Galley proofs of part of this MS, set in type for publication by C. Kegan Paul and Company in April 1880 but withdrawn, Yale. These proofs have been marked by Sidney Colvin, C. Kegan Paul, and by Stevenson himself. Proof sheets of "Across the Plains" as published in *Longman's Magazine*, Anderson 1914, I, 639. "Across the Plains: Leaves from the Notebook of an Emigrant Between New York and San Francisco," *Longman's Magazine*, 2 (July 1883), 285-304; and 2 (August 1883), 372-86. Signed at the end of each installment R. L. Stevenson. This publication includes only the last seven chapters of the work as written, according to Sidney Colvin "abridged and recast" by Stevenson in 1883 for publication in this form. Differences between this publication and the 1880 MS of these seven chapters, however, are few. *Across the Plains* (1892). This publication reprints the seven chapters first published in *Longman's Magazine*, abridged by the deletion of three passages in the chapter "Despised Races." First published as "The Amateur Emigrant" after Stevenson's death, in the Edinburgh Edition, 3 (1895), 1-166. This publication includes for the first time the first part of the work as written, abridged by Stevenson himself in 1894, together with the seven chapters already published in *Longman's Magazine* taken from the version published in *Across the Plains*. As written in 1880, the work is titled as a whole "The Amateur Emigrant, with some first impressions of America." Part 1 is called "The Emigrant Ship," consists of seven chapters, and ends with the chapter "Personal Experience and Review." Part 2, eight chapters, is called "America: The Emigrant Train" and begins with the chapter "New York." But to preserve the integrity of the seven chapters already published as "Across the Plains" Stevenson made the chapter "New York" the last in the first part of the work and retitled the two parts "From the Clyde to Sandy Hook" and "Across the Plains." These consist of eight and seven chapters respectively. Tusitala 18, which follows the text first published in the Edinburgh Edition. Stevenson's MS was used to supply passages which he deleted in 1894 in the edition of this work which appears in James D. Hart, ed., *From Scotland to Silverado* (1966), pp. 1-147. This edition follows the text published in the Edinburgh Edition except for passages restored from the MS. Stevenson's MS was first published in its entirety, divided and subtitled as in 1880, in Roger G. Swearingen, ed., *The Amateur Emigrant*, 2 vols. (Ashland: Lewis Osborne, 1976-77). This edition also includes comment on the suggestions made by Sidney Colvin and C. Kegan Paul on the galley proofs returned to Stevenson in the early summer of 1880.

Stevenson began work on the first part of "The Amateur Emigrant," his account of his trans-Atlantic voyage aboard the *Devonia*, 7-17 August 1879, in early September 1879 in Monterey, and by the first week of October he had this part "about half drafted" (*Letters, 2*, 76). In mid-October, having then 68 pages written, he laid it aside to work instead on "A Vendetta in the West" and, shortly, to finish "The Pavilion on the Links." In early December he added the three final pages of the first part and sent the manuscript to Sidney Colvin, commenting on the work and suggesting that as "the need for coin is pressing" Colvin negotiate the publication of this part alone (Beinecke 3042, partly published in *Letters, 2*, 85-86). Colvin received the manuscript shortly before Christmas 1879 and was very disappointed with its quality, remarking to Charles Baxter on 22 December that he found it "quite unworthy" of Stevenson (Beinecke 4179). W. E. Henley shared Colvin's opinion, remarking to Stevenson on 12 February 1880 that he found it "feeble, stale, pretentious" (Beinecke 4733). But both proceeded vigorously in their efforts to find a publisher for it (see Beinecke 4731, 4734, and Donald Macleod to James Runciman, 4 February 1880, and Runciman to Colvin, 5 February 1880, uncatalogued letters, Beinecke Collection). When it proved impossible to place the work with *Good Words*—"It is capital—full of force and character, fine feeling, and quite the kind of thing which would suit 'Good Words,' " wrote the editor Macleod. "My difficulty is getting room for it"—Henley and Colvin turned to C. Kegan Paul and Company, publisher of Stevenson's *An Inland Voyage* (1878) and *Travels with a Donkey* (1879). Paul accepted it, and by late April 1880 the whole manuscript of the first part of this work had been set in type.

Stevenson took up the second part of "The Amateur Emigrant" in San Francisco early in 1880, pressing on with the work even in the face of his friends' disappointment. "Well, God's will be done," Stevenson wrote to Colvin in February; "if it's dull, it's dull; it was a fair fight, and it's lost, and there's an end. But, fortunately, dulness is not a fault the public hates; perhaps they may like this vein of dulness. If they don't, damn them, we'll try them with another. . . . Only, frankly, Colvin, do you think it a good plan to be so eminently descriptive, and even eloquent in dispraise? You rolled such a lot of polysyllables over me that a better man than I might have been disheartened.—However, I was not, as you see, and am not. The *Emigrant* shall be finished and leave in the course of next week" (*Letters, 2*, 98-99). Illness delayed him, however, and Stevenson does not seem to have sent the second part of "The Amateur Emigrant" until April or early May 1880. "God only knows how much courage and suffering is buried in that MS.," he wrote to Colvin then. "The second part was written in a circle of hell unknown to Dante—that of the penniless and dying author. . . . There is one page in Part II., about having got to shore, and sich, which must have cost me altogether six hours of work as miserable as ever I went through. I feel sick even to think of it" (*Letters, 2*, 113).

In the same letter Stevenson also wrote, referring to the first part of this work: "recover the sheets of the *Emigrant*, and post them registered to me. And now give me all your venom against it; say your worst, and most incisively, for now it will be a help, and I'll make it right or perish in the attempt" (*Letters, 2*, 113). Acknowledging receipt of these proofs in late May he wrote: "I have received the first sheets of the *Amateur Emigrant*; not yet the second bunch, as announced. It is a pretty heavy, emphatic piece of pedantry; but I don't care; the public, I verily believe, will like it. I have excised all you proposed and more on my own movement. But I have not yet been able to rewrite the two special pieces which, as you said, so badly wanted it; the easiest work is still hard to me. But I am certainly recovering fast; a married and convalescent being" (*Letters, 2*, 116). Among the sheets to which Stevenson refers are the proofs of galleys 17-20 (photostats only), 25-28, and 33-40, now in the Beinecke Collection. These contain material from the three consecutive chapters "Steerage Scenes," "Steerage Types," and "The Sick Man" and are marked by Colvin, C. Kegan Paul, and, where he agrees with a proposed change or wishes a passage modified, by Stevenson himself.

Nevertheless, after his return to Britain in August 1880 Stevenson agreed with his father that it would be best not to publish the work. As Graham Balfour writes: "both Stevenson and his father now considered it undesirable to publish the account of his recent experiences as an emigrant in its existing form. It was necessarily somewhat personal, and the circumstances under which it was written had told against its success. It had been sold, but it was the work which his friends had criticised most severely, and there no longer existed the dire need for making money by any possible means. The sum paid by the publishers was refunded by Mr. Stevenson, and for the time being the book was withdrawn" (*Life, 1*, 177-78; see also *Letters, 2*, 126).

Announcement of the withdrawal appeared in *The Athenaeum*, 23 October 1880, and no doubt elsewhere: "Mr. R.L. Stevenson has determined to suppress his *Amateur Emigrant*, announced by us some little time ago, and has withdrawn it from his publishers' hands."

Early in 1883 Stevenson prepared the last seven chapters of "The Amateur Emigrant" for publication separately in *Longman's Mazagine* under the title of "Across the Plains." He made few changes from his original manuscript and returned corrected proofs to Edmund Gosse in London on 20 May 1883 (*Letters, 2*, 240). For this separate publication Stevenson received forty-five pounds, paid to his account with Mitchell and Baxter on 24 April 1883 (Beinecke 7268). Under the same title this material was reprinted, in slightly condensed form, in *Across the Plains* (1892), possibly from corrected sheets supplied by Stevenson himself.

Except for these seven chapters Stevenson left *The Amateur Emigrant* entirely aside from the time of its writing in 1879-80 until 1894, when it was proposed to publish it in the Edinburgh Edition. The idea was Sidney Colvin's. As Colvin wrote to Charles Baxter on 7 February 1894: "As to the arrangement of the matter, I had written to R.L.S. by last mail suggesting that the *Inland Voyage* and the *Donkey* should make one vol. of travels . . . and that a second volume might very appropriately be made if he chose, out of *The Amateur Emigrant* and *The Silverado Squatters. The Amateur Emigrant* would include the suppressed ocean passage which would need some recasting, etc. (I have sent him out my old proofs in case he catches on to the idea), as well as *Across the Plains" (Baxter Letters*, p. 346). On 19 April 1894 Colvin, as he wrote to Baxter then, was still unsure whether Stevenson was "willing to reprint the first part of the Amateur Emigrant" (Beinecke 4282). But on 18 March 1894 Stevenson replied. "Your proposals are entirely to my mind," he wrote. "About the *Amateur Emigrant*, it shall go to you by this mail well slashed. If you like to slash some more on your own account, I give you permission. 'Tis not a great work; but since it goes to make up the first two volumes as proposed, I presume it has not been written in vain" (*Letters, 5*, 127-28; see also Colvin to Baxter, 22 June 1894, Beinecke 4300). Although Stevenson did not live to see this volume through the press, Colvin made no additional changes and the work as published in the Edinburgh Edition represents Stevenson's final revision of it made in the spring of 1894. See Colvin's note in *Baxter Letters*, p. 370.

Contributions to THE MONTEREY CALIFORNIAN. 7 October-23 December 1879. MSS untraced. Anne R. Issler, *Pacific Historical Review*, 34 (August 1965), 319, attributes to Stevenson fifteen articles and announcements in the weekly newspaper *The Monterey Californian*, 7 October through 23 December 1879. Anne B. Fisher, *No More A Stranger* (1946), pp. 131-36, 245, supplies evidence for one of these attributions and suggests an additional attribution, "The Morals of Monterey" (probably 4 November). George R. Stewart establishes Stevenson's authorship of "San Carlos Day" (11 November) in the introduction to his reprinting of it, *Scribner's Magazine*, 68 (August

1920), 209-11. Except for "San Carlos Day," reprinted also in James D. Hart, ed., *From Scotland to Silverado* (1966), pp. 168-71, none of these articles has been published since its first appearance.

A VENDETTA IN THE WEST. Begun October 1879. MS untraced. Unpublished. According to Sidney Colvin, *Letters, 2*, 79, this work was "three parts written and then given up and destroyed." On 21 October 1879 Stevenson wrote to Sidney Colvin that he had laid aside "The Amateur Emigrant" for the moment, having carried it nearly to the end of the first part, "and I have now, by way of change, more than seventy pages of a novel, a one-volume novel, alas! to be called either *A Chapter in the Experience of Arizona Breckonridge* or *A Vendetta in the West*, or a combination of the two. The scene from Chapter IV. to the end lies in Monterey and the adjacent country; of course, with my usual luck, the plot of the story is somewhat scandalous, containing an illegitimate father for a piece of resistance" (*Letters, 2,* 82). By mid-November Stevenson had written 85 of what he expected would be 140 pages (see *Letters, 2,* 84, 80), and in February 1880 W. E. Henley was anxious to begin finding a publisher for it. "If 'tis good and exciting, I'll try the *Glasgow Herald* with it, or try & work off a sepduplicate of country journals—seven at a blow—for it, as [James] Payn does" (Beinecke 4733). But even though he referred to it often during the winter and spring and at the end of May 1880 was still hoping to finish the novel "this summer," Stevenson does not seem to have worked on the novel at all after he left Monterey in December 1879. See *Letters, 2*, 95-100, 105, 107, 116. His sister-in-law Nellie Sanchez recalled that it was to have been based "upon some of his [Stevenson's] impressions of western America," that the heroine's name Arizona "came out of his intense delight in the 'songful, tuneful' nomenclature of the United States, in which terms he refers to it in *Across the Plains*," and that "some story that we told him about a man who named his numerous family of daughters after the States—Indiana, Nebraska, California, etc.—took his fancy and suggested the name of Arizona Breckinridge to him" (*The Life of Mrs. Robert Louis Stevenson*, 1922, pp. 60-61). In a separate article, she wrote that the novel was to be "an American story based on the southern feuds, which seemed to appeal to his imagination" ("Some Stevenson Legends," *Overland Monthly*, 88, January 1930, 10).

PADRE DOS REALES. Late November 1879. MS untraced, probably destroyed. Two hundred copies of this broadsheet, 121 words of text berating the parsimony of Padre Angelo Casanova of Monterey, were printed in San Jose by Crevole M. Bronson, publisher of *The Monterey Californian*, and were posted late one November night by Stevenson and his friends. See his account of the mischief, *Letters, 2*, 86. Three copies survive, in the Widener Library, Harvard University; in the Huntington Library; and pasted into one of Stevenson's mother's scrapbooks, Monterey State Historical Monument Stevenson House Collection, California (xerox, Yale). The text is reprinted in James D. Hart, ed., *From Scotland to Silverado* (1966), pp. xxvii-xxviii; a facsimile appears in the catalogue of the February 1923 Lloyd Osbourne sale, Sotheby's, at which one of the extant copies was offered.

STORIES. Planned December 1879. MSS untraced. Unpublished except for "The Pavilion on the Links" (1880). In a letter to Sidney Colvin in early December 1879, having outlined a collection of "Fables and Tales" to be made from work already published, Stevenson writes: "I have heaps of short stories in view. The next volume will probably be called *Stories* or *A Story-Book*, and contain quite a different lot: *The Pavilion on the Links: Professor Rensselaer: The Dead Man's Letter: The Wild Man of the Woods: The Devil on Cramond Sands*. They would all be carpentry stories; pretty grim for the most part; but of course that's all in the air as yet. . . . I may even send another story 'Marjory Bonthron' straight to this volume, instead of first to a Maga" (Beinecke 3043: partly published in *Letters, 2*, 89). Of these stories only the first and last are known except as titles in this and other lists of projected stories. "The Pavilion on the Links" is entered above under date of November 1878, and at the time he wrote of the present collection Stevenson had only just finished it. "The Devil on Cramond Sands" is entered above under date of late 1860s or early 1870s and appears in Stevenson's 1868-69 list for "A Covenanting Story-Book" and in lists of November 1874 and June 1881; see *Letters, 1*, 213-14, and *2*, 150-51. "The Dead Man's Letter" appears again in Stevenson's list of June 1881 (*Letters 2*, 150-51) but is otherwise unknown. "Marjory Bonthron" appears in Stevenson's list of November 1874 (*Letters, 1*, 213-14) but is otherwise unknown. "Professor Rensselaer" and "The Wild Man of the Woods" are unknown except as titles in the present list.

HENRY DAVID THOREAU: HIS CHARACTER AND OPINIONS. December 1879-January 1880. MS untraced. *Cornhill Magazine*, 41 (June 1880), 665-82; signed R.L.S. *Familiar Studies of Men and Books* (1882), where in the "Preface" Stevenson comments on his discussions with A.H. Japp about this essay in September 1881; see *Letters, 2*, 164-65, 169-70. Tusitala 27.

Having finished his essay on Burns in July 1879 Stevenson then planned to write on Thoreau, and he spent the autumn in Monterey reading for the essay. "Thoreau was another favorite of his," the rancher Edward Berwick recalled of Stevenson in Monterey, "and, as I had never even heard of Thoreau, he kindly offered to lend me a volume" (MS, Monterey State Historical Monument Stevenson House Collection, California, item 1490). Stevenson's copy of A. H. Japp's *Thoreau: His Life and Aims* (London, 1878) was sold as Anderson 1914, I, 680, and contains marginal notes and some verses by Stevenson written in Monterey on the fly leaf.

Stevenson wrote the essay in December 1879 and January 1880 in San Francisco. Charles Warren Stoddard, *Exits and Entrances* (1903), p. 16, recalls visiting Stevenson in San Francisco and finding him "submerged in billows of bedclothes; about him floated the scattered volumes of a complete set of Thoreau; he was preparing an essay on that worthy, and he looked at the moment like a half-drowned man—yet he was not cast down" (rpt. in J. A. Hammerton, ed., *Stevensoniana*, 2nd ed., 1907, p. 48). By 23 January the essay had been sent off, and on 5 February 1880 Leslie Stephen wrote to C. E. Norton that he had received this essay and expected to publish it soon (see F. W. Maitland, ed., *The Life and Letters of Leslie Stephen*, 1906, pp. 339-40). On 5 June Stevenson wrote to Charles Baxter that it had brought him £18.18, a sum already paid to his account with Mitchell and Baxter on 1 June 1880 (*Letters, 2*, 97, 102; Stevenson to Baxter, uncatalogued letter, Beinecke Collection; Beinecke 7268).

When the essay was published in June 1880, A. H. Japp wrote immediately to the *Spectator* about it. In his letter, published under the heading "Thoreau's Pity and Humour" (*Spectator*, 12 June 1880, pp. 749-50), Japp found Stevenson's knowledge of Thoreau decidely limited: "I think the most charitable assumption is that Mr. R.L.S.'s studies of Thoreau have not been quite so extensive as they might have been, but at all events, one ounce of fact is surely worth a bushel of theory and 'smart' writing, even in these days of exact science and agnosticism." Thoreau did not lack pity, nor was he a skulker—as Japp tried to show from anecdotes about him. "Should Mr. R.L.S. wish it, I can, through you, give him reference to authority for this anecdote, and to a dozen similar instances."

Stevenson returned to Britain on 17 August 1880, and in due course Japp's letter came to his attention. As Japp writes, *Robert Louis Stevenson . . .* (1905), p. 4, Stevenson replied privately and "expressed the wish to see me, and have some talk with me on that and other matters," and the following summer he invited Japp to visit him at Braemar—as he did in late August and early September, carrying away with him the early chapters of *Treasure Island*. "To him who knew the man from the inside," Stevenson remarked of Japp in his "Preface" to *Familiar Studies of Men and Books*, "many of my statements sounded like inversions made on purpose; and yet when we came to talk of them together, and he understood how I was looking at the man through the books, while he had long since learned to read the books through the man, I believe he understood the spirit in which I had been led astray" (Tusitala, *27*, xviii).

Fanny Price, "R.L.S. and Thoreau," *Notes and Queries*, 2 January 1943, p. 18, suggests that the last two lines of Stevenson's poem "Requiem," written early in 1880 in San Francisco (see *Letters, 2*, 108) may echo a couplet in Thoreau's *A Week on the Concord and Merrimac Rivers* (1845).

1880

MEMOIRS OF HIMSELF. Early 1880, augmented later. MSS: (1) Book I—Childhood, Widener Collection, Harvard University, 23 pp. at the beginning of a 72 pp. quarto notebook, the remaining pages blank. (2) Book II, untraced except for the last 2 pp., sold with the MS of Book III as Anderson

1914, I, 336, and the material quoted by G. S. Hellman in "Stevenson and the Streetwalker," *American Mercury*, 38 (July 1936), 349. (3) Book III—From Jest to Earnest, Anderson 1914, I, 336. (4) Additional material dictated to Isobel Strong in Samoa, untraced but published in the Vailima Edition, 26 (1923), 224-37. Publication: (1) *Memoirs of Himself* (Philadelphia: For Private Distribution Only, 1912) and from this source in *The Cornhill Booklet*, 4 (Christmas 1914), 55-68, and in the Vailima Edition, 26 (1923), 203-24. This material comprises the whole of Book I, from the MS now at Harvard. Tusitala *29*, 145-60. (2) Book II has been published only in Balfour, *Life, 1*, 83-84, a fragment from the end of Book II, and—another fragment—in the article by G. S. Hellman cited above. (3) Book III has been published only in Balfour, *Life, 1*, 86-94. (4) The additional material Stevenson dictated to Isobel Strong commences with the words "I have long given up all idea of autobiographical writing." First published in the Vailima Edition, as cited above, it appears immediately after the text of Book I in Tusitala, *29*, 160-68. "I am living absolutely alone in San Francisco," Stevenson writes at the very beginning of this work, and he appears to have written the first three parts of it there early in 1880, adding the dictated material in Samoa sometime during the 1890s.

YOSHIDA-TORAJIRO. Before 23 January 1880. MS untraced. *Cornhill Magazine*, 41 (March 1880), 327-34; signed R.L.S. *Familiar Studies of Men and Books* (1882). Tusitala 27. Stevenson's interest in Yoshida dates from the visit to Edinburgh in early June 1878 of a Japanese official, Taiso Masaki, who at dinner at Professor Fleeming Jenkin's told Stevenson and others the story of Yoshida's career. See Sir Alfred Ewing, "Stevenson and the Fleeming Jenkins," in Masson, ed., *I Can Remember Robert Louis Stevenson* (1922), p. 125, and the detailed commentary in Yukinobu Tanabe, "Robert Louis Stevenson's View of the Japanese," *Ôbun-ronsô*, 6 (30 January 1976). Later in 1878, Stevenson added the title "A Japanese Hero" to a list of "Essays" projected for eventual collection, this on a page in the notebook he kept for *An Inland Voyage* (Yale). But not until he was in San Francisco, more than a year later, does Stevenson appear actually to have returned to the project. Probably he wrote the essay in late December and early January 1879-80. On 23 January 1880 he wrote to Edmund Gosse that this essay and another on Thoreau were both "postulant," having just been submitted to Leslie Stephen for the *Cornhill Magazine*, and on 1 February he was still awaiting a decision (*Letters, 2*, 102-3). On the same date Professor Fleeming Jenkin wrote to Stevenson agreeing to read the proofs; in doing so he also added two footnotes supplying further matters of detail (Beinecke 4987).

BENJAMIN FRANKLIN AND THE ART OF VIRTUE. Projected January-February 1880, November 1881. MS untraced if written. MS notes, Princeton University Library. Unpublished. Stevenson first mentioned the idea of writing on Franklin in a letter to Sidney Colvin on 10 January 1880 (*Letters, 2*, 93), and in February he wrote to W. E. Henley about a proposed collection of "Studies" that he had already sent essays on Thoreau and Yoshida-Torajiro to Leslie Stephen for the *Cornhill Magazine*. "But I want *Benjamin Franklin and the Art of Virtue* to follow; and perhaps also *William Penn*, but this last may be perhaps be delayed for another volume— I think not, though" (*Letters, 2*, 105). His copy of *The Life of Benjamin Franklin, Written by Himself*, ed. John Bigelow, 3 vols. (Philadelphia and London, 1874-75) is now held as Beinecke 2530. Passages are marked in these volumes but there are no marginal comments. On 9 November 1881 Stevenson wrote to Edmund Gosse, who was acting for R.W. Gilder of the *Century Magazine*, "Benj. Franklin — do you want him?" (*Letters, 2*, 175). See the entry of this work under date of November 1881. But on neither occasion does Stevenson appear actually to have written this essay.

[William Penn.] Projected January-May 1880. MS untraced if written. Unpublished. Stevenson's projected study was inspired by his finding Penn's *Fruits of Solitude, in Maxims and Reflections . . .*, 10th ed. (Phildelphia: Benjamin Johnson, 1792) at a San Francisco bookseller's. In late January 1880 he asked Sidney Colvin to send him William Hepworth Dixon's *History of William Penn* (2nd ed., 1872) and Penn's *Select Works* (1771). He acknowledged receipt of Dixon's study in May 1880; his copy of the *Select Works*, 4th ed. (London, 1825) was sold as Anderson 1914, II, 444. Stevenson later gave his copy of Penn's *Fruits of Solitude* to Horatio F. Brown, writing in it two lengthy presentation inscriptions commenting both on Penn and this particular copy. For the inscriptions see *Letters, 2*, 145; Stevenson's copy was offered in 1979 by Bernard M. Rosenthal, Inc., San Francisco. Stevenson's copy of S. M. Janney's *Life of William Penn* (1852) was sold as Anderson 1914, II, 443. His copy of *A Concise Biographical Sketch of William Penn* (Philadelphia: For Sale at Friends' Book-Store, No. 304 Arch Street, n. d.) is among the uncatalogued Stevenson materials in the Beinecke Collection. See also *Letters, 2*, 105, 112, 117, 145, and the previous entry. Stevenson comments briefly on Penn in "Books Which Have Influenced Me" (1887), Tusitala *28*, 67.

ESSAYS, REFLECTIONS AND REMARKS ON HUMAN LIFE. January-February 1880. MS, Yale: 22 pp. originally from a notebook, comprising a table of contents, 9 pp. in ink containing the first six pieces, and 12 pp. mostly in pencil containing the rest. The last three pieces are in ink, and the division between ink and pencil also appears in the table of contents, suggesting that Stevenson wrote or copied these pieces chiefly on two separate occasions. Edinburgh Edition, 28 (1898), 26-41. Tusitala 26.

In letters to W. E. Henley on 23 January 1880 and in February 1880 Stevenson referred to the third of these pieces, the "Dialogue on Character and Destiny Between Two Puppets" (Tusitala, *26*, 77-82), as among various pending projects (*Letters, 2*, 98, 106). Probably he wrote some or all of these pieces during the spring of 1880 in San Francisco.

[Contributions to San Francisco newspapers.] January-May 1880. None traced. It seems certain that Stevenson never worked as an ordinary reporter for any San Francisco newspaper during his stay from December 1879 through May 1880, and that he never worked for the San Francisco *Chronicle* in any capacity. He may have contributed two or three articles to the San Francisco *Bulletin,* but if so these have never been identified.

Two separate accounts claiming that Stevenson wrote for newspapers when he was in San Francisco exist. Howard Wilford Bell, "An Unpublished Chapter in the Life of Robert Louis Stevenson," *Pall Mall Magazine*, 24 (June 1901), 267-71 (substantially rptd. in J. A. Hammerton, ed., *Stevensoniana*, 2nd ed., 1907, pp. 42-46), asserted that Stevenson was employed by the San Francisco *Chronicle,* first as a regular reporter and then as a contributor of articles on Sundays. Bell's account was denied in its entirety by the newspaper's then editor, James DeYoung, in a letter to the *Times,* 2 July 1901 (rpt. *Stevensoniana*, pp. 46-47). In addition, on 6 May 1901, Nellie Sanchez wrote to her sister Fanny, Stevenson's wife, mentioning these forthcoming claims and saying that she knew of no articles written by Stevenson for San Francisco newspapers in 1879-80. On this letter Fanny wrote by way of annotation: "While Louis was living in San Francisco the two people that [he] saw almost every day were Nellie and Mrs [Dora] Williams. He talked anything over with them, and Nellie wrote to his dictation, and copied everything else for him. Neither of them ever heard of such a thing as his being a Chronicle reporter. They both knew of two or three letters published by the Bulletin." As to Stevenson's ever having worked as a reporter, she added: "he would have told me had he taken any such position—why should he have kept it such a dead secret that only Mr Bell knows it?" (NLS 9891, f. 62).

Anne R. Issler, *Happier for his Presence: San Francisco and Robert Louis Stevenson* (1949), pp. 90-94, finds Bell's story about the *Chronicle* conceivable, on the grounds that perhaps Bell knew "more than Stevenson's indignant relatives were willing to believe" (p. 94; she seems unaware of DeYoung's emphatic denial). But chiefly she tells the story of Stevenson's having contributed to the San Francisco *Bulletin.* This story Mrs. Issler had from Bailey Millard, whose friend George K. Fitch was editor of the San Francisco *Bulletin* when Stevenson was in San Francisco. According to Fitch, Stevenson came to the *Bulletin* office one Saturday afternoon and left with him a number of manuscripts for consideration. "When he called for the verdict a few days later," Issler writes, "he was told that two [articles] had been selected and that he would . . . [receive] payment at the rate of five dollars a column," a total of just over twenty dollars. Stevenson protested that the articles were worth more, but he accepted the twenty dollars nevertheless (pp. 91-92). The titles or contents of these articles seem to have been unknown to Issler's informants, but she speculates that one of them might have been "San Francisco Restaurants" (*Daily Evening Bulletin*, 11 February 1880, p. 4). This article, which in any event is not even a column in length, clearly was not written by Stevenson, however, for it is signed at the end "*Corr. N. Y. Trib.*," shows a much greater familiarity with New York restaurants that Stevenson could have acquired in his one-day stay there in August 1879, and refers to restaurants in other American cities which Stevenson never visited or only passed through on the train.

Graham Balfour, *Life, 1*, 172, seems to have had some knowledge of all of the above-mentioned facts and claims. He cites DeYoung's denial that Stevenson ever wrote for the *Chronicle* and adds that Stevenson didn't write for the *Bulletin* either, because its rate of payment was too low. Balfour's authority for this last statement is unknown—certainly he would have consulted Fanny Stevenson, and on 16 April 1901 he wrote to Charles Warren Stoddard about the matter (Beinecke 3940)—but Balfour's account is consistent with Fitch's recollection of his interview with Stevenson, at least as to the paper's rates. Whether the "two or three letters" in the *Bulletin* which Nellie Sanchez and Dora Williams "both knew of," or the two articles for which its editor George Fitch recalled having paid Stevenson slightly more than twenty dollars were ever actually published, however, remains unknown. None has been identified, and Balfour's statement that Stevenson did not write for the *Bulletin* can be reconciled with the other accounts of the matter simply by assuming that while the articles in question were written and even perhaps submitted to the *Bulletin*, Stevenson withdrew them rather than see them published at rates he considered too low.

THE HUMAN COMPROMISE. Projected February 1880. Stevenson mentions this work he has in mind, one of "two (or three) essays," in a letter to W. E. Henley in February 1880 (*Letters, 2*, 106). But it is otherwise unknown.

ON THE ART OF LITERATURE. February 1880. MS, Silverado Museum, St. Helena, California: 15 pp. of text written at the beginning of a notebook, remaining pages blank. Unpublished. Probably this draft represents work toward the essay titled "Thoughts on Literature as an Art" which Stevenson mentioned among other pending projects in a letter to W. E. Henley written in February 1880 (*Letters, 2*, 106).

A HOUSE DIVIDED; FATE OF THE HOUSE. February-June 1880. MS list of characters, Yale. MS untraced. Unpublished. W. E. Henley wrote to Stevenson on 12 February 1880 proposing nihilism as a dramatic subject, and in late February Stevenson conveyed his enthusiasm in a letter to Sidney Colvin. "Tell Henley I have a new play for him: drama in 3 acts: A House Divided: three thrilling situations: the last ghastly; he had better be reading up Nihilism, as hard as he is able" (Beinecke 3045, 4733). Stevenson worked on the play, apparently also under the title "Fate of the House," at intervals during the next two or three months in San Francisco. But on 15 June 1880, having received a draft of this play from Stevenson, Henley conveyed his great disappointment and the project was apparently dropped (Beinecke 4737).

THE FOREST STATE; THE GREENWOOD STATE. Spring 1880. MS untraced. Unpublished. See the entry of *Prince Otto*, 10 April-December 1883; *Letters, 2*, 105-6; and the entry "Stylistic Imitations and Exercises," late 1860s and 1870s. Early in 1880, Stevenson wrote to Henley that "my old [play] Semiramis, our half-seen Duke and Duchess . . . suddenly sprang into sunshine clearness as a story." Therefore he was writing it out under the title of *The Forest State* or *The Greenwood State: A Romance*. "I mean we shall quarry [a play] from it. . . . Certain scenes are, in conception, the best I have ever made" (*Letters, 2*, 105-6). Stevenson's letter to Henley makes it clear that the work in question was that eventually published as the novel *Prince Otto* (1885), and later in the spring of 1880 Stevenson first mentioned it under this title, remarking in a letter to Sidney Colvin that "Prince Otto" was one of three novels he then had in view, estimating its eventual length at about 200 pages (Beinecke 3045). Nellie Sanchez, *The Life of Mrs. Robert Louis Stevenson* (1922), p. 64, recalls Stevenson dictating "the first rough draught of *Prince Otto*" to her during his stay with her and her sister Fanny, soon to become Stevenson's wife, in Oakland, California, in the late spring of 1880. Stevenson himself, dedicating *Prince Otto* to Nellie, remarks that in Oakland the novel was "no bigger in fact than a few sheets of memoranda written for me by your kind hand." Stevenson did not return to the work for more than two years, however, taking it up again at Kingussie in August 1882. Thus Stevenson's early play "Semiramis" became, first, an idea for a play discussed with W. E. Henley in 1878 or early 1879 ("our . . . Duke and Duchess"); then a prose tale intended as quarry for a play, the tale called *The Forest State* or *The Greenwood State: A Romance*. Under the new title *Prince Otto*, a synopsis of the work was dictated in the spring of 1880; and eventually the work was resumed, again as a novel, in 1882 and 1883. In the biography of Stevenson which he began and then abandoned in the 1890s, Sidney Colvin says that Stevenson began recasting his early play in Monterey in 1879. A play of his "boyish days," Colvin writes, was "re-cast during walks on the seashore at Monterey into the guise of a prose narrative" (Beinecke 7225, p. 35).

ADVENTURES OF JOHN CARSON. Begun spring 1880. MS, Yale. Unpublished. In a letter to Sidney Colvin written in the spring of 1880, Stevenson remarks that he has now "three novels before me": "A Vendetta in the West," which he estimates as "160 pp."; *Prince Otto*, "say 200"; and a third, "Adventures of John Carson in Several quarters of the world: dictated by himself: including the exploits of Diamond Charlie. perhaps 100. pertemps 200. This is still vagueish, but most promising. Real life, throughout" (Beinecke 3045). Presumably this novel was to be based on reminiscences by his landlord at 608 Bush Street, San Francisco. Stevenson's untitled manuscript (Beinecke 6062) consists of seven pages of reminiscences, written by Stevenson but in the first person, of life in California during the 1850s and 1860s. Probably Stevenson wrote them to his landlord's dictation during the spring of 1880. But the projected novel seems to have gone no further.

[Nathaniel Hawthorne.] Projected spring 1880. On Stevenson's projected "blast" against Henry James's *Hawthorne* (1879) see *Letters, 2*, 117, and Stevenson's brief doggerel sent to W. E. Henley in 1882, quoted in Janet Adam Smith, ed., *Collected Poems*, 2nd ed. (1971), p. 476. Stevenson apparently proposed the subject to Leslie Stephen in the late spring of 1880 but was persuaded to abandon the idea by Stephen's polite demurral, 16 June 1880 (Beinecke 5565). Stevenson and James were not at this time the intimate acquaintances they ultimately became.

[Gods and demi-gods in exile.] Projected April 1880. In a letter to Sidney Colvin probably written in April 1880 Stevenson writes of his many requests for books: "now, to make matters worse . . . I do earnestly desire the best book about mythology (if it be German, so much the worse; send a bunctionary along with it, and pray for me). This is why. If I recover, I feel called on to write a volume of gods and demi-gods in exile: Pan, Jove, Cybele, Venus, Charon, etc.; and though I should like to take them very free, I should like to know a little about 'em to begin with" (*Letters, 2*, 112; see also *2*, 43). Nothing came of this project, however.

SAMUEL PEPYS. Begun June 1880, completed at intervals through spring 1881. MS untraced. *Cornhill Magazine*, 44 (July 1881), 31-46; signed R.L.S. *Familiar Studies of Men and Books* (1882). Tusitala 27.

During the early 1870s, compiling a personal "*Catalogus Librorum Carissimorum*," Stevenson included "Pepys, his *Diary, esp. the Trip to Bristol, Bath, etc.*," (Beinecke 6073; quoted in Balfour, *Life, 1*, 98). On 16 June 1880, evidently replying to a proposal of Stevenson's, Leslie Stephen wrote to him: "I shall be glad of Pepys. I had been vaguely thinking of him myself: but you will do it so much better & I am very busy with other things" (Beinecke 5565). Stevenson probably began reading at once, and he seems to have turned to the essay in earnest at Davos that winter. In a letter written to his parents on 21 November 1880 Stevenson remarked of this essay and his then newly begun reading in the history of the Highlands for which they were sending him a box of books: "I have got Lord Mahon to read, to give me patience till my box turns up, and rest me from unmitigated Pepys" (Brick Row Book Shop, 1921, 41). In the biography of Stevenson which he began writing and then abandoned in the late 1890s Sidney Colvin wrote that in late 1880 Stevenson had sent to him at Davos Mynors Bright's new edition of Pepys' *Diary* "and began to prepare the paper on that subject" (Beinecke 7225, p. 10).

Stevenson refers unfavorably to Bright's *Diary and Correspondence of Samuel Pepys*, 6 vols. (1875-79) in the first paragraph of his essay, where too he discloses a preference for Lord Braybrook's more copious edition and H. B. Wheatley's commentary (Tusitala, *27*, 179). Stevenson's copy of Richard Lord Braybrooke's *Diary and Correspondence of Samuel Pepys . . .with a Life by Lord Braybrooke*, 6 vols. (London: Bickers and Son, 1875-79), was sold as Anderson 1914, I, 470. It is described as containing many marked passages and marginal comments by Stevenson, especially in the first three volumes. His copy of H. B. Wheatley's *Samuel Pepys and the World He Lived In* (London: Bickers and Son, 1880) is now held as Beinecke 2605. Stevenson presented a copy of another edition of Lord Braybrooke's *Diary and Correspondence of Samuel Pepys*, 4 vols. (London: George Bell, 1876), to the Apia Public Library; the fourth volume is now held as Beinecke 2566.

It is unknown exactly when Stevenson finished this essay, but probably he submitted the manuscript before he left Davos in the late spring of 1881. On 30 July 1881, £18.18 was credited to Stevenson's account with Mitchell and Baxter from Smith, Elder, publishers of the *Cornhill Magazine*. Presumably this was payment for this essay (Beinecke 7268). Sometime during the mid-1880s, Stevenson and Henley seem to have considered collaborating on "Pepys' Diary: Comedy," although nothing came of this project. See the list of plays quoted in Balfour, *Life, 2*, 4.

THE OLD PACIFIC CAPITAL. Summer or autumn 1880. MS untraced. *Fraser's Magazine*, 131 (November 1880), 647-57; signed Robert Louis Stevenson. *Across the Plains* (1892). First published with the essay on San Francisco, "A Modern Cosmopolis" (1883), in the Edinburgh Edition, 3 (1895), 169-91. In this edition, for the first time, these essays appeared under the joint title "The Old and New Pacific Capitals" and the names of the two cities were given as subtitles. Stevenson himself suggested the idea; see *Letters, 5*, 153. Tusitala 18.

On 29 January 1880, Andrew Lang wrote to Stevenson that he had just been dining with Charles Longman and John Tulloch, the editor of *Fraser's Magazine*, and that Longman was "very anxious you should do somewhat for Frazer, as much as you can. They pay £1.1 a page" (Beinecke 5035). Stevenson lived in Monterey, California, from the very end of August until mid-December 1879, and it seems likely that he mentioned this request to Tulloch when he visited the Stevensons at the Ben Wyvis Hotel, Strathpeffer, in September 1880. In her diary, 6 September 1880, Stevenson's mother noted that their old friend John Tulloch had arrived at Strathpeffer and that during his visit Stevenson read "a humorous Scotch poem to him which he [begged] for Fraser" (Beinecke 7304). "The Scotsman's Return from Abroad" appeared in the same issue of *Fraser's Magazine* as the essay on Monterey; the poem and the essay may have been intended as companion pieces, and may have been discussed at the same time in September 1880. On Stevenson in Monterey see Anne B. Fisher, *No More A Stranger* (1946) and Anne R. Issler, "Robert Louis Stevenson in Monterey," *Pacific Historical Review*, 34 (August 1965), 305-21. See also the entry "[Simoneau's at Monterey]" under the date of winter 1880-81.

SCOTLAND AND THE UNION; THE TRANSFORMATION OF THE SCOTTISH HIGHLANDS. Late summer 1880, winter 1880-81. MS notes, source books, and source materials transcribed and sent to Stevenson by his parents, Yale. Unpublished. The fullest record of Stevenson's research for these projected historical works is in his letters to his father. See especially *Letters, 2,* 121-23, 134-35, 138-40, 173-74, and Beinecke 3458-60, 6529, and Stevenson's father's notebook 52, Beinecke 7316, 7325, 7354, and 7356. Although, as Sidney Colvin remarked (*Letters, 2,* 123), Stevenson "read much, but composed little or nothing, and eventually this history went to swell the long list of his unwritten books," the value of this research to Stevenson's Scottish historical novels is obvious. On the awakening of Stevenson's interest in the Highlands in 1880 see his mother's comments, "Notes from his Mother's Diary," Vailima Edition, *26,* 335-36. She remarks of the family's trip to Blair Athol and Strathpeffer after Stevenson's return from the United States: "On this visit for the first time Louis acknowledged that the Highlands of Scotland was the most beautiful place in the world; before that he used to say it was too gloomy and declared that coming down from Dalnaspidal the river and the train seemed to be trying which could get out first. . . . [He and John Tulloch] had long talks together and Louis planned writing [A History of the Union] of which [Tulloch] highly approved." See also the entry of "[A History of the Union]" above under date of ca. 1876.

[Christmas story.] Projected October 1880. The only surviving record of this project appears in the biography of Stevenson which Sidney Colvin began writing and then abandoned in the late 1890s. During the three weeks he spent in London in October 1880, Colvin wrote, Stevenson was busy "seeing his friends, among them the late Mr. Randolph Caldecott, with whom he discussed the plan of a Christmas story and its illustration; a plan never carried out" (Beinecke 7225, p. 7).

VIRGINIBUS PUERISQUE. Collected and augmented late 1880, published mid-April 1881. MSS untraced except for the two parts of "'Virginibus Puerisque'" and the essay "On Falling in Love." See the entries of these works under dates of 18 May 1876 and November 1876. Fifteen essays, all but two published previously in periodicals from 1874 to 1879. The exceptions are "Some Portraits by Raeburn," written but not published in October 1876, and the second part of "'Virginibus Puerisque,'" which, like Stevenson's note at the end of "Ordered South" as published in this collection and his dedicatory letter to W. E. Henley prefacing the volume, was written at Davos in late 1880. Although originally published separately and without connection, "On Falling in Love" (1877) and "Truth of Intercourse" (1879) were here made the third and fourth of the group of four essays collectively titled "Virginibus Puerisque." *Virginibus Puerisque and Other Papers* (London: C. Kegan Paul and Company, 1881); published mid-April 1881. Tusitala 25.

Stevenson had long wanted to publish a collection of his essays, and in *The Athenaeum*, 27 September 1879, p. 401, there actually appeared a report that Stevenson was planning to publish such a collection. See *Letters, 1,* 174-75, *2,* 28, 79, 105, 117, and Leslie Stephen to Stevenson, 1 March 1877, Beinecke 5560. Arrangements for the present collection seem to have been made by Sidney Colvin while Stevenson was still in the United States (see

Letters, 2, 79, 105, 117), and they were complete by early December 1880. As Stevenson wrote to his mother from Davos on 12 December: "I only got £20 for Virg. Puer. I could take Paul by the beard and knock his head against the wall" (Chrysler, 1952, 296). In the C. Kegan Paul *Publication Books*, vol. 4, p. 200, it is noted that on 29 March 1881 Stevenson was paid twenty pounds in cash for the copyright; see *The Archives of Kegan Paul . . . 1853-1912,* ed. Brian Maidment, 27 microfilm reels (1973), reel 2. Sales were poor, however, and this fact and others led, by a complicated set of transactions not complete until 1884, to Stevenson's adopting Chatto and Windus as his regular publishers. In the C. Kegan Paul *Publication Account Books*, vol. 3, p. 117, the entry of *Virginibus Puerisque* is closed out by a payment of £35.9.0 apportioned from the sum of £101 or more paid in January 1884 to recover Stevenson's interest in the three books of his first published by C. Kegan Paul and Company (Maidment, ed., reel 7). See also the recollections of A. C. Trench quoted in F. A. Mumby, *The House of Routledge* (1934), pp. 192-93. Graham Balfour, *Life, 1*, 211, notes that by early 1884 "only nine hundred copies" of *Virginibus Puerisque* had been sold. Stevenson's copy of Horace's *Oeuvres. Traduction nouvelle par Leconte de Lisle. Avec le texte latin.*, 2 vols. (Paris, 1873) was sold as Mrs. W. E. Safford, 1926, 17. In this copy the words "virginibus puerisque" (*Odes,* 3.1.4) are underscored in ink and an "X" placed opposite them in the margin. At the end of several of the essays in the copy of *Virginibus Puerisque* which he gave to his father (C. Gerhardt and Company, 1915, 54), Stevenson wrote where the essay was written. According to the catalogue description, the dedication and the second part of the title essay are marked as having been written at Davos; Stevenson's other annotations are included in the entries of the individual essays above. Stevenson also corrected *Robinson* to *Robieson* on p. 232 in the essay on Raeburn in this copy.

[Essays planned at Davos.] Winter 1880-81. MS list, Yale. Unpublished. Except for the essay described in the next entry, none of these five essay was ever written. On five MS pages Stevenson lists by title and briefly outlines the following five essays: "The beginnings of a soul," "Health Resorts," "Simoneau's Inn," "Relations of children," and "My Russians." Only the third was written; see the next entry.

[Simoneau's at Monterey.] Winter 1880-81. MS outline and drafts, Yale. Partially published in Balfour, *Life, 1*, 168-69. First published in full, as a sequential text combining both MS fragments, in James D. Hart, ed., *From Scotland to Silverado* (1966), pp. 172-78. On Stevenson's outline see the previous entry.

[Protest on behalf of Boer independence.] Winter 1880-81. MS, Yale. *Hitherto Unpublished Prose Writings* (Boston: Bibliophile Society, 1921), pp. 97-99; a facsimile of the first MS page faces p. 96. Tusitala 28. Stevenson's untitled notebook draft was probably conceived as a letter to the newspapers supporting the Transvaal rebellion of Paul Kruger begun 16 December 1880 and settled 3 August 1881 by the Pretoria Convention.

1881

[Swiss Notes.] Published 17 February-17 March 1881. MSS untraced. Five unsigned articles published in the *Pall Mall Gazette*: "Health and Mountains" (17 February); "Davos in Winter" (21 February); "Alpine Diversions" (26 February); "The Stimulation of the Alps" (5 March); "The Misgivings of Convalescence" (17 March). Quotations from the second and third essays appear in Balfour, *Life, 1*, 180-83, 186. The first four essays were first reprinted in *Essays and Criticisms by Robert Louis Stevenson* (Edinburgh: Herbert B. Turner and Company, 1903), and then in *Essays of Travel* (London: Chatto and Windus, 1905). "The Misgivings of Convalescence," unpublished since its original appearance, appears in facsimile in the Beinecke Collection catalogue, *A Stevenson Library . . .* , facing p. 485. Tusitala 30, which reprints only the first four of these essays.

[A mock trial.] March or April 1881. MS, Columbia University Library. Published in Louis L. Cornell, "A Literary Joke By R.L.S.: Interpretation and Commentary," *Columbia Library Columns*, 17 (Februrary 1968), 17-26. Stevenson's MS is headed "From The Daily Telegraph of 12th July, 1881" and purports to be an account of the evidence given by Stevenson in the trial of Mr. Cornish, an acquaintance of his at Davos, on the events of the ——th of March 1881. Stevenson reluctantly discloses that he found Cornish still abed in the afternoon and both Cornish and his room "in a state of great uncleanness." Asked to describe and account for the prisoner's state that day Stevenson remarks: "Well, there was a large cylindrical stove, such as are common in Switzerland, in one corner of the room; and it did occur to me he might, by some mistake, have got inside it. But then there was no door; and besides . . . [the] stove was white." But Stevenson faints just as he is about to disclose the real reason for what he observed. As Cornell observes, "the basis of the joke is a trifle obscure" and this mock trial must have been "a private joke, never intended for publication" (pp. 18-19). Probably it was written shortly after the events to which it alludes, in March or April 1881. Stevenson's poem to Miss Cornish, on her birthday, is now held as Beinecke 7016.

THE MORALITY OF THE PROFESSION OF LETTERS. Early 1881. MS untraced. *Fortnightly Review*, n.s. 157 (April 1881), 513-20; signed Robert Louis Stevenson. Tusitala 28. See also the next entry.

Letter: THE MORALITY OF THE PROFESSION OF LETTERS. 27 April 1881. MS untraced. *The Academy,* 7 May 1881, p. 339. Unpublished since its original appearance. Stevenson replies, in a letter dated Paris, April 27, 1881, to criticism of his essay of this title which had appeared in the "Magazines and Reviews" section of *The Academy*, 9 April 1881, p. 261.

COLONEL JEAN CAVALIER. June 1881. MS note of title, notes, draft paragraph, Yale. Unpublished. Stevenson's interest in Jean Cavalier, commander of the Camisards, began during the writing of *Travels with a Donkey* (1878-79), and in June 1881 he seems to have become interested in writing a general study of him. See *Letters, 2*, 149. Of this study, however, only the opening paragraph was ever written.

THRAWN JANET. June 1881. MS untraced *Cornhill Magazine,* 44 (October 1881), 436-43; signed R.L.S. *The Merry Men and Other Tales and Fables* (1887). Tusitala 8. Leslie Stephen accepted this story for publication on 23 June 1881, and Stevenson received proofs in August (Beinecke 5567; *Letters, 2*, 163). On 24 August 1881, £8.8 was credited to Stevenson's account with Mitchell and Baxter from Smith, Elder, publishers of the *Cornhill Magazine.* Presumably this was payment for "Thrawn Janet" (Beinecke 7268). But the story had long been in Stevenson's mind. In 1868-69 he listed "The Story of Thrawn Janet" among stories for "A Covenanting Story-Book," and in 1871 he acquired George Sinclair's *Satan's Invisible World Discovered* (1685), a major source. Stevenson may well have worked from a draft written during the 1870s in bringing the story into final form—as he did, very quickly, in June 1881 at Pitlochry, intending it to be one of various stories to be called "The Black Man and Other Tales" or "Tales for Winter Nights." See *Letters, 2*, 150-51, 158; Fanny Stevenson's "Prefatory Note," Tusitala, *8*, xii-xiii; and the next entry.

Commenting on "Thrawn Janet" in a preface to *The Merry Men* which he began in 1887, Stevenson remarked that he was pleased with the story in spite of the defect that it was "true only historically, true for a hill parish in Scotland in old days, not true for mankind and the world. Poor Mr. Soulis' faults we may equally recognise as virtues; and feel that by his conversion he was merely coarsened; and this, although the story carries me away every time I read it, leaves a painful impression on the mind" (Tusitala, *8*, xv-xvi).

Coleman O. Parsons, "Stevenson's Use of Witchcraft in *Thrawn Janet,*" *Studies in Philology*, 43 (July 1946), 551-71, shows in detail Stevenson's debts to such Scottish historical works as the Rev. Robert Wodrow's *Analecta* (1842-43) and George Sinclair's *Satan's Invisible World Discovered; or a Choice Collection of Modern Relations* (1685). Stevenson's copy of the *Analecta* is now held as Beinecke 2606. His copy of Sinclair's book (London: James Clark, 1814) was sold as Anderson 1914, II, 509, and is now in the Monterey State Historical Monument Stevenson House Collection, item 642-B. Stevenson's signature and "Kirkcudbright, 1871" are written on the flyleaf.

THE BLACK MAN AND OTHER TALES. Planned June 1881. MSS untraced. Unpublished. In a letter to Sidney Colvin written from Kinnaird Cottage, Pitlochry, in early or mid-June 1881 Stevenson sent a table of contents for "the new work on which I am engaged with Fanny," a collection of eight or nine stories, "all supernatural," to be called "The Black Man and Other Tales" (*Letters, 2*, 150-51). Later in the summer, reporting his progress, he gave the title as "Tales for Winter Nights" (*Letters, 2*, 158). The first two stories were to be titled jointly "The Black Man," a Scottish name for the devil. The first of these, "Thrawn Janet," was then already finished and is discussed in the previous entry. The second, "The Devil on Crammond Sands," is discussed above under date of late 1860s or early 1870s. Then followed in Stevenson's list six other stories, and "maybe another—*The Dead Man's Letter*." The first of these six stories, "The Shadow on the Bed," Fanny Stevenson finished in July, at which time she was already "hammering at a second, for which we have 'no name' as yet" (*Letters, 2*, 158; see also Beinecke 4751-52 on the story). "The Body-Snatchers" is discussed in the next entry. "The Case Bottle" is probably "The Curate of Anstruther's Bottle" under a new title; see the entry above under date of late 1860s or early 1870s. "The King's Horn" is probably the story Stevenson listed as "King Matthias's Hunting Horn" in another list of stories in November 1874 (*Letters, 1*, 213-14). "The Actor's Wife" is otherwise unknown. "The Wreck of the *Susanna*," as Sidney Colvin suggests (*Letters, 2*, 150), probably became "The Merry Men" later in the summer. See the entry after next. Stevenson's possible additional story, "The Dead Man's Letter," is mentioned in a similar list of stories projected in December 1879 (*Letters, 2*, 89) but is otherwise unknown. Except for writing "Thrawn Janet," "The Body Snatcher," and "The Merry Men" during June and July 1881, and having "The Travelling Companion" and a story temporarily titled "The Torn Surplice" both "*in germis*" on 1 August (*Letters, 2*, 163), Stevenson does not seem to have kept on with this project much after he left Pitlochry for Braemar in early August 1881.

THE BODY SNATCHER. June-July 1881. MS, Yale. *Pall Mall Christmas "Extra" —No. 13* (December 1884), pp. 3-12; signed R. Louis Stevenson. Tusitala 11. Although laid aside shortly after it was begun, "in a justifiable disgust, the tale being horrid," a draft of this story under the title "The Body-Snatchers" was complete by 1 August 1881, being the second of the stories Stevenson wrote for the collection "The Black Man and Other Tales" discussed in the previous entry. See *Letters, 2*, 151, 158, 163. It was not published until 1884, however, when "Markheim" proved too short for the space already allotted Stevenson in the Christmas extra number of the *Pall Mall Gazette*. See the discussion of "Markheim" under date of November 1884. See also *Letters, 3*, 16-17, 21-22, 27-28; Beinecke 3084; Edmund Gosse's introduction in the Pentland Edition, 3 (1906), 293-94; and the note on the advertising used for the story in J. A. Hammerton, ed., *Stevensoniana*, 2nd ed. (1907), pp. 317-18. On 31 December 1884, thirty pounds was credited to Stevenson's account with Mitchell and Baxter from Smith, Payne, and Smith. Presumably this was for "The Body Snatcher," the sum reduced at Stevenson's request by ten pounds from the forty pounds promised originally for "Markheim" (Beinecke 7268).

On the career of Robert Knox (1793-1862), the anatomist whom Burke and Hare supplied with bodies and on whom Stevenson's protagonist K. is clearly based, see Isobel Rae, *Knox the Anatomist* (1964), especially pp. 150-51, 188-89. Rae discusses "The Body Snatcher" in detail and also quotes from the unpublished reply (MS, NLS) written by Professor John Goodsir in response to the "Key to Mr. Stevenson's 'Body Snatcher'" published in the *Pall Mall Gazette*, February 1885. Goodsir writes that Stevenson "must have been ill advised when he gave to the public for Christmas reading this gruesome—and he must forgive me if I say,—coarse sketch. . . . [And] if Mr. Stevenson has been unjust to the memory of Knox he has been still more so to the memories of his Demonstrators or Assistants" (MS pp. 3, 14).

THE MERRY MEN. June-July 1881. MS draft outline, Yale. MS untraced. *Cornhill Magazine*, 45 (June 1882), 676-95; and 46 (July 1882), 56-73; unsigned. Published without the benefit of Stevenson's corrections on the proof; see Beinecke 3214. *The Merry Men and Other Tales and Fables* (1887). Tusitala 8. This was the third of the stories which Stevenson wrote during June and July 1881 for the collection "The Black Man and Other Tales." See the previous three entries and his detailed comments on this story in *Letters, 2*, 158-60. W. E. Henley liked the draft of the story which he read during a visit to Braemar in July 1881, calling it "first-chop indeed" and commenting briefly on it in a letter to Sidney Colvin quoted in E. V. Lucas, *The Colvins and Their Friends* (1928), p. 130. Stevenson revised it at Davos during the winter of 1881-82; as he wrote to George Iles, 29 October 1887, the story was "begun at Pitlochrie, finished at Davos" (*Bookman*, London, 7, February 1895, 136). Stevenson received £18.18 for this story, paid to his account with Mitchell and Baxter on 12 July 1882 (Beinecke 7268).

On 19 March 1884, some time after the story had been published, Stevenson wrote to his father: "*The Merry Men* I mean to make much longer, with a whole new dénouement, not yet quite clear to me" (*Letters, 2*, 303). Stevenson did not revise the story extensively for publication in volume form in 1887, but he did make many minor changes in wording and, especially in the last two chapters, deleted sentences and a number of scattered paragraphs to condense it. Fanny Stevenson remarks in her "Prefatory Note," Tusitala, *8*, xiii, that the story "never quite satisfied its author, who believed that he had succeeded in giving the terror of the sea, but had failed to get a real grip on his story." See also Stevenson's own remarks on the story quoted in Balfour, *Life, 2*, 141-42.

John Robert Moore, "Stevenson's Source for 'The Merry Men,'" *Philological Quarterly*, 23 (April 1944), 135-40, suggests that Stevenson was to some degree indebted to W. E. Aytoun's story, "The Santa Trinidada: A Tale of the Hebrides" (1842). The locale was also drawn from observation. As Stevenson remarked in his draft preface to *The Merry Men* (1887), the real name of the island in this story was Earraid, and as a locale "[it] has done me yeoman service" (Tusitala, *8*, xvi). Stevenson first visited Earraid, an island off the western tip of Mull, near Iona, for three weeks during

August 1870 to observe construction of the Dhu Heartach lighthouse offshore by his father's engineering firm; it figures prominently in *Kidnapped* (1886); and he wrote on it in "Memoirs of an Islet" (1887). See also L. M. Buell, "Eilean Earraid: The Beloved Isle of Robert Louis Stevenson," *Scribner's Magazine*, 71 (February 1922), 184-95.

Stevenson probably also drew upon his knowledge of the coast nearer Edinburgh. For in 1922 his cousin Mrs. Thomas Dale of Scoughall, East Lothian, wrote: "It was a letter from me, R.L.S. said, that made him write *The Wreckers* [i.e. "The Merry Men"]. We used to have a great many wrecks, fifty years ago, on the coast beside my home at Scoughall . . . and I had described one of these wrecks, when many poor fellows were drowned. My husband was first officer of a volunteer rocket apparatus there, and when the tide went back, crowds of men with lanterns searched the rocks for bodies. . . . My husband said it was a most weird scene, and like olden times, when 'the Pagans of Scoughall' had the worst of reputations;—they were said to tie a horse's neck to its knee and attach a lantern to the rope, and then drive the horse slowly along the cliffs, so that a vessel out at sea should think it a ship riding at anchor, and come in, only to be wrecked on our rocks and plundered by the ghoulish people" (in Masson, ed., *I Can Remember Robert Louis Stevenson,* 1922, pp. 9-10). See also Stevenson's remarks on his father's eyewitness account of a wreck in the Pentland Firth, *Records of a Family of Engineers* (1893), chap. 2, sect. 1, Tusitala *19*, 191-92; and the entry for "The School Boys Magazine" under date of October 1863, above.

THE TRAVELLING COMPANION. Begun August 1881. MS destroyed by Stevenson. Unpublished. Although Stevenson listed this story among those intended for "The Black Man and Other Tales" on 1 August 1881, indicating that it was then "*in germis*" (*Letters, 2*, 163), and though he also twice listed this story among various published and unpublished stories in a notebook he used during the early 1880s at Davos (Yale), it is not clear how much work he did on this story until he mentioned it again in correspondence in October and November 1883. At that time Stevenson called it "an unpleasant tale" (*Letters, 2*, 163; see also Beinecke 3468); but once more he seems to have laid it aside. In June 1886, in the interval having written *Dr. Jekyll and Mr. Hyde*, Stevenson remarked of this story to Sidney Colvin: "O! the Trav. Comp. won't do; I am back on it entirely: it is a foul, gross, bitter ugly daub . . . a carrion tale!" (*Letters, 3,* 95). Nevertheless the story was actually finished and submitted for publication. It was, Stevenson wrote in "A Chapter on Dreams" (1887), "returned by an editor on the plea that it was a work of genius and indecent." And, not agreeing with this estimate, Stevenson continues his account of the story by remarking that he "burned [it] the other day on the ground that it was not a work of genius and that *Jekyll* had supplanted it" (Tusitala, *30*, 51-52).

THE TORN SURPLICE. Projected August 1881. The only surviving record of this composition is Stevenson's listing of it as "*in germis*" for the collection "The Black Man and Other Tales" in a letter to Sidney Colvin, 1 August 1881

(*Letters, 2*, 163). He notes that this was "*not* [its] *final title*" and the story itself seems never to have been written.

TREASURE ISLAND. September-November 1881. MS untraced except notebook entries of characters and scenes, Yale. "Treasure Island; or, The Mutiny of the Hispaniola. By Captain George North." *Young Folks*, 19-20, seventeen weekly installments, 1 October 1881-28 January 1882. Stevenson received 12.6 per column, £30 for the whole, for publication in this form. *Treasure Island* (London: Cassell and Company, 1883); published 14 November 1883 in an edition of two thousand copies. Stevenson received £100 initially, "a sight more than *Treasure Island* is worth," he told Henley shortly after negotiations for book form publication had been completed (*Letters, 2,* 245). Stevenson made numerous word changes, deletions, and revisions in the text for its publication in book form and he divided it into the six parts which it now has. As originally published, *Treasure Island* consisted of six chapters titled "Prologue.—The Admiral Benbow" followed by the remaining twenty-eight chapters, collectively titled "The Story." Now held as Beinecke 1008 is a leatherbound scrapbook which contains the text of *Treasure Island* clipped from the serial publication in *Young Folks*. It bears scattered minor corrections and alterations throughout and was evidently owned by Stevenson. But the book form edition was set from his revised original manuscript, not this copy. As Stevenson wrote in "My First Book: *Treasure Island*" (1894): "The time came when it was decided to republish, and I sent my manuscript and the map along with it to Messrs. Cassell" (Tusitala, *3*, xxx). American edition (Boston: Roberts Brothers, 1884) published in mid-February 1884, with four illustrations by F. T. Merrill. This was the first illustrated edition, and it was followed eighteen months later by the first English illustrated edition (London: Cassell and Company, 1885), which contains twenty-one illustrations and an illustrated title page. Two of these illustrations are from the American edition, the rest by various other illustrators. In October 1887, a new edition of *Treasure Island* then being in prospect under the Scribner imprint, Stevenson wrote to Charles Scribner that he found the Roberts Brothers illustrations "disgusting" and therefore urged that Scribner recover from Cassell and Company "Roux's very spirited pictures—the best of which Cassell omitted to reproduce!" Howard Pyle would have done the illustrations even better, Stevenson added, and he wished he had known of his work earlier: "the French faces [in Roux] jar" (Beinecke 3234, received 26 October 1887). This plan was not carried out, however, and the only edition of *Treasure Island* published by Charles Scribner's Sons (1902) was illustrated by Wal Paget. Tusitala 3.

On the composition and publication of *Treasure Island* see especially Stevenson's own acount, "My First Book: *Treasure Island* " (1894), Tusitala *3*, xxiii-xxxi; Lloyd Osbourne's "Note" and Fanny Stevenson's "Prefatory Note" to *Treasure Island*, Tusitala *3*, xvii-xxii; *Letters, 2*, 168-71, 174-75, 177; and the various accounts gathered together in J. A. Hammerton, ed., *Stevensoniana*, 2nd ed. (1907), pp. 53-61. As Stevenson wrote to George Iles, 29 October 1887, *Treasure Island* was "begun at Braemar, finished at Davos;

the whole in two bursts of about fifteen days each, my quickest piece of work" (*Bookman*, London, *7*, February 1895, 136).

Treasure Island was begun in the late summer of 1881 at Braemar, initially as an amusement for Stevenson's stepson Lloyd Osbourne, then twelve years old. One of the rooms in the cottage, Stevenson wrote, "with aid of pen and ink and a shilling box of water-colours," Lloyd had "turned . . . into a picture-gallery." While his own duty was merely to be showman of the gallery, Stevenson wrote, he would sometimes join his stepson in his efforts. "On one of these occasions I made the map of an island; it was elaborately and (I thought) beautifully coloured; the shape of it took my fancy beyond expression; it contained harbours that pleased me like sonnets; and with the unconsciousness of the predestined, I ticketed my performance *Treasure Island*" (*3,* xxv). Lloyd Osbourne takes credit for drawing and coloring the map himself, remarking that "Stevenson came in as I was finishing it, and with his affectionate interest in everything I was doing, leaned over my shoulder, and was soon elaborating the map, and naming it" (*3*, xviii). But both agree that Stevenson immediately thereafter began the story: "as I pored upon my map of *Treasure Island*," Stevenson wrote, "the future characters of the book began to appear there visibly among imaginary woods; and their brown faces and bright weapons peeped out upon me from unexpected quarters, as they passed to and fro, fighting and hunting treasure, on these few square inches of a flat projection. The next thing I knew, I had some paper before me and was writing out a list of chapters" (*3*, xxvi).

"On a chill September morning, by the cheek of a brisk fire, and the rain drumming on the window, I began *The Sea Cook*, for that was the original title," Stevenson wrote (*3*, xxvi). Actually the date was in late August, Stevenson asking W. E. Henley on 25 August 1881 to send him "the *best* book about the Buccaneers that can be had" for his new story, *The Sea Cook, or Treasure Island: A Story for Boys (Letters, 2*, 168-69). A chapter a day was written and read aloud by Stevenson after lunch, at first only to his stepson, wife, and parents. As Fanny Stevenson remarked, "before the advent of our visitors, [it] had been thought of simply as an amusement for a small boy condemned to the inaction of an indoor life by the inclement weather" (*3*, xx). "It seemed to me original as sin," Stevenson wrote; and though he had counted only on one boy in his original audience he soon found that he had two. "My father caught fire at once with all the romance and childishness of his original nature . . . and he not only heard with delight the daily chapter, but set himself actively to collaborate," preparing the inventory of Billy Bones's chest, asking that Flint's old ship be called the *Walrus*, and, no doubt, recognizing in Jim's hiding in the apple barrel (chap. 11) a recollection of his own boyhood experience with Captain Soutar aboard the *Regent* (*3*, xxvii-xxviii; on the apple barrel incident see Stevenson's *Records of a Family of Engineers*, chap. 2, sect. 1, Tusitala *19*, 194).

In late August, Alexander Hay Japp came to Braemar, invited by Stevenson to discuss their differences on Thoreau (see *Letters, 2*, 164-65,

169-70; Stevenson's preface to *Familiar Studies of Men and Books*, Tusitala, *27*, xviii; and Japp's *Robert Louis Stevenson . . .* , 1905, pp. 3-7, 270-75). And, Stevenson wrote, as "we would by no means stop our [daily] readings . . . the tale was begun again at the beginning, and solemnly redelivered for the benefit of Doctor Japp" (*3,* xxviii). Japp was so delighted with the story that he urged its publication, and when he left Braemar he was carrying the manuscript of the early chapters to see if he couldn't find a publisher for them in London — as he did. Japp recalls taking with him from Braemar revised manuscript of seven or eight chapters and "the pencil outline of incident or plot" for the whole (p. 272). In early September he took these to James Henderson at *Young Folks*, with whom he was not previously acquainted, and Henderson promptly accepted it. On 24 September Stevenson authorized publication at 12.6 per column, by his own calculations approximately £30 for the whole; see Beinecke 8040, 3175, *Letters, 2*, 170, and the discussion below. Stevenson wrote that Japp had been "charged by my old friend, Mr. Henderson, to unearth new writers for *Young Folks*" (*30*, xxviii), but in this his memory erred. "I had no connection with Mr. James Henderson," Japp wrote, "whom I [only] knew as coming from my own district in Scotland" (Hammerton, p. 59). Another, later visitor was Edmund Gosse, who stayed at Braemar from 26 August to 5 September 1881 and also heard the early chapters of *Treasure Island* read aloud. On Gosse's visit see especially Arthur C. Young, "Edmund Gosse Visits Robert Louis Stevenson," *Journal of the Rutgers University Library*, 20 (June 1957), 33-41.

"He had written the greater half of it when I went [to Braemar]," Japp wrote, and it was "the first half of it" that he carried with him when he returned to London (Hammerton, pp. 58-59). In *The Academy*, 10 March 1900, p. 209, Japp wrote that "I . . . heard the whole of the story in first pencil draft before I left," but by this he can only have meant that he heard it from the beginning. For just before the midpoint of the narrative Stevenson's inspiration suddenly failed. "Fifteen days I stuck to it, and turned out fifteen chapters," he wrote; "and then, in the early paragraphs of the sixteenth, ignominiously lost hold. My mouth was empty; there was not one word more of *Treasure Island* in my bosom; and here were proofs waiting me at the *Hand and Spear*!" (*30*, xxviii). Having left Braemar on 21 September Stevenson corrected the proofs of the early chapters at Weybridge, according to his wife also writing there "several" more chapters (*30*, xxi). But by the time serial publication began on 1 October 1881 Stevenson seems to have completed no more than nineteen or twenty chapters altogether (*Letters, 2*, 171).

Stevenson returned the corrected proofs of the early chapters to James Henderson in London at the very end of September, and it was at this time that the work's title was changed, from *The Sea Cook* to *Treasure Island.* As Henderson wrote: "Before the story commenced . . . Stevenson called on me, bringing the corrected proofs of the opening chapters, and it was at that interview—my first with him—I expressed my dislike to the title *The Sea Cook*, and suggested *Treasure Island* (the name of the 'map'), which he readily agreed to" (Hammerton, pp. 59-60). See also James Dow, "Robert Louis Stevenson and the *Young Folks* Reader," in Masson, ed., *I Can Remember Robert Louis Stevenson* (1922), p. 209.

Treasure Island was finally finished in November 1881 at Davos. "We carried the unfinished novel with us on the journey," Fanny Stevenson wrote, but *Treasure Island* "went back in the parcel as it came out," and it was not until they had arrived in Davos that it was resumed (*3*, xxi). According to Stevenson, at Davos "down I sat one morning to the unfinished tale, and behold! it flowed from me like small talk; and in a second tide of delighted industry, and again at the rate of a chapter a day, I finished *Treasure Island*" (*3*, xxix). On the other hand, Fanny Stevenson says that it was completed "intermittently," and that if it had not already begun appearing as a serial "I doubt if it would ever have been finished" (*3*, xxi). On 22 November 1881, thirty pounds was credited to Stevenson's account with Mitchell and Baxter for the serial publication of *Treasure Island* (Beinecke 7268). Presumably this was paid upon receipt of Stevenson's manuscript of the end of the novel.

Unlike *The Black Arrow*, which raised the circulation of *Young Folks* eighteen months later "by many hundreds of copies a week," *Treasure Island*, according to a later editor of *Young Folks* Robert Leighton, was "as a serial a comparative failure." It did not raise circulation "by a single copy" (Hammerton, p. 56). Some young readers even wrote to the paper complaining about *Treasure Island* (see *Letters, 2*, 174). Nevertheless, from the beginning Stevenson had anticipated publication of the novel in book form, and on 26 January 1882, just after the serialization was complete, he wrote to his father: "You may be pleased to hear that I mean to re-write Treasure Id in the whole latter part, lightening and *siccating* throughout. Any suggestions will be very welcome: above all to know what parts *you like* would much help me, as I mean to cut down like a fiend" (NLS, Acc. 7165; see also *Letters, 2*, 184). A month later, on 26 February 1882, his father wrote to him that he had now "gone over 17 Chapters of the Treasure Island & I think all these should do." A few small changes in wording seemed necessary, and unavoidably "the character painting which is so well done in the early chapters drops a good deal after getting to the island." "But I think you should intermit this tragic work if possible & I think you have a good opportunity with Ben Gunn," Stevenson's father continued. "I would interject a long passage there of a religious character. I would have him ask if Jim had ever been at some little coast village say Mousehole . . . & whether he had ever heard of his father or mother. The want of such an inquiry strikes me as unnatural. Then I would have him regret the fatal day on which he had run away from his home & some pathetic passage should follow as to what he had lost & what troubles he had passed through & something about the Minister of the place & the sayings of his father or his mother & so forth. So far as I can see this is the only way of harking back to something higher than mere incident" (Beinecke 5771). Stevenson did not agree, however, and despite his plans, the revisions in *Treasure Island* for book form publication, although numerous, did not greatly alter the main outline of the work.

Negotiations with Casell and Company for publication of *Treasure Island* in book form were conducted through William Ernest Henley, who was then employed in the educational department of Cassell and Company. According to Sir Newman Flower, Henley "entered the room of the chief editor, threw the cuttings of 'The Sea Cook' . . . on to his desk, and exclaimed in his usual abrupt manner, 'There's a book for you!' Having said this he went out and climbed to his office again. Therefore it was Henley who was the prime mover in the book publication of 'Treasure Island'" (undated clipping, letter to the editor of the *Daily Telegraph*, Edinburgh Room, Central Public Library, Edinburgh). By the end of April Henley had secured an offer of one hundred pounds for the book. As Stevenson wrote to his parents on 5 May 1883: "I have had a great piece of news. There has been offered for *Treasure Island* . . . [a] hundred pounds, all alive, O! A hundred jingling, tingling, golden, minted quid" (*Letters, 2*, 238). Stevenson's actual contract, dated 2 June 1883 and signed by Thomas D. Galpin for Cassell and Company, grants to Cassell and Company "sole and exclusive property" in the copyright of *Treasure Island*, for which Stevenson was to receive fifty pounds upon signing the agreement, fifty pounds when the book was passed for the press (this amount was sent to him on 24 September 1883), and a royalty of twenty pounds per thousand copies sold after the first four thousand. In addition, Stevenson was to receive half the net proceeds of selling advance sheets or stereotype plates in the United States and one-fourth royalty on copies of the English edition sold there. See his contract and the letter to him from Cassell and Company, 24 September 1883, in the Society of Authors Archive, British Museum, MS. Add. 56638, ff. 4-6. See also *Letters, 2*, 238, 245, and Beinecke 3404. Simon Nowell-Smith, *The House of Cassell 1848-1958* (1958), pp. 99-100, 132-35, notes that Cassell and Company continued paying royalties on *Treasure Island* until 1944, and he reproduces Cassell and Company's royalty receipts for the book.

Stevenson's original map went astray during preparation of the book for publication, however. "The proofs came, they were corrected, but I heard nothing of the map," Stevenson wrote. "I . . . was told it had never been received, and sat aghast. It is one thing to draw a map at random, set a scale in one corner of it at a venture, and write up a story to the measurements. It is quite another to have to examine a whole book, make an inventory of all the allusions contained in it, and with a pair of compasses painfully design a map to suit the data. I did it, and the map was drawn again in my father's office, with embellishments of blowing whales and sailing ships; and my father himself brought into service a knack he had of various writing, and elaborately *forged* the signature of Captain Flint and the sailing directions of Billy Bones. But somehow it was never *Treasure Island* to me" (*3*, xxx). "I have just sent off the title sheet of T. Id, which only wants the map," Stevenson wrote to his father on 30 August 1883: "marche-t-elle" (Brick Row Book Shop, 1921, 49). Used as the frontispiece when *Treasure Island* was finally published in book form, on 14 November 1883, this map was sold as Chrysler, 1952, 292, for $3,500 to Hamell and Barker.

According to Stevenson's own reckoning of his sources, the map which he drew at Braemar was "the chief part of my plot . . . I might almost say it was the whole" (*3*, xxx). Incidental sources he mentions are: Charles Kingsley's narrative of a cruise in the Caribbean, *At Last* (1871); Charles Johnson's *General History of the Robberies and Murders of the Most Notorious Pirates* (1724), actually written by Daniel Defoe and undoubtedly the work sent by W. E. Henley in response to his request for "The *best* book about the Buccaneers that can be had" (*Letters, 2*, 169); Washington Irving's *Tales of a Traveller* (1824); Edgar Allan Poe's "The Gold Bug" (1845); and Defoe, probably *Robinson Crusoe* (1719). In his prefatory poem, "To the Hesitating Purchaser," first published in the book form edition of *Treasure Island* (1883), Stevenson refers to "Kingston . . . Ballantyne the brave, / [And] Cooper of the wood and wave" (Tusitala, *3*, vi); and their adventure novels and those of Frederick Marryat and Captain Mayne Reid might be included generally as sources also.

Treasure Island, Stevenson wrote to Sidney Colvin in 1884, "came out of [Charles] Kingsley's *At Last*, where I got the Dead Man's Chest—and that was the seed—and out of the great Captain Johnson's *History of Notorious Pirates*. The scenery is Californian in part, and in part *chic*" (*Letters, 2*, 315-16; see also Tusitala, *3*, xxx). Maurice Kingsley, "Concerning 'The Dead Man's Chest,'" *Book Buyer*, 12 (March 1895), 73-74, quotes his father's description in *At Last: A Christmas in the West Indies* (1871) and adds a description of his own. See also Burton E. Stevenson, *Famous Poems and the Controversies which have Raged Around Them* (1923), pp. 321-40; David Barnett, *A Stevenson Study: Treasure Island* (1924), pp. 10-16, where he argues that the prospect of Edinburgh seen from the Pentland Hills much resembles the topography of the island and that there is a man named Pew buried in the cemetery at Pilrig near the Balfours; G. A. England, "The Real Treasure Island," *Travel*, 52 (January 1929), 17-21, 41-45, who argues that Stevenson's description best suits the Isle of Pines, near Cuba; Vincent Starrett, "The Dead Man's Chest: A Stevensonian Research," *The Colophon*, 17 (1934), who shows that the island which Kingsley described is in fact named Dead Chest Island, Dead Man's Chest Island lying off the south coast of Puerto Rico; and Andrew Cluness, "Could Unst Have Been Treasure Island?" *Scotsman,* 17 November 1962 (clipping, Edinburgh Room, Central Public Library, Edinburgh), who argues that in tides, anchorages, topography, and the like, the island of Unst in the Shetland Islands much resembles Treasure Island. Stevenson visited Unst briefly in June 1869 aboard the lighthouse yacht *Pharos*. On the verses see Vincent Starrett, "The History of a Chanty," *The Freeman*, 15 November 1922, pp. 228-30, and James Milne, *Memoirs of a Bookman* (1934), pp. 168-75.

Stevenson himself never visited the Caribbean, and when asked by an interviewer whether the real island was in the Pacific "smiled humorously." Treasure Island, he said, "is not in the Pacific. In fact, I only wish myself that I knew where it was. When I wrote the book I gave no indication as to its whereabouts, for fear that there might be an undue rush towards it. However, it is generally supposed to be in the West Indies" (Sydney *Morning Herald*, 14 February 1893, in Stevenson's mother's scrapbooks, Monterey

State Historical Monument Stevenson House Collection, California, vol. 3, p. 118; xerox, Yale). Pursuing Stevenson's own hint, George R. Stewart, "The Real Treasure Island," *University of California Chronicle*, 28 (April 1926), 207-13, argues that the scenery is in fact chiefly Californian, derived from Stevenson's stay in Monterey and the Napa Valley in 1879-80.

Stevenson's copy of Defoe's pseudonymous *General History* (1724) was sold as Anderson 1914, II, 261: Captain Charles Johnson, *The History of the Lives and Actions of the Most Famous Highwaymen, Street-Robbers, &c. To which is added, A Genuine Account of the Voyages and Plunders of the Most Noted Pirates* (Edinburgh, 1814). His indebtedness to this work is discussed by John Robert Moore, "Defoe, Stevenson, and the Pirates," *ELH*, 10 (March 1943), 35-60; Tom Burns Haber, "RLS and Israel Hands," *English Journal*, 32 (September 1943), 399; Harold Suits, "The Pirate Lore in *Treasure Island* " (M.A. thesis, Univ. of North Carolina, 1956); and by Manuel Schonhorn in the introduction to his edition of the *General History* (1972). Similarities between *Treasure Island* and James Fenimore Cooper's *The Sea Lions* (1848) are discussed in W. H. Bonner, *Pirate Laureate: The Life and Legends of Captain Kidd* (1947), p. 197, and Harold F. Watson, *Coasts of Treasure Island* (1969), pp. 160-63. Watson's book-length study of the sources of *Treasure Island* also includes discussion of Stevenson's debts to Defoe's *General History*, Washington Irving's "Wolfert Webber," the fifth tale in the section "The Money Diggers" in *Tales of a Traveller* (1824), Ballantyne, Kingston, and Marryat. Pursuing an inquiry of Stevenson's own (*Letters, 2,* 315-16), F. D., " 'Treasure Island' and 'Captain Singleton,' " *Notes and Queries,* 15 January 1944, p. 51, inquired in vain what similarities Edward Burne-Jones might have seen between *Treasure Island* and Defoe's *Captain Singleton* (1720), which Stevenson first read in 1884.

"A few reminiscences of Poe, Defoe, and Washington Irving, a copy of Johnson's *Buccaneers*, the name of the Dead Man's Chest from Kingsley's *At Last*," Stevenson wrote, "some recollections of canoeing on the high seas, a cruise in a fifteen-ton schooner yacht, and the map itself with its infinite, eloquent suggestion, made up the whole of my materials" (*3*, xxx). Canoeing was a recreation with Sir Walter Simpson and others during the late 1860s and 1870s in the Firth of Forth and elsewhere; the "cruise in a fifteen-ton schooner yacht" took place in June 1869, when Stevenson accompanied his father and the Commissioners of Northern Lights on their annual inspection of Scottish lighthouses aboard the lighthouse yacht *Pharos*. F. W. Robertson, Caithness County Librarian, has pointed out to me that *Treasure Island* also owes something to Stevenson's stay in Wick in September 1868: "In Caithness we always think that 'Ben Gunn' in 'Treasure Island' derives from Stevenson's Wick days. . . . The Gunns are a Caithness clan and Ben Gunn a very common name here" (letter, 30 January 1969).

Finally, as Stevenson acknowledged obliquely in "My First Book" (*3*, xxvi), Long John Silver was drawn from his friend W. E. Henley. "Henley was John Silver," he wrote to Lloyd Osbourne in the autumn of 1890 (Lloyd Osbourne, 1914, 585), having earlier written to Henley himself, in May 1883: "It was the sight of your maimed strength and masterfulness that begot John

Silver in *Treasure Island.* Of course, he is not in any other quality or feature the least like you; but the idea of the maimed man, ruling and dreaded by the sound, was entirely taken from you" (*Letters, 2*, 242).

JERRY ABERSHAW: A TALE OF PUTNEY HEATH; THE LEADING LIGHT: A TALE OF THE COAST. Projected September 1881, during the writing of *Treasure Island.* MSS untraced if written. Unpublished. See *Letters, 2*, 170, where Stevenson remarks that he would like to follow *Treasure Island* "at proper intervals" with these two adventure stories, neither of which was apparently written, and a third, discussed in the next entry.

THE SQUAW MAN. Projected September 1881, during the writing of *Treasure Island*; begun but abandoned winter 1881-82. MS, Anderson 1914, II, 389: 6 pp. folio, comprising the whole of the first chapter and part of the second chapter of this "romance of the Western country and the Indians." This title also appears in a notebook list of various works projected or written at Davos, Yale. Unpublished. See *Letters, 2*, 170, and Lloyd Osbourne's comments on the writing of this story, *An Intimate Portrait of R.L.S.* (1924), p. 26. Osbourne mistakenly dates this story from the previous winter; it cannot have preceded *Treasure Island.*

FAMILIAR STUDIES OF MEN AND BOOKS. Collected autumn 1881, at which time the "Preface, by way of Criticism" was written. Nine essays, published mostly in the *Cornhill Magazine* between 1874 and 1881. MSS untraced except for "Victor Hugo's Romances" and "The Gospel According to Walt Whitman" and notes for the essays on John Knox, Charles of Orleans, and Villon; see the entries of these essays individually above. MS draft of dedication, Yale. The last page of Stevenson's preface appears in facsimile in A. H. Japp, *Robert Louis Stevenson . . .* (1905), facing p. 262, but the manuscript itself is untraced. *Familiar Studies of Men and Books* (London: Chatto and Windus, 1882); published 22 February 1882. Tusitala 27.

Returning to Davos in October 1881, Stevenson placed this collection with Chatto and Windus for one hundred pounds, a sum no doubt given with the further understanding that Chatto and Windus would thus acquire the rights to Stevenson's three earlier books, published by C. Kegan Paul and Company, and first refusal of future books. On 2 March 1882, a week after *Familiar Studies of Men and Books* was published, Stevenson signed a receipt for one hundred pounds by bill due on 5 June from Chatto and Windus, assigning them all rights in the volume (Society of Authors Archive, British Museum, MS. Add. 56638, f. 30). The same sum was credited to Stevenson's account with Mitchell and Baxter on 14 March 1882 (Beinecke 7268). C. Kegan Paul and Company proved reluctant to surrender their original interest, however, and final agreement was not reached until January 1884, when Stevenson's father paid them slightly more than one hundred pounds to close Stevenson's account.

By November 1881 Stevenson was correcting proofs of the essays and still discussing his great reluctance to reprint the essay on Knox (*Letters, 2*, 175-76). He returned proofs of the preface on 30 December (Beinecke 7951), having in the meantime, as he wrote to A. H. Japp, "lost a great quire of corrected proofs" and experienced other difficulties almost past bearing. "I was never so sick of any volume as I was of that," he wrote to Japp: "I was continually receiving fresh proofs with fresh infinitesimal difficulties. I was ill; I did really fear, for my wife was worse than ill" (Stevenson to Japp, 1 April 1882, in Japp's *Robert Louis Stevenson* . . . , 1905, p. 28, partly published in *Letters, 2*, 194). Probably due to these difficulties, Stevenson left final proofreading of the preface to Japp. Stevenson was in Davos, Japp wrote, and "felt so much the disadvantage of being there in the circumstances (both himself and his wife ill) that he begged me to read the proofs of the Preface for him" (p. ix). For the reasons he gives in the preface, Stevenson revised none of these essays for publication in book form.

THE MURDER OF RED COLIN: A STORY OF THE FORFEITED ESTATES. Projected October 1881. MS untraced. Notes, fragments, source books: Yale, Huntington. Unpublished. Shortly after he returned to Davos in 1881 Stevenson wrote to his father that "last night in bed" it struck him that he could write this essay from the books he had with him if his father would send him two or three others, and that this essay would be "my first for the electors," then considering him (not very seriously) for the vacant chair of Constitutional Law and History at the University of Edinburgh (*Letters, 2*, 173-74). But this appears to be almost as far as the project ever went. Stevenson returned to the subject itself, the Appin murder of Colin Campbell of Glenure, in "[Famous murders]" (December 1881) and, of course, in *Kidnapped* (1886).

Letter: YOUNG ROB ROY. Published 21 October 1881. MS untraced. Published in the *Stirling Observer*, 21 October 1881, and from this source reprinted in that newspaper's *Local Notes and Queries* (1883), pp. 287-88, with other letters on the subject; signed R.L.S. Reprinted in J. A. MacCulloch, *Robert Louis Stevenson and the Bridge of Allan* (1927), pp. 83-85, and in D. B. Morris, *Robert Louis Stevenson and the Scottish Highlanders* (1929), pp. 69-72. Probably Stevenson became involved in this antiquarian controversy over Rob Roy's physical appearance as a result of clippings sent him by one or both of his parents after he had left Braemar to return to Davos in October 1881.

BYWAYS OF BOOK ILLUSTRATION: BAGSTER'S *PILGRIM'S PROGRESS*. October-November 1881. MS untraced. *The Magazine of Art*, 5, n.s. part 16 (February 1882), 169-74; signed Robert Louis Stevenson. Tusitala 28. Stevenson comments at some length on the Bagster illustrations in a letter to his cousin Bob written in late 1868 (Beinecke 3553), having been given his own copy some ten years earlier. Sold as Edith B. Tranter, 1952, 367,

Stevenson's own copy of the Bagster edition of *Pilgrim's Progress* (London: Samuel Bagster and Sons, n. d.) is inscribed: "Robert L. Stevenson. From Pappa and Mamma, Jan. 1, 1858." A selection of the illustrations appears in the essay itself and as it was reprinted in the Edinburgh Edition, but these have not since been reprinted. In an undated letter to W. E. Henley written in 1882, Stevenson complained about a mistake in the fifth paragraph from the end of the essay: "Why the hell did you and your printers—a lousy lot whom I abominate—pass over a correction of mine and send me down to posterity as an ignoramus who though the ill-favoured ones were in the first part; when I was nine years old I knew better than that" (Christie's sale, 6 March 1962, lot 125). This correction, whatever it was, has never appeared in any published version of the essay.

BENJAMIN FRANKLIN AND THE ART OF VIRTUE. Summer-autumn 1881, abandoned November. See also the entry for this work, to which Stevenson returned in 1881 but again did not write or finish, under date of January-February 1880. In late June or early July 1881 W. E. Henley wrote to Sidney Colvin of dining with the American writer and critic Brander Matthews: "He was full of amiability, & volunteered any amount of assistance in the States. When this was made plain to me, I began asking for information for Louis' sake. I found his 'Whitman' & his 'Thoreau' very well known & very highly esteemed in the States; I heard that for the 'B. Franklin' he has in view there would be instant & splendid sale: & it was intimated to me that if he would print his Americanisms in a volume for sale in the States he would make a good thing of it. The idea is indeed admirable. I have communicated it to Louis" (in E. V. Lucas, *The Colvins and Their Friends*, 1928, pp. 131-33). Stevenson took up the matter with Edmund Gosse, since 1880 acting as the London agent of the *Century Magazine*, and on 7 November 1881 Gosse wrote to Stevenson that he had at last heard from New York. Although very interested in publishing his work, Richard Watson Gilder, editor of the *Century Magazine*, had written of the Franklin project: "He would have to say something remarkably fresh about our dear old household divinity Franklin to justify him in tackling that exhausted subject" (in Evan Charteris, *The Life and Letters of Edmund Gosse*, 1931, p. 149). Gosse's letter anticipated Stevenson's own inquiry on 9 November, "Benj. Franklin —do you want him?" (*Letters, 2*, 175), and presumably the project was dropped at this point.

[Scottish writers.] Projected November 1881 for writing that winter; apparently abandoned. Beginning his reading on the history of the Highlands and the Union between Scotland and England, Stevenson remarked in late 1880 that among the pleasures of the task was the "vast number of delightful writers I shall have to deal with: Burt, Johnson, Boswell, Mrs. Grant of Laggan, Scott." Stevenson had in mind Edward Burt's *Letters from a Gentleman in the North of Scotland* (1754); Samuel Johnson's *Journey to the Western*

Isles of Scotland (1775); James Boswell's *A Journal of a Tour to the Hebrides with Samuel Johnson* (1785); Mrs. Anne Grant's *Letters from the Mountains* (1803) and *Essays on the Superstitions of the Highlands* (1811); and Sir Walter Scott's historical novels. In November 1881, he wrote to his father: "this winter I mean to write an article on" Burt and the others except Johnson. But nothing further came of this project. See *Letters, 2,* 140, 176.

WILLIAM HAZLITT. Projected December 1881-late 1882. MS list of works to consult, miscellaneous notes, Yale. MS untraced if written. Unpublished. "I tried for nearly a year to get Morley to admit Hazlitt," Stevenson wrote about the English Men of Letters series to A. W. Ireland on 25 February 1882, "but whether he was shy of the subject or the writer, he would have none of it." Just as he was abandoning hope, in December 1881, an offer came from Richard Bentley "proposing just such a work as I wished to undertake," and Stevenson began assembling sources as well as writing to such an authority as Ireland. Stevenson worked on the project at intervals during much of 1882; but by early 1883, as Stevenson wrote to Ireland, he had abandoned it at least temporarily. "The Hazlitt scheme lies, for the present, high and dry." See *Letters, 2*, 179, 181-82, 189, 191; additional letters published by Mrs. Ireland, *Atlantic Monthly*, 82 (July 1898), 122-28; Beinecke 3174; and E. M. Clark, "The Kinship of Hazlitt and Stevenson," *Univ. of Texas Bulletin: Studies in English*, 4 (1924), 97-114.

Commenting on Stevenson's abandonment of this work on Hazlitt, Graham Balfour remarked that "a wider study of his [Hazlitt's] writings produced a cooler feeling, and the *Liber Amoris* is said to have created a final distaste, which rendered any continued investigation or sympathetic treatment impossible" (*Life, 1,* 193). Augustine Birrell repeated this statement in his study of Hazlitt (1902), giving Balfour as his authority, but Edmund Gosse immediately wrote to correct him. In a letter to Birrell on 28 June 1902 Gosse wrote: "People give different reasons for the same act to different people. . . . But at the time . . . when R.L.S. was so full of Hazlitt, he talked a great deal to me about the project, and never gave that as a reason. The reason he gave was that he did not feel in Hazlitt the substance of a biography, that when you took the writer from the man, there seemed so little left." Gosse added: "I don't think R.L.S. was the man to be shocked at the *Liber Amoris.* He would see the vulgarity, and, what is worse, the slight insanity of it all. But the processes of desire are so mysterious, and Stevenson so fully realized that, in the case of an artist, it is what art he deposits, not what desire he takes in, which is of interest, and he was, moreover, so devoid of the least touch of cant, that I rather resent your words on this subject, although I perfectly understand your writing them on your knowledge. . . . Only to my ear, they sound false to R.L.S. " (in Evan Charteris, *The Life and Letters of Edmund Gosse*, 1931, pp. 284-85).

[Famous murders.] Projected December 1881-September 1882. As early as 1879, Stevenson and Edmund Gosse had considered a collaboration in which they would retell the stories of famous murders, and in late 1881 Richard Watson Gilder accepted Gosse's proposal for a series of such articles in the *Century Magazine*. On 26 December 1881 Stevenson promised to turn at once to his part in the scheme, and on 17 March 1882 Gosse inquired: "Do you get on with your Glencoe Tragedy for us? I look forward to something in your best style" (in Evan Charteris, *The Life and Letters of Edmund Gosse*, 1931, p. 150). Evidently Stevenson was then planning to write on the Glencoe massacre, 13 February 1692. He replied that although not yet begun, his first essay was "early on my list . . . and when once I get to it, three weeks should see the last bloodstain—maybe a fortnight" (*Letters, 2*, 193). Gosse elaborates: "About this time Louis and I had a good deal of correspondence about a work which he had proposed that we should undertake in collaboration—a retelling, in choice literary form, of the most picturesque murder cases of the last hundred years. We were to visit the scenes of these crimes, and turn over the evidence. The great thing, Louis said, was not to begin to write until we were thoroughly alarmed. 'These things must be done, my boy, under the very shudder of the goose-flesh.' We were to begin with the 'Story of the Red Barn,' which indeed is a tale pre-eminently worthy to be retold by Stevenson. But the scheme never came off, and is another of the dead leaves in his Vallombrosa" (*Critical Kit-Kats*, 1903, p. 292).

During the summer of 1882 Stevenson investigated the Appin murder of Colin Campbell of Glenure which figures prominently in *Kidnapped* (1886) apparently also for this series. He visited Lochearnhead with his father and, as he wrote to Gosse after his return, found "*living traditions* not yet in any printed book; very startling," and he paid £1.17 to have photographs made (*Letters, 2*, 202; *Baxter Letters*, p. 103). On 19 August 1882, John Cameron sent Stevenson a long letter in answer to his various inquiries earlier that summer (Beinecke 4158). But thereafter the project seems to have languished. See *Letters, 2,* 57, 181, 193, 202, and the other sources and letters cited above.

[Stevenson at Play: war games correspondence.] Winter 1881-82. MSS: Yale; Silverado Museum, St. Helena, California. "Stevenson at Play," *Scribner's Magazine*, 24 (December 1898), 709-19. Tusitala 30. See Lloyd Osbourne's discussion of the elaborate war games he and his stepfather, Stevenson, played at Davos during the two winters they spent there: "Prefatory Note," Tusitala, *30*, 191-96, and *An Intimate Portrait of R.L.S.* (1924), pp. 26-27, 36-39. These facetious journalistic accounts of the campaigns appear in Stevenson's notebooks along with work which suggests that these were a recreation of the second winter at Davos, in 1881-82. In "The Ideal House" (?1884) Stevenson writes that he would always have a war game set up and recommends having one of the players "every day or so, write a report of the operations in the character of army correspondent" (Tusitala *25*, 194).

THE ROYAL FORTUNE. Possibly planned winter 1881-82. MS list of seventeen chapter titles, Yale. Unpublished. Stevenson's list is written at the back of a notebook otherwise devoted to material for the humorous series of poems on the publican Thomas Brash which he was writing at Davos in 1881-82. No other record of this work survives; the list may have been written some time after the poems.

1882

THE SILVERADO SQUATTERS. Rewritten early 1882 from Stevenson's journal of 1880; finished by late April 1882. MS journal, Huntington HM 650. MS untraced. "The Silverado Squatters: Sketches from a California Mountain," *Century Illustrated Monthly Magazine*, 27 (November 1883), 27-39; 27 (December 1883), 183-93; both installments signed Robert Louis Stevenson. *The Silverado Squatters* (London: Chatto and Windus, 1883); published 8 January 1884. American edition (Boston: Roberts Brothers, 1884) published January 1884, presumably from Chatto and Windus sheets. Stevenson inscribed a copy of this edition to Will H. Low on 19 January 1884 (Beinecke 234). Stevenson's journal was first published, partially, as "The Silverado Diary," Vailima Edition, 2 (1922), 579-608; complete, as *Robert Louis Stevenson's Silverado Journal*, ed. John E. Jordan (1954). Tusitala 18, which contains the work itself and "The Silverado Diary."

Stevenson was married on 19 May 1880 in San Francisco, and after three weeks spent in Calistoga took up residence at the abandoned Silverado mine north of Calistoga on the slopes of Mt. St. Helena. Here Stevenson, his wife, and his stepson Lloyd stayed through the end of June 1880, when they returned to Calistoga and, later in July, left California to return to Britain. Stevenson's journal, like the book itself, covers his whole stay in the Napa Valley, not only his weeks at Silverado. See Anne R. Issler, *Stevenson at Silverado* (1939).

Stevenson rewrote his journal early in 1882 at Davos, and in April 1882 he sent the completed MS to W. E. Henley in London for placement with Chatto and Windus. Not until almost a year later, however, did Stevenson actually find a publisher. On 17 February 1883 Richard Watson Gilder of the *Century Magazine* wrote to Stevenson praising his work and added: "May we not hope that you will let us see some of your handwriting—especially of the fictitious sort—with a view to publication in the magazine" (*Letters of Richard Watson Gilder*, 1916, p. 121). Stevenson offered Gilder *The Silverado Squatters* and had Henley send the MS to New York; and by the third week in May Stevenson had accepted Gilder's offer of forty pounds for publication in the *Century Magazine* later in 1883. See *Letters, 2*, 191, 195-96, 198, and 240-41.

Stevenson had proofs of the *Century Magazine* version in early October; much to his distress, the manuscript at first returned to him was incomplete; and during October and November he revised the proofs extensively. As he wrote to his mother in mid-November: "I have been hard at [*Prince*] *Otto*, hard at *Silverado* proofs, which I have worked over again to a tremendous extent; cutting, adding, rewriting, until some of the worst chapters of the original are now, to my mind, as good as any. I was the more bound to make it good, as I had such liberal terms; it's not for want of trying if I have failed" (*Letters, 2*, 277).

On 17 October 1883 Chatto and Windus had bound and issued as a pamphlet ten copies of the uncorrected November magazine installment. One of these Stevenson eventually inscribed to his friend and physician at Hyères, Walter A. Powell, remarking in his inscription that "This Strange and Imperfect Publication" offered "a handy compendium of mis-readings and errors of the press" (Beinecke 230; Stevenson's inscription and the first page of this copy appear in facsimile in the Beinecke Collection catalogue, *A Stevenson Library* . . . , after p. 102). In November, Chatto and Windus ordered 1,000 copies of *The Silverado Squatters* printed; they sent 750 of these for binding on 22 November, and on 2 January 1884 they sent the remainder. (Further copies of this edition must have been ordered, for there exist copies with advertisements dated November 1887, and copies without advertisements, as well as copies with advertisements dated October 1883. See the discussion of Beinecke 231-33, 7500-1, in *A Stevenson Library* . . . , pp. 103-4, 2252-53.)

The book was published by Chatto and Windus on 8 January 1884, the Roberts Brothers edition published in Boston the same month having been set from advance sheets sent them by Chatto and Windus. Stevenson's contract with Chatto and Windus, 28 January 1884, stipulated that Stevenson was to be paid one hundred pounds within three months (less ten pounds for the advance sheets sent to Roberts Brothers), and that Chatto and Windus would thereby acquire exclusive rights of republication for five years (Society of Authors Archive, British Museum, MS. Add. 56638, fol. 31). Stevenson was not paid until September, however; only on 21 September was the one hundred pounds for this work finally paid to his account with Mitchell and Baxter (Beinecke 7268).

In his copy of the first American edition (Beinecke 7502) Stevenson made more than a dozen small corrections; he also made corrections in his copy of the second English edition, published by Chatto and Windus in 1886 (Beinecke 7503).

THE FOREIGNER AT HOME. Winter 1881-82, probably finished January or February 1882. MS fragment, one-page draft of the fifth paragraph, Yale. *Cornhill Magazine,* 45 (May 1882), 534-41; signed R.L.S. *Memories and Portraits* (1887). Tusitala 29. As Graham Balfour notes, *Life, 1*, 52-53, Stevenson's remarks about English schoolboys in this essay derive from his experience during the autumn term he spent at the Burlington Lodge Academy, Spring Grove, Isleworth, Middlesex.

TALK AND TALKERS. Winter 1881-82, probably finished January or February 1882. MS untraced. *Cornhill Magazine*, 45 (April 1882), 410-18; signed R.L.S. *Memories and Portraits* (1887). Tusitala 29. See *Letters, 2*, 197, where Stevenson identifies the various talkers for his mother, and *Baxter*

Letters, p. 102, where he tells his friend Charles Baxter that the man "speaking, I declare, as Congreve wrote" (*29*, 81) is "yourself." See also the entry of "Talk and Talkers (A Sequel)" below under date of spring 1882.

BYWAYS OF BOOKS ILLUSTRATION: TWO JAPANESE ROMANCES. Probably early 1882. MS untraced. *The Magazine of Art*, 5, n.s. part 25 (November 1882), 8-15; signed Robert Louis Stevenson. Original illustrations not reprinted. Tusitala 28. Stevenson's commentary is on the illustrations in Frederick V. Dickins, trans., *Chiushingura; or the Loyal League* (1876; new ed., London: Allen and Co., 1880) and Bernard-Henri Gausseron, trans., *Les Fidèles Ronins* (Paris: A. Quantin, 1882), both of which, as Stevenson notes in the essay, are versions of "the gem of Mr. Mitford's collection," the tale attributed to Shunsui Tamenaga called "The Forty-Seven Ronins" in A. B. F. Mitford's *Tales of Old Japan* (1871). Probably he wrote the essay early in 1882. He was paid £8.8 for it, a sum credited to his account with Mitchell and Baxter on 2 November 1882 (Beinecke 7268).

A GOSSIP ON ROMANCE. February 1882. MS untraced. *Longman's Magazine*, 1 (November 1882), 69-79; signed R. L. Stevenson. *Memories and Portraits* (1887). Tusitala 29. Stevenson discussed the subject of this essay at length in a letter to his cousin Bob written not long after he had finished it; see *Letters, 2*, 270-72. He remarked that although it had been written "very popularly" the essay was still "all loose ends." Publication was delayed until the whole first issue of *Longman's Magazine* was ready, but Stevenson was paid at once, nine pounds being credited to his account with Mitchell and Baxter on 13 March 1882 (Beinecke 7268).

A MODERN COSMOPOLIS. Spring 1882, possibly finished later. *The Magazine of Art,* 6, n.s. part 31 (May 1883), 272-76; signed Robert Louis Stevenson. Not reprinted in *Across the Plains* (1892), this essay was first published with the essay on Monterey, "The Old Pacific Capital" (1880), in the Edinburgh Edition, 3 (1895), 169-91. In this edition, for the first time, these essays appeared under the joint title "The Old and New Pacific Capitals" and the names of the two cities were given as subtitles. Stevenson himself suggested the idea; see *Letters, 5*, 153. Tusitala 18.

Stevenson lived in San Francisco from mid-December 1879 until his marriage there on 19 May 1880; he returned briefly eight years later, departing on the yacht *Casco* on 24 June 1888. See Anne R. Issler, *Happier for his Presence: San Francisco and Robert Louis Stevenson* (1949). He probably began this essay at Davos in the spring of 1882, at the same time as, or shortly after, he revised his journal for *The Silverado Squatters*. Having only a few final touches to add to "A Gossip on Romance" for *Longman's Magazine*, Stevenson wrote to W. E. Henley in late February 1882: "Tomorrow, having once finished off the touches still due on this I shall tackle *San Francisco* for you" (*Letters, 2*, 85). Probably he also finished the essay at Davos. In April he remarked how much magazine work he had recently written, and a year later, in May 1883, he complained of "eight months and more of perfect idleness at the end of last [year] and beginning of this." See *Letters, 2*, 195, 198, 240. Stevenson received £6.15 for this essay, paid to his account with Mitchell and Baxter on 4 May 1883 (Beinecke 7268).

THE ADVENTURES OF JOHN DELAFIELD. Planned February 1882, possibly begun that spring. Stevenson's only reference to this work at the time of its writing is in a letter to Sidney Colvin, February 1882: "My new long story, *The Adventures of John Delafield*, is largely planned." On 1 April he wrote that he had written forty thousand words since December, including both essays and "stories," but it is unclear whether this work should be included with the others. See *Letters, 2,* 185, 195, and *3,* 282. See also the entry of "The Shovels of Newton French" under date of early 1891.

NEW ARABIAN NIGHTS. Stories collected spring 1882, all published in periodicals from 1877 to 1880, chiefly written in 1877-78. MSS untraced except for a partial draft of "A Lodging for the Night," Yale. *New Arabian Nights*, 2 vols. (London: Chatto and Windus, 1882); published 17 July 1882. Vol. 1 contains the seven stories published in *London*, 8 June-26 October 1878, as "Latter-Day Arabian Nights," here under the collective headings used as subtitles in the periodical publication: "The Suicide Club" and "The Rajah's Diamond." Vol. 2 contains "The Pavilion on the Links," "A Lodging for the Night," "The Sire de Malétroit's Door," and "Providence and the Guitar." Only the first of these four stories was revised for publication in book form; see the entry for "The Pavilion on the Links" above under date of November 1878. Tusitala 1.

Chatto and Windus had succeeded C. Kegan Paul and Company as Stevenson's regular publishers with their publication of *Familiar Studies of Men and Books* on 22 February 1882, and within a month afterwards Stevenson was offering still more work to them, probably this collection and *The Silverado Squatters*, through his friend W. E. Henley. On 15 April 1882 Henley wrote to Charles Baxter that he had sold *New Arabian Nights* for twenty pounds: "As much, that is, as Louis got for [*An Inland Voyage* and *Travels with a Donkey*] put together" (Beinecke 4578). *New Arabian Nights*, Stevenson told an interviewer in 1890, was "the first book that ever returned me anything, and it also established my name" (Melbourne *Daily Telegraph*, 14 February 1890, in Stevenson's mother's scrapbooks, Monterey State Historical Monument Stevenson House Collection, California, vol. 3, p. 120; xerox, Yale). Inscribing this volume in a set of the Scribner edition of his books which he presented to Dr. E. L. Trudeau, Stevenson denounced the printer's error he found in the fifth paragraph of the second story in "The Suicide Club." Instead of *devilry*, which had appeared correctly in the first edition, the word was printed *deviltry*, an error which also appears in the first one-volume edition published by Chatto and Windus in 1884. On p. 39 Stevenson wrote: "I will stand being missspelled; but not this *reveltry* / Of nonsense. Deviltry ! ! ! ! ! ! O Devilry!" See "Stevensoniana: The Trudeau Dedications," *The Book Buyer*, 12 (February 1895), 12-14, rpt. in J. A. Hammerton, ed., *Stevensoniana*, 2nd ed., 1907, pp. 322-34. On other errors in the texts of *New Arabian Nights* see the note inserted in Beinecke 1799, a copy of the 1914 Grolier Club exhibition catalogue, *First Editions of the Works of Robert Louis Stevenson* (1915).

WHERE IS ROSE? Spring 1882 and later. MS untraced if written. Unpublished. Andrew Lang proposed this collaboration to Stevenson sometime during the spring of 1882, writing to him as follows: "A man asking me to write a short story, I have just invented a sensational plot. *Where is Rose?* Where indeed? Her lover led her to her carriage, from the gilded saloon; her carriage returned without her. Presently, an advertisement appearing in the agony column that Rose was to be found in No 19 Anything Street, her friends hurried to the spot, and found, tied up, a Russian girl, and an ex ticket of leave man. Won't you help me write *Where is Rose?* You would enjoy it. If you will, I will send you a scenario. Rose, I must inform you is *really* in a convent on the shores of the White Sea" (Beinecke 5038). Lang elaborated still further in this letter; for as he noted in his discussion of "Where is Rose?" in *Adventures Among Books* (1905), pp. 252-54, the projected story contained "quantities of plot, nothing but plot." Stevenson responded favorably to the idea and sent Lang some notes. Lang continued work and wrote to Stevenson on 20 April 1882 that "Longman says *Longman's Magazine* is the place for *Rose*." Even in November Lang was still enthusiastic: "Why don't you do *Rose*?" he wrote to Stevenson. "We'd make a fortune out of Longman if you would." Nevertheless the project languished, in part due to the success of Hugh Conway's *Called Back* (1883), which, Lang wrote, unfortunately "anticipated part of the idea" (*Adventures Among Books*, p. 252). See Beinecke 5038-39, 5042, 5044, 5046, 5072; and Roger Lancelyn Green, "'Dear Andrew' and 'Dear Louis,'" *Scots Magazine*, 43 (August 1945), 375-81.

[Collaborative novel-writing scheme.] Spring 1882. Two press clippings, from the *Evening News*, 1 May 1882, and the *Northern Chronicle*, 3 May 1882, are pasted in Stevenson's mother's scrapbooks, Monterey State Historical Monument Stevenson House Collection, California, vol. 2, p. 10 (xerox, Yale). These state, on what authority is not specified, that Stevenson, W. E. Henley, Andrew Lang, and George Saintsbury were about to form a novel-writing consortium for the popular market. Probably these reports originated with Andrew Lang, on whose projected collaboration with Stevenson on a popular novel, *Where is Rose?,* see the previous entry.

TALK AND TALKERS (A SEQUEL). Spring 1882. MS untraced. *Cornhill Magazine,* 46 (August 1882), 151-58; signed R.L.S. *Memories and Portraits* (1887). Tusitala 29. The article which, as Stevenson notes, inspired this extension of his essay "Talk and Talkers" (winter 1881-82) was a long critique, "The Restfulness of Talk," *Spectator*, 1 April 1882, pp. 420-21. Leslie Stephen accepted this second essay on 1 July 1882 (Beinecke 5568).

THE TREASURE OF FRANCHARD. August 1882, finished in October or November. MS untraced. *Longman's Magazine*, 1 (April 1883), 672-94; 2 (May 1883), 83-112; both installments signed R. L. Stevenson, the first containing the first three chapters, the second the rest. *The Merry Men and Other Tales and Fables* (1887). Tusitala 8.

Although mostly written at Kingussie, Inverness-shire, in August 1882, "The Treasure of Franchard" was not finished for publication until Stevenson had moved into Campagne Delfli, St. Marcel, near Marseilles, in the late autumn of 1882. Stevenson first submitted it to the *Cornhill Magazine*, then no longer edited by Leslie Stephen, where it was refused. "This is a poison-bad world for the romancer," Stevenson wrote to Sidney Colvin in recollection of this refusal in 1892: "When I remember I had the *Treasure of Franchard* refused as unfit for a family magazine, I feel despair weigh upon my wrists" (*Letters, 4*, 149; see also Stevenson to James Payn, 21 December 1882, Beinecke 3214). *Longman's Magazine* accepted it, however, for sixty-five pounds, a sum paid to Stevenson's account with Mitchell and Baxter on 10 January 1883 (Beinecke 7268). Stevenson was reading proofs in February (Beinecke 3071), and on 14 February he wrote to W. E. Henley asking him to tell Chatto and Windus that this story would shortly be available for republication, with others, in a volume (Beinecke 4666). Not until 1887, however, did such a collection actually appear.

Letter: PLAGIARISM. 16 October 1882. MS, Yale. MS copy sent to *The Athenaeum*, untraced. New York *Tribune*, 28 October 1882, p. 12; *The Athenaeum*, 21 October 1882, p. 531; both signed Robert Louis Stevenson and dated Marseilles, 16 October 1882. *Letters, 2*, 214-15. Stevenson writes to correct a misinterpretation of his "Note" in *New Arabian Nights* (1882). He had referred there to a "gentleman who had condescended to borrow the gist of one of my stories, and even to honour it with the addition of his signature," and in a *Tribune* item signed G.W.S. (George W. Smalley, the editor) this gentleman had been identified as James Payn. This is not correct, Stevenson writes, but he does not say who in fact was meant. See the various items mounted in the copy of *New Arabian Nights* (1882) once owned by G. A. Arthur, Beinecke 140.

1883

[Dramatic version: *Great Expectations.*] Projected winter 1882-83 but abandoned. MS untraced if extant. See *Letters, 2*, 233-35. Writing to his father on

17 March 1883, Stevenson says that he and his wife had reread Dickens's *Great Expectations* that winter: "The object being a play; the play, in its rough outline, I now see: and it is extraordinary how much of Dickens had to be discarded. . . . I have great hopes of this piece." But the project does not seem to have gone beyond a "prologue, which is pretty strong" in which were explained the many changes it was found necessary to make in dramatizing the novel.

AUTOLYCUS IN SERVICE. Early 1883. See the entry for this work, to which Stevenson appears to have returned in early 1883 planning a play and also a story, under date of February 1879. On 14 February 1883 Stevenson wrote to W. E. Henley asking him to tell Chatto and Windus that they could expect from him a volume containing this and other stories in the autumn (Beinecke 4666). But nothing seems to have come immediately of this project. On Stevenson's various versions of this work as a play see Nancy Blonder Schiffman's edition of the manuscripts now in the Folger Library, Washington, D. C. (Ph. D. dissertation, Univ. of South Carolina, 1973). She suggests that the play may have been quarried for *Prince Otto* later in 1883.

ACROSS THE PLAINS. Early 1883. See the entry for "The Amateur Emigrant," of which this material represents the last seven chapters, under the date of its actual composition, September 1879-June 1880. Stevenson received forty-five pounds for these chapters, paid to his account with Mitchell and Baxter on 23 May 1883 (Beinecke 7268); he returned the corrected proofs to Edmund Gosse in London on 20 May 1883 (*Letters, 2,* 240). They were published in two installments in *Longman's Magazine*, July-August 1883, only slightly revised from the original manuscript of 1879-80.

[The Arethusa.] Planned March 1883. The only surviving record of this projected work appears in Fanny Stevenson's comment on Sidney Colvin's visit to Hyères in March 1883: "I can remember few things more exciting than the evenings we spent with Mr. Colvin inventing a play to be called *The Arethusa*" (Tusitala, *4.* xvi).

THE CHARACTER OF DOGS. Spring 1883, finished and sold by midsummer. MS untraced. *The English Illustrated Magazine*, 5 (February 1884), 300-5; signed Robert Louis Stevenson. *Memories and Portraits* (1887). Tusitala 29. Presumably Stevenson finished this essay, which was inspired by J. Comyns Carr's *Male Dogs* (1882), before he turned to *Prince Otto* in April and *The Black Arrow* in late May 1883. In a letter to Alison Cunningham written in midsummer he mentions it as forthcoming (*Letters, 2,* 256.) Stevenson's copy of Edward Mayhew's *Dogs, Their Management* (London, n. d.), signed by him, "R. L. Stevenson, 17 Heriot Row, Edinburgh," was sold as Anderson 1914, II, 415.

FONTAINEBLEAU: VILLAGE COMMUNITIES OF PAINTERS. Spring 1883. MS untraced. *The Magazine of Art,* 7, n.s. part 43 (May 1884), 265-72; 7, n.s. part 44 (June 1884), 340-45; both signed Robert Louis Stevenson, the first containing the first three sections, the second the rest. Tusitala 30. Stevenson left this essay aside temporarily to work on *The Black Arrow* in May 1883, but it was already almost finished and he seems to have completed it that summer. Henley was expressing his pleasure with it in the autumn (*Letters, 2,* 243, 267), discussing the illustrations in mid-February, and asking for a little more copy at the end of March, both parts presumably then being in type (Beinecke 4778, 4785). Publication was probably delayed in order to run the parts consecutively.

PRINCE OTTO. 10 April-December 1883, and at intervals before and after. MS untraced. Notebook prefaces, list of characters, unpublished dedicatory poem, Yale. *Longman's Magazine*, 5-6, seven monthly installments, April through October 1885; each installment signed Robert Louis Stevenson. *Prince Otto: A Romance* (London: Chatto and Windus, 1885); published 1 November 1885. Tusitala 4.

Prince Otto, Stevenson wrote to George Iles on 29 October 1887, "was written at Hyères; it took me about five months, in the inside of a year, not counting the first chapter, which was written before at Kingussie [August 1882]" (*Bookman*, London, *7*, February 1895, 136). According to his 1883 diary, Stevenson "began Prince Otto" at Hyères on 10 April; had drafted eleven chapters after three weeks, on 30 April; had drafted seventeen chapters and begun rewriting after four weeks, on 7 May; and left it aside to work on *The Black Arrow* after slightly more than six weeks, on 26 May 1883 (Beinecke 6154). Graham Balfour notes that Stevenson was again at work on *Prince Otto* in October and November 1883 (*Life, 1*, 207). By mid-December, Stevenson had arranged for serial publication of the novel in a year's time. At his wife's suggestion he had asked £250 for the serial rights. Husband and wife soon repented of the figure as too high, however, and they had nearly rescinded it when Longmans replied "that they considered two hundred and fifty pounds a very moderate price for the story" (Tusitala *4*, xvii). On 3 January 1884, £100 was paid to Stevenson's account with Mitchell and Baxter from Longmans. Presumably this was part payment of the £250 sum agreed upon (Beinecke 7268).

At the time of the agreement, December 1883, the novel lacked only one chapter and revision of several others, but Stevenson continued writing and rewriting at least until March 1884. As he wrote to George Iles: "'Otto' was my hardest effort, for I wished to do something swell, which did not quite come off. Whole chapters of 'Otto' were written as often as five or six times, and one chapter, that of the Countess and the Princess, eight times by me and once by my wife—my wife's version was second last." Consenting to Gerald Gurney's request for permission to dramatize *Prince Otto*, Stevenson added that it was "originally a tragedy, and, by my sooth! in blank verse. I still think it has much that is very suitable to the boards" (*Academy*, 19 May 1900, p. 419). On the earlier versions of *Prince Otto* see the entries, "[Stylistic imitations and exercises]" (late 1860s and 1870s) and "The Forest State; The Greenwood State" (spring 1880). On 31 August 1884 W. E. Henley sent the manuscript to Chatto and Windus for consideration, reporting to Stevenson their offer of one hundred pounds for the book rights on 11 September 1884 (Beinecke 4667, 4613).

THE BLACK ARROW. Begun 26 May 1883 and written during the next two months. MS untraced except notebook outlines of chapters, map, and list of characters, NLS (Acc. 7165), and a notebook outline of chapters, Yale. "The Black Arrow, A Tale of Tunstall Forest. By Captain George North." *Young Folks*, 22-23, seventeen weekly installments, 30 June-20 October 1883. *The Black Arrow: A Tale of the Two Roses* (New York: Charles Scribner's Sons, 1888); published 16 June 1888. English edition (London: Cassell and Company, 1888) published 2 August 1888 from Scribner sheets. Tusitala 9.

James Henderson, editor of *Young Folks*, where *Treasure Island* had first appeared in 1881-82, asked Stevenson for another serial sometime early in 1883, and he left aside both *Prince Otto* and the essay "Fontainebleau" to begin *The Black Arrow* at Hyères on 26 May 1883. From the outset Stevenson derided the work as "tushery," remarking to W. E. Henley that he had begun it at all because he was fit for little else: "The influenza has busted me up a good deal; I have no spring, and am headachy" (*Letters, 2*, 242). Stevenson wrote the novel rapidly, even carelessly, during the next month or two. According to his 1883 diary, he began *The Black Arrow* on Saturday 26 May, writing one and one-half chapters; by Monday 28 May, four chapters had been written; by Wednesday 30 May, six chapters; and, after Stevenson spent a week in Marseilles, by Monday 11 June 1883, 8 chapters (Beinecke 6154). In late June and July, when he was finishing the novel, Stevenson even had trouble keeping it consistent with itself. He had actually "forgotten what had last happened to several of his principal characters," Graham Balfour reports from Stevenson's own recollections, and had to wait for proofs of the early installments to reach him before he could continue (*Life, 1*, 208). Henderson's proofreader, James Dow, adds that when Stevenson sent the last installment he had forgotten to account for the fourth black arrow or to tell the fate of Sir Oliver, "for whom the fourth arrow was evidently intended." Dow wrote to Stevenson, alerting him to this lapse, and Stevenson abashedly corrected it. "Nowhere do I send worse copy than to *Young Folks*," he wrote to Dow, "for, with this sort of story, I rarely rewrite; yet nowhere am I so well used." (For both letters and Dow's further comments see Masson, ed., *I Can Remember Robert Louis Stevenson,* 1922, pp. 206-8; the letters alone appear in *Letters, 2*, 309-10.)

Stevenson was not altogether ashamed of the novel, however. In October he wrote to Sidney Colvin, pleased that Colvin had thought well of the characterization of Richard of Gloucester and looking forward to an eventual revision (*Letters, 2*, 226). Seven years later, after *The Black Arrow* finally appeared in book form, he returned to this point in response to Marcel Schwob's request for permission to translate it into French. "I warn you," Stevenson wrote, "I do not like the work." But he added: "I had indeed one moment of pride about my poor *Black Arrow*: Dicon Crookback I did, and I do, think is a spirited and possible figure" (*Letters, 3*, 308).

Publication of *The Black Arrow* in book form did not occur until 1888 and was preceded by its reserialization in the United States. Neither Stevenson nor any of his British publishers seems to have considered it worth reprinting, and here matters rested until October 1887, when S. S. McClure visited Stevenson at Saranac Lake, New York. McClure came to convey Joseph Pulitzer's offer of ten thousand dollars for a year's weekly essays for the New York *World*; but as he writes in *My Autobiography* (1914), McClure also told Stevenson "that I would publish 'The Black Arrow' serially in my newspaper syndicate, and pay him a good price for it" (p. 185). Stevenson had William Archer send him a copy of the *Young Folks* serialization from London (*Letters, 3*, 152-53), and when it arrived he wrote to McClure: "I believe I see my way to make something of it for your purpose" (Beinecke 3185).

Stevenson then sent the original serialization to McClure, who writes in his autobiography: "I read the story, and told him that I would take it if he would let me omit the first five chapters. He readily consented" (p. 186). "In the hope of keeping possible pirates in the dark," McClure continues, "I advertised and published the story under the title 'The Outlaws of Tunstall Forest.' I had it illustrated by Will H. Low, an old friend of Stevenson's . . . the first illustrated story we ran in the syndicate, and it brought in more money than any other serial novel we ever syndicated" (pp. 186-87). Correcting an article in *The Critic*, Stevenson's mother notes in her scrapbook that Stevenson was actually paid five hundred dollars for the serial rights in the United States (Monterey State Historical Monument Stevenson House Collection, California, vol. 3, p. 54; xerox, Yale). Her scrapbook also contains an announcement from the Philadelphia *Press*, 24 March 1888, that Stevenson's "The Outlaws of Tunstall Forest" would commence serialization the next day (vol. 3, p. 59). Stevenson does not appear to have revised the work for its reserialization.

Meanwhile, Charles Scribner's Sons, already Stevenson's regular American publisher, was arranging publication of *The Black Arrow* in book form. On 22 December 1887 Charles Scribner wrote to Stevenson that his firm was not interested in McClure's proposal that Howard Pyle illustrate both newspaper and book versions (Beinecke 5451), and this probably influenced McClure's choice of Will H. Low to illustrate the newspaper version. The first edition, published by Scribner's on 16 June 1888, had a frontispiece by Low and eleven illustrations by Alfred Brennan; the first English edition (1888) was not illustrated; in 1891 appeared the first illustrated English edition, with eight illustrations by H. M. Paget.

Robert Louis Stevenson

On Stevenson's historical sources see Ruth Marie Faurot, "From Records to Romance: Stevenson's *The Black Arrow* and *The Paston Letters*," *SEL*, 5 (1965), 677-90, and A. W. Mahaffy, "A Visit to the Library of R. L. Stevenson, at Vailima, Samoa," *Spectator*, 30 November 1895, pp. 762-63 (rpt. *The Book Buyer*, 12 January 1896, pp. 816-17, and partially in Hammerton, ed., *Stevensoniana*, 1907, pp. 113-14). Now held as Beinecke 1869 is an edition of the *Original Letters* . . . , 5 vols. (London: Robinson, 1787-1823), but this was not necessarily Stevenson's own. Taking issue with the usual dismissal of *The Black Arrow*, the historian G. M. Trevelyan remarked in the *Times*, 25 May 1919, that it "reproduces a real state of society in the past" and does this "well, like a good historical novel. The book reads like the outcome of an eager and imaginative study of the Paston Letters. (Appleyard, by the way, is a real name from them.)"

A NOTE ON REALISM. Summer 1883, in proof by 3 September. MS untraced. Galley proofs with a marginal note by W. E. Henley dated 3/9/83, Yale. *The Magazine of Art*, 7 (November 1883), 24-8; signed Robert Louis Stevenson. Tusitala 28. See *Letters, 2*, 270-72, where Stevenson comments at some length to his cousin Bob on his "breathless note" shortly before its publication.

OLD MORTALITY. Autumn-winter 1883. MS untraced. *Longman's Magazine*, 4 (May 1884), 74-81; signed Robert Louis Stevenson. *Memories and Portraits* (1887). Tusitala 29. Stevenson's college friend James Walter Ferrier, recalled in the third section of this essay, died 19 September 1883. The essay was written in the months following. Stevenson's wife notes that he originally "hesitated to publish" the essay due to its personal nature. "Finally, he sent the proof sheets to his friend's sister, leaving it to her to say whether it should see the light or not. She responded with an urgent request for its publication" (Tusitala, *3*, ix).

LAY MORALS. October 1883. See the entry of this work, to which Stevenson returned in October 1883 but made little more progress toward completing, under date of March 1879. On his work on it in 1883 see especially Stevenson to his father, 12 October 1883, *Letters, 2*, 272-74.

"A PENNY PLAIN AND TWOPENCE COLOURED." Autumn 1883. MS untraced. *The Magazine of Art,* 7, n.s. part 42 (April 1884), 227-32; signed Robert Louis Stevenson. *Memories and Portraits* (1887). Tusitala 29. Original illustrations not reprinted, nor was Stevenson's paragraph discussing them near the end of the essay. Benjamin Pollock, mentioned in the last paragraph of the essay, wrote three letters on Stevenson's visit to his shop in London in 1884, the year the essay was published but after it was written. These were given to the Stevenson Society of America, Saranac Lake, New York, by Charles Bradbury and are described in the Society's *General Report for 1930,* pp. 6-7. W. E. Henley had the finished essay in London before Christmas 1883, although he did not publish it until April (Beinecke 4774). Presumably Stevenson began writing it soon after his return to Hyères in September 1883 (see *Letters, 2,* 267).

HOKUSAI. Projected autumn 1883 but never written. "I think I can give you a good article on Hokusai," Stevenson wrote to W. E. Henley in May 1883; "but that is for afterwards; *Fontainebleau* is first in hand." In September he wrote: "Glad you like *Fontainebleau. . . . Hokusai* will really be a gossip on convention, or in great part" (*Letters, 2,* 243, 267). But Stevenson seems to have carried this project no further. Thirteen printed volumes of Hokusai drawings published in Japan mostly in the late 1870s are in the Silverado Museum, St. Helena, California. None is marked in any way, but there is with them a note by Isobel Field that the volumes were in Stevenson's library in Samoa and had been brought from Scotland.

A MISADVENTURE IN FRANCE. Begun autumn 1883; presumably laid aside, then revised for publication as "Epilogue to 'An Inland Voyage,'" March 1888. See the entry for this work below.

THE TRAVELLING COMPANION. See the entry for this work, to which Stevenson returned in October and November 1883 but again did not finish, under date of August 1881.

1884

MORE NEW ARABIAN NIGHTS: THE DYNAMITER. Begun at Hyères, spring 1884; mostly written at Bournemouth, autumn and winter 1884-85; finished February 1885. Stevenson wrote "Zero's Tale of the Explosive Bomb" alone; his wife, "The Destroying Angel" and "The Fair Cuban"; the other stories are collaborations between them. MSS untraced. *More New Arabian Nights: The Dynamiter* (London: Longmans, Green, and Co., 1885); published 28 April 1885. Stevenson's wife is listed as coauthor on the title page. Tusitala 3.

Stevenson was very ill during the first six months of 1884, and these stories were originally devised as entertainment for him in the afternoons at Hyères. As his wife writes of his confinement to bed during this illness: "He went on to say that there was something that he greatly wished me to do. I was to go out for an hour's walk every afternoon, if it were only back and forth in front of our door, and invent a story to repeat when I came in—a sort of Arabian Nights Entertainment where I was to take the part of Scheherezade and he the sultan. There had been several dynamite outrages in London about this time, the most of them turning out fiascos. It occurred to me to take an impotent dynamite intrigue as the thread to string my stories on. I began with the Mormon tale ["The Destroying Angel"], and followed it with innumerable others, one for each afternoon." As Stevenson's health improved, he gradually returned to his own work and "the stories of Scheherezade were thought of no more" until after the move to Bournemouth in the summer of 1884: "Money was absolutely necessary, [and] we cast about for something that could be done quickly and without too much strain; the Scheherezade stories came to mind, and we both set to work to write out what we could remember of them. We could recall only enough to make a rather thin book, so my husband added one more to the list, *The Explosive Bomb*" (Tusitala, *3*, xi-xii).

Stevenson and his wife turned to the actual writing of these stories in October 1884, after Stevenson and Henley had finished collaboration on *Admiral Guinea* and *Beau Austin*. After a month Stevenson described himself and his wife as "heavily handicapped with Arabs." By December the collection was undergoing revision and reorganization. On 27 January 1885 Stevenson wrote to Charles Baxter: "I am in treaty with *P.M.G.* [the *Pall Mall Gazette*] for *The Dynamiters*" (*Baxter Letters,* p. 156). Publication in the *Pall Mall Gazette* did not occur, but on 26 February 1885 Stevenson executed a contract with Longmans, Green and Company for the collection. Stevenson was to receive royalties of one-sixth of the retail price on all copies sold, Longmans to pay £150 against royalties in advance of publication, half that sum immediately, the rest when the proofs were passed for the press. Stevenson retained the American rights and was to receive half the proceeds from translation. (Society of Authors Archive, British Museum, MS. Add. 56638, f. 25.) On 16 March 1885 Andrew Lang wrote to Stevenson that the title *The Dynamiter* struck him as "catch penny," an attempt to exploit interest in the recent Fenian dynamite outrages. He proposed "The Man in the Sealskin Coat" instead, but Stevenson stuck with his original title. See *Letters, 3*, 12, 23, 36, 39, and Lang to Stevenson, Beinecke 5070. Stevenson's copy of the first edition, with notes by his wife about changes worth making in two passages, is now held as Beinecke 323.

[Assasinat par amour.] Spring or summer 1884 (uncertain). MS, Yale: 4 leaves, folio; G. Stewart and Company paper watermarked 1883; written in ink, pages numbered [1]-4 with a catchword at the foot of p. 4 suggesting that at least one more page of this MS was written. On the versos appears a pencil draft of Stevenson's poem "The Builder's Doom." Unpublished. Stevenson's untitled beginning of an essay, two long paragraphs and the beginning of a third, is an attack on the vulgarities of the popular press, in particular the sensationalized coverage given a recent murder under the heading "*Romantic Murder and Suicide*" in "a leading paper." Stevenson begins the essay, "*Assasinat par amour*, is one of those insidious elegancies, which journalism and the bar invent," refers unfavorably to the gossip columns of Edmund

Yates, and states his general theme at the end of the first paragraph: the ways in which "the small journalist, making phrases, telling us from day to day the story of our lives, steadily degrades the tone of thought" (Beinecke 5987, p. 1). He continues: "The hurt thus done, it would be hard to overestimate; if good books, true words and clear ideas have influence for good, by so much and something more their opposites have influence for ill. Thoughtless levity (not to be confused with antiseptic ridicule) and maudlin sentiment; the one absolving the reader from intellectual effort, the other indoctrinating lies: these are the two headmarks of bad journalism" (p. 2). In the rest of the manuscript Stevenson turns to the recent murder as a specific instance. Stevenson's argument resembles that in "The Morality of the Profession of Letters" (1881), but clearly he began this essay not earlier than 1883—possibly in the closing months of his residence at Hyères or early in his residence at Bournemouth.

ADMIRAL GUINEA. Summer or early autumn 1884. MS notebook devoted to communications with W. E. Henley about this play and *Beau Austin*, Yale. MS untraced. *Admiral Guinea: A Melodrama in Four Acts. By William Ernest Henley and Robert Louis Stevenson*. Edinburgh: privately printed by R. and R. Clark, 1884. Printed dedication to Andrew Lang dated 27 September 1884. W. E. Henley inscribed copies of this edition, of which perhaps as many as two dozen copies were printed, on 29 October 1884 — e.g. to Stevenson's father (Beinecke 7543), Sidney Colvin (Beinecke 2619), Arthur Egmont Hake (Ashley Library, British Museum), and Charles Warner (Princeton University Library). Stevenson himself inscribed the copy sent or given to Walter A. Powell (Beinecke 5943). Copy XXII (Beinecke 7544) is not inscribed to any particular recipient. Nor is copy V (Free Library of Philadelphia), which is marked throughout in pencil to indicate deletions and transpositions; in many places passages are merely circled. First published, with *Deacon Brodie* and *Beau Austin*, in *Three Plays by W. E. Henley and R. L. Stevenson* (London: David Nutt, 1892). First performed, Avenue Theatre, London, 29 November 1897. First separately published, *Admiral Guinea: A Drama in Four Acts by W. E. Henley & R. L. Stevenson*. (London: William Heinemann, 1897). Tusitala 24.

Stevenson took up residence in Bournemouth in July 1884, and soon he and W. E. Henley were energetically collaborating on various plays, projecting others, and looking forward, sometimes seriously, to the immense sums these would surely bring. Stevenson had first written plays during the late 1860s and early 1870s when he was a student at the University of Edinburgh, and in 1878 he and Henley had first collaborated—in revising Stevenson's *Deacon Brodie*, begun during his boyhood and reworked by him at the University of Edinburgh. Stevenson returned to Britain too late in July 1884 to see any of the London performances of *Deacon Brodie* earlier in the month; but as Graham Balfour writes, its reception "had been sufficiently promising to serve as an incentive to write a piece which should be a complete success, and so to grasp some of the rewards which now seemed within reach" (*Life, 2,* 3). Thus inspired, the collaborators concentrated on *Admiral Guinea,* which Henley had begun as early as 1881 (*Letters, 2,* 169), and shortly *Beau Austin.*

The plays were written according to the general procedure which Stevenson's wife described in her account of the collaborations at Bournemouth: "The plays were invented and written in the fervid, boisterous fashion of Mr. Henley, whose influence predominated, except in the actual literary form. A very thin, elastic scenario was first sketched out, which was afterwards elaborated in a series of paragraphs contributed alternately by each author. It was agreed between them that did one object to what the other had written, it should be stricken out without argument—a procedure that I cannot but believe was damaging to the work of both" (Tusitala, *5,* xvi). Thus for practical purposes it is impossible to separate the work of the two collaborators, although in general Henley seems to have done the most work. As Lloyd Osbourne noted, "In the interval of Henley's absences he [Stevenson] very gladly returned to his own work, and had as a playwright to be resuscitated by his unshaken collaborator, who was as confident and eager as ever" (*An Intimate Portrait of R.L.S.,* 1924, p. 57).

Henley was also chiefly responsible for getting the plays produced and for circulating the printed copies—a practice about which Stevenson expressed reservations in a letter to Henley in the spring of 1885. "Do you think you are right to send *Macaire* and the *Admiral* about?" Stevenson wrote. "Not a copy have I sent, nor (speaking for myself personally) do I want sent. . . . What I mean is that I believe in playing dark with second and third-rate work." Although he had defended the play in a letter to his father on 5 November 1884 (*Letters, 3,* 16), in his letter to Henley in the spring Stevenson remarked that reading *Admiral Guinea* again "was a sore blow; eh, God, man, it is a low, black, dirty, blackguard, ragged piece: vomitable in many parts—simply vomitable. Pew is in places a reproach of both art and man" (*Letters, 3,* 43). Except for work on *Macaire* during the winter of 1884-85 and perhaps some additional work on other plays in 1885, Stevenson collaborated with Henley on no more plays after *Admiral Guinea* and *Beau Austin* were written during the late summer and early autumn of 1884. See also the next two entries.

On 23 April 1891 it was agreed with the publisher David Nutt that the proceeds from the separate publication of *Deacon Brodie, Admiral Guinea, Beau Austin,* and *Robert Macaire* would be divided equally among Nutt, Henley, and Stevenson; none of the plays was in fact so published until 1897, and then the publisher was William Heinemann. On 15 February 1892 it was agreed that of the proceeds from *Three Plays* one quarter would go to David Nutt and the rest be divided equally between Henley and Stevenson (Society of Authors Archive, British Museum, MS. Add. 56638, ff. 71-72.)

BEAU AUSTIN. Summer or early autumn 1884. MS notebook devoted to communications with W. E. Henley about this play and *Admiral Guinea,*

Yale. MS untraced. *Beau Austin: A Play in Four Acts. By William Ernest Henley and Robert Louis Stevenson.* Edinburgh: privately printed by R. and R. Clark, 1884. Printed dedication to George Meredith dated 1 October 1884. On the differences between the first and second states of this printing see the Beinecke Collection catalogue, *A Stevenson Library* . . . , pp. 139, 2271. W. E. Henley inscribed a number of copies of this edition, of which perhaps as many as two dozen copies were printed, in October 1884 — e.g. to Sidney Colvin on 4 October 1884 (Princeton University Library). Other copies were certainly sent to Stevenson's father, Professor Fleeming Jenkin, Henry Arthur Jones, and George Meredith. See the letters, Beinecke 5396, 5783, 4992, 5011, and Meredith to Stevenson, 25 October 1884, Beinecke 5223, in *The Letters of George Meredith,* ed. C.L. Cline (1970), *2,* 750-51. Stevenson himself inscribed the copy sent or given to Una Ashworth Taylor (Beinecke 320). Copy XIX is not inscribed to any particular recipient, nor is the copy which bears only Henley's address in Edinburgh (both copies, Princeton University Library). First published, with *Deacon Brodie* and *Admiral Guinea*, in *Three Plays by W. E. Henley and R. L. Stevenson* (London: David Nutt, 1892). First performed, Theatre Royal, Haymarket, London, 17 November 1890, with H. Beerbohm Tree in the title role. First separately published, *Beau Austin: A Drama in Four Acts by W. E. Henley & R. L. Stevenson.* (London: William Heinemann, 1897). Tusitala 24.

According to Lloyd Osbourne, *Beau Austin* "was written in four days" at Bournemouth during the late summer or early autumn of 1884 (*An Intimate Portrait of R.L.S.,* 1924, p. 56). On 9 October 1890, H. Beerbohm Tree was granted exclusive London performance rights to *Beau Austin* and *Macaire* for two years, and in addition exclusive American performance rights to *Macaire* for the same period. The authors were to receive 5 percent of each night's gross receipts for the two plays performed together in London, up to a total of £100, after which their share was to be 7 percent. For each London performance of *Beau Austin* alone they were to receive £5.5, for each such performance of *Macaire*, £2.2. Terms for American performances were not specified. (Society of Authors Archive, British Museum, MS. Add. 56638, f. 74.) On the 1890 production see especially the correspondence, Beinecke 4657-59, and *Baxter Letters*, pp. 281-82, 285-86.

[Plays in collaboration with W. E. Henley.] Projected summer 1884 and at other times. Nearly throughout the time of their close friendship, from February 1875 until the spring of 1888, Stevenson and Henley were often discussing plays on which they might collaborate, among them those mentioned in the previous two entries. Henley was by far the more energetic and interested of the two, and in many instances Stevenson's collaboration seems to have consisted mostly of advice rather than actual writing. "The theatre is a gold mine; and on that I must keep my eye," Stevenson wrote to his father in 1883, expressing the view both collaborators sometimes took (quoted in Balfour, *Life, 2,* 3). But by the spring of 1885 Stevenson had clearly grown weary of the whole idea of writing plays. As he wrote to

Henley: "I have thought as well as I could of what you said; and I come unhesitatingly to the opinion that the stage is only a lottery, must not be regarded as a trade, and must never be preferred to drudgery. If money comes from any play, let us regard it as a legacy, but never count upon it in our income for the year. . . . It is bad enough to have to live by an art—but to think to live by an art combined with commercial speculation—that way madness lies" (*Letters, 3*, 33; see also *2*, 90).

Although it is by no means complete, confined as it seems to be to plays which had actually been written by the autumn of 1884 or were then under discussion (neither *Macaire* nor "Hester Noble" is included, for example), the list of Stevenson's own which Graham Balfour quoted from his notebook for *Beau Austin* (Yale) gives an indication of the range of the collaborators' interests and plans. In addition to *Deacon Brodie, Admiral Guinea,* and *Beau Austin*, Stevenson listed twelve other plays of various kinds; and in his review of Balfour's biography, *Pall Mall Magazine*, 25 (December 1901), 512-13, Henley added further comments on a number of them.

The plays were: "Honour and Arms: Drama in Three Acts and Five Tableaux," discussed at some length and described by Henley as "of its essence English, Jacobitish, romantic"; "The King of Clubs: Drama in Four Acts," on which Henley comments at some length, remarking that he took the idea originally from Dickens's *The Old Curiosity Shop*; "Pepys' Diary: Comedy"; "The Admirable Crichton: Romantic Comedy in Five Acts"; "Ajax: Drama in Four Acts," on which Henley remarks that they once decided to take all their dramatic situations from the Greeks and with this in mind "sketched, and partly wrote, our *Ajax*: whose hero is one Sir Robert Trelawney, an elderly Anglo-Indian engineer, who—brave, honest magnificent—plays the unconscious criminal as one of several directors in a fraudulent bank"; "The Passing of Vanderdecken: (Legend!) in Four Acts"; "Farmer George: Historical Play in Five Acts," described by Balfour as planned to cover "the whole reign of George the Third, ending with a scene in which the mad King recovered for a while his reason"; "The Gunpowder Plot: Historical Play"; "Marcus Aurelius: Historical Play"; "The Atheists: Comedy"; "The Mother-in-Law: Drama," which Henley says was to have been a tragedy; and "Madame Fate: Drama in a Prologue and Four Acts," of which Henley had no recollection save that the title "Madame Destiny," which also appears in Stevenson's list, was an alternate title. See also *Baxter Letters*, pp. 281-82 and 285-86, where Stevenson and Henley comment on "Hester Noble," "The King of Clubs," "Ajax," "Honour and Arms," and the collaborations of theirs which were actually published.

A HUMBLE REMONSTRANCE. Autumn 1884. MS untraced. *Longman's Magazine*, 5 (December 1884), 139-47; signed Robert Louis Stevenson. *Memories and Portraits* (1887), in which the concluding paragraph on Howells appears for the first time. Tusitala 29. Stevenson's essay in reply to "The Art of Fiction" (*Longman's*, September 1884) led to his lasting friendship with Henry James, on which see *Henry James and Robert Louis*

Stevenson: A Record of Friendship and Criticism, ed. Janet Adam Smith (1948). Writing to Will H. Low, 13 March 1885, Stevenson remarked: "I was terribly tied down to space, which has made the end congested and dull" (*Letters, 3*, 40). But he made only trivial changes reprinting it. Smith follows the 1884 versions of both essays. Stevenson presumably wrote this essay shortly after he read "The Art of Fiction" in the September 1884 issue of *Longman's Magazine*.

Letters: THE BELL ROCK LIGHTHOUSE. 3 October, 20 October 1884. MSS untraced. *The Athenaeum,* 11 October 1884, p. 465, and 25 October 1884, p. 529. Unpublished since their original appearance. In a letter dated Bournemouth, 3 October 1884, Stevenson complains of errors in *The Sea: its Stirring Story of Adventure, Peril and Heroism*, 4 vols., 2nd ed. (London: Cassell and Company, 1882-85). "I have visited both the Bell Rock and the Skerryvore, and I am in a position to state that the cuts representing those lighthouses have been made from models," Stevenson writes; "in neither case is the reef even approximately like the original." Even more alarming, though, is the claim made that David Rennie, not Robert Stevenson, deserves the credit for designing and building the Bell Rock lighthouse. "Who is the man who thus brings against my dead grandfather a wholesale charge of imposition and untruth, and who, while doing so, witholds his own name from the cover of his work? This is not merely a question of the fair name of Robert Stevenson, too well established to be shaken, but of the decency of letters" (11 October 1884, p. 465).

To Stevenson's question the book's author, Frederick Whymper, replied immediately, in a letter published in *The Athenaeum,* 18 October 1884, p. 497. He had nothing to do with the illustrations, Whymper writes. His name does indeed appear on the title pages. And for his remarks on Robert Stevenson he drew upon Samuel Smiles's *Lives of the Engineers* (1861-62) and the correspondence on Rennie and Stevenson cited by Smiles from the *Civil Engineer and Architects' Journal*, 12 (1849).

Stevenson's reply, dated Bournemouth, 20 October 1884, was published in *The Athenaeum*, 25 October 1884, pp. 529-30. In it, he reviews the whole question at length and refers to further material on the controversy in the *Civil Engineer and Architects' Journal*, May 1862, this being a long letter by Stevenson's uncle David Stevenson explaining the various contributions of the two engineers. "That Mr. Rennie was consulted; that he gave advice, sometimes taken, frequently rejected; and that he held a dignified consultative position, is not and has never been, denied," Stevenson concludes. "It merely and peremptorily denied that he either designed or executed the Bell Rock lighthouse" (p. 530).

Stevenson comments on this exchange of letters in a letter to Miss Coggie Ferrier, 12 November 1884 (*Letters, 3*, 18). His father wrote to him, probably about his second letter: "I have seen the letter & have no fault to find or criticism of any kind to make excepting that I think it very good and there is of course a considerable store of facts to fall back upon" (Beinecke

5785; see also Beinecke 5784). See also Stevenson's remarks at the beginning of chap. 3 of his *Records of a Family of Engineers* (1893) and the annotations there supplied by Sidney Colvin (Tusitala, *19*, 216-19).

OLIVER LEAF. Begun November 1884 but soon abandoned. MS untraced. Unpublished. See the next entry.

MARKHEIM. Late November 1884, revised 1885. MSS: (1) Houghton Library, Harvard University, fifteen leaves, folio, comprising the whole of the MS which Stevenson submitted to the *Pall Mall Gazette* in 1884; the MS was cut into sixty-six printers' takes for setting in type and has since been reassembled and mounted. (2) Revised version, being the MS eventually published, untraced. A facsimile of the first page of this revised MS faces the first page of text in vol. 10 of the Vailima Edition (1922). Publication: (1) unpublished; (2) *The Broken Shaft: Tales in Mid-Ocean*, ed. Henry Norman (London: T. Fisher Unwin, 1886 [for 1885]), pp. 27-38; signed Robert Louis Stevenson. *The Merry Men and Other Tales and Fables* (1887). Tusitala 8.

On 12 November 1884 Stevenson confirmed to Charles Morley of the *Pall Mall Gazette* an agreement made in his behalf by Edmund Gosse, whom Morley had approached seeking a story by Stevenson for the Christmas number. Stevenson was to provide Morley with a story of between seven and nine thousand words by 10 December, payment to be forty pounds on delivery. "My birthday [13 November] was a great success," Stevenson wrote to W. E. Henley two days later: "I was better in health; I got delightful presents; I received the definite commission from the P.M.G., and began the tale" (*Letters, 3*, 20). The tale thus begun was "Oliver Leaf," but when Morley sent for Stevenson's approval a printed advertisement for the Christmas number it became clear, as Stevenson wrote to Morley, that "you desire the blood to be curdled." Therefore "Oliver Leaf" was abandoned and Stevenson, as he wrote further to Morley, "telegraphed for a draft story left elsewhere which is ugly enough and ought to chill the blood of a grenadier." This was "The Body Snatcher," which Stevenson had drafted in 1881, but even so he did not abandon the attempt to write a story expressly for the occasion. During the next two weeks he wrote "Markheim," sending it to Morley on 1 December 1884. "Pray let me have a proof, *before you send me the money,*" Stevenson wrote, "as I wish to rejudge the work." And on 4 December, even before he received the proof, he wrote Morley that in his opinion the story was not his best work and, as a result, he wished to be paid only thirty pounds for it. When set in type "Markheim" proved to be fifteen hundred words too short for the space Morley had already budgeted, and so Stevenson hastily retouched "The Body Snatcher," which had arrived from Edinburgh, and submitted it instead. "The Body Snatcher" proved acceptable, and long enough, and was accordingly published in the 1884 *Pall Mall Christmas "Extra"* and "Markheim" returned to Stevenson. On 31 December 1884, thirty pounds was credited to Stevenson's account with

Mitchell and Baxter from Smith, Payne, and Smith. Presumably this was for "The Body Snatcher," the sum reduced at Stevenson's request by ten pounds from the forty pounds promised originally for "Markheim." See Beinecke 7268; Stevenson's correspondence with Morley in the Widener Collection *Catalogue*, 1912, pp. 240-43; and *Letters, 3*, 20-21, 27-28.

Stevenson left "Markheim" aside to work on other projects in 1885. But when Henry Norman approached him, probably during the summer of that year, for a story for Unwin's Christmas Annual, he returned to his manuscript and brought "Markheim" into the form eventually published. On Stevenson's reading of Dostoevsky's *Crime and Punishment* (1866; French trans., Dérély, 1884) see *Letters, 3*, 81; letters to him by W. E. Henley, November 1885, and John Addington Symonds, 3 March 1886, Beinecke 4846 and 5829; and Edgar C. Knowlton, "A Russian Influence on Stevenson," *Modern Philology*, 14 (December 1916), 449-54. Symonds's letter appears in *The Letters of John Addington Symonds*, ed. Schueller and Peters (1969), *3*, 120-21. Stevenson may also have known Eugène-Melchior de Vogüé's article on Dostoevsky first published in the *Revue des Deux Mondes*, 15 January 1885, rpt. June 1886 in de Vogüé's *Le roman russe.*

ON STYLE IN LITERATURE: ITS TECHNICAL ELEMENTS. December 1884. MS untraced. *The Contemporary Review*, 47 (April 1885), 548-61; signed Robert Louis Stevenson. Tusitala 28. See *Letters, 3*, 29-30, 40. Balfour, *Life, 2*, 11, notes that this essay was "the work of five days in bed."

MACAIRE. Autumn and winter 1884-85. MS untraced. Galley and page proofs, the latter stamped 25 February 1885, Princeton University Library. *Macaire: A Melodramatic Farce in Three Acts. By William Ernest Henley and Robert Louis Stevenson.* Edinburgh: privately printed by R. and R. Clark, 1885. Printed dedication to Arthur Egmont Hake dated 24 January 1885. W. E. Henley inscribed copies of this edition to various persons, among them Sidney Colvin (Beinecke 339; inscription dated 11 March 1885) and Edmund Gosse (Princeton University Library). First published in *The Chap Book* (Chicago), 1 and 15 June 1895, pp. 43-71, 92-101; signed Robert Louis Stevenson, William Ernest Henley. Simultaneously in *The New Review*, 12 (June 1895), 685-706. Published first in book form as magazine sheets bound and entered for United States copyright, 27 May 1895, and then in a regular edition: *Macaire: A Melodramatic Farce by Robert Louis Stevenson and William Ernest Henley* (Chicago: Stone and Kimball, 1895). Also published in England as *Macaire: A Melodramatic Farce in Three Acts by W. E. Henley & R. L. Stevenson* (London: William Heinemann, 1897), uniform with the Heinemann editions of *Deacon Brodie, Admiral Guinea,* and *Beau Austin* published at the same time. First performed, Strand Theatre, London, 4 November 1900. But there was a reading of the play to secure performance rights on 12 December 1887 at the Athenaeum Hall, Godolphin Road, Shepherd's Bush, London. A playbill from this reading was sold as Anderson 1914, I, 643. Tusitala 24.

Stevenson and Henley both knew Frederic Dumont's *L'Auberge des Andrêts* (1823), a play made famous in the 1820s by the French actor Frédérick-Lemaître and successful in England in Charles Selby's version, *Robert Macaire* (1835). In "'A Penny Plain and Twopence Coloured'" (1884) Stevenson even mentions having put on *Robert Macaire* in his toy theatre during his childhood. See the discussion of this play and its adaptations in M. W. Disher, *Blood and Thunder* (1949), p. 167, and Allardyce Nicholl, *A History of English Drama . . . IV. Early Nineteenth-Century Drama* (1955), pp. 397-98, 428, 610. But it was H. Beerbohm Tree who suggested that they adapt the play, during one of his visits to Bournemouth in the autumn of 1884. See Hesketh Pearson, *Beerbohm Tree: His Life and Laughter* (1956), pp. 48-50, and Coulson Kernahan, *Celebrities: Little Stories about Famous Folk* (1923), pp. 21-23. This they did during the autumn and winter of 1884-85, and throughout 1885 Tree was in correspondence with both Stevenson and Henley about the play, even revising it considerably himself. But on 8 December 1885 he withdrew, stipulating also that the authors were to send him a copy of the play on which he would mark the passages indebted to his suggestions. These were not to be used in any future productions. See the voluminous correspondence on the whole matter, Beinecke 3589-90, 4058, 4638-40, 4645, 5883-87, 8042. See also the entry of *Beau Austin* above under date of summer 1884; *Letters, 3*, 43-44; and *Baxter Letters*, pp. 282, 286.

THE GREAT NORTH ROAD. Late 1884-June 1885. MS, Berg Collection, New York Public Library. Notebook list of characters and sketch map, Yale. *Illustrated London News*, Christmas 1895, pp. 5-14, illustrated by R. Caton Woodville; signed "by the late Robert Louis Stevenson." Also published in *The Cosmopolitan*, New York, 20 (December 1895), 147-57; 20 (January 1896), 289-300, titled "A Tragedy of the Great North Road" and illustrated by Eric Pape. Tusitala 16. According to Sidney Colvin (*Letters, 3*, 2-3), Stevenson began "The Great North Road" during the autumn of 1884 at Bournemouth. In December 1884 he suggested to W. E. Henley that it be offered eventually to Cassell and Company; in February 1885 he was definitely at work on the novel; but it was still unfinished in June and the project seems to have languished thereafter. See *Letters, 3*, 23, 36, 49, and the remarks by Stevenson quoted in Sidney Colvin's "Editorial Note" to this unfinished novel, Tusitala, *16*, 234-35.

1885

THE DUKE OF WELLINGTON. Begun January 1885 but at length abandoned. MS, 6 pp., and many notes and source books, Yale. Other source books: Anderson 1914, I, 249, 700, 701. Vailima Edition, 24 (1923), 26-9. Tusitala 24.

Late in 1884, Andrew Lang wrote to Stevenson that Longmans was contemplating a series of books, English Worthies, and wondered whether Stevenson might care to contribute. They will pay not less than one hundred pounds, Lang wrote. As to subject: "Bar politicians, the field is almost unlimited" (Beinecke 5055). By the end of the year Stevenson had agreed to write on Wellington, and early in 1885 he signed a contract dated 31 December 1884 with Longmans, Green and Company for *The Duke of Wellington* in the English Worthies series. The section providing for submission of the manuscript within a year was deleted on the printed form. Stevenson was to be paid fifty pounds upon receipt of the manuscript and royalties of one-sixth of the retail price on all copies sold after the first five hundred. He had earlier rejected an offer of one hundred pounds outright for the volume. (Society of Authors Archive, British Museum, MS. Add. 56638, f. 21; *Letters, 3*, 30-31.) He began work at once, assembling books and writing letters—among these a letter to W. E. Gladstone, 6 January 1885, of which two copies survive (Silverado Museum, St. Helena, California; Beinecke 8400). Stevenson's letter to his neighbor at Bournemouth, Sir Henry Taylor, thanking him in January 1885 for an anecdote Sir Henry had supplied is now in the private collection of Waverley B. Cameron, Edinburgh. See also Stevenson to the bookseller Walter Scott ordering books on Wellington (Sotheby's, 6 June 1978, 497) and A. W. Mahaffy, "A Visit to the Library of R. L. Stevenson, at Vailima, Samoa," *Spectator*, 30 November 1895, pp. 762-63 (rpt. in *The Book Buyer*, 12 January 1896, pp. 816-17, and partially in J. A. Hammerton, ed., *Stevensoniana*, 2nd ed., 1907, pp. 113-14). Mahaffy recalls seeing "a fine and complete edition of 'Wellington's Despatches' and several military treatises," but he does not comment further on them.

Stevenson continued to work on his study of Wellington at intervals during the next eighteen months. Andrew Lang, editor of the English Worthies series, was in correspondence with him about details in 1885 and 1886, writing on 22 October 1885 for instance, "*don't forget the Duke*" (Beinecke 5074; see also 5059, 5061, 5077). Even as late as August 1886, according to Will H. Low, Stevenson was still "much preoccupied" with his study of Wellington. "He was full of his subject," Low recalled of Stevenson's visit to Paris in August 1886, "and his many tales of the Iron Duke made that theretofore conceived (to me) rather wooden—or iron—hero wonderfully living and human" *(A Chronicle of Friendships*, 1908, p. 335). But the study never progressed beyond the assembling of notes and Stevenson's writing the opening paragraphs. See also *Letters, 3*, 30-36.

Letter: A WARNING. 10 January 1885. MS untraced. *The Athenaeum*, 24 January 1885, p. 121. Unpublished since its original appearance except in the variously titled edition, *The Works of Robert Louis Stevneson*, ed. C. C. Bigelow and Temple Scott, 10 vols. (New York, 1906), *9*, 265-66. In a letter dated Bournemouth, 10 January 1885, Stevenson denounces as "an imposture" Augustin Filon's *Histoire de la littérature anglaise* (1883). "M. Filon is a rash and ignorant compiler; he has read but few of the books of which he treats, many he has not seen," Stevenson writes. "Such a book can only be called an imposture."

KIDNAPPED. Begun March 1885 but shortly laid aside; resumed January 1886, under which date it is entered below.

[Contribution to THE SCOTTISH CHURCH.] Promised April 1885 but apparently never written. MS untraced. Unpublished. On 7 April 1885, Stevenson's friend Charles Baxter wrote telling him of a new magazine being started in Edinburgh, *The Scottish Church*. It was intended "primarily to meet the falsehoods of the Liberation party, but also as a moderate-priced literary periodical for the Scotch Country Folk," and Baxter hoped that "some of your old Scotch stories" might be suitable for it. "Look at it not only from a pecuniary point," Baxter worte, "but from a patriotic one" (*Baxter Letters*, p. 162n.). Stevenson replied immediately that he would be glad to contribute (*Baxter Letters*, p. 162), and on 13 April 1885 Baxter wrote to him that the editor R. H. Story had proposed paying 30s. per page (Beinecke 4017). But more than a year later, on 1 May 1886, Story wrote to Baxter that Stevenson had still not sent his promised contribution; on 3 May Baxter wrote to Stevenson about this (Beinecke 5805, 4021). Nevertheless, nothing seems to have come of the request, although Stevenson did eventually contribute two poems, "A Lowden Sabbath Morn" and "Ille Terrarum," to the April 1887 issue.

Baxter mentions fiction, but it is possible that Stevenson planned to contribute an essay to *The Scottish Church*. An anonymous writer in *The British Weekly*, 20 December 1894, p. 135, remarks: "His favourite religious writer was John Bunyan. More than nine years ago he [Stevenson] promised the present writer an article for a religious magazine, and though this purpose was not carried out," Stevenson did leave some remarks on Bunyan in "Bagster's *Pilgrim's Progress*" (1882). More information than this, however, is lacking.

Obituary: PROFESSOR FLEEMING JENKIN. Mid-June 1885. MS, Yale. *The Academy*, 20 June 1885, p. 441; signed Robert Louis Stevenson. Unpublished since its original appearance. See the next entry.

MEMOIR OF FLEEMING JENKIN. Autumn 1885-summer 1887. MS untraced. "Memoir of Fleeming Jenkin," in *Papers Literary, Scientific, &c. by the Late Fleeming Jenkin, F.R.S., LL.D. Professor of Engineering in the University of Edinburgh*, ed. Sidney Colvin and J. A. Ewing, 2 vols. (London and New York: Longmans, Green, and Co., 1887), I, xi-cliv. *Memoir of Fleeming Jenkin* (New York: Charles Scribner's Sons, 1887); published 7 January 1888. Tusitala 19. Stevenson's friend (and teacher in 1871, when Stevenson was still studying engineering), Professor Henry Charles Fleeming Jenkin, died 12 June 1885 at the age of fifty-three. Stevenson wrote his obituary, published in *The Academy,* 20 June 1885, and immediately felt a desire to write more. "To try to draw my friend at greater length, and say what he was to me and his intimates, what a good influence in life and what an example, is a desire that grows upon me," he wrote to Mrs. Jenkin before the end of June 1885 (*Letters, 3*, 48). According to Graham Balfour, Stevenson "had begun to write" the *Memoir* itself by September, and Balfour quotes Mrs. Jenkin's own account of Stevenson's attentive work with her when she visited Bournemouth later in the year (*Life, 2*, 20-21). On 1 January 1886 Stevenson described himself as "much and hopefully occupied with dear Jenkin's life" (*Letters, 3*, 65). But the work went slowly, in part due to illness, and it was not until more than a year later that Stevenson neared completion of his task. On 15 April 1887 he reported to Mrs. Jenkin that he was "getting on well with" the biography; a few weeks later he wrote that it was "all drafted," that he would soon send her several chapters for review, and that chapters 6 and 7 were still giving him trouble (*Letters, 3*, 124-5, 130). By midsummer Stevenson had the MS ready for the press. "I have just read the memoir," Jenkin's son wrote to him on 9 August 1887; and by late September Mrs. Jenkin had returned proofs of the American edition to Scribner's in New York, Stevenson by then having already arrived in the United States. Publication of this separate edition, which contained only Stevenson's memoir of Jenkin, not reprints of Jenkin's works and other contributions, was delayed until the complete Longmans work could appear. See the correspondence, Beinecke 5474-75, 5444, 5447, 4978-82, 4390, and the entries of Stevenson's obituary of Jenkin and his protest of P. G. Tait's review of the complete collection under dates, respectively, of mid-June 1885 and March 1888.

STRANGE CASE OF DR. JEKYLL AND MR. HYDE. September-October 1885; submitted by 1 November; in proof by mid-November. MSS: (1) Yale, Princeton University Library, notebook fair copy, incomplete. (2) Pierpont Morgan Library, Silverado Museum, St. Helena, California, final version, complete except for pages missing in the middle. Described with some inaccuracies in E. Limedorfer, "The Manuscript of Dr. Jekyll and Mr. Hyde," *Bookman*, 12 (New York, September 1900), 52-58, with facsimiles of three pages of the manuscript. (3) Proofs of title page and front matter dated 14 and 19 November 1885, Yale. (4) Proof of title page stamped 14 November 1885, Princeton University Library. *Strange Case of Dr Jekyll and Mr Hyde* (London: Longmans, Green, and Co., 1886); published 9 January 1886. American edition (New York: Charles Scribner's Sons, 1886) published 5 January 1886 but from Longmans sheets. Stevenson originally offered the story for serialization in *Longman's Magazine*, submitting the manuscript by 1 November 1885 (Beinecke 3726). Longmans suggested separate publication instead, and on 3 November 1885 Stevenson executed a contract with them for "The Story of Dr Jekyll and Mr Hyde." Stevenson was to receive royalties of one-sixth of the retail price on all copies sold, Longmans to pay the royalty on the first ten thousand copies immediately and on all copies above that number sold through Christmas 1885 on 1 January 1886. In addition, Stevenson was to receive half the proceeds of foreign sales (Society of Authors Archive, British Museum, MS. Add. 56638, f. 27). Longmans went to press with the book immediately, but by the time it was ready, according to Charles Longman, "the bookstalls were already full of Christmas numbers, etc., and the trade would not look at it." Therefore it was withdrawn until January, and though forty thousand copies were sold in Britain alone during the first six months the book had little success until it was noticed in the *Times*, 26 January 1886. See Balfour, *Life, 2*, 14. Tusitala 5.

"*Jekyll* was conceived, written, re-written, re-re-written, and printed inside ten weeks," Stevenson wrote to F.W.H. Myers on 1 March 1886 (*Letters, 3*, 83). It was drafted in three days and written in six weeks, he told the San Francisco *Examiner,* 8 June 1888, having already given an account of the story's composition in "A Chapter on Dreams" (1888). Due to "financial fluctuations," Stevenson had written there, "for two days I went about racking my brain for a plot of any sort; and on the second night I dreamed the scene at the window, and a scene afterwards split in two, in which Hyde, pursued for some crime, took the powder and underwent the change in the presence of his pursuers. All the rest was made awake, and consciously. . . . All that was given me was the matter of three scenes, and the central idea of a voluntary change becoming involuntary" (*30*, 52). "Byles the butcher," Stevenson called his initial monetary impulse (*Letters, 3*, 83). His physician at Bournemouth, Dr. T. B. Scott, recalls not only that Stevenson was pressed for funds but that it was his publishers who had suggested writing a shilling shocker, presumably for the Christmas trade, an idea which Stevenson viewed with reluctance (see Masson, ed., *I Can Remember Robert Louis Stevenson*, 1922, p. 213). The dream itself Stevenson had described in somewhat more limited terms to the New York *Herald,* 8 September 1887: "All I dreamed about Dr. Jekyll was that one man was being pressed into a cabinet, when he swallowed a drug and changed into another being. I awoke and said at once that I had found the missing link for which I had been looking so long, and before I again went to sleep almost every detail of the story, as it stands, was clear to me. Of course, writing it was another thing" (in Hammerton, ed., *Stevensoniana*, 2nd ed., 1907, p. 85). Thus, at the earliest stage, Stevenson was pressed for money, anxious to find a workable plot, and in a dream hit upon one or more details which made the story he was seeking fall into place. In "A Chapter on Dreams" he notes that he had long been "trying to write a story on this subject, to find a body, a vehicle, for that strong sense of man's double being, which must at times come in upon and overwhelm the mind of every thinking creature" (*30*, 51). But it is not apparent that it was to write a story on this particular subject, rather than a story of any kind (which turned out to *be* on this subject), that Stevenson actually began.

Several accounts of the actual writing of *Dr. Jekyll and Mr. Hyde* exist.

According to Fanny Stevenson, "My husband's cries of horror [one night] caused me to rouse him, much to his indignation. 'I was dreaming a fine bogey tale,' he said reproachfully, following with a rapid sketch of Jekyll and Hyde up to the transformation scene, where I had awakened him." Next morning, she says, Stevenson began the first draft, finishing its thirty thousand words in three days. This draft, however, was then "entirely destroyed and immediately re-written from another point of view,—that of the allegory, which was palpable and had yet been missed, probably from haste, and the compelling influence of the dream. In another three days, the book, except for a few minor corrections, was ready for the press" (Tusitala, *5*, xvii-xviii).

Lloyd Osbourne adds that it was Fanny Stevenson herself who suggested the rewriting, and he too says that Stevenson destroyed a whole first draft—mostly, it would appear, due to his wife's keen disappointment with the original. "When my mother and I both cried out at the folly of destroying the manuscript," Osbourne wrote, Stevenson "justified himself vehemently. 'It was all wrong,' he said. 'In trying to save some of it I should have got hopelessly off the track. The only way was to put temptation beyond my reach'" (*An Intimate Portrait of R.L.S.,* 1924, pp. 65-66).

In 1944, Isobel Field repeated most of this but said that Stevenson initially wrote "only a few pages telling of a man taking a potion that changed him from a good man into his evil self!" and sent these to Fanny for criticism. She suggested treating the tale allegorically; Stevenson destroyed these few pages; and upon Fanny's urging he wrote the story at length from this new standpoint in the next few days. When this version, the first of any length, was finished, Fanny still felt that a "horrible deed" was needed to establish Hyde's evil. "R.L.S. replied, 'you write that yourself' . . . [and] did not change a word of her description of Hyde's evil deed" (Beinecke 7372).

Graham Balfour's concise account, *Life, 2*, 12-14, brings coherence from these disparate versions, including Stevenson's own, and is based upon earlier recollections by both Fanny and Lloyd. Stevenson "read nearly half the book aloud" the day after his dream, Lloyd told Balfour, "and then, while we were still gasping, he was away again, and busy writing." Balfour continues: Fanny Stevenson, "according to the custom then in force, wrote her detailed criticism of the story as it then stood." Her main objection, at this point, writes Balfour, was that "it was really an allegory, and he had treated it purely as if it were a story. In the first draft Jekyll's nature was bad all through, and the Hyde change was worked only for the sake of a disguise." Not long after giving Stevenson her written criticisms, Fanny returned to find the first draft in ashes. Balfour continues: "It was written again in three days ('I drive on with Jekyll: bankruptcy at my heels'); but fear of losing the story altogether prevented much further criticism." After this version was written, Stevenson "was working hard for a month or six weeks bringing it into its present form."

In short, Stevenson wrote and then destroyed at least one initial treatment of the story; then wrote, probably in three days and with the benefit of his wife's criticism and stepson Lloyd's reactions, a fairly complete second draft;

and finally he subjected this draft to detailed revision over a period of weeks. (Isobel Field's suggestion that Fanny Stevenson contributed one scene is uncorroborated and contradicts what Fanny herself once told Sidney Colvin. Probably the suggestion originated in the collaborations on *Prince Otto* or *The Dynamiter*.)

Stevenson's ultimate inspiration for *Dr. Jekyll and Mr. Hyde*, according to his wife, was "a paper he read in a French scientific journal on subconciousness." This "deeply impressed" Stevenson, and, "combined with memories of Deacon Brodie, gave the germ of the idea that afterwards developed into the play, was used again in the story of *Markheim*, and finally . . . culminated in the dream of Jekyll and Hyde" (Tusitala, *5*, xvi). This article, which has never been identified, presumably appeared in the 1870s or late 1860s, Stevenson's collaboration revising his early play on Deacon Brodie being a project begun with W. E. Henley in 1878. Stevenson told an interviewer in 1893 that he had never heard of any actual case of "double personality" when he wrote the book: "After the book was published I heard of the case of 'Louis V.,' the man in the hospital at Rochefort. Mr. Myers sent it to me" ("Mr. R. L. Stevenson and Literature," Wellington, N. Z., April 1893, in Stevenson 's mother's scrapbooks, Monterey State Historical Monument Stevenson House Collection, California, vol. 5, p. 164; xerox, Yale). But as he notes in "A Chapter on Dreams" Stevenson had long been seeking a vehicle for his concern with this general subject and in 1881 had actually written "The Travelling Companion," a story to which he returned in 1883 and eventually destroyed as having been "supplanted" by *Dr. Jekyll and Mr. Hyde* (*30*, 51).

Although no real-life model for Dr. Jekyll need be found—"I believe you will find he is . . . quite willing to answer to the name of Low or Stevenson," Stevenson remarked to his friend the painter Will H. Low (*Letters, 3*, 67-8)—C.H.E. Brookfield asserted in 1902 that "I was in his company at the moment that he [Stevenson] conceived the germ of the idea of 'Dr. Jekyll and Mr. Hyde.'" Stevenson was furious with a local tradesman, possibly called Samuel Creggan, for feigning a cooperativeness he did not have: "Creggan's the *real* man: Samuel's only superficial," Stevenson remarked. T. P. O'Connor, commenting on the anecdote, suggests that the "tradesman" was in fact Stevenson's early publisher C. Kegan Paul. "Oh, yes," Stevenson is recalled saying, "Kegan is an excellent fellow, but Paul is a publisher" (in J. A. Hammerton, ed., *Stevensoniana*, 2nd ed., 1907, pp. 80-81).

A recent theory is that Dr. Jekyll is based on Horace Wells (1815-48), a dentist in Hartford, Connecticut, whose pioneering work with nitrous oxide anaesthesia preceded a very unhappy end. Disappointed in establishing the priority of his discoveries to those of a former colleague, Wells moved to New York, fell increasingly prey to self-intoxication with chloroform, and was arrested for throwing vitriol on a prostitute, apparently not the first such attack he had made when thus intoxicated. Before killing himself in his cell, he wrote a long letter filled with self-abhorrence to the New York *Journal of Commerce*, which published it on 25 January 1848. Stevenson may have known something of anaesthesia through his friend Sir Walter Simpson, son of Sir James Y. Simpson, who pioneered the use of chloroform, or perhaps through W. E. Henley. But there is no reason to think that Stevenson had ever heard of Horace Wells, and plainly the story need not have been based on a real person at all.

Myron G. Schultz, M. D., "The 'Strange Case' of Robert Louis Stevenson," *Journal of the American Medical Association*, 216 (5 April 1971), 90-94, suggests that Stevenson's seemingly prodigious energy in writing the earliest draft of this story may have been due to his taking cocaine for respiratory complaints. The evidence is at best circumstantial, and Schultz's speculations are in addition reviewed skeptically in an article on the history of cocaine use by Charles Perry, *Rolling Stone*, 115 (17 August 1972), 24-26.

THOMAS STEVENSON. Autumn 1885 (uncertain). MS, Huntington HM 2405: 12 pp. titled "Thomas Stevenson" written at the beginning of a notebook, 7⅛" x 9⅛". Followed by an untitled very early draft of the beginning of "The Misadventures of John Nicholson" (begun November 1885), 5 pp.; an untitled list of some three dozen English prose writers from Sir Thomas Malory to John Ruskin, each classified by Stevenson into one of five broad stylistic categories, 1 p.; and some miscellaneous jottings including draft stanzas of a poem in Scots about W. E. Gladstone. Unpublished except for extensive quotations in Balfour, *Life, 1*, 16-20. No information exists as to the date or occasion of Stevenson's unfinished account of his father's childhood except its appearance in a notebook immediately before material for "The Misadventures of John Nicholson," which Stevenson is known to have begun in November 1885. Graham Balfour dates the account 1887 on the assumption that Stevenson wrote it after his father's death, but this seems contradicted by the manuscript evidence. See also the entry of Stevenson's obituary of his father, "Thomas Stevenson: Civil Engineer," under date of late May 1887.

THE MISADVENTURES OF JOHN NICHOLSON. Begun November 1885, finished December 1886. MS, Huntington HM 2405: untitled very early draft of the beginning of this story (5 pp.) and an untitled list of ten chapters for the work (1 p.), both in the notebook described in the previous entry. "The Misadventures of John Nicholson: A Christmas Story," *Yule Tide . . . Cassell's Christmas Annual*, December 1887, pp. 3-12; signed Robert Louis Stevenson. Tusitala 13. E. B. Simpson, *Robert Louis Stevenson's Edinburgh Days,* 2nd ed. (1898), p. 153, notes that the story would not have been reprinted even in the Edinburgh Edition had not T. N. Foulis of the publishers Douglas and Foulis, Edinburgh, "reminded the editors of its existence."

Stevenson began this story in November 1885, intending it as a Christmas story for the *Court and Society Review* edited by Charles Gray Robertson. But he soon ran into trouble and laid it aside, probably after completing no more of it than now survives in the Huntington Library manuscript. "John has broken down, and its place has been taken by one 'Olalla,'" Stevenson wrote to Robertson on 4 November 1885 (Beinecke 3229). He left "The Misadventures of John Nicholson" aside for nearly a year before finishing it, his only other references to the writing of the story appearing in letters to Sidney Colvin, 14 December 1886, and to Henry James, early January 1887 (*Letters, 3*, 112, 115). To Colvin he remarks in December that he is writing "a damn tale to order, which will be what it will be: I don't love it, but some of it is passable in its mouldy way, *The Misadventures of John Nicholson.*" To Henry James, in January, he mentions having completed "a silly Xmas story (with some larks in it) which won't be out till I don't know when." Presumably Stevenson left the manuscript with Cassell and Company early in 1887 for publication at their pleasure. See also *Letters, 4*, 56.

OLALLA. November-December 1885. MS untraced. *Court and Society Review*, Christmas 1885, pp. 3-15. *The Merry Men and Other Tales and Fables* (1887). Tusitala 8. Sometime during the autumn of 1885 Stevenson seems to have agreed to provide a story for the Christmas number of Charles Gray Robertson's *Court and Society Review*. Relations were naturally strained by Stevenson's sending *Dr. Jekyll and Mr. Hyde* to Longman instead, and in late October he even asked to have that story back, a request which Longman of course refused. Meanwhile he had begun "The Misadventures of John Nicholson" expressly for Robertson, and when he found progress halted on that story he began "Olalla" instead. "John has broken down," Stevenson wrote to Robertson on 4 November 1885, "and its place has been taken by one 'Olalla'" (Beinecke 3229). By early December "Olalla" was finished, Stevenson's wife communicating his thanks "for the cheque" in a letter to Robertson postmarked 11 December 1885. See the correspondence with Robertson, Beinecke 3227-30, 3725-27. Graham Balfour, *Life, 2*, 15-16, notes the resemblance between "Olalla" and E. G. Bulwer Lytton's *A Strange Story* (1861), calls attention to Stevenson's remarks on the genesis of the story in "A Chapter on Dreams" (1888) and his passing comment on the character Felipe (*In the South Seas*, "The Gilberts—Apemama," chap. 5; Tusitala *20*, 310), and notes that Stevenson was "never well satisfied" with the story. Balfour also quotes Stevenson's letter on the stories in *The Merry Men*, written to Lady Taylor, January 1887: "The trouble with *Olalla* is that it somehow sounds false. . . . *Markheim* is true; *Olalla* false; and I don't know why, nor did I feel it when I worked on them" (*Letters, 3*, 114). See also Ramon Jaén, "Notes on Stevenson's 'Olalla,'" *University of California Chronicle*, 25 (July 1923), 376-84, on the story's Spanish atmosphere and setting; and Edwin M. Eigner, *Robert Louis Stevenson and Romantic Tradition* (1966), pp. 201-11.

1886

KIDNAPPED. January to April or May 1886; begun but laid aside spring 1885. MS, Huntington HM 2410, complete except for the last two chapters; see

Mildred Wilsey, "*Kidnapped*, in Manuscript," *American Scholar*, 17 (Spring 1948), 213-20. Draft dedication, miscellaneous notes and source materials, Yale. Source books, Princeton University Library. "Kidnapped; or The Lad With the Silver Button. By Robert Louis Stevenson." *Young Folks*, 28-29, fourteen weekly installments, 1 May—31 July 1886, *Kidnapped: Being Memoirs of the Adventures of David Balfour in the Year 1751*... (London: Cassell and Company, 1886); published 14 July 1886, and on the same date by Charles Scribner's Sons, New York. Tusitala 6.

Stevenson began *Kidnapped* early in 1885 at Bournemouth, "partly as a lark, partly as a pot-boiler" he told Theodore Watts-Dunton (*Letters, 3*, 104), and on 17 March 1885 James Henderson of *Young Folks* accepted Stevenson's proposal for another serial. Henderson offered 15s. per column and added that Stevenson should avoid having "much broad Scotch in it... a little of that goes a long way with our readers" (Beinecke 4356). But other projects intervened and it was not until *Dr. Jekyll and Mr. Hyde* was published in January 1886 that Stevenson returned to *Kidnapped.*

By 25 January 1886 Stevenson had finished sixteen chapters (*Letters, 3*, 75-76). Two days later he reported his progress to James Henderson (Beinecke 3160) and remarked to his father: "I am at David again, and have just murdered James Stewart semi-historically. I am now fairly in part two: the Highland part. I don't think it will be so interesting to read, but it is curious and picturesque" (NLS typescript 9898). A letter from Henderson having come in the meantime, Stevenson wrote to him on 3 February that the novel "goes on its way still" and that he was "in great hopes you may go ahead at Easter in safety." He would send notes for the illustrations and expected that the novel would be at least thirty chapters (Princeton University Library; facsimile in *Princeton University Library Chronicle*, 17, Winter 1956, 74).

Stevenson finished *Kidnapped* sometime in April or May 1886, the work as a whole having taken "probably five months actual writing, and one of these months entirely over the last chapters, which had to be put together without interest or inspiration, almost word by word, for I was entirely worked out" (Stevenson to George Iles, 29 October 1887, *Bookman*, London, 7, February 1895, 136). He had accepted Sidney Colvin's suggestion to end the novel in Edinburgh, leaving the rest for a sequel. "It will deal with Edinburgh, Gulane, Bass Rock, Leyden and Dunkirk," Stevenson wrote of this sequel to his father on 23 May 1886; and on 18 June, also to his father, he wrote that he had also accepted both of his father's earlier suggestions, to include something on religion—i. e., the material on Mr. Henderland—and to have David decoyed onto the *Covenant* "instead of being knocked on the head at Queensferry" (NLS typescripts 9898; see also *Letters, 3*, 75).

On 6 April 1886, three weeks before serialization in *Young Folks* commenced on 1 May, Stevenson executed a contract with Cassell and Company for *Kidnapped.* The manuscript was to be delivered on or before 15 May 1886, the book published on 1 July 1886 or as soon thereafter as possible. Cassell was to have sole book-form rights in the United Kingdom. Stevenson was to receive royalties of 15 percent on the retail price, reckoning thirteen copies as twelve, against which £150 was to be paid when the proofs were passed for the press. Stevenson retained the American rights and was to receive half the proceeds from translation. (Society of Authors Archive, British Museum, MS. Add. 56638, f. 9.)

Publication of the novel in book form on 12 July 1886 found Stevenson wishing a few small changes made. See the comments by G. L. McKay in the Beinecke Collection catalogue, *A Stevenson Library . . .*, pp. 163-65, 1024, 2280. Referring to a copy of the first issue of the first English edition, Stevenson wrote to Charles Scribner's Sons on 16 July 1886 that in the ninth paragraph of chap. 5 (p. 40 in the Cassell edition) the correct reading was *pleasure*, not *business*; that in the first paragraph of chap. 8 (p. 64) the time should be *twelve* o'clock, not *nine*; and that in the second paragraph of chap. 12 (p. 101) *Long Island* was correct, not *Long Islands*. Only the second of these is an actual change. In *Young Folks*, the readings are, respectively, *pleasure, nine,* and *Long Island.* In the Edinburgh Edition (1895), the time was changed again, to *eleven* o'clock.

Replying to a letter from Edmund Gosse, Stevenson agreed that a phrase in the sixth paragraph of chap. 17 should also be changed. "You are right about 'ferny dells'," Stevenson wrote on 17 July 1886, "damn, it's like Claribel's po'try. I shall change it to ferny howes, which would be unexceptionable" (Silverado Museum, St. Helena, California; a reply to Gosse's letter of 15 July 1886 published in Evan Charteris, *The Life and Letters of Edmund Gosse*, 1931, pp. 187-89). This change was not made until the Edinburgh Edition was published, after Stevenson's death. Two further changes appear in the Edinburgh Edition. In the twelfth paragraph of chap. 28 the correct reading *Thomson* appears, as it had in *Young Folks*. In some of the book-form editions it had appeared wrongly as *Johnson*. In the twenty-fifth paragraph of chap. 28 the Edinburgh Edition reads *quite out of countenance*. This corrects a misprint in the English book-form editions but does not in fact restore the reading in *Young Folks: quite put out of countenance*. In the book's elaborated general title, in the eight paragraph from the end of chap. 7, and in the fourth paragraph from the end of chap. 13, the Edinburgh Edition gives the correct readings—*Acquaintance, child*, and *Earraid*, respectively—as they had also appeared in *Young Folks*. All three were misprinted in the first English issue (as *Acquaintancc, chlid*, and *Erraid*) and only the first was ever corrected in Cassell and Company editions published during Stevenson's lifetime.

The changes and corrections which appeared for the first time together in the Edinburgh Edition (eleven o'clock, ferny howes, Thomson, quite out of countenance, Acquaintance, child, Earraid) also appeared in the new edition of *Kidnapped* which Cassell and Company published, also in 1895, as part of a two-volume edition of *Kidnapped* and its sequel called, in accord with a suggestion of Stevenson's own, "The Adventures of David Balfour." This 1895 edition of *Kidnapped* has 319 pp. of text; earlier Cassell editions have 311 pp. The title page and half-title are both headed "THE ADVENTURES OF

DAVID BALFOUR," and the half-title of *Kidnapped* continues, "PART ONE: /KIDNAPPED.," the half-title of the sequel, "PART TWO:/CATRIONA." The 1895 Cassell text and the Edinburgh Edition text both derive from a corrected copy of *Kidnapped* which in December 1893 Stevenson wrote that he was "just sending home" (*Letters, 5*, 95-96). It is unknown which of the two was set in type first, or whether one was set from the other. Nor is it known where Stevenson's corrected copy of *Kidnapped* is now, if it survives. But it is clear that Stevenson's last revisions in *Kidnapped* are embodied for the first time in these 1895 texts.

In American editions the corrections which Stevenson requested in his letter to Charles Scribner's Sons on 16 July 1886 were not made immediately. Only one of the correct readings appears in the first American edition, probably by spontaneous amendment by the printer rather than due to Stevenson's request. But there is in the Princeton University Library collection (I, 31E) a copy of the 1887 American edition, illustrated by W. B. Hole, in which all three of the corrections which Stevenson requested have been incorporated into the text. This copy Stevenson inscribed to Mr. and Mrs. George Saxby, Saranac Lake, 30 December 1887, and in it Stevenson also corrected by hand six misprints unique to the American editions.

Kidnapped originated in Stevenson's interest in Scottish history, in particular that interest in the history of the Highlands in the eighteenth century which he dated from visits there in the late summer of 1880 and, especially, the summer of 1881. "The best of all my designs," Stevenson wrote later in his unfinished "Note to *Kidnapped*" (early 1894), "a History of the Highlands from the Union to the Present day; social, literary, economical and religious, embracing the 15, and the 45, the collapse of the Clan System, and the causes and growth of existing discontents, I bequeath to a more qualified successor." But this interest led to his acquiring, "in the city of Inverness, the printed trial of James Stewart bound up with a critical examination of the evidence; I suppose the volume cost me a few shillings, and has proved certainly the best of my investments. I was taken with the tale from the beginning . . . " (in W. H. Arnold, "My Stevensons," *Scribner's Magazine*, 71, January 1922, 65; see also *Letters, 5*, 81). This volume, now in the Princeton University Library, was *The Trial of James Stewart in Aucharn in Duror of Appin, for the Murder of Colin Campbell of Glenure* . . . (Edinburgh: G. Hamilton and J. Balfour, 1753), and it is bound with *A Supplement to The Trial of James Stewart* . . . (London, 1753) and a four-page folio printing of *An Authentick Copy of the Dying Speech of James Stewart*. . .(n.p., n.d.). Stevenson has marked passages in this volume and made a list of page references at the end. (Another copy of *The Trial of James Stewart*, identical with the above and also bearing Stevenson's bookplate, is held as Beinecke 1879, but it lacks the supplementary items and is unmarked. Possibly this is the copy Stevenson's wife recalls as having been sent to them in Bournemouth; see Tusitala, *6*, vii-viii.) This was Stevenson's principal source of historical information in *Kidnapped*, although it was not the only one and he also gathered some information personally during a trip to the west of Scotland in 1882. On this trip, made to gather material for an article he was to write on the Appin murder, see the entry "[Famous murders]" under date of December 1881. Stevenson's detailed knowledge of the terrain of the island of Earraid and of the extreme western tip of Mull derives from his three-week visit there in August 1870 during construction of the Dhu Heartach lighthouse offshore by his father's engineering firm. See also his "Memoirs of an Islet" (*Memories and Portraits*, 1887) and L. M. Buell, "Eilean Earraid: The Beloved Isle of Robert Louis Stevenson," *Scribner's Magazine*, 71 (February 1922), 184-95. According to Stevenson's wife (Tusitala *6*, x), the recipe for Lily-of-the-Valley Water in the first chapter came from an old cook book she was reading at the time: E. Smith, *The Compleat Housewife* . . . , 8th ed. (London: Pemberton, 1737). This volume is now in the Princeton University Library. Further on Stevenson's sources and his interest in Scottish history see the entry of "The Murder of Red Colin: A Story of the Forefeited Estates" under date of October 1881.

Letter: AMERICAN RIGHTS AND WRONGS. 15 March 1886. MS, Yale. *The Academy*, 20 March 1886, p. 203. Unpublished since its original appearance. In a letter dated Skerryvore, Bournemouth, 15 March 1886, Stevenson offers several remarks on copyright for the benefit of English authors. "There is always a little money to be got from advance sheets" sent to America, he remarks. "I have known it to be near a third of what the author could raise (in money down) at home; and this is too great a consideration to be let slip." He commends the "good faith and generosity" of Charles Scribner's Sons and hopes that eventually an international agreement will be reached. Meanwhile, he concludes, it would be worthwhile "to get our own copyright law amended, and wait, with such civility as we can muster, for the States to follow in our wake."

[Dramatic version: *The Mayor of Casterbridge.*] Projected June 1886 but never written. Stevenson first met Thomas Hardy in early September 1885, when he and Fanny were "almost the first visitor[s]" to the Hardys in their new home, Max Gate (*The Life of Thomas Hardy 1840-1928*, 1962, p. 174). Stevenson had written to Hardy, asking to visit, on 24 August 1885, and after their visit Fanny wrote to Stevenson's mother: "We saw Hardy the novelist at Dorchester . . . a pale, gentle, frightened little man, that one felt an instinctive sympathy for" (10 September 1885; NLS typescript 9898). To Sidney Colvin she wrote: "We saw Hardy the novelist. . . and liked him exceedingly" (Beinecke 3643; in *Scribner's Magazine,* 75, March 1924, 321). Ten months later, Stevenson wrote to Hardy: "I have read 'The Mayor of Casterbridge' with sincere admiration: Henchard is a fine fellow, and Dorchester is touched with the hand of a master. Do you think you would let me try and dramatize it?" (Stevenson to Hardy, late May or early June 1886; in *The Life of Thomas Hardy*, pp. 179-80). Hardy was delighted. "I feel several inches taller at the idea of your thinking of dramatizing the *Mayor*," he wrote to Stevenson on 7 June 1886. "Yes, by all means" (*Collected Letters of Thomas Hardy*, ed. Richard L. Purdy and Michael Millgate, 1978, *1*, 146-47). Nevertheless nothing came of this project.

THE GOLD FEVER. Outlined 16 July 1886 but never written. The only surviving record of this projected novel is in the correspondence between Stevenson and Charles Scribner's Sons in July and August 1886 (Beinecke 3262, 5479, and Pierpont Morgan Library MA 1598, Stevenson to Charles Scribner's Sons, received 8 September 1886). Stevenson supplied a list of chapter titles for this projected novel on 16 July. Scribner's replied on 13 August offering $1800 for the serial rights, estimating that it would run for about eight months in *Scribner's Magazine*. Stevenson then replied: "Good heavens, into what an error are you fallen!" He couldn't possibly have a book ready by autumn, although he might have one in a year, and was sorry he had misled them into thinking otherwise. Nothing eventually came of this project.

Letter: HONOUR AND CHASTITY. 22 July 1886. MS untraced. *Court and Society Review*, 29 July 1886, pp. 677-78; signed Robert Louis Stevenson. Unpublished since its original appearance except in *The Stevensonian: The Journal of the Robert Louis Stevenson Society of London*, no. 3 (August 1967), 3-7, with a commentary by Ernest J. Mehew. In a letter dated 22 July 1886 Stevenson comments on the conduct of Sir Charles Dilke, the Liberal politician, in relation to the Crawford divorce case in which Dilke was named as corespondent. "I have really no concern with Sir Charles's morals, which it appears impossible to mend," Stevenson writes; "the morals of my fellow-countrymen at large are what I care about." What is appalling is not Dilke's "unchastity," then the only subject of public comment, but his insistence that the whole case, settled in February, be reopened to clear his own name, as it had been in July when Stevenson wrote. Rather than "let the case go, and handsomely sacrifice himself," Dilke chose "to save his own reputation, and heartlessly destroy that of a woman who had trusted him." This is the conduct for which Dilke deserves censure, Stevenson writes: "and yet I observe . . . that what strikes me most seems to strike my contemporaries least. They are justly enough horrified to find him guilty: the question of his guilt is to me but the dust of the balances; and even accepting his own story in every particular, I still find him the meanest figure of a man that I remember to have read of." Andrew Lang wrote to Stevenson about this letter: "You don't mean you've been writing on Dilke and the Elections? 'Not here, o Apollo'" (Beinecke 5093). Further on Dilke's career and this divorce case which ended it see Roy Jenkins, *Sir Charles Dilke: A Victorian Tragedy* (1958).

[French story.] August-September 1886. MS untraced. Publication details unknown if published. During a fortnight's stay in Paris in August 1886,

Stevenson spent much time with the sculptor Auguste Rodin who was then finishing a portrait bust of W. E. Henley. Not long after Stevenson returned to Bournemouth, Rodin communicated to him the request of the sculptor Adrien Gaudez, a friend of Stevenson's and Will H. Low's from the 1870s who had unfortunately been absent from Paris during Stevenson's visit, for a contribution to "son journal" (Beinecke 5409). Stevenson evidently complied. On 5 September 1886 he wrote to his mother: "I have just written a French (if you please!) story for a French magazine. Heaven knows what it is like; but they asked me to do it, and I was only too pleased to try" (quoted in Balfour, *Life, 2*, 20). But Stevenson seems to have changed his mind about actually submitting the story. Arthur Johnstone, *Recollections of Robert Louis Stevenson in the Pacific* (1905), pp. 105-6, quotes from the office diary of the editor of the *Pacific Commerical Advertiser* an interview with Stevenson in September 1893 in which Stevenson says of this work: "I once wrote a story in a foreign language—by request, as your reporters say. It was written in French, of a kind; but I was not brave enough to send it to the publishers, so I destroyed it, as one should all literary temptations of every class."

Letter: RODIN AND ZOLA. September 1886. MS untraced. *The Times* (London), 6 September 1886, p. 8. Unpublished since its original appearance. In an undated letter from Skerryvore, Bournemouth, Stevenson takes exception to a recent correspondent's comparison of Rodin and Zola, especially to his calling Rodin "the Zola of sculpture." This is most inaccurate, Stevenson writes. "M. Zola is a man of personal and fanciful talent, approaching genius, but of diseased ideals; a lover of the ignoble, dwelling complacently in foulness, and to my sense touched with erotic madness. . . . M. Zola presents us with a picture, to no detail of which we can take grounded exception. It is only on the whole that it is false. We find therein nothing lovable or worthy; no trace of the pious gladnesses, innocent loves, ennobling friendships, and not infrequent heroisms by which we live surrounded; nothing of the high mind and the pure aims in which we find our consolation. Hence we call his work realistic in the evil sense, meaning that it is dead to the ideal, and speaks only to the senses. M. Rodin's work is the clean contrary of this. His is no triumph of workmanship lending an interest to what is base, but to an increasing degree as he proceeds through life the noble expression of noble sentiment and thought. . . . The public are weary of statues that say nothing. Well, here is a man coming forward, whose statues live and speak, and speak things worth uttering. Give him time, spare him nicknames and the cant of cliques, and I venture to predict . . . he will take a place in the public heart." See also the entry for Stevenson's "[Essay on Rodin]," early 1887, and the previous entry.

SOME COLLEGE MEMORIES. Autumn 1886. MS, Huntington HM 44527: 12 pp., quarto, in a bound volume of manuscripts containing Stevenson's and all the other contributions. *The New Amphion: Being the Book of the Edinburgh University Union Fancy Fair* . . . (Edinburgh: David Douglas, 1886), pp. 221-40; signed Robert Louis Stevenson. The separate, purportedly 1886, issue of Stevenson's essay (Beinecke 407) is a forgery by Thomas J. Wise. *Memories and Portraits* (1887). Tusitala 29. Stevenson's is one of various literary contributions to the book published to raise money for the Edinburgh University Union and sold at a "Fancy Fair" held for this purpose late in 1886. The volume was published on 30 November 1886; presumably Stevenson wrote and submitted his contribution sometime during October or early November.

THE MERRY MEN AND OTHER TALES AND FABLES. Dedication written, preface begun but neither finished nor used, and the stories collected, late 1886; published 9 February 1887. MS draft dedication, Yale; draft dedication and unfinished preface, Princeton University Library. Six stories, all written and published between 1881 ("The Merry Men") and 1885 ("Markheim"). *The Merry Men and Other Tales and Fables* (London: Chatto and Windus, 1887); published 9 February 1887. American edition (New York: Charles Scribner's Sons, 1887) published 19 February 1887. Draft preface first published, partially, in Balfour, *Life, 1*, 189. First published complete, with a facsimile of the first page and many misreadings of Stevenson's hand, in *Hitherto Unpublished Prose Writings* (1921), pp. 73-76, and from this source in the Vailima Edition, 26 (1923), 477-78. Tusitala 8, which also includes Stevenson's draft preface. Stevenson had been anxious to make a second collection of his short stories for a number of years before *The Merry Men* was agreed upon. On 14 February 1883, reading proofs of "The Treasure of Franchard," he wrote to W. E. Henley asking him to tell Chatto and Windus that this story would shortly be available for republication, with others, in a volume (Beinecke 4666). More than a year later, writing to his father about revisions he wanted to make in various stories, Stevenson remarked: "When they are all on their legs this will make an excellent collection" (19 April 1884, *Letters, 2,* 303). Not until late 1886, however, was Stevenson able to see his hopes realized; and even then, as he wrote to Lady Taylor on 1 January 1886, the collection was most heterogeneous (*Letters, 3*, 112-13; see also *3*, 114-16). On 24 January 1887 Stevenson executed a contract with Chatto and Windus for *The Merry Men.* He was to receive royalties of one-sixth of the retail price on all copies sold of the 6 shilling edition, Chatto and Windus to pay one hundred pounds against royalties on the day of publication. On 13 April 1891, W. E. Henley, acting for Stevenson, agreed to payment of forty pounds for the Tauchnitz edition. (Society of Authors Archive, British Museum, MS. Add. 56638, ff. 21, 53.)

MEMORIES AND PORTRAITS. Collected late 1886, augmented 1887, published 21 November 1887. MS draft of "Note," Yale. Sixteen essays written from the winter of 1881-82 ("The Foreigner at Home," "Talk and Talkers") to the early summer of 1887, including three essays previously unpublished: "A College Magazine," "Memoirs of an Islet," and "A Gossip on a Novel of Dumas's." *Memories and Portraits* (London: Chatto and Windus, 1887); published 21 November 1887. American edition (New York: Charles Scribner's Sons, 1887) published 2 December 1887 from Chatto and Windus sheets. Tusitala 29. Stevenson had proofs of part of this volume in early January 1887, when he sent them to Henry James (*Letters, 3*, 115). Having received a second batch of proofs a few weeks later, he explained to James his general plan at that time: "I am on the start with three volumes, that one of tales [*The Merry Men*], a second one of essays [*Memories and Portraits*], and one of—ahem—verse [*Underwoods*]. . . . All new work stands still. . . . I shall re-issue *Virg*[*inibus*] *Puer*[*isque*] as vol. I of *Essays*, and the new vol. as vol. II of ditto; to be sold, however, separately" (*Letters, 3, 117;* see also *3*, 133). *The Merry Men* was published 9 February 1887, and at about this time it seems to have been decided to delay publication of *Memories and Portraits* until Stevenson had a few more essays ready for it, including some which would appear for the first time in this volume. By 2 August 1887 copy for *Memories and Portraits* and for a new edition of *Virginibus Puerisque* was in the hands of Chatto and Windus (Beinecke 7947), and on 16 August 1887 Stevenson executed a contract with them for the publication of *Memories and Portraits* and the reprinting of *Virginibus Puerisque*, his royalty being one shilling per volume sold at six shillings (Society of Authors Archive, British Museum, MS. Add. 56638. f. 34). Stevenson read proofs of *Memories and Portraits* and wrote the introductory matter for it during the voyage of the *Ludgate Hill* to New York, 22 August-7 September 1887. On 29 September, Chatto and Windus ordered one thousand copies of *Virginibus Puerisque*; presumably at the same time they ordered the two thousand copies of *Memories and Portraits* which constituted the first edition. This was published on 21 November 1887, *Virginibus Puerisque* for the first time under the Chatto and Windus imprint two weeks later on 5 December.

THE HANGING JUDGE. Winter 1886-87. MS untraced. Typewritten copy, Yale. *The Hanging Judge: A Drama in Three Acts and Six Tableaux. By Robert Louis Stevenson and Fanny Van De Gript* [*sic*] *Stevenson.* Edinburgh: privately printed by R. and R. Clark, 1887. Printed in March, or possibly June, 1887. See the discussion of this item (Beinecke 441) in the Beinecke Collection catalogue, *A Stevenson Library* . . . , pp. 187-88. See also John Carter, "The Hanging Judge Acquitted," *Colophon*, n.s. 3 (Spring 1938), 238-42, and Michael Balfour, "In Defense of *The Hanging Judge,*" *New Colophon*, 3 (1950), 75-77. Privately printed in 1914 for Thomas J. Wise, with an introduction by Edmund Gosse. On this 1914 printing see the discussions by John Carter and Michael Balfour, already cited, and Fred B. Warner, "*The Hanging Judge* Once More Before the Bar," *PBSA*, 70 (January-March 1976), 89-96. First published in the Vailima Edition, 6 (1922), 316-414. Tusitala 24.

According to William Ernest Henley: "*The Hanging Judge* idea was suggested by a story in Sheridan Lefanu's *Through a Glass Darkly*; a book for which R.L.S. had a profound respect. *I* brought it on the cloth, as a *motif* for a play. One was written . . . [and] submitted to Beerbohm T. [H. Beerbohm Tree]. But it came to nothing; & it wasn't for years that he (Lewis) took up the Hanging Judge thing, & incarnated it in McQueen of Braxfield, who is Weir of Hermiston" (Henley to Sidney Colvin, 10 November 1895, in E. V. Lucas, *The Colvins and Their Friends*, 1928, p. 247). Fanny Stevenson wrote that she herself suggested the idea, proposing that Henley and Stevenson base a play upon it. This came to nothing, and eventually she took up the challenge herself, "emboldened by my husband's offer to give me any help needed." Accounts of Old Bailey trials were ordered from London as background, and soon both husband and wife found themselves "absorbed, not so much in the trials as in following the brilliant career of a Mr. Garrow, who appeared as counsel in many of the cases. We sent for more books, and yet more," Fanny Stevenson continues, "still intent on Mr. Garrow, whose subtle cross-examination of witnesses and masterly, if sometimes startling, methods of arriving at the truth seemed to us more thrilling than any novel" (Tusitala, *6*, vii).

The play itself was written, and perhaps the typewritten copy of the manuscript also made in London, during the winter of 1886-87. Stevenson's request to R. and R. Clark, Edinburgh, instructing them to print the work was dated, according to a pencil note on the letter, 11 March 1887 (Beinecke 7955). Copies may not have been printed at once, however, for on 30 May 1887 Stevenson wrote to R. and R. Clark: "Please strike off a dozen or two dozen copies as it stands; but on a large quarto page with broad margins, and printed only on one side. I do not want it stitched, simply in loose, numbered single leaves, as (when I have time) I must work a great part of it afresh" (Beinecke 7956).

In his discussion of *The Hanging Judge* in the Beinecke Collection catalogue, *A Stevenson Library . . .*, p. 187, G. L. McKay writes that the play "was submitted to Beerbohm Tree but he declined to produce it. A revised version was submitted in manuscript to Richard Mansfield. In the Beinecke Collection is Stevenson's receipt for the manuscript returned by Mansfield: "Received M. S. of / Hanging Judge / Robert Louis Stevenson / May 1st 1888." When this revision was made is unknown, but on 6 December 1887 Fanny Stevenson wrote to Sidney Colvin: "*The Hanging Judge*, amid much dissension and general acrimony, has been finished" (in Lucas, *The Colvins and Their Friends*, p. 209). And in a letter postmarked the same day, 6 December 1887, Stevenson thanked E. L. Burlingame for "your promptitude about the Hanging Judge" (Beinecke 2899; see also Beinecke 3246). Stevenson may have sent the work to Charles Scribner's Sons for an opinion, or for suggestions who might want to produce it.

H. L. Simpson, "Island Treasure: A Visit to Samoa," in Sir George Douglas, ed., *A Cadger's Creel . . .* (1925), p. 110, recalls meeting Dion Boucicault's actor son Darley (Dot) Boucicault in Sydney not long after Stevenson's death. "Boucicault," Simpson writes, "showed us the place where Stevenson tried to persuade the young actor to produce *The Hanging Judge*. To him it seemed as if the sick man could not last through the interview." This interview probably took place in February 1891. Stevenson's stepdaughter Isobel Field remarks that in Australia in 1890-91 she lived at Miss Leaney's, 17 St. Mary's Terrace, Sydney, where "the boarders . . . being stage folk, . . . [the] stage was discussed morning, noon and night" (*This Life I've Loved*, 1937, pp. 259-61; see also Stevenson's mother's *Letters from Samoa 1891-1895*, 1906, pp. 25-26). But even in 1895, after Stevenson's death, the play remained unstaged, Fanny Stevenson asking Sidney Colvin at that time to see whether he couldn't get it produced somewhere (Beinecke 3683-86).

1887

[Essay on Rodin.] Planned early 1887 for writing in July, but never written. Stevenson's only reference to this essay, probably a discussion of Rodin's sculptures based on photographs and intended for publication in the *Art Journal*, appears in a letter to W. E. Henley written in late March 1887. "You have never sent me the names of those photographs," Stevenson wrote. "I do not know what they represent, and wish that you would see to have this remedied. I am much behind with my work now . . . but if all goes as I hope, and the information comes, I should be able to tackle the matter in early July, which I hope will do" (*Baxter Letters*, p. 199). On Stevenson's acquaintance with Rodin see especially Will H. Low, *A Chronicle of Friendships* (1908), pp. 325-29. See also the entries "[French story]" and "[Letter: Rodin and Zola]" under date of September 1886.

PASTORAL. Spring 1887, published April. MS untraced. *Longman's Magazine*, 9 (April 1887), 596-602; signed Robert Louis Stevenson. *Memories and Portraits* (1887). Tusitala 29. One paragraph of this essay is analyzed at length in F. C. Riedel, "A Classical Rhetorical Analysis of Some Elements of Stevenson's Essay Style." *Style*, 3 (Spring 1969), 182-99. Riedel finds "juxtaposition of opposites" a leading stylistic feature.

THE DAY AFTER TO-MORROW. Spring 1887, published April. MS untraced. *The Contemporary Review*, 51 (April 1887), 472-79; signed Robert Louis Stevenson. Tusitala 26.

Letter: LIFE OF FLEEMING JENKIN. 28 March 1888. MS untraced. *Nature*, 12 April 1888, p. 559. Unpublished since its original appearance. In a letter dated 28 March, Stevenson writes about the review (*Nature*, 8 March 1888, pp. 433-35) of *Papers Literary, Scientific, &c. by the Late Fleeming Jenkin* (1887), in which his own "Memoir of Fleeming Jenkin" had appeared.

Signed P.G.T., the review had been written by Professor P. G. Tait of the University of Edinburgh. "I have read with singular pain a paragraph in your notice (signed with the initials of one whom I admire and respect) of my Life of Fleeming Jenkin," Stevenson writes. "The Biographer's story of his Class Certificate in Engineering," Tait had written, "will, we are certain, find no credence with any one who knew Prof. Jenkin." Stevenson replies that the story is true—"the terms of the document are at the reviewer's service to-morrow, if he be curious"—and if Tait had read more carefully he would have found it reflecting no discredit whatever on Jenkin (see Stevenson's "Memoir," chap. 6, part 4; Tusitala, *19*, 127-29). Nor is Stevenson pleased with Tait's general view that the "Memoir" was a great success as an imaginative work, "fresh proof of the versatility of his genius" as Tait had written, but inadequate as a biography due to its slighting of Jenkin's habits as a scientist and Stevenson's predilection for striking details. "I dwell upon this," Stevenson writes in his letter defending his accuracy, "because it is plain your reviewer scarcely understands what literature is, and I fear others may be equally at sea. . . . To accuse a man of falsehood in private life is a strong step. But I must explain to your reviewer, I might lie to him all day long and not be so disgraced as if I put one single falsehood in a book."

Letter: INTERNATIONAL COPYRIGHT. 31 March 1887. MSS untraced; copies made by Stevenson of Harper and Brothers' letter to him, 11 March 1887, and his reply, 31 March 1887, Yale. *The Times* (London), 2 April 1887, p. 6. Unpublished since its original appearance. Enclosing his recent correspondence with Harper and Brothers, New York, in which that firm sent him twenty pounds for their recent publication of several of his works and Stevenson replied that the money was more justly due to Charles Scribner's Sons and so he was sending it to them, Stevenson observes that such unauthorized republication of British authors' works in the United States will only continue unless some form of internationally recognized copyright is enacted. See also the entries "Letter: American Rights and Wrongs" (15 March 1886) and "Authors and Publishers" (1890-91).

THE MANSE: A FRAGMENT. Spring 1887, published May. MS untraced. *Scribner's Magazine*, 1 (May 1887), 611-14; signed Robert Louis Stevenson. *Memories and Portraits* (1887). Tusitala 29. Charles Scribner's Sons acknowledged receipt of the MS on 22 April 1887 (Beinecke 5482). See also Balfour, *Life, 1*, 11-13, 39-48, and the entry of "Reminiscences of Colinton Manse" (early 1870s).

BOOKS WHICH HAVE INFLUENCED ME. April or early May 1887. MS, 7 pp. folio, item 115 in the *Catalogue* (1901) of the George M. Williamson collection but untraced thereafter. The MS is described, with a facsimile of the first and last sentences, in *Bookman* (New York), 8 (January 1899), 417. *British Weekly*, 13 May 1887, pp. 17-19; signed Robert Louis Stevenson. Collected with the other eleven contributions to this series as *"British Weekly" Extras, No. I. Books Which Have Influenced Me* (London: British Weekly, 1887), published August 1887. Stevenson's essay is on pp. 3-16. Tusitala 28.

THOMAS STEVENSON: CIVIL ENGINEER. Late May 1887. MS draft portion, Ashley Library, British Museum, written on the back of part of Stevenson's manuscript of "Ticonderoga" (1887). MS untraced. *The Contemporary Review*, 51 (June 1887), 789-93. The separate, purportedly 1887, issue of Stevenson's essay (Beinecke 458) is a forgery by Thomas J. Wise. *Memories and Portraits* (1887). Tusitala 19.

Stevenson's father, born on 22 July 1818, died in Edinburgh on 8 May 1887, aged sixty-eight, and was buried there in the New Calton Burial Ground on 13 May. Stevenson wrote this obituary shortly thereafter, remarking to Sidney Colvin in thanks for Colvin's own note in the *Pall Mall Gazette*: "I have written four pages in the *Contemporary*, which Bunting found room for: they are not very good, but I shall do more for his memory in time" (*Letters, 3*, 132). On 1 May 1888 the Edinburgh publishers Adam and Charles Black inquired whether Stevenson would care to write a biography of his father for them (Beinecke 4453). Apparently he declined this suggestion, although he did write about his father in the history of his family which he began in 1891 and worked on at intervals thereafter and indirectly in such later essays of reminiscence as "Contributions to the History of Fife: Random Memories" (1888) and "Rosa Quo Locorum" (1893). See also the entry of *Records of a Family of Engineers,* under date of August 1891, and "Thomas Stevenson," autumn 1885. Much biographical information about the whole family appears in Craig Mair's *A Star for Seamen: The Stevenson Family of Engineers* (1978).

In the margin opposite the next-to-last paragraph of this essay in the copy of *Memories and Portraits* which he gave to George Iles (Beinecke 456) Stevenson wrote the following note on his father's views favoring "a marriage law under which any woman might have a divorce for the asking": "Any man or woman who wants a divorce should have it by registering his or her wish for 25 cts or 10 cts or nothing. The children should be a charge on parents property or earnings."

A COLLEGE MAGAZINE. Spring-summer 1887. MS untraced. *Memories and Portraits* (1887). Tusitala 29. This essay was first published in *Memories and Portraits*, serving as an introduction to the only essay of the six Stevenson contributed to the *Edinburgh University Magazine* in 1871 which he ever reprinted, "An Old Scotch Gardener." See the entry of his contributions above under date of January-April 1871.

MEMOIRS OF AN ISLET. Spring-summer 1887. MS untraced. *Memories and Portraits* (1887). Tusitala 29. This essay was published for the first time in *Memories and Portraits* and is based on the three weeks Stevenson spent on Earraid in August 1870 during construction of the Dhu Heartach lighthouse offshore by his father's engineering firm. See the entry for "The New Lighthouse on the Dhu Heartach Rock, Argyllshire" under date of summer 1872. Earraid was the setting for "The Merry Men" (1881) and "The Islet," chap. 14 in *Kidnapped* (1886). It is also the subject of L. M. Buell, "Eilean Earraid: The Beloved Isle of Robert Louis Stevenson," *Scribner's Magazine*, 71 (February 1922), 184-95.

A GOSSIP ON A NOVEL OF DUMAS'S. Spring-summer 1887. *Memories and Portraits* (1887). Tusitala 29. This essay on Alexandre Dumas's *Dix ans plus tard, ou le vicomte de Bragelonne* (1848-50) was published for the first time in *Memories and Portraits*. Edward Latham, "Stevenson and Miss Yonge," *Notes and Queries*, 8 January 1921, p. 79, remarks that the novel of Charlotte Yonge's in which Stevenson recalls first finding d'Artagnan was *The Young Stepmother*, serialized in *The Monthly Packet*, 1857-60. Yonge's character Gilbert Kendal is found reading "one of the worst and most fascinating of Dumas's romances" and d'Artagnan is mentioned.

[Essays for *Scribner's Magazine*.] October 1887-April 1888. Entered individually below. Stevenson reached New York aboard the *Ludgate Hill* on 7 September 1887, and after a short visit to Newport, Rhode Island, he returned there on 19 September, remaining until 30 September. During this stay in late September he was offered $10,000 (£2,000) for a year's weekly articles in the New York *World*, an offer which he declined. But he did accept an offer of $3,500 (£720) made him for twelve monthly articles in *Scribner's Magazine*. These were to be "as long or as short as I please," Stevenson remarked in October, "and on any mortal subject. I am sure it will do me harm to do it; but the sum was irresistible" (*Letters, 3*, 148).

Scribner's had for some time been Stevenson's regular American publishers, in fact although not by formal arrangement. Theirs, for example, were the only authorized American editions of *Dr. Jekyll and Mr. Hyde* and *Kidnapped*, both published in 1886. On 13 August 1886 Scribner's offered him $1,800 to serialize a novel Stevenson had outlined, "The Gold Fever," in their new *Scribner's Magazine*, begun the previous January; see the entry for that work under date of July-August 1886. In 1887, this close relation continued with their publication of *The Merry Men* on 19 February; "The Manse" in the May issue of *Scribner's Magazine*; the poem "Ticonderoga," accepted in June, paid for in July ($250, or £51), and published in the December issue of *Scribner's Magazine*; and, ten days before Stevenson's arrival in New York, the volume of poems, *Underwoods*, published on 26 August. So it was only natural that Stevenson would continue this association when he arrived in the United States.

In addition to arranging to write this series of essays for *Scribner's Magazine*, Stevenson also granted to Scribner's "power over all my work in this country," an agreement which of course made awkward his contracting with S. S. McClure in October to reserialize *The Black Arrow*, his promising McClure three essays for newspaper syndication, and his agreement with McClure, on 1 November 1887, to give him "the next story I finish of the same character as Kidnapped." See *Letters, 3*, 157-59, and Beinecke 2899-2900, 3186, 3241, 3243-47, 5443-44, and 5449-50. See also the extensive treatment of Stevenson's relations and correspondence with Scribner's in Roy A. Riggs, "The Vogue of Robert Louis Stevenson in America, 1880-1900" (Ph.D. dissertation, Ohio State Univ., 1959; *DA, 20*, 1959, 304-5); the Charles Scribner's Sons archives are now in the Princeton University Library and the materials in them are listed in Alexander D. Wainwright's *Robert Louis Stevenson: A Catalogue* (1971), pp. 108-19. See also Roger Burlingame, *Of Making Many Books: A Hundred Years of Reading, Writing and Publishing* (1946), pp. 18-19, 93, 96, 212-13, 231-33, 250-51, and 260-61.

Stevenson wrote these twelve essays—thirteen counting "Confessions of a Unionist," which Scribner's declined after it was in type—during his stay at Saranac Lake, New York, from October 1887 through April 1888. They were published, one a month, in *Scribner's Magazine* during 1888, and each is entered individually below. From the beginning it was planned to collect these twelve essays into a volume, a plan which was later dropped, no doubt due to their very diverse character and subject matter. "I shall be glad to hear from you or Mr Burlingame as to a name," Stevenson wrote to Charles Scribner in early October. "The papers will all likely be *gossips*" (Beinecke 3239). In mid-October, still at a loss for a name for the volume, Stevenson was considering *Familiar Essays* and listed the first six essays as: "Dreams," "The Lantern-Bearers," "Beggars," "Gentlemen," "Clergymen and Others," and "Artists" (Beinecke 3241). Toward the end of the month he offered two more possible titles for the volume, *Variations* or possibly *Airs and Variations* (Beinecke 3235, received 27 October 1887). But thereafter discussion of this question ceased. The twelve essays were never published together as a distinct volume. Although nine of them appeared in *Across the Plains* (1892), three did not appear even in the Edinburgh Edition. These three essays—"Popular Authors," "Gentlemen," and "Some Gentlemen in Fiction"—were first collected in the Scribner's counterpart of the Edinburgh Edition, the Thistle Edition, vol. 14 (1896). On Stevenson's idea of undertaking another such series of essays for *Scribner's Magazine*, see *Letters, 3*, 287, 298-99, *4*, 33, and the entries of "An Onlooker in Hell" and "[Water of Leith]," both under date of late 1890.

A CHAPTER ON DREAMS. Early October 1887. MS untraced. *Scribner's Magazine*, 3 (January 1888), 122-28; signed Robert Louis Stevenson. *Across the Plains* (1892). Tusitala 30. Stevenson's first essay for *Scribner's Magazine* was in the publisher's hands before 20 October 1887, less than a month after he agreed to write the series of twelve (Beinecke 4118). It took him five days, he wrote to his wife (*Letters, 3*, 190), and it was probably inspired by the questions interviewers in New York asked him about his methods of composition. See especially the long interview published in the New York *Herald*, 8 September 1887, and substantially reprinted two days later in *The Critic*, from which source it is excerpted in J. A. Hammerton, ed., *Stevensoniana*, 2nd ed. (1907), pp. 83-84.

THE LANTERN-BEARERS. Early or mid-October 1887. MS untraced. *Scribner's Magazine*, 3 (February 1888), 251-56; signed Robert Louis Stevenson. *Across the Plains* (1892). Tusitala 30. "The first paper took me five days," Stevenson wrote to his wife in mid-October 1887 about the series of essays he was writing for *Scribner's Magazine*, "the second, eight, and very hard and rather hopeless six of them were till light broke on the seventh morning, and the thread ran off the reel right merrily" (*Letters, 3*, 190). This second essay was in the publishers' hands by 20 October 1887, on which date E. L. Burlingame wrote to Stevenson suggesting "New Lamps for Old" as its title, a suggestion which Stevenson rejected (see Beinecke 3233, 4118, 2895). Burlingame acknowledged receipt of the corrected proofs on 12 November 1887 (Beinecke 5447). Further on Stevenson's early visits to North Berwick, recalled in this essay, see the article signed A Lantern-Bearer, "Some Notes on the Boyhood of R.L.S.," *Chambers's Journal*, 28 May 1910, pp. 410-11, and the same author's "R.L.S. as Playmate," (*Chambers's Journal,* September 1919) in Masson, ed., *I Can Remember Robert Louis Stevenson* (1922), pp. 23-32.

BEGGARS. October-November 1887. MS untraced. *Scribner's Magazine*, 3 (March 1888), 380-84; signed Robert Louis Stevenson. *Across the Plains* (1892). Tusitala 25. "I have written two of my papers, and have begun the third this morning," Stevenson wrote to his wife in mid-October 1887 (*Letters, 3*, 190). "Herewith a third paper," he wrote to E. L. Burlingame in mid-November: "it has been a cruel long time upon the road, but here it is, and not bad at last, I fondly hope" (*Letters, 3*, 159). The essay reached Charles Scribner's Sons on 18 November 1887 (Beinecke 4119). Stevenson read proofs before the end of the year, submitting "Pulvis et Umbra," the fourth essay in the series, in the meantime (see *Letters, 3*, 158). The incident upon which this essay is based is probably that recorded in Stevenson's letter to his cousin Bob, 7 January 1870 (Beinecke 3554).

PULVIS ET UMBRA. November-December 1887. MS untraced. Uncorrected galley proofs marked "Extra Set," Yale. *Scribner's Magazine*, 3 (April 1888), 509-12; signed Robert Louis Stevenson. *Across the Plains* (1892). Tusitala 26. "The fourth article is nearly done; and I am the more deceived, or it is *A Buster*." Thus Stevenson wrote to E. L. Burlingame in late November 1887;

in a letter to Sidney Colvin he mentions it by title and comments briefly on the merits he sees in it (*Letters, 3*, 158, 169-70; see also Beinecke 2902). Stevenson returned corrected proofs early in 1888, having begun *The Master of Ballantrae* and submitted a fifth essay, "Confessions of a Unionist," in the meantime (*Letters, 3*, 179). M. M. Bevington, "Locke and Stevenson on Comparative Morality," *Notes and Queries,* February 1960, p. 73, argues that Stevenson echoes Locke's *Essay on the Human Understanding* (1690), I, iii, paragraph 10, in the third sentence of "Pulvis et Umbra," and he finds other similarities of outlook, prose rhythm, and argument as well. One paragraph of this essay is analyzed at length in F. C. Riedel, "A Classical Rhetorical Analysis of Some Aspects of Stevenson's Essay Style," *Style*, 3 (Spring 1969), 182-99. Riedel finds "juxtaposition of opposites" a leading stylistic feature.

THE MASTER OF BALLANTRAE. Early December 1887-May 1889. MS preface and two chapter outlines, Silverado Museum, St. Helena, California. MS table of contents for "Author's Edition" printed spring 1888, Yale. MS pages from chaps. 6 and 7, Huntington HM 2462 (1 p., numbered 3), Yale (20 pp., numbered 5-8, 10-25, with fragments of p. [9]): this was the material acknowledged by E. L. Burlingame on 22 January 1889 (Beinecke 4131) and it was written during Stevenson's stay in Tahiti, 29 September-25 December 1888. Stevenson's "Note to *The Master of Ballantrae*" was written later and is entered below under date of early 1894. *The Master of Ballantrae*, "Author's Edition," 1888; printed spring 1888, copies distributed autumn 1888 (see Beinecke 5466). Probably ten or fewer copies of this version of the novel were printed; they were distributed in pamphlet form to secure copyright. The text in this edition corresponds to the first five chapters of the novel as eventually published, but in unrevised form. One copy is now held as Beinecke 486, on which see also *Letters, 3*, 174, 180, and E. L. Burlingame to Stevenson, 29 September 1888, Beinecke 4126. "The Master of Ballantrae," *Scribner's Magazine*, 4-6, twelve monthly installments, November 1888-October 1889; each installment signed Robert Louis Stevenson. *The Master of Ballantrae: A Winter's Tale* (New York: Charles Scribner's Sons, 1889); published 21 September 1889. English edition (London: Cassell and Company, 1889) published 20 September 1889 but from Scribner's sheets. Stevenson's "Preface" (MS, Silverado Museum) was first published in the Edinburgh Edition, 28 (1898), 48-51. As he wrote to Charles Baxter in May 1894 about the Edinburgh Edition: "There was in the original plan of *The Master of Ballantrae* a sort of introduction describing my arrival in Edinburgh on a visit to yourself and your placing in my hands the papers of a story. I actually wrote it, and then condemned the idea as being a little too like Scott, I suppose. Now I must really find the MS and try to finish it for the E. E." (*Letters, 5*, 127). Tusitala 10, which also includes Stevenson's "Preface" and his "Note to *The Master of Ballantrae*."

Stevenson's immediate inspiration for *The Master of Ballantrae* was Robert Marryat's *The Phantom Ship* (1839). Stevenson had been reading it again at Saranac Lake in October 1887, and on 1 November he even proposed to Charles Scribner that his firm reissue it with illustrations by Howard Pyle: "And if you will do your part, I will do mine and write a preface" (Beinecke 3236; see also Beinecke 3242, 5446). His rereading of *The Phantom Ship*, Stevenson wrote later, had given him some insight into its artistic workings, and this was his immediate inspiration for *The Master of Ballantrae*. "Inspired by some such possibly imaginary insight into the merits of the Phantom Ship," he wrote, "I reminded myself it was a long time since I had cast a plot . . . and determined to design one there and then; this was to be a story on a great canvas; it was to cover many years, so that I might draw my characters in the growth and the decay of life; and many lands, so that I might display them in changing and incongruous surroundings. Above all, it was to be such as should present the large, conspicuous features of incident, and might be treated in the summary, elliptic method of the book I had been reading" ("Note to 'The Master of Ballantrae,'" MS, Silverado Museum).

By late November or early December 1887 Stevenson had begun planning the novel, in one outline calling it first "The Familiar Incubus" and then "Brothers," and subtitling it first "A Romantic tale," then "A Fantastic tale," and then "A Fantasy." He also experimented with both Ballantrae and Colinwell as alternatives to the name Lord Irongray in the list of characters. In another outline, which is untitled, Stevenson introduced Durrisdeer as the family's name and Mackellar as one of the characters. (Both outlines are now in the Silverado Museum, St. Helena, California.)

Stevenson began writing sometime after he and his mother were left alone at Saranac Lake on 8 December 1887. "Memories of Chevalier Johnstone and Johnsons lives of notorious pirates by swiftest conveyances," Stevenson telegraphed to Charles Scribner on 15 December (Beinecke 3248), following this with a letter written on the same day remarking that he had telegraphed for Johnstone, "*on which I depend*—I cannot go on without it," because he needed the book for a new story which he was writing for Scribner and which he would, when it was further advanced, copyright as a pamphlet. In the same letter he also asked Scribner to send him recent works on life in the United States during the colonial period by Edward Eggleston and John B. McMaster, an original account of a journey in the North American woods around 1760, and materials of like date on missionaries, military expeditions, and buccaneers in North American, original works whenever possible (Beinecke 3249, received 19 December; Scribner's reply, 31 December, Beinecke 5452, is partially quoted in Roger Burlingame, *Of Making Many Books*, 1946, p. 19). A day or two later Stevenson told Scribner that "the new tale [was] finally christened," as *The Master of Ballantrae* (Beinecke 3250, received 20 December); and by Christmas, as he wrote to Sidney Colvin with a lengthy description of the novel, Stevenson had drafted ninety-two pages (*Letters, 3*, 170-71). Further requests for books followed in the next week—"small manners are what I am especially after" (Beinecke 3252; see also 4120)—including one to the London bookseller James Bain for "all the available information as to the people in Hindustan who are buried alive." Stevenson recalled having once read "a very accurate article" in

Blackwood's Magazine on the subject. "Can you find me that? And what else can you lay hands on? I put my trust in you; and the time presses exceedingly" (Beinecke 7930).

Early in 1888, Stevenson was revising "the first four numbers," each of these consisting of "from twenty to thirty pages of my manuscript," and wished to have these set in type at once and copyrighted as a pamphlet (*Letters, 3*, 174). The first page of Stevenson's fair copy of these installments in now held as Beinecke 6563; in this manuscript the work is titled "Durrisdeer" and four chapters listed with page numbers opposite each (pp. 1, 23, 50, 77). It was from this manuscript, only the first page of which survives, that the "Author's Edition" mentioned above was printed, during the spring of 1888. Its four chapters were eventually made five in book form by dividing the first chapter in two. Stevenson also referred to the work as "Durrisdeer" in a letter to E. L. Burlingame after he sent him the manuscript (Beinecke 2908), but he reverted to his former title, *The Master of Ballantrae*, immediately upon Burlingame's suggesting that he do so (*Letters, 3*, 179).

Before he received the printed copy of these opening chapters, however, Stevenson found himself facing a major problem, to which at first he sought a drastic solution. As he described it afterwards: "How, with a narrator like Mackellar, should I transact the melodrama in the wilderness? How with his style, so full of disabilities, attack a passage which must be either altogether seizing or altogether silly and absurd? The first half [through the duel, chapter 5 in final book form] was already in type, when I made up my mind to have it thrown down, and recommence the tale in the third person; friends advised, one this way, one that; my publishers were afraid of the delay; indolence had doubtless a voice; I had besides a natural love for the documentary method in narration; and I ended by committing myself to the impersonation of Mackellar, and suffering the publication to proceed" ("Note to *The Master of Ballantrae,*" Tusitala *10*, 239). In asking that the type be distributed, a decision he probably made in February 1888, Stevenson nevertheless asked that Chevalier Burke's narration be kept standing, "as I *may* leave that in the first person" (Stevenson to Burlingame, photostat, Beinecke 7943; in *Scribner's Magazine,* 26, September 1899, 346), And by the end of March Stevenson had returned to his original plan entirely, no doubt helped in this decision by E. L. Burlingame of Scribner's, who visited him that month at Saranac Lake.

Stevenson seems mostly to have left the work aside, however, during the rest of his stay at Saranac Lake—to wait for and correct the printed copy of the first part of the novel, to write the last of his essays for *Scribner's Magazine*, and to begin rewriting Lloyd Osbourne's draft of *The Wrong Box* for publication. Probably he carried the novel no further than the end of Mackellar's narration (chap. 6), if indeed he carried it that far, before leaving for San Francisco at the end of May 1888. The summer was occupied by Stevenson's first South Seas voyage, aboard the *Casco*, and not until his stay in Tahiti, 29 September-25 December 1888, does Stevenson appear really to have engaged himself again with the novel. From Tahiti he sent the seventh serial installment, acknowledged by Burlingame on 22 January 1889; in mid-February he sent three more installments from Honolulu (Beinecke 4131-32; *Letters, 3*, 226-29). But once more problems arose with the narration. As Stevenson wrote later: "I never thought of the business in the wilderness [the last two chapters] but I fell back aghast; and when the remainder of the book, down to the departure from New York, had been finished in the adorable island of Tahiti, and I found myself after another voyage face to face in the suburbs of Honolulu with the first page of my conclusion, I came near to confessing a defeat. Months passed before I saw how to attack the problem, how the pen of Mackellar was to relate a series of incidents so highly coloured, so excessive, and so tragic; the magazine was already on my heels, when desperation helped me; and in a few days of furious industry the novel was, for good or evil, rushed to its last word" ("Note to *The Master of Ballantrae*," MS, Huntington; in E. N. Caldwell, *Last Witness for Robert Louis Stevenson*, 1960, p. 117). In April the novel was still unfinished, "this cursed end of *The Master*," Stevenson wrote to Burlingame, hanging over him "like the gallows" (*Letters, 3*, 245). Stevenson finally finished it in May 1889 (*Letters, 3*, 252), and dispatched it before leaving on the *Equator*, 24 June; Burlingame acknowledged receipt of the last two chapters on 22 July 1889 (Beinecke 4135).

1888

CONFESSIONS OF A UNIONIST. January 1888. MS untraced. Corrected galley proofs, Widener Collection, Harvard University. Uncorrected galley proofs, Yale, NLS. *Confessions of a Unionist: An Unpublished 'Talk on Things Current' By Robert Louis Stevenson* (Cambridge, Mass.: privately printed, 1921); this edition was printed from the galley proofs at Harvard and embodies Stevenson's corrections. Unpublished otherwise. On 18 January 1888 Stevenson sent this essay to E. L. Burlingame at Charles Scribner's Sons, "to publish in the earliest possible number, displacing all the rest" (Beinecke 2905). In April 1887 Stevenson's distress over the violence in Ireland, in particular the terrorist raids on the house and family of John O'Connell Curtin (killed in an earlier attack, 13 November 1885) led him to wonder whether he shouldn't involve himself personally by going to Ireland, perhaps even to become a political martyr there at the cost of his own life (see *Letters, 3*, 124-28, 130-31). Stevenson supported the policies of Salisbury's coalition government of Conservatives and Liberal-Unionists formed after Gladstone's defeat on the issue of Home Rule in August 1886, mostly on the grounds that the alternative to firmness from England was mere anarchy and bloodshed. But in the United States he found considerable sympathy for the opposite cause: immediate Home Rule, and an end to English interference. The "Bloody Sunday" demonstration and violence in Trafalgar Square, 13 November 1887, no doubt only increased this sympathy; and it was to explain to American readers why, even then, he and others still could not espouse the cause of Home Rule that Stevenson wrote this article, because of its urgency pressing for immediate publication. Nevertheless, at the last minute Scribner's decided against publication—a decision which Stevenson accepted with equanimity. "Of course then don't use it," he wrote to Burlingame. "Dear man, I write these [essays] to please you: not myself, and you know a main sight better than I do what is good" (*Letters, 3*, 179). Further on Stevenson's views and the issues involved see G. A. Hayes-McCoy, "Robert Louis Stevenson and the Irish Question," *Studies: An Irish Quarterly Review*, 39 (June 1950), 130-40, and Balfour, *Life*, 2, 21-23.

GENTLEMEN. January or early February 1888. MS untraced. *Scribner's Magazine*, 3 (May 1888), 635-40; signed Robert Louis Stevenson. Tusitala 26. E. L. Burlingame refers to this essay in a letter to Stevenson on 18 February 1888 (Beinecke 4122). Presumably it was in his hands at that time, Stevenson having written it in January or early February.

SOME GENTLEMEN IN FICTION. February 1888. MS untraced. *Scribner's Magazine*, 3 (June 1888), 764-68; signed Robert Louis Stevenson. Tusitala 26. On 5 March 1888 E. L. Burlingame wrote to Stevenson that he had received this essay, which presumably Stevenson had written in February (Beinecke 4123). Charles Dickens (1837-96), the novelist's son, wrote very critically of this essay, especially the second part on his father's inability to depict a gentleman without marring the portrait, in *All the Year Round*, 15 February 1890, pp. 163-65. According to a note in his mother's scrapbooks, Monterey State Historical Monument Stevenson House Collection, vol. 3, p. 74 (xerox, Yale), Stevenson made no response. On 30 June 1890, however, the younger Dickens wrote to Stevenson apologizing that he had done him an "injustice," apparently in the article itself and in a New York newspaper interview (Beinecke 8221).

POPULAR AUTHORS. February or March 1888, possibly earlier. MS untraced. *Scribner's Magazine*, 4 (July 1888), 122-28; signed Robert Louis Stevenson. Tusitala 28. Stevenson's fondness for popular fiction began during his childhood, with the stories by J. F. Smith and others in *Cassell's Illustrated Family Paper*; see his remarks on rereading that magazine with great pleasure in 1886, *Letters, 3*, 100-6. Not long after he moved to Saranac Lake, in October 1887, Stevenson wrote to Charles Scribner asking him to send him quite a number of popular books, especially by Mrs. Emma Southworth and Pierce Egan the younger (*Fair Lilias* and *The Marvel of Kingswood Chase* above all). He was well up on Stephens Hayward, M. J. Errym (James Malcolm Rymer), Edward Viles, and J. F. Smith, Stevenson wrote, "and know all I want to know of E. P. Roe, [Bracebridge] Hemming and [G.W.M.] Reynolds" (Beinecke 3234, received 26 October 1887). He may have had this essay in mind then, but it is not among the first six he lists in a letter to Scribner about the same time (Beinecke 3241), and probably he wrote it in the new year, after "Confessions of a Unionist." In a passage in *The Amateur Emigrant* (1879-80) which he later deleted, Stevenson recalled the incident with which he begins this essay, even using the same language as he had eight years before. One of the sailors aboard the *Devonia* warmly recommended to him *Tom Holt's Log*. Stevenson had not read the work, but he ventures the opinion that "it is either excellent or downright penny trash. There seems to be no medium in the taste of the unliterary class; mediocrity must tremble for its judgement; either strong, lively, matter solidly handled, or mere ink and banditti, forms its literary diet" (*The Amateur Emigrant*, ed. Roger G. Swearingen, 2 vols., 1976-77, *1*, 80; also in James D. Hart, ed., *From Scotland to Silverado*, 1966, p. 75).

EPILOGUE TO "AN INLAND VOYAGE." March 1888. MS untraced. *Scribner's Magazine*, 4 (August 1888), 250-56. *Across the Plains* (1892). Tusitala 17, where it appears as the last chapter of *An Inland Voyage*. Of the incident in 1875 of which this essay is a narration Stevenson's mother wrote in her diary, 2 September 1875: "Lou arrives today [from France] with only a knapsack . . . looking well and strong. He was taken up as a vagabond & put in a dungeon for two hours—everything taken from him even his pocket handk[erchief] lest he commit suicide with it!" (Beinecke 7304; also in her "Notes from his Mother's Diary," Vailima Edition, *26*, 328). Stevenson began this essay under the title "A Misadventure in France" in 1883 (*Letters, 2*, 278). Probably he revised and finished it for publication at Saranac Lake in March 1888.

A LETTER TO A YOUNG GENTLEMEN WHO PROPOSES TO EMBRACE THE CAREER OF ART. March or April 1888, definitely finished by May. MS untraced. *Scribner's Magazine*, 4 (September 1888), 377-81; signed Robert Louis Stevenson. *Across the Plains* (1892). Tusitala 28. Will H. Low, *A Chronicle of Friendships* (1908), pp. 413-17, recalls Stevenson reading this essay, probably in proof, aloud during his stay at Manasquan, N. J., in May 1888. Low found its point of view so provoking—"I protested that we were not prostitutes . . . I arrayed all the arguments at my command" (p. 414)—that Stevenson suggested that he write a reply to be published along with his own essay. Low's "A Letter to the Same Young Gentleman" follows Stevenson's essay in the September 1888 *Scribner's Magazine*, the two essays together comprising the last contribution in that issue. In January 1879 Stevenson had submitted an essay, "On the Choice of a Profession, In a letter to a young gentleman," to Leslie Stephen for possible publication in the *Cornhill Magazine*. Stephen declined it, and according to Lloyd Osbourne Stevenson rewrote this essay at Saranac Lake for *Scribner's Magazine*—where it was again declined, at least in its original form. See the entry of "On the Choice of a Profession" under date of January 1879 and Osbourne's remarks with the reprinting of it in the Tusitala Edition, *28*, 12–19.

CONTRIBUTIONS TO THE HISTORY OF FIFE: RANDOM MEMORIES. Spring 1888. MS untraced. *Scribner's Magazine*, 4 (October 1888), 507-12; signed Robert Louis Stevenson. *Across the Plains* (1892), where this essay appears under its subtitle alone, "Random Memories," and "The Education of an Engineer" appears as "Random Memories Continued." In the Edinburgh Edition, 1 (1894), the two essays are both headed "Random Memories." They are subtitled, respectively, "I. The Coast of Fife," and "II. The Education of an Engineer." Tusitala 30.

THE EDUCATION OF AN ENGINEER: MORE RANDOM MEMORIES. Spring 1888. MS untraced. *Scribner's Magazine*, 4 (November 1888), 636-40; signed Robert Louis Stevenson. *Across the Plains* (1892). See the previous entry on the various retitlings of this essay. Two sentences at the very end of this essay were struck from the version reprinted in *Across the Plains* and subsequently; they comment on the inspiration for "The Pavilion on the Links," begun in 1878 and published in 1880. Tusitala 30.

A CHRISTMAS SERMON. Spring 1888. MS untraced. *Scribner's Magazine*, 4 (December 1888), 764-68; signed Robert Louis Stevenson. *Across the Plains* (1892). Tusitala 26. Stevenson probably finished this essay, the last of the twelve he had agreed to write for *Scribner's Magazine*, before he left Saranac Lake in mid-April 1888, reading proofs of it at Manasquan, N. J., in May.

THE WRONG BOX. Revised by Stevenson, March-May 1888, February-March 1889, from the work as written by Lloyd Osbourne, October-November 1887. MS and corrected proof sheets, Yale. See the discussion of these materials by Ernest J. Mehew, *TLS*, 13 November 1970, p. 1328. *The Wrong Box* (New York: Charles Scribner's Sons, 1889); published 15 June 1889. English edition (Longmans, Green and Co., 1889) published simultaneously but from Scribner's sheets. Lloyd Osbourne is listed as coauthor on the title page in both editions. Tusitala 11. On the composition and publication of this work see Lloyd Osbourne, *An Intimate Portrait of R.L.S.* (1924), pp.7-8, 79-81; Balfour, *Life, 2,* 32-34; the contribution by Ernest J. Mehew cited above; *Letters, 3,* 156, 161-62, 227, 235; and Stevenson's correspondence with E. L. Burlingame, 1888-89, Beinecke 2912-22.

Stevenson's stepson Lloyd Osbourne began the novel which became *The Wrong Box* at Saranac Lake, New York, in October 1887. By early December he had a complete first draft—then titled *The Finsbury Tontine*—Stevenson writing to J.A. Symonds on 6 December: "Lloyd has learned to use the typewriter, and has most gallantly completed upon that the draft of a tale, which seems to me not without merit and promise, it is so silly, so gay, so absurd, in spots (to my partial eyes) so genuinely humorous" (*Letters, 3*, 161-62). On 17 January 1888, S. S. McClure came to visit at

Saranac Lake. In her "Notes from his Mother's Diary" Stevenson's mother remarked of McClure's visit: "He reads Lloyd's story *The Wrong Box* and likes it" (Vailima Edition, *26*, 355). Stevenson was then still occupied writing his essays for *Scribner's Magazine*, and shortly with *The Master of Ballantrae* as well; but he did find the manuscript promising enough to offer to revise it for publication. By mid-March he was at work, and by the end of May 1888 (when he left for California and the Pacific) Stevenson had finished revising the first eleven chapters, the work as a whole now being called *A Game of Bluff*. This manuscript (Beinecke 7186) Stevenson left for safekeeping with Scribner's together with Lloyd's unrevised typescript of the remaining chapters. Of its 128 pages, all but 23 are in Stevenson's hand; the others, which survive from Lloyd's typescript, are in many instances considerably revised by Stevenson.

For the next six months Stevenson was busy cruising the Pacific aboard the *Casco*. On 15 October 1888, however, he wrote to E. L. Burlingame at Scribner's and asked that a typewritten copy of *A Game of Bluff* be made and sent to him, this to consist of a typewritten copy of the chapters in his hand together with Lloyd's unrevised typescript of the rest. "What I shall want will be the *copy* of the XV [actually eleven] chaps, and the *original* of the type-written remainder" (Beinecke 2912). Stevenson received this in Honolulu in January, and on 8 March 1889 he sent the whole revised text, since January called *The Wrong Box*, to Burlingame for publication. (Stevenson's manuscript of the last five chapters, those written in Honolulu, is held as Beinecke 7186. But unlike the manuscript of the first eleven chapters, which were set from the typewritten copy sent to Stevenson in Honolulu, the manuscript of these chapters bears compositors' names and obviously was used directly in setting type of the first edition.) In April, Burlingame agreed to Stevenson's terms of five thousand dollars for the American rights only (in March Burlingame had offered five thousand dollars for both English and American rights)—provided that Stevenson's name come first on the title page and in the preface, reversing their order in the manuscript.

Stevenson received proofs of *The Wrong Box* early in May 1889, the novel having been set from the typescript copy and Stevenson's manuscript of the closing chapters, and he returned the first batch with corrections early in June. "I keep the rest to rewrite a part, which is not up to the mark," Stevenson wrote then: "I have there overdone confusion, the meaning is obscure, and the joke does not tell, in consequence" (Beinecke 2921). Stevenson soon sent these revisions as well. But Scribner's seems not to have waited for the return of any proofs at all, publishing the book uncorrected on 15 June. As Ernest J. Mehew writes: "He [Stevenson] had asked his American friend the artist Will H. Low to look over the proofs, and since he had seen and corrected the typescript of most of the work Scribner's apparently did not think Stevenson wanted to make any revisions on the proofs." Nor have Stevenson's revisions ever been embodied in an edition of *The Wrong Box* since that time, even though the complete set of corrected proofs, long in the hands of Scribner's and now held as Beinecke 7589, survives. As Mehew writes, having made a detailed comparison between manuscript, proofs, and book: "As well as revealing a surprising number of misreadings of Stevenson's hand and some interesting first thoughts and deleted passages, the manuscript . . . show[s] that Stevenson followed Osbourne's plot and characters very closely, particularly in the early chapters." Stevenson himself revised the proofs throughout, chapter 14 extensively. As Mehew writes of chapter 14: "He re-wrote a number of pages (amounting to five pages of manuscript) and introduced a new Chapter XV called 'The Battle of Waterloo Station.'" None of these changes has appeared in any edition of *The Wrong Box*.

FIGHTING THE RING. March-April 1888. MS photostats, Yale, Silverado Museum, St. Helena, California: typescript by Lloyd Osbourne, 15 pp. comprising the first four chapters of this work. Original typescipt untraced. Unpublished. "Lloyd and Louis are engaged to write a story for the *New York Ledger*," Stevenson's mother wrote of the visit to Saranac Lake of Robert Bonner, the proprietor, and S. S. McClure on 19 March 1888. "The proprietor is a very wealthy man, who wishes to raise the literary tone" (*Baxter Letters*, p. 199). "Fighting the Ring," which Lloyd Osbourne had perhaps already begun, was first decided upon. It deals in highly melodramatic terms with one firm's heroic resistance against a monopolistic syndicate in the copper market. But shortly this work was put aside in favor of "The Gaol Bird," on which see the next entry.

THE GAOL BIRD. March-April 1888. MS untraced if written. Unpublished. Having agreed to write a story for the New York *Ledger,* Stevenson apparently thought at first that "Fighting the Ring" would be suitable. But he soon concluded otherwise, remarking in a letter quoted in Balfour, *Life, 2*, 32-33: "Study of the *Ledger* convinced me that 'Fighting the Ring' would not do. Accordingly, at about nine one night Lloyd and I began, and next day before lunch we had finished the design of a new and more sensational tale, 'The Gaol Bird.' 'Tis the correct *Ledger* subject of a noble criminal, who returns to prove his innocence; but it seems picturesquely designed, and we flatter ourselves that the relations between the criminal and the man whom he suspects (Donald, first Baron Drummond of Drummond and Raracaroo, late Governor-General of India) are essentially original, and should quite blind all but the most experienced." But this project too was abandoned in favor of another. As Balfour writes: "Mr. Osbourne laboured at this tale by himself for many a long day in vain; but the plot was hardly sketched before the collaborators were again deep in the plan of a new novel dealing with the Indian Mutiny" (*Life, 2*, 33). This new novel, "The White Nigger," is discussed in the next entry. On 25 May 1888, S. S. McClure wrote to Osbourne that he thought he could arrange newspaper syndication of "The Gaol Bird" (Beinecke 5187; see also McClure to Stevenson, 31 May 1888, Beinecke 5188), and on 10 December he wrote to Stevenson that the London

Globe had offered five hundred pounds to serialize "your Ledger serial" (Beinecke 5191). By that time, however, "The Gaol Bird" had been supplanted by "The White Nigger," itself supplanted by the novel which became *The Ebb-Tide*, begun by Lloyd Osbourne in Honolulu in the spring of 1889. See the principal entry of *The Ebb-Tide* under the date of its final writing by Stevenson, February-June 1893.

THE WHITE NIGGER. April-May 1888. MS photostats, Yale, Silverado Museum, St. Helena, California: typescript by Lloyd Osbourne, 3 pp., comprising a list of characters and a summary of the plot. Original typescript untraced. Unpublished. As Graham Balfour remarks of "The Gaol Bird" (*Life, 2*, 33), its plot was hardly sketched before Stevenson and Lloyd Osbourne were again "deep in the plan of a new novel dealing with the Indian Mutiny." This was "The White Nigger," which Stevenson described without mentioning the title in a letter to Sidney Colvin on 10 April 1888. "I am reading with extraordinary pleasure the life of Lord Lawrence," Stevenson wrote: "Lloyd and I have a mutiny novel . . . on hand—a tremendous work—so we are all at Indian books. The idea of the novel is Lloyd's. I call it a novel. 'Tis a tragic romance, of the most tragic sort: I believe the end will be almost too much for human endurance—when the hero is thrown on the ground with one of his own (Sepoy) soldier's knees upon his chest, and the cries begin in the Beebeeghar. O truly, you know it is a howler! The whole last part is—well the difficulty is that, short of resuscitating Shakespeare, I don't know who is to write it" (*Letters, 3,* 188).

In his typescript, Lloyd Osbourne listed more than a dozen characters, chief among these the hero Christopher St. Ives, the heroine Honoria Norman, her father, her uncle Brigadier Norman, and Colonel Neil. The first part of the novel was to be set at Cawnpore in January 1857, the second part at Allahabad and elsewhere from 3 June to 15 July 1857. The plot, as outlined, is sketchy and complicated but chiefly turns on St. Ives's attentions to Honoria and his proposal of marriage, his quarrel with her father, his throwing in his lot with the mutineers, and a confused multitude of dangers, rescues, and escapes during the mutiny itself. Except for this typescript, nothing survives of this projected novel. Probably it was abandoned soon after Stevenson wrote to Sidney Colvin about it—in April 1888 or soon afterwards. On Stevenson's reading about the Indian Mutiny see the letters, Beinecke 3244, 3246, 3253, and 5536.

1889

Letters to THE TIMES, PALL MALL GAZETTE, etc. 10 February 1889 and other dates through 9 October 1894; ten letters in all. MSS untraced except for letter VII, Ashley Library, British Museum. Beinecke 3585 is a draft of

Stevenson's letter of 9 and 12 April 1892; Beinecke 8104 is the MS of his postscript to the letter of 14 September 1892. First publication of these letters was as follows:

I. 10 February 1889. "Recent German Doings in Samoa," *The Times* (London), 11 March 1889, p. 10.
II. 12 and 14 October 1891. "Samoa," *The Times* (London), 17 November 1891, p. 7.
III. 9 and 12 April 1892. "The Latest Difficulty in Samoa," *The Times* (London), 4 June 1892, p. 18.
IV. 22 June 1892. "Samoa," *The Times* (London), 23 July 1892, p. 12.
V. 19 July 1892. "Mr. Stevenson and Samoa," *The Times* (London), 19 August 1892, p. 4.
VI. 14 September 1892. "Mr. Stevenson and Samoa," *The Times* (London), 17 October 1892, p. 7.
VII. 4 September 1893. "War in Samoa," *Pall Mall Gazette*, No. 8877 (September 1893), pp. 1-2.
VIII. 23 April 1894. "The Deadlock in Samoa," *The Times* (London), 2 June 1894, pp. 17-18.
IX. 22 May 1894. "Mr. Stevenson on Samoa," *The Times* (London), 30 June 1894, p. 6.
X. 7 October 1894. "Robert Louis Stevenson's Swan Song; His Dying Appeal for Mata'afa. Letter to J. F. Hogan, Esq., M. P.," *Daily Chronicle*, 18 March 1895, p. 3.

First published together in the Edinburgh Edition, 25 (1897), 249-311, under the collective title "Letters to the 'Times,' 'Pall Mall Gazette,' Etc." Tusitala 21. The pamphlet issue of letter VII, *War in Samoa* (London: Reprinted from The Pall Mall Gazette./September, 1893.) is spurious, having in fact originated with Thomas J. Wise. See the entry of this item as Beinecke 597.

As Oscar Wilde remarked: "I see that romantic surroundings are the worst surroundings possible for a romantic writer. In Gower Street Stevenson could have written a new *Trois Mousquetaires*. In Samoa he wrote letters to *The Times* about Germans" (Wilde to Robert Ross, 6 April 1897, in *The Letters of Oscar Wilde*, ed. Hart-Davis, 1962, p. 520). These letters, the first written ten months before Stevenson first came to Samoa in 1889, the last written less than two weeks before his death there in 1894, reflect his concern with the behavior of the diplomatic and other representatives of the various nations—Britain, Germany, and the United States—then involved in Samoan affairs.

THE EBB-TIDE. Begun in Honolulu by Lloyd Osbourne, spring 1889. See the principal entry of this work under the date of its final writing by Stevenson, mid-February to early June 1893.

A SAMOAN SCRAPBOOK. Spring 1889, at Honolulu. MS, Yale. Unpublished. See the brief discussion of this work, which was intended as text for photographs taken by Joseph D. Strong during the Hawaiian expedition to Samoa in 1887-88, in J. C. Furnas, *Voyage to Windward* (1951), pp. 332-34. Stevenson takes a slightly different view of the expedition in chapter 3 of *A Footnote to History* (1892), but he obviously drew on this earlier manuscript in writing the later, shorter account of what is described in the heading of this manuscript as "the late ill-starred Hawaiian mission to Samoa."

Although he himself had not yet visited Samoa, in his commentary Stevenson wrote of the Hawaiian mission as nobly motivated, especially given that the only alternative to Polynesian self-government seemed then to be iron-handed German control. "German activity in the [Samoan islands] group is confined to a little coffee and a great deal of gunpowder," he writes. Malietoa is now being kept prisoner in the Marshall Islands "on a serious charge of not appreciating German influence" (Beinecke 6925, pp. 6-7). Commenting on Strong's photographs, Stevenson remarks that the best qualities of the Samoan natives seem to have survived the arrival of Christianity. The people seem happy and to be working hard, and all of this is a great credit to the missionaries. "There is another pleasing feature in these illustrations," he continues. "After so much that we have heard of the missionary, it is good to see these people unashamed in their own costume. The pastor's daughter has indeed modestly concealed her breasts; but this was in honour of that one-eyed and unfamiliar spectator, the camera; and as soon as the photograph was taken, the young lady of the vicarage would drop her veil, and reappear in her natural costume of a single petticoat" (p. 2).

THE WRECKER. Summer 1889-November 1891. MS portions: Yale (1 p. discarded fragment of chap. 5); Princeton University Library (5 pp., folio, numbered 32-36, comprising the beginning of chap. 20); Anderson 1914, II, 407 (22 pp., folio, numbered 15-36, comprising the text of chap. 19 and the beginning of chap. 20; pp. 32-36 are now at Princeton, the balance untraced). Page proofs of pp. 163-65 (chap. 8) with an inserted change by Stevenson incorporated into the final text, Yale. "The Wrecker. By Robert Louis Stevenson and Lloyd Osbourne." *Scribner's Magazine*, 10-12, twelve monthly installments, August 1891-July 1892. *The Wrecker* (New York: Charles Scribner's Sons, 1892); published 27 June 1892. English edition (London: Cassell and Company, 1892) published 25 June 1892 but from Scribner's sheets. Lloyd Osbourne is listed as coauthor on the title page in both editions. Tusitala 12.

Stevenson himself comments on the genesis and composition of *The Wrecker* at the end of its "Epilogue: To Will H. Low" (Tusitala, *12*, 404-6). See also *Letters, 3*, 268, through *4*, 210; Beinecke 2926-51, 4136-54; Fanny Stevenson's "Prefatory Note" (Tusitala, *12*, xv-xxiv); Lloyd Osbourne, *An Intimate Portrait of R.L.S.* (1924), pp. 107-8; and Balfour, *Life, 2*, 33-34, 75, 137-38. On the strange disappearance of the *Wandering Minstrel*, news of which reached Honolulu as the Stevensons were preparing to leave aboard the *Equator*, see Andrew Farrell, ed., *John Cameron's Odyssey* (1928).

The Wrecker was conceived shortly after Stevenson and his party left Honolulu, 24 June 1889, aboard the trading schooner *Equator*. "My husband tried in vain to solve the mystery of the *Wandering Minstrel*," Fanny Stevenson wrote of the weeks before their departure, "and it was more or less in his mind when we started on our new cruise" (*12*, xvi). "On board the schooner *Equator*," Stevenson himself wrote, "almost within sight of the Johnstone Islands . . . and on a moonlit night when it was a joy to be alive, the authors were amused with several stories of the sale of wrecks. The subject tempted them; and they sat apart in the alley-way to discuss its possibilities" ("Epilogue," *12*, 404). A fine complication would be to have another ship's crew manning the ship when it was wrecked, and immediately the *Wandering Minstrel* affair came to mind. "Before we turned in, the scaffolding of the tale had been put together. But the question of treatment was as usual more obscure." Attracted by "that very modern form of the police novel or mystery story, which consists in beginning your yarn anywhere but at the beginning, and finishing it anywhere but the end," the collaborators resolved to mitigate its defect of "insincerity and shallowness of tone" by approaching the tale itself "gradually." Characters and atmosphere would be developed before the mystery itself so that "this defect might be lessened and our mystery seem to inhere in life itself." At length it occurred to them, Stevenson wrote in conclusion, that the method "had been invented previously by some one else, and was in fact—however painfully different the results may seem—the method of Charles Dickens in his later work" (*12*, 404-5).

At the same time, as Fanny Stevenson wrote, Stevenson decided "to make his home for ever in the islands, and to that end projected the purchase of a schooner . . . which was to be half-yacht, half-trader, and wholly self-supporting" (*12*, xviii). This vessel was to be called the *Northern Light*, and it was to be purchased in part from proceeds of the new novel, which was to be written and sent from Samoa as soon as possible. The trading scheme soon faded away in the light of both practical and ethical difficulties, but the collaborators' enthusiasm for the novel remained and they began writing *The Wrecker* during their eight weeks at Apemama in the Gilbert Islands, 31 August—25 October 1889.

Lloyd Osbourne would write a chapter, he recalled later of the collaboration, Stevenson would rewrite it, and the two would discuss the chapter next to come. "We never had a single disagreement as the book ran its course," Osbourne wrote; "it was a pastime, not a task, and I am sure no reader ever enjoyed it as much as we did. Well do I remember him [Stevenson] saying: 'It's glorious to have the ground ploughed, and to sit back in luxury for the real fun of writing—which is rewriting'" (*An Intimate Portrait of R.L.S.*, 1924, pp.107-8). Earlier, Osbourne had told Graham Balfour of their collaboration: "in *The Wrecker*, the storm was mine; so were the fight and the murders on the *Currency Lass*; the picnics in San Francisco, and the commercial details of Loudon's partnership. Nares was mine and Pinkerton to a great degree, and Captain Brown was mine throughout. . . . The Paris parts of *The Wrecker* . . . I never even touched" (*Life, 2*, 33-34; see also *Letters, 5*, 166-67).

On 4 December 1889, having left Apemama and at length nearing Samoa, Stevenson wrote to E. L. Burlingame at Scribner's: "Will you be likely to have space in the Magazine for a serial story, which should be ready, I believe, by April, at latest by autumn? It is called *The Wrecker*; and in book form will appear as number 1 of *South Sea Yarns* by R.L.S. and Lloyd Osbourne" (*Letters, 3*, 227). Two months later, by early February 1890, Osbourne had finished nearly the whole first draft of the novel and Stevenson had revised about half of this into final form (*Letters, 3*, 288); and on 11 March 1890 Stevenson sent the first ten chapters to Burlingame in New York (Beinecke 2926). Thereafter the revision went slowly, however, and by midsummer, having revised and dispatched at most three or four more chapters during the spring and early summer, Stevenson found himself "[at] a period when I cannot well go on until I can refresh myself on the proofs of the beginning" (13 July 1890, *Letters, 3*, 299).

These proofs Stevenson found waiting him in Sydney when he returned there in August 1890 after his cruise aboard the *Janet Nichol,* and he returned them with corrections on 2 September (Beinecke 2928, 4137). But even so the work continued only intermittently. Stevenson wrote chaps. 15-17 during September and October, Burlingame acknowledging receipt of them "the day before yesterday" on 6 November (Beinecke 4138; see also Beinecke 2936 and *Letters, 4*, 11). But he left *The Wrecker* aside to continue work on *The South Seas*, and on 5 November he finally advised Burlingame that the end of the novel would be delayed for at least six more months, partly because Lloyd Osbourne was still in Britain winding up affairs there (Beinecke 2930). Stevenson returned some revised proofs from Sydney at the end of January 1891 (Beinecke 4140), but not until May and June of that year, after Lloyd Osbourne's return, was he again able to send new material.

In mid-May 1891 Stevenson sent Burlingame an outline of the last nine chapters (17-25); he sent him manuscript of "two more chapters," possibly chaps. 18 and 19, on 22 June; and on 14 August Burlingame acknowledged receipt of chap. 21 (Beinecke 2937-39, 4143). But despite this activity during the summer of 1891 Stevenson was not finally able to send off the end of the novel until mid-November—an installment in manuscript of "seventy or eighty pages" (*Letters, 4*, 118; see also *4*, 108-9, 112, and Beinecke 4145-46). The writing had extended over a period slightly longer than two years, in three more or less separate bursts of activity: September 1889-March 1890 (chaps. 1-10), autumn 1890 (through chap. 17), and summer and autumn 1891 (chaps. 18-25 and the epilogue).

At the end of January 1892 Stevenson had proofs of the concluding installments, which he returned, apparently giving Scribner's the impression that he planned to revise chaps. 13-25 extensively for publication in book form (*Letters, 4*, 149, Beinecke 5469). Accordingly, on 25 March 1892, Scribner's sent proofs of chaps. 1-12 to Cassell and Company in London, reserving the rest; but on 22 April, not having received corrections after all, they sent the remaining chapters as well (Beinecke 5469-70). Stevenson had changed his mind as to corrections (see *Letters, 4*, 204) and seems to have been content to have the book published without revision from the serial version—as it was, on 24 June 1892, publication coinciding with the appearance of the last installment serially. Having received a copy of the finished book, he wrote to Burlingame on 1 August 1892 that it seemed on the whole "very satisfactory" except for "a devil of a miscarriage" in the Latin quotation ("Qui nunc it per iter tenebricosum—nos precedens") in the "Epilogue: To Will H. Low" (*Letters, 4*, 210). The English words from "as it were" through "in no haste to" appear, correctly, after the whole quotation in the serial version; but in the first edition they appeared between the two parts of the quotation, after the dash, and so made nonsense of the quotation. This error was corrected in the Edinburgh Edition.

The illustrations, however, Stevenson found disastrous. Commenting on the illustrations by W. L. Metcalf, Stevenson remarked in the same letter to Burlingame, 1 August 1892: "All the points in the story are missed. The series of little pictures of chance interviews in rooms might have illustrated any story (or nearly any story) that ever was written. The different appearances (all wrong) that he has given to my Captain Wicks would make the head of any reader spin." As to the frontispiece, typical of the whole: "Consider the attitude of the tonsured priest who is sitting on the cabin table. If (in such a position) the rev. gentleman shall be able to drive his knife through his hand, or even through a Swedish match box, I will give Mr. W. L. Metcalf two and sixpence and a new umbrella" (Beinecke 2950; quoted in Roger Burlingame, *Of Making Many Books*, 1946, p. 231; see also pp. 212-13, on revisions in chap. 7 Burlingame requested Stevenson make in proof.)

On 6 November 1891, Scribner's agreed to pay Stevenson royalties of 15 percent on the published price of $1.25 (Beinecke 4145), and 1 February 1893 they reported to Stevenson royalty earnings on *The Wrecker* during the first seven months from its publication on 25 June through 31 December 1892 of $1,067.37, this being 18¾¢ per copy on sales of 4,866 copies of the American edition, $912.37, and an additional $155, being half the profit on 2,000 copies sold in Canada (Beinecke 7285). Stevenson, as he wrote to Burlingame on 16 April 1893, was shocked by the poor sales and consequently small financial reward and determined to alter his arrangements with Scribner's, as he did (Beinecke 2196; see also 3949, 4154, and 5456). Sales were worse in 1893, Scribner's reporting sales of 414 copies on which the 15 percent royalty yielded $77.65 (Beinecke 7285).

On 8 October 1891 it was agreed with Cassell and Company that they would have sole British rights to *The Wrecker* in book form. The authors were to receive royalties of 15 percent of the retail price reckoning 13 copies as 12, £200 to be paid against royalties when the proofs were passed for the press. (Society of Authors Archive, British Museum, MS. Add. 56638, f. 11.) On 12 July 1892, £200 was paid to Stevenson's account with Mitchell and Baxter in accord with this agreement, and on 7 February 1894 royalties of £66.5.7 were similarly paid on *The Wrecker*, possibly on sales for the eighteen months from publication through the end of 1893 (Beinecke 7268). On 4 October 1890, Robert McClure executed an agreement with Stevenson and Osbourne to pay £40 each on the day of publication for *The Pearl Fisher* (ultimately published as *The Ebb-Tide*) and *The Wrecker,* and to divide equally with them the proceeds of serial publication (Society of Authors Archive, British Museum, MS. Add. 56638, ff. 61-62). Possibly this was for the Continental rights, although these were ordinarily negotiated directly with the Tauchnitz firm, for on 2 July 1892 there was paid to Stevenson's account with Mitchell and Baxter £40, listed as from McClure for the Continental rights to *The Wrecker* (Beinecke 7268).

Isobel Field comments on the originals of the main characters in this novel in *This Life I've Loved* (1937), pp. 275-76. See also Fanny Stevenson's "Prefatory Note" (Tusitala, *12*, xxiii-xxiv) and her *The Cruise of the "Janet Nichol"* (1914). Beinecke 1438 is a scrapbook which contains 159 pp. of reviews and notices of *The Wrecker* on its first appearance. Arthur Conan Doyle's high opinion of the book appears in a sentence in the "News Notes" section of the *Bookman*, 3 (London, October 1892), 6: "Dr. Conan Doyle thinks 'The Wrecker' the best of Mr. Stevenson's books." It was also thoughtfully reviewed by Lionel Johnson in *The Academy*, 6 August 1892, pp. 103-4. Stevenson's plan to make *The Wrecker* part of a series of *South Sea Yarns* (*Letters, 3*, 227) was not carried out during his lifetime, at least not in the physical production of his books. Although not so presented on the title pages, *The Wrecker, Island Nights' Entertainments,* and *The Ebb-Tide* were, however, designated *South Sea Yarns* on the spines of the volumes in the Edinburgh Edition which contained them. *The Wrecker* comprises vols. 1 and 2, the other works vol. 3.

THE SOUTH SEAS. Rewritten October 1889-autumn 1891 from material written during cruises from June 1888 through July 1890.

Manuscripts:

1. Huntington HM 2412: 140 pages headed "Cruise of the *Casco,*" Stevenson's day-to-day record of events in the Marquesas and Paumotus, 15 July-21 September 1888; 6 pp. beginning "Tahiti. October 14th [1888]," Stevenson's notes on things told him about Tahiti and the Marquesas by Captain Hart; 20 pp. headed "Kona Coast Hawaii," Stevenson's day-to-day record of events, 28 April-2 May 1889; 70 pp. beginning "Butaritari. July [1889]," Stevenson's day-to-day record of events during his second South Seas cruise, aboard the *Equator*, from the time of his arrival at Butaritari in the Gilbert Islands, 12 July 1889, through 1 November, three days before Stevenson and his party left the Gilberts for Samoa. HM 20534: 6 pp. of miscellaneous notes on Hawaii clearly part of the same MS and probably written before the "Kona Coast" material described above. HM 2417-8: two pencil sketches made in the Marquesas.

2. Beinecke 6224: 57 pp. in continuation of HM 2412; pages numbered 71-128, headed on the first page after some material carried over from HM 2412, "Samoa." This manuscript consists mainly of a detailed summary of historical events in Samoa from 1887 to the time of writing in late 1889 or early 1890. Much of the information was evidently provided by H. J. Moors;

p. 89 has the heading "Mr Moors continued." Stevenson drew upon this information in *A Footnote to History* (1892). All of this MS material, Huntington and Beinecke MSS alike, is written on yellow wove paper, 7¾ inches by 12¼ inches, ruled on the front only with horizontal blue lines and a left-hand side margin consisting of a double rule in red. Stevenson used the same paper for the portion of *The Master of Ballantrae* which he sent from Tahiti in late 1888 (Huntington HM 2462, Beinecke 6564) and for his detailed outline of *The South Seas* (HM 2421). Material written on this yellow wove paper typically represents day-to-day material intended by Stevenson for later revision.

3. Huntington HM 2421: 5 pp. comprising a detailed part and chapter outline of *The South Seas*, written on the same yellow wove paper as HM 2412. The first page is in the form of a title page and reads: "The South Seas: / A Record of Two Years' Travel, / with / sketches of scenery, manners, history, legend and song / by / Robert Louis Stevenson / Cassell & Co / London, Melbourne, and New York / 189 ." Above the words "Two Years' Travel" the alternative "3 cruises" is written in. The second page represents a false start, being an outline headed, "Part I—Whites in the Pacific," followed by three subdivisions marked with Roman numerals: "Seafaring," "Crime at Sea," and "Beachcombers." The remaining three pages comprise a detailed outline of *The South Seas* divided into six parts and twenty-two chapters: "Part I—'Of Schooners, Islands, and Maroons'" (4 chaps.); "Part II—The Marquesas" (3 chaps.); "Part III — The Dangerous Archipelago" (3 chaps.); "Part IV—Tahiti" (6 chaps.); "Part V—The Eight Islands" (3 chaps.); "Part VI—The Kingsmills" (3 chaps.). The last two parts Stevenson later renumbered in this MS, placing the material on Hawaii (Part V) last and numbering parts of chapters as well as whole ones. In this renumbering he seems to have had in mind the newspaper serialization of *The South Seas*: in this new system he lists fifty installments altogether. This outline was probably made in October 1889 at Apemama; compare the similar outline sent at about the same time to Sidney Colvin, *Letters, 3*, 273-75. Beinecke 6426, 6440, 6445: 3 other lists of contents.

4. David Scott Mitchell Library, Sydney: 97 pp. comprising Stevenson's revised text of Part I of *The South Seas* as it appeared in the 1890 copyright edition. The text in this MS, as it does in the 1890 copyright edition, consists of fifteen chapters. But in the eventual dispostition of this material—when *The South Seas* was first published other than serially, in the Edinburgh Edition after Stevenson's death—one chapter not represented in this MS or in the copyright edition ("The Two Chiefs of Atuona") was added at the end and the original chapters 11-12 were combined ("Long Pig" and "A Cannibal High Place").

5. Beinecke 6428-30, 6826: four one-page fragments of Stevenson's revised text of Part II of *The South Seas.* Beinecke 6431-34; Huntington HM 2421; Princeton University Library: appoximately 40 pp. of Stevenson's revised text of the Gilbert Islands part(s) of *The South Seas*, including more than one version of several portions. Stevenson's chapter numbering and pagination in this material—e. g. "LIX. The King of Apemama: Equator

Town and the Palace," which begins on p. 49—show that he was at this time writing with newspaper serialization in mind, not writing a text divided according to his book outline into parts and chapters. In addition, although he began numbering anew at the beginning of the Gilbert Islands material he did not begin again when he turned to the material on Apemama. This same lack of division obtained when this material was serialized in the New York *Sun* (it did not appear at all in *Black and White*), but in the Edinburgh Edition the material on Apemama was made a separate part of *The South Seas*. Like much of what Stevenson wrote during the 1890s in Samoa, nearly all of this material (presumably also including the MS in the Mitchell Library) is written on white laid paper watermarked "E. Towgood / Fine" or with a seated figure of Britannia surrounded by an oval border, the individual pages having been created by tearing in half what were originally folders. The resulting leaves, faintly ruled horizontally, measure 7⅞ inches x 12⅝ inches. Material written on this E. Towgood paper is later than the material written on yellow wove paper—often much later, even when the events or places described are the same.

6. Beinecke 6435-39; Princeton University Library ("A Ride in the Forest"); Houghton Library, Harvard University, 47M-36 ("Kaahumanu"): approximately 15 pp. of holograph material and 114 pp. of typescript material comprising revised text for the Hawaiian part of *The South Seas*, "The Eight Islands," often in several forms. Although published serially both in the United States and in England, none of this material appeared when *The South Seas* was first collected, in the Edinburgh Edition.

7. Beinecke 6441-2 (Penrhyn); Beinecke 6443-4, 7069, and Huntington (Tutuila): notebook and revised versions of the material on these two islands, meant ultimately for *The South Seas* and published serially in the United States and in England (Penrhyn material only). Because the two islands in question were not in the Marquesas, Paumotus, Gilberts, or the Hawaiian islands, the material about them could not be accommodated under any of the geographical part headings of *The South Seas*. As a result, the material was not immediately collected, and when collected was misleadingly separated from *The South Seas* itself, as if it really were separate material. See the discussion below.

Publication:

1. *The South Seas: A Record of Three Cruises* (London: Cassell and Company, 1890). Twenty-two copies printed in London on 12 November 1890: two were actually sold, to secure copyright, and the rest were distruibuted by Stevenson. According to W. F. Prideaux, *A Bibliography of the Works of Robert Louis Stevenson*, 2nd ed. (1917), p. 112, fifteen were cut up and used for setting the serial versions, which if so would leave five for Stevenson's own use and for presentation. Beinecke 7596: page proofs of this edition. Beinecke 523: copy of this edition marked by Isobel Strong. McCutcheon, 1925, 639: copy of this edition marked by Sidney Colvin. Princeton University Library: copy of this edition owned by Edmund Gosse, annotated by him with the information as to the number of copies printed and their disposition given in Prideaux. Beinecke 524, Princeton University

Library: two unmarked copies. This edition was set from the manuscript now in the Mitchell Library; see the commentary on MS (4) above. It was of this group of chapters, in this edition, that Henry James wrote to Stevenson on 12 January 1891: "I loved 'em and blessed 'em quite. But I did make one restriction—I missed the *visible* in them" (in Smith, ed., *Henry James and Robert Louis Stevenson*, 1948, p. 198).

2. "The South Seas: Life Under the Equator: Letters from a Leisurely Traveller." *The Sun* (New York), thirty-four installments signed Robert Louis Stevenson, weekly from 1 February to 13 December 1891 except the weeks of 22 February-8 March, 19 July-30 August, and 29 November-8 December. "The South Seas: A Record of Three Cruises." *Black and White* (London), 1-2, twenty-seven installments signed Robert Louis Stevenson, weekly at irregular intervals, 6 February-19 December 1891. Both serial versions were set, independently, from the 1890 copyright edition for the material in Part I. Then the remaining material was set for the New York *Sun* version from revised manuscript sent by Stevenson to S. S. McClure, and for the *Black and White* version from proofs of the New York *Sun* version sent to England by McClure. Stevenson expected his manuscript to be edited by McClure as it arrived, as it was. Stevenson, McClure says, "told me to use my own judgment . . . [and] cut wherever I thought it would be advantageous. After the series was well started . . . he wrote and asked me why I was not cutting the stuff down more" (*My Autobiography*, 1914, pp. 195-96). Proofs of the New York *Sun* version were also sent to Stevenson: Beinecke 525 comprises proofs of nearly the whole of the second part of *The South Seas* with markings by Stevenson not followed in either serial version; NLS 9892 comprises similar material for the portion on Hawaii. These were sent to Stevenson for reference and his later use when the time came to bring all of the material together into a book. The actual serial publication of this material was left entirely to McClure. Nor are the New York *Sun* and the *Black and White* versions identical either as to what chapters were printed or what in each chapter was included or left out.

In the seven installments published in the New York *Sun* from 1 February through 5 April 1891 appeared the whole of the text now known as Part I of *The South Seas* (The Marquesas), except for three chapters (5, 7, and 11). Two of these chapters (7 and 11) did, however, appear in the *Black and White* version, making it relatively the more complete serial text of this material. In the six installments next published in the New York *Sun,* from 12 April through 17 May 1891, appeared the six chapters now known as Part II of *The South Seas* (The Paumotus). All of this material also appeared in the *Black and White* version. From 24 May through 12 July 1891 there appeared in the New York *Sun* eight installments. Three of these—the second, third, and fourth—contain the whole of the text now known as Part III of *The South Seas* (The Eight Islands). The first, 24 May 1891, deals with the island of Penrhyn and is titled "XIV. A Pearl Island: Penrhyn," with a subtitle in the text, later, "Leprosy at Penrhyn." The last four installments, 21 June through 12 July 1891, contain the material on the leper settlement at Molokai, installments XVIII and XIX titled "The Lazaretto," XX titled

"The Lazaretto of To-day," and XXI titled "The Free Island." In the *Black and White* version, the installment on Penrhyn and the first of the Hawaiian chapters ("The Kona Coast") were omitted, but all of the rest of this material was included. Nothing else from *The South Seas* appeared in *Black and White*. In the New York *Sun*, from 6 September through 22 November 1891 (twelve installments), appeared the whole of the text now known as Parts IV and V of *The South Seas* (The Gilberts, The Gilberts—Apemama). Finally in the New York *Sun*, 13 December 1891, appeared the last portion of Stevenson's South Seas material published serially, an unnumbered installment titled "Tutuila: The Cruise of the Schooner Nukunono." Another version of this was eventually reprinted by the Bibliophile Society (1921) and in the Vailima Edition (1923). See the discussion below.

3. *In the South Seas*, Edinburgh Edition, 20 (1896). Sidney Colvin edited this volume, in which Stevenson's individual chapters appeared for the first time together other than serially, and as a distinct work. For text he drew upon the 1890 copyright edition, proofs sent in 1891 by S. S. McClure, possibly including those with Stevenson's annotations, the detailed plan of the work which Stevenson had sent him (*Letters, 3*, 273-75), and possibly upon Stevenson's revised or unrevised manuscripts. See the comments on Beinecke 525 in the catalogue of the Beinecke Collection, *A Stevenson Library . . .* , pp. 230-31. The work as published in 1896 consists of four parts, thirty-five chapters, selected from the whole series. It is divided as follows: I. The Marquesas (15 chapters), II. The Paumotus (6 chapters), III. The Gilberts (7 chapters), IV. The Gilberts—Apemama (7 chapters). From the text edited by Colvin derive the editions of *In the South Seas* published by Charles Scribner's Sons, New York, on 26 September 1896, and by Chatto and Windus on 11 December 1900.

4. *In the South Seas*, Swanston Edition, vol. 18 (1912). In this edition Andrew Lang augmented *In the South Seas* by including Stevenson's material on Hawaii in a new third section titled, as Stevenson had titled this material in the serial version and in his original outline, "The Eight Islands." The additional text published here is divided into five chapters and seems to have been edited from a typescript (Beinecke 6436-37) made from Stevenson's MS (Beinecke 6435, 7 pp. portion of chap. 1) rather than from, or only from, the serial versions published in 1891. It includes material not found in the serial version and its division into chapters differs both from the serial version and the typescript.

5. Additional material written for *The South Seas* and published, although from other MS sources or in different form, serially in the New York *Sun* in 1891, appeared in the Bibliophile Society volume, *Hitherto Unpublished Prose Writings* (1921), pp. 116-56 ("Tutuila"), and 177-83 ("Historical Sketch of the Lazaretto"). "Tutuila" was here printed from the MS titled by Graham Balfour "Malaga in Tutuila Samoa March April 1891" (Beinecke 7069), portions of which Balfour had quoted, *Life, 2*, 96-101. This is a notebook version of the material in the Huntington Library manuscript called "The Circumnavigation of Tutuila" (11 pp.) and in Beinecke 6443-4 (10 pp.), some of which appeared in the New York *Sun*, 13 December 1891.

It was published, from the Bibliophile Society version, in the Vailima Edition, 25 (1923), 381-415. "Historical Sketch of the Lazaretto" was printed from the MS Stevenson had titled "The Lazaretto today" and marked "For chapter XLII of The South Seas" (Beinecke 6439). In revised form it had appeared in the New York *Sun*, 5 July ("The Lazaretto Today") and 12 July 1891 ("The Inn"). It was not reprinted in the Vailima Edition because the New York *Sun* material was reprinted instead: see the next paragraph.

In the Vailima Edition, 25 (1923), Lloyd Osbourne reprinted "Tutuila" from the Bibliophile Society version and printed "A Ride in the Forest" (*25*, 289-99) from the MS now in the Princeton University Library—not then realizing that in revised form it had appeared in the New York *Sun*, 7 June 1891, and as the second chapter of "The Eight Islands" part of *The South Seas* in the Swanston Edition (1912). Osbourne then supposed that "A Ride in the Forest" was an unfinished story and he so presented it in the Vailima Edition. In preparing the Tusitala Edition (1924) he corrected the error by dropping this earlier version of "A Ride in the Forest" altogether. In the Vailima Edition, 26 (1923), 425-76 Obsourne reprinted as "Letters from the South Seas" five installments from the New York *Sun* version of *The South Seas* not previously reprinted. These installments were "A Pearl Island: Penrhyn" (24 May 1891) and the four installments—made into three in the reprinting—on the leper settlement at Molokai (21 June-12 July). Tusitala 20-21.

Composition:

During the last few months of 1887, Stevenson's mother recalled, Lloyd Osbourne was much troubled by toothache. "To amuse him Louis plans a yacht trip," she wrote, "and they discuss all the arrangements even to where the piano is to stand in the saloon, how many rifles and other instruments of war they are to have, and where they are to be hung" (Vailima Edition, *26*, 353-54). S. S. McClure recalled that it was during his first visit to Stevenson at Saranac Lake, in November 1887, that he first heard him mention "his desire to take a long ocean cruise" (*My Autobiography*, 1914, p. 191). As Stevenson had written already to his cousin Bob, the voyage on the *Ludgate Hill* "proved the sea agrees heartily with me, and my mother likes it; so if I get any better, or no worse, my mother will likely hire a yacht for a month or so in the summer. . . . I was so happy on board that ship, I could not have believed it possible" (*Letters, 3*, 146). "Fame is nothing to a yacht," he wrote to Sir Walter Simpson at about the same time: "*experto crede*" (*Letters, 3*, 148). And when he heard of Stevenson's ambition, McClure wrote, "I . . . told him that if he would write a series of articles describing his travels, I would syndicate them for enough money to pay the expenses of his trip" (p. 191).

When he returned to New York, McClure sent Stevenson various books on the South Seas, including (he recalled) a South Pacific sailing directory (p. 191). "How we zigzagged over the charts, and sailed through this channel or avoided that in accordance with the great poet's instructions," Lloyd Osbourne wrote of their reading Alexander G. Findlay's directories at Saranac Lake (*An Intimate Portrait of R.L.S.*, 1924, p. 84). After

Stevenson's death, Fanny Stevenson gave his copies of the directories for the Mediterranean and the Indian Ocean to Captain Joshua Slocum; see his *Sailing Alone Around the World* (1900), pp. 155-56, and Osbourne, p. 82. Stevenson's copy of Findlay's *A Directory for the Navigation of the South Pacific Ocean* (London, 1884) was sold as Anderson 1914, I, 230. Of it Stevenson wrote to Charles Baxter on 10 April 1890: "Persons with friends in the islands should purchase Findlay's *Pacific Directories*: they're the best of reading anyway, and may almost count as fiction" (*Baxter Letters*, p. 267).

McClure came again to Saranac Lake for a few days on 17 January 1888, and at that time the scheme was pursued in detail. "We planned that when he came back he was to make a lecture tour and talk on the South Seas," McClure wrote; "that he was to take a phonograph along and make records of the sound of the sea and wind, the songs and speech of the natives, and that these records were to embellish his lectures. We planned the yacht and the provisioning of the yacht, and all possible adventures" (pp. 191-92). On 20 March 1888 McClure entered into a formal arrangement with Stevenson: "Should you go upon a yacht cruise, or other expedition, this year or next, and should you write letters descriptive of your experiences and observations for publication, I will undertake to sell such letters to syndicates of newspapers, (or such other periodicals as we may agree upon), in all countries where such sales can be effected." Stevenson was to receive three-fourths of the proceeds, McClure the rest. (Society of Authors Archive, British Museum, MS. Add. 56638, ff. 59-60.) The cruise was decided upon. Fanny Stevenson left for San Francisco to look into hiring a yacht, at length choosing Dr. Samuel Merritt's ninety-four-foot schooner *Casco*, chartered under Captain A. H. Otis with a crew of five for seven months to "various islands in the Pacific Ocean, including the Galapagos, Marquisas, Society, Sandwich, and other Islands which in the judgment of the Captain . . . can be visited with safety." Stevenson was to pay five hundred dollars per month and bear the entire cost of the voyage, "which may be extended one, two or three months with the approval of the captain" (Beinecke 6071, 1699). On 31 May 1888 McClure wrote from London that he thought he could get altogether three hundred dollars per letter, a figure he repeated in another letter on 8 December (Beinecke 5188-89). And on 28 June 1888, Stevenson, Fanny, Lloyd Osbourne, and Stevenson's mother all sailed from San Francisco bound for the Marquesas.

By the end of 1888 or early in 1889 McClure had arranged with the New York *Sun* to supply Stevenson's letters to them exclusively in the United States: ten thousand dollars was to be paid for the American rights to fifty letters, and McClure had found another five thousand dollars in Britain (see Peter Lyon, *Success Story: The Life and Times of S. S. McClure*, 1963, pp. 105-7). On 9 March 1889 McClure wrote to him that (as Stevenson had requested) the *Sun* "simply purchases the serial use of the letters, exclusively for North America for $200 per letter of 2,000 to 3,000 words" and that the paper was willing to take up to fifty such letters (NLS 9891, ff. 21-23). Presumably McClure made the arrangements for serialization in England at about the same time, although it was not until 1891 that Charles Baxter was informed by McClure that the terms were twenty pounds per letter for up to fifty letters, less McClure's commission of one-fourth (Beinecke 5172).

Stevenson, meanwhile, was finding voyaging everything he had hoped, writing accounts of his most recent experiences, discoveries, and conversations nearly every day during the voyages of the *Casco* (28 June 1888-24 January 1889), the *Equator* (24 June-7 December 1889), and the *Janet Nichol* (11 April-26 July 1890), although during this last voyage he was chiefly occupied with revising earlier material rather than with his day-to-day accounts. On these voyages see especially Balfour, *Life, 2*, 41-103; Stevenson's mother's *From Saranac to the Marquesas* (1903), on the *Casco* voyage; Thomson Murray MacCallum, *Adrift in the South Seas* (1934), pp. 217-46, on the *Equator* voyage; Fanny Stevenson's *The Cruise of the "Janet Nichol"* (1914); and Stevenson's own account in *The South Seas* (Tusitala 20-21).

Stevenson began working on *The South Seas* as distinct from his day-to-day accounts during the eight weeks (31 August-25 October 1889) he spent at Apemama in the Gilbert Islands while the *Equator* was trading elsewhere. On 2 December, after he had left Apemama and was nearing Samoa, he wrote to Sidney Colvin: "My book is now practically modelled; if I can execute what is designed, there are few better books now extant on this globe, bar the epics, and the big tragedies, and histories, and the choice lyric poets and a novel or so—none. . . . At least, nobody has had such stuff; such wild stories, such beautiful scenes, such singular intimacies, such manners and traditions, so incredible a mixture of the beautiful and horrible, the savage and civilised." Stevenson then outlined the work in detail for Colvin: seven parts, twenty-three chapters, most with several subdivisions, titles for each subdivision—all this not even including Samoa, "which I have not reached yet," and Fiji and Tonga "or even both." "Anyway, you see it will be a large work," Stevenson wrote, "and as it will be copiously illustrated, the Lord knows what it will cost" (*Letters, 3*, 273-75).

At all times during the project he remained enthusiastic—and equally ambitious. See, for example, Fanny Stevenson's complaints a year later about her "desperate engagements with the man of genius over the South Sea book," which Fanny and others wished would be about "his adventures in these wild islands" while Stevenson was busy with "his own theories on the vexed questions of race and language" (Fanny Stevenson to Sidney Colvin, autumn 1890, in E. V. Lucas, *The Colvins and Their Friends*, 1928, p. 219); or Stevenson's own remarks to the editor of the *Pacific Commercial Advertiser* during his visit to Honolulu in late September and October 1893, that the book "will take somewhat the form of a prose-epic . . . [bearing on] the unjust (yet I can see the inevitable) extinction of the Polynesian Islanders by our shabby civilization" (in Arthur Johnstone, *Recollections of Robert Louis Stevenson in the Pacific*, 1905, p. 103).

Samoa, especially its recent history, proved much more absorbing than had been anticipated, and after arriving from Apemama Stevenson spent most of the time during his first visit to Samoa (December 1889-January 1890) gathering material for the work eventually published as *A Footnote to*

History (1892). But in Sydney and later in 1890 during the cruise of the *Janet Nichol* Stevenson turned to the actual writing of *The South Seas*, to the point that by 19 August 1890 he could report that he was then "about waist-deep in my big book on the South Seas" (*Letters, 3*, 309). He sent the manuscript of the first part to England with Lloyd Osbourne that autumn, and by 12 November 1890 this material had been printed, constituting the 1890 copyright edition.

Before the end of his cruise on the *Janet Nichol* Stevenson had written to McClure, on 19 July 1890, telling him that he had finished the first fifteen chapters of *The South Seas* and explaining his intentions more or less fully. He was sending his manuscript to England to be printed, Stevenson wrote, and then this printed copy would be sent to McClure in New York for serialization. Stevenson wanted McClure clearly to understand, therefore, "that what you are to receive is not so much a certain number of letters, as a certain number of chapters in my book. The two things are identical but not coterminous. It is for you to choose out of the one what is most suitable for the other." But even though McClure was welcome not to print individual letters, letters chosen at all were to be printed complete, "as you receive them without suppression and without typographical embellishments," except insofar as mere cutting might be required for reasons of space. (McClure's account of this matter differs slightly in that he says that once the series began Stevenson actually wanted him to omit more; see *My Autobiography*, pp. 195-96, and the discussion of the periodical publication of *The South Seas* above.) Finally, Stevenson wrote, he hoped to have the whole series of fifty-two letters ready by the end of the year or by Easter 1891. (NLS 9891, ff. 24-27.)

When in December 1890 McClure received the 1890 copyright edition material in New York—the first of any kind sent him for publication—he was very dismayed that Stevenson had not sent the manuscript directly to him. He was right. The New York *Sun* refused to take the material under the original agreement, arguing that (as McClure wrote to Stevenson early in 1891) "the letters did not come as letters are supposed to come. They were not a correspondence from the South Seas, they were not dated and . . . in no way . . . fulfil[led] the definition of the word 'letter' as used in newspaper correspondence" (quoted in Lyon, *Success Story*, p. 106). Therefore McClure had to syndicate the material, in the New York *Sun* and elsewhere, at much reduced rates. Thirty-seven installments (not fifty, as had been anticipated) appeared in the New York *Sun* from 1 February through 13 December 1891, and in England twenty-seven of these appeared in *Black and White* from 6 February through 19 December 1891. Payments from McClure to Stevenson's account with Mitchell and Baxter for the various serializations began on 28 July 1891 and continued at intervals through 5 January 1893. Altogether McClure paid £644.12 for the American serializations (an average of £17.8 per installment), £305 for the English (£11.16), and £74.13.12 for the Australian serialization—a total paid to Stevenson of just over £1,000, about a third of what had been anticipated originally (Beinecke 7268).

Except for the material, Part I of *The South Seas*, which he sent to London for the 1890 copyright edition, all the rest of his revised manuscript Stevenson sent to McClure in New York, no doubt partly because of the great trouble which his not doing so for the earlier material had caused. McClure would then have the material set in type and send proofs to London and to Stevenson in Samoa to serve, in both places, as quarry for further publication. Stevenson's intentions, however, seem never to have been well understood. "No one ever seems to understand my attitude about that book," Stevenson wrote to Sidney Colvin on 22 April 1891; "the stuff sent was never meant for other than a first state; I never meant it to appear as a book. . . . I hoped some day to get a 'spate of style' and burnish it—fine mixed metaphor. I am now so sick that I intend, when the Letters are done and some more written than will be wanted, simply to make a book of it by the pruning-knife. Of the little volume [the 1890 copyright edition], for instance, Chapter I, a page or two of II, III, IV, some of VIII, some of IX, X, XII, XIV, and XV, with some excisions and rewriting are to stand. The rest I shall simply drop, and by similar drastic measures make up a book of shreds and patches: which will not be what I had hoped to make, but must have the value it has and be d —— d to it. I cannot fight longer . . . [and] really five years were wanting, when I could have made a book; but I have a family, and — perhaps I could not make a book after all, and anyway, I'll never be allowed for Fanny has strong opinions and I prefer her peace of mind to my ideas" (Vailima Letters, Widener Collection, Harvard University; partly published in *Letters, 4*, 67). Colvin and others having written of their great disappointment with the material, by then appearing serially, Stevenson had to write to Colvin again on 18 May 1891, stating emphatically that "*these letters were never meant, and are not now meant, to be other than a quarry of materials from which the book may be drawn" (Letters, 4*, 77). But in spite of all this almost no one shared Stevenson's hopes for the book which was to come.

Especially after taking up residence permanently in Samoa in October 1890 Stevenson seems to have proceeded rapidly in the acutal writing of *The South Seas*, and except for occasional delays in the spring of 1891 he carried the work steadily forward to its present state of completion by the end of the summer of 1891. He never lived to fulfill his intention of reshaping all of this material eventually into "*the* big book on the South Seas" (*Letters, 3*, 309). This material did not appear during his lifetime except serially, and as the complicated publishing history of *The South Seas* as a distinct single work shows, both in contents and order of arrangement it was subject to continual evolution in the hands of others for some thirty years after Stevenson's death.

THE BEACHCOMBERS. October 1889. Stevenson's only reference to this planned collaboration with his stepson Lloyd Osbourne is in a letter to Sidney Colvin written at Apemama in the Gilbert Islands in October 1889. "The Beachcomber" is listed as the third of three "South Sea Yarns" on which he and Osbourne were planning to collaborate, the other two being *The Wrecker*, which they were then writing, and *The Pearl Fisher*, which Osbourne had begun earlier in 1889 in Honolulu and which Stevenson finished as *The Ebb-Tide* in 1893. "*The Pearl Fisher* is for the *New York Ledger*," Stevenson wrote: "the yarn is a kind of Monte Cristo one. *The Wrecker* is the least good as a story, I think; but the characters seem to me good. *The Beachcombers* is more sentimental" (*Letters, 3*, 268-69). Nothing came of this third project.

THE BOTTLE IMP. December 1889-January 1890; possibly begun at Honolulu, May or June 1889. MS untraced. Fanny Stevenson's "notes" on this story (Beinecke 7286) are simply surviving bits of her MS for the introductory material she wrote for the Biographical Edition, vol. 15 (1909), also published in the Tusitala Edition. New York *Herald*, four weekly installments, 8 February-1 March 1891; each installment signed Robert Louis Stevenson. *Black and White* (London), 28 March and 4 April 1891; both installments signed Robert Louis Stevenson. Translated into Samoan by the Rev. Arthur E. Claxton, "O Le Fagu Aitu," *O Le Sulu Samoa*, seven monthly installments, May-December 1891 except the month of September; subtitled "O le tala lenei a le Tusitala," thus identifying the work as Stevenson's. See the facsimile of the first installment in the Beinecke Collection catalogue, *A Stevenson Library* . . . , facing p. 500. As Stevenson remarked to Arthur Conan Doyle, this translation gave rise to certain difficulties. The Samoans, Stevenson wrote on 23 August 1893, "do not know what it is to make a fiction. . . . Parties who come up to visit my unpretentious mansion, after having admired the ceilings by Vanderputty and the tapestry by Gobbling, manifest toward the end a certain uneasiness . . .and at last the secret bursts from them: 'where is the bottle?' "(*Letters, 5*, 71). The story seems to have been pirated almost immediately, from the New York *Herald,* by M. J. Ivers and Company, New York: see Beinecke 433. It was also reprinted in *The Herald* (London), 13 and 20 December 1891. *Island Nights' Entertainments* (1893). Tusitala 13.

In his "Note" to "The Bottle Imp," published with the story, Stevenson wrote that for its "name and root idea" he was indebted to a play "once rendered popular by the redoubtable O. Smith" (Tusitala, *13*, 78). This was *The Bottle Imp*, a melodrama by Richard Brinsley Peake first produced at the English Opera House in 1828 in which the actor Richard John Smith, nicknamed Obi Smith from his success as the character of that name in *Three Fingered Jack*, had starred. Stevenson first encountered it, according to his wife, among the collection of plays which their neighbors at Bournemouth, Sir Percy and Lady Shelley, kept for private theatricals (Tusitala, *13*, xi-xii). George Speaight, *Notes and Queries*, 16 November 1946, p. 218, remarks that it was available in two popular collections, Dicks's *Standard Plays* and Webster's *Acting National Drama*, although which of these, if either, Stevenson encountered is unknown.

During their residence in Honolulu, according to Fanny Stevenson,

Stevenson spoke of this play, which he knew was itself based on a German folk-tale, "several times," especially as being, "in its ingenuity and imaginative qualities, singularly like the Hawaiian tales" (*13*, xii). Stevenson visited the Kona Coast of the island of Hawaii for a week at the end of April and the beginning of May 1889, continuing his active inquiry into contemporary and historical Polynesian culture. (Stevenson's account of his stay became "The Eight Islands" in *The South Seas*; Tusitala, *20*, 177-210.) His host there, Judge Monsarrat, recalled of Stevenson that after visiting the ruins of Hale Keawe he "spent his days in applying himself to his work, with the result that instead of returning to Honolulu with a description of my property, he arrived . . . with *The Bottle Imp* tucked away in his travelling-case" (quoted in Eleanor Rivenburgh, "Stevenson in Hawaii—II," *Bookman*, New York, 46, November 1917, 305). Paul Newman, New York *Evening Post*, 26 December 1925, recalled Stevenson's telling him and his sister "The Bottle Imp" as a bedtime story sometime during May or June 1889. So it seems certain that Stevenson had written or at least conceived a first version of "The Bottle Imp" before he left Honolulu aboard the *Equator* on 24 June 1889.

Sidney Colvin is probably also correct, however, in stating that Stevenson wrote the story in Apia, Samoa, during his first visit there in December 1889 and January 1890 (*Letters, 4*, 200). Graham Balfour, moreover, seems to date the writing of the story even later, remarking that it was translated into Samoan "almost as soon as it was written" (*Life, 2*, 130)—a statement which places the writing of "The Bottle Imp" in late 1891 or early 1892, eighteen months after Stevenson left Honolulu and a year after he first visited Samoa. According to H. J. Moors, it was at his house in Apia that Stevenson "stated that he had written, or that he proposed to write, this story for the natives" and offered it to the Rev. J. E. Newell for the missionary newspaper. Newell replied that he would be glad to have it if it were suitable and lent itself to translation. "Whereupon," says Moors, "Stevenson unfolded the story." Moors continues: "Speaking of the incident recently, Mr. Newell remarked, 'I never had such an entertaining hour in all my life.' When the manuscript was afterwards handed to him he found that the work of translation was an easy task" (*With Stevenson in Samoa*, 1919, p. 98). For more on Newell and the translation see the paragraph after next.

What appears likely, given all these accounts, is that like "The Beach of Falesá" and not a few of his other works "The Bottle Imp" occupied Stevenson on several distinct occasions in various locations. Probably he drafted it in the Hawaiian Islands in May and June 1889, returned to it in Samoa at the end of the year, and finished it there almost a year later. Probably "The Bottle Imp" was among the various manuscripts which S. S. McClure acknowledged receiving from Stevenson on 4 December 1890 (Beinecke 5195). The translation into Samoan was begun in March 1891 (see Beinecke 4900 and *Letters, 4*, 62), probably from proofs sent to Stevenson early in the year or from one of the periodical publications.

It is possible that "The Bottle Imp" was conceived from the outset as a story for translation. In his "Note" on the story Stevenson himself remarked that it had been "designed and written for a Polynesian audience" (*13*, 78), and Graham Balfour remarks that it was translated into Samoan "almost as soon as it was written" (*Life, 2*, 130). But its translator, the Rev. Arthur E. Claxton, wrote that "Mr. Newell (then our Senior missionary), at my suggestion, sounded R.L.S. as to his willingness to let me translate and publish one of his stories in the *Sulu*. To this he agreed, and *The Bottle Imp* was the one selected" (in Masson, ed., *I Can Remember Robert Louis Stevenson*, 1922, p. 249). This wording implies that the story had already been written when the idea of making a Samoan translation occured. Claxton may have been mistaken about the order of events or, which is more likely, Stevenson may have written the story in the manner of Polynesian tales, and with a Polynesian setting, without having any particular "Polynesian audience" in mind—or forseeing any need of translation. When the idea of translation was proposed, naturally he was happy, and according to Claxton he threw himself enthusiastically into the work: "By mutual agreement, Stevenson and I spent an evening together each month, going over each chapter before it was printed, and discussing my translation. He was rapidly picking up a knowledge of the Samoan language and seemed to enjoy the balancing of rival expressions in the Samoan idiom" (p. 249). For more on Stevenson's interest in the Samoan language see the entries of "Talofa, Togarewa!" (summer 1891) and "Eatuina" (summer 1892) below. See also Beinecke 4900 and *Letters, 4*, 62.

Stevenson's sources for "The Bottle Imp" have been the subject of two articles: Bacil F. Kirtley, "The Devious Genealogy of the 'Bottle-Imp' Plot," *American Notes and Queries*, 9 (January 1971), 67-70, and Joseph Warren Beach, "The Sources of Stevenson's *The Bottle Imp," Modern Language Notes*, 25 (January 1910), 12-18. Kirtley's is the more comprehensive, and he writes that "the fountainhead of the Bottle-Imp plot, for both literary and 'folk' versions, seems to be an episode (chapters 18-22) in Hans Jacob Christoffel von Grimmelhausen's *nouvelle 'Trutz Simplex'* (printed in 1610)" (p. 68). This *nouvelle* undoubtedly did derive from folktales, but it rather than oral tradition seems to be the source of later renderings. "The plot," Kirtley writes, "was utilized repeatedly from the 17th to the 19th century" (p. 67), notably in LaMotte-Foque's *Das Galgenmännlein* (1810) and in the Grimm tale "Spiritus Familiaris" (*Deutsche Sagen*, 1816). Joseph Warren Beach takes up the history of the tale in English, arguing that for his melodrama R.B. Peake drew on the story translated as "The Bottle Imp" in the collection *Popular Tales and Romances of the Northern Nations* (London: Simpkin and Marshall, J. H. Bohte, 1823). Beach says that the translation is of LaMotte-Foque's "Das Galgenmännlein." But in reprinting the translation in his collection, *Gothic Tales of Terror*, 2 vols. (1972; rpt. Penguin, 1973), *2,* 136-64, Peter Haining attributes the original to J.K.A. Musäus (1735-87), whose folktales were first translated into English, apparently by William Beckford, as *Popular Tales of the Germans* (1791).

Whatever was the actual source of Peake's melodrama, there is no evidence that Stevenson knew the story of "The Bottle Imp" except in that dramatic version. He did know that there was such a source, however, and indeed remarked in 1893 that he had always intended "The Bottle Imp" to be "the centre-piece of a volume of *Märchen* which I was slowly to elaborate" (*Letters, 5*, 5). Further on this plan see the entry of *Island Nights' Entertainments*, where this story was first collected, below under date of late 1892. For more on the sources of "The Bottle Imp" see Martha M. McGaw, *Stevenson in Hawaii* (1950), pp. 76-79; Beinecke 1085 and 1871; and the anonymous comment, *Bookman* (London), 1 (February 1892), 159, that it seemed odd that in acknowledging his debt to the old melodrama Stevenson "was not aware that the story was published over sixty years ago in the Romanticist's and Novelist's Library," probably the earliest comment on the prose sources of Stevenson's story. George Speaight, *Juvenile Drama: The History of the English Toy Theatre* (1946), p. 237, notes that sheets for *The Bottle Imp* were issued by at least four publishers, although there is no evidence that Stevenson ever encountered the play in this form.

[A Malaga in Samoa.] December 1889-January 1890. MS, Yale. Stevenson's untitled notes are dated 30 and 31 December 1889 and 1-2 January 1890 and represent almost his earliest impressions of Samoa; the title was supplied by Graham Balfour. Partly published in Balfour, *Life, 2*, 85-88. Unpublished otherwise. At the turn of the year during his first visit to Samoa Stevenson accompanied the Rev. W. E. Clarke of the London Missionary Society by boat west along the coast of Upolu, Samoa, as far as Fagaloa—partly, Graham Balfour writes, "on mission business, and partly on his own account to visit Tamasese, the chief whom the Germans had formerly set up as king" (*Life, 2*, 85). No doubt Stevenson planned to use the material he wrote about this trip in some form in *The South Seas;* and certainly it was of use to him in writing *A Footnote to History* (1892).

AUTHORS AND PUBLISHERS. Late 1889-early 1890 (uncertain). MS, Yale. Unpublished. Stevenson's main point in this essay is that authors and publishers have different views of their relations and business: "The author will always continue to regard his venture [by] itself, the publisher must always continue to think of it as one of many; and the two points of view are hard to bring in focus" (Beinecke 5997, p. 5). Even so, publishers should become much more open and truthful with their authors, above all in reporting honestly their costs and sales. Publishers are probably not robbers, they are simply in the habit of some very shabby procedures which ought to be changed. In a pencil revision on this essay Stevenson refers to his experience "after 17 years of active authorship" and in the essay itself he refers to an island king, surely Tembinonka, with whom he was acquainted. These references would date the essay after Stevenson's stay at Apemama in the Gilbert Islands, 31 August-25 October 1889, but other information than this about when or why Stevenson wrote it is lacking. See also the entries of "Letter: American Rights and Wrongs" (15 March 1886), "Letter: International Copyright" (31 March 1887), and "Imaginary Dispatches" (Additional Works).

1890

[Address to the Samoan students at Malua.] January 1890. MS, Yale. Published in Balfour, *Life, 2*, 233-38. Unpublished otherwise. At the invitation of the Rev. J. E. Newell of the London Missionary Society Stevenson visited the mission school at Malua, Upolu, Samoa, in early January 1890. Here he gave this address to the students, for whose benefit it was also translated into Samoan.

FATHER DAMIEN. Dated 25 February 1890. MS untraced. *Father Damien: An Open Letter to the Reverend Doctor Hyde of Honolulu from Robert Louis Stevenson* (Sydney: n.p., 1890). Twenty-five copies, the title page headed *With Mr. R.L. Stevenson's Compliments.*, which Stevenson had printed in Sydney in late February and March 1890. Printing was in progress on 5 March, completed by 12 March, and copies were sent out on 27 March. Stevenson corrected three misprints in these copies before sending them. "Father Damien. An Open Letter to the Reverend Dr. Hyde of Honolulu." *The Scots Observer*, 3 and 10 May 1890, pp. 659-61, 687-89; signed Robert Louis Stevenson at the end of both installments. *Father Damien: An Open Letter to the Reverend Doctor Hyde of Honolulu from Robert Louis Stevenson* (London: Chatto and Windus, 1890); published 16 July 1890 in an edition of one thousand copies. Further on these and other appearances of this work in 1890 see the discussion of items 506-10, 7593, and 7701 in the Beinecke Collection catalogue, *A Stevenson Library . . .*, pp. 222-24, 2292-93, 2353. Facing p. 932 is a facsimile of Stevenson's letter to Andrew Chatto, Beinecke 2974, declining all remuneration for this work (text in *Baxter Letters*, p. 271). Tusitala 21.

Stevenson visited the Hawaiian Board of Health leprosy settlement at Kalawo, Molokai, for a week at the end of May 1889, six weeks after the death there of Father Damien, Joseph DeVeuster (1840-89). The first shipload of leprosy victims had been landed on 6 January 1866; Damien came to serve as Catholic priest to the settlement seven years later, in May 1873; after more than a decade there, he contracted leprosy, his case being confirmed medically late in 1884; and on 15 April 1889 he died, famous around the world as the leper-priest of Molokai. (On Damien's life and work see Gavan Daws, *Holy Man: Father Damien of Molokai*, 1973.) Stevenson's friend Charles Warren Stoddard had visited Kalawo in October 1884 and written of it in *The Lepers of Molokai* (1885), and this no doubt strengthened Stevenson's desire to see the settlement himself. "I can only say that the sight of so much courage, cheerfulness, and devotion stung me too high to mind the infinite pity and horror of the sights," Stevenson wrote to Sidney Colvin just after his return to Honolulu in early June 1889. "I have seen sights that cannot be told, and heard stories that cannot be repeated: yet I have never admired my poor race so much, nor (strange as it may seem) loved life more than in the settlement" (*Letters, 3*, 259). See also Stevenson's letters to wife, to James Payn, and to his mother, *Letters, 3*, 255-63, and his two articles originally published in the New York *Sun* in 1891 as part of *The South Seas*, "The Lazaretto" and "The Lazaretto of To-day," Tusitala, *21*, 317-55.

"He talked very little to us of the tragedy of Molokai, though I could see it lay heavy on his spirits," Stevenson's wife wrote, "but of the great work begun by Father Damien and carried on by his successors he spoke fully. He had followed the life of the priest like a detective until there seemed nothing more to learn" (Preface, *Lay Morals and Other Papers*, Biographical Edition, 1911, pp. viii-ix). Therefore, Stevenson was outraged six months later to discover, from newspapers awaiting them in Samoa in December 1889, that due to an attack on Damien written by a prominent Protestant missionary in Honolulu it was likely that no monument would be erected in his honor. "I'll not believe it," Stevenson's wife recalled him saying of this attack, "unless I see it with my own eyes; for it is too damnable for belief!" (p. x).

Graham Balfour says that Stevenson did not hear about the monument question until after he read the letter itself in Sydney (*Life, 2*, 89-90). But all accounts agree that it was in Sydney, during the third week of February 1890, that Stevenson first read the offending letter, and that his reaction was immediate and intense. On 2 August 1889 the Rev. Charles McEwen Hyde (1832-99), an important Congregational minister in Honolulu, had written privately to the Rev. Henry Bartlett Gage in San Francisco attacking Damien and claiming that those who knew the priest's work in Honolulu were "surprised at the extravagant newspaper laudations, as if he [Damien] was a most saintly philanthropist." Gage made the letter public, apparently first in *The Congregationalist*, Boston, a widely circulated Protestant weekly, during August or September 1889. It was reprinted in *The Presbyterian*, Sydney, 26 October 1889, in which publication and from which source Stevenson quoted it in *Father Damien* (Tusitala, *21*, 28).

Robert Scot-Skirving, whom Stevenson had first known years before in Edinburgh when they had both taken part in private theatricals at Professor Fleeming Jenkin's, recalled seeing Stevenson again in Sydney in February 1890 and asking what he was then doing. "Well," Scot-Skirving recalls Stevenson saying, "I propose to devote myself to writing a libel, but it will be a justified and righteous one." Scot-Skirving continues: "It seems that, on the previous evening, over the dinner table, reference had been made to Father Damien and the Molokai lepers. Someone asked Stevenson whether he had seen a letter written by the Rev. Dr. Hyde, a Presbyterian minister at Honolulu, whom Stevenson had met there. . . . When R.L.S. read the account, he leaped to his feet in furious anger, declaring that he must reply at once—must smash the traducer of the dead man for whom he had conceived an ardent admiration" (quoted in George MacKaness, *Robert Louis Stevenson: His Associations with Australia*, 1935, pp. 12-13; also in his *The Art of Book-Collecting in Australia*, 1956, pp. 83-4).

Stevenson wrote his reply, *Father Damien*, quickly. According to his wife, Stevenson actually read Hyde's offending letter one morning, began writing immediately, and read the finished work to her, Lloyd Osbourne, and Isobel

Strong, "that afternoon" (ix). Isobel Strong wrote of the reading itself: "One afternoon we were summoned to the Oxford Hotel, the whole family assembling. Giving instructions that no one was to be admitted under any circumstances, Louis announced with unusual gravity that he had written something he wanted us to hear. . . . I had never seen him so serious or so deeply stirred. He explained that the article he had written would probably involve him in a suit for libel, which, if lost, might mean poverty for us all. He felt he had no right to print it without consulting us. . . . He would abide by our decision." Stevenson then read the work, and when he finished his wife "rose to her feet, and holding out both hands to him in a gesture of enthusiasm, cried, 'Print it! Publish it!'" (Isobel Field, *This Life I've Loved*, 1937, pp. 270-71).

Stevenson consulted a lawyer, according to his wife's recollection by the name of Mr. Moses, and—again according to his wife—learned what he already knew: that publication was risky, probably so risky that no one in Sydney would publish the work. This proved to be true, and so Stevenson "hired a printer by the day, and the work was rushed through" (pp. xi-xii; but on the legal matters cf. *Baxter Letters*, pp. 264-65). On 5 March 1890 Stevenson wrote to his mother that his reply to Hyde's attack was "in the press" and would soon appear as a pamphlet. "I have struck as hard as I knew how," Stevenson wrote, "nor do I think my answer can fail to do away (in the minds of all who see it) with the effect of Hyde's incredible and really villainous production" (*Letters, 3*, 293).

The printing of *Father Damien* was carried out under W. M. Maclardy at the Ben Franklin Printing Office in Sydney. According to James Grant: "At that time (1890) I was employed at the old Ben Franklin Printing Office, the proprietor of which was a member of the *Cercle Francais*, a coterie of literary and musical men whose meeting place was in Wynyard Square. . . . I do not think his visit made much stir, but the *Cercle* entertained him, and to my employer was entrusted the job of printing the *Apologia* [*Father Damien*]. It was only a small job—I think 100 copies, demy 8vo" (quoted from the *Australasian,* Melbourne, 29 July 1922, in MacKaness, p. 16, rpt, p. 85).

By 12 March 1890 the pamphlet had been printed. On that date Stevenson sent a copy of *Father Damien* to Charles Baxter, leaving it to him to decide all questions of further publication, in particular whether to send it to W. E. Henley for *The Scots Observer*, which Baxter did, or to withhold it as too dangerous: "I don't want to give him a serpent for a fish" (*Baxter Letters,* p. 265). Presentation copies were sent from Sydney on 27 March 1890, recipients including (according to Stevenson's stepdaughter) "the Pope of Rome, Queen Victoria, [and] the President of the United States" (*This Life I've Loved*, p. 271). Further on the publication history of this work see the first paragraph of the present entry and the sources cited there. F. W. Heron's collection of materials on *Father Damien* is now held as item 794 in the Monterey State Historical Monument Stevenson House Collection, California. Beinecke 1282 is a photostatic copy of clippings from the *Pacific Commercial Advertiser* on the controversy.

Hyde's public response to Stevenson's pamphlet appeared as "Father Damien and his Work," *The Congregationalist*, Boston, 7 August 1890, p. 268, from which source it was summarized and quoted under the heading *"Father Damien.* Dr. Hyde's Reply to Mr. Stevenson." in *The British Weekly*, 22 August 1890, pp. 262-63. "Father Damien and his Work" was apparently also reprinted as a pamphlet. In his reply Hyde insisted: "The attempt made to glorify Father Damien, the leper priest . . . is not merely an exaggeration or perversion of the facts, but many statements made in his behalf are in direct contravention of the truth" (*The Congregationalist*, p. 282; all quotations in this paragraph are from this source and were not reprinted in the summary in *The British Weekly*). Of Stevenson's *Father Damien* in particular he wrote: "I am indebted to Mr. R.L. Stevenson for sending me the pamphlet which he published in Sydney in relation to Father Damien, with special reference to the statements I had made on Damien's character and work. But I am sorry that he should have written his own condemnation as one indifferent to truth and justice, not to say Christian charity, in such a philippic against me, without making any inquiry as to my personal knowledge of Hawaiian leprosy, or the concurrent testimony I could cite for my statements in regard to Father Damien. His invective may be brilliant, but it is like a glass coin, not golden, shivered into fragments of worthless glitter when brought to the test of truthfulness. He has been in hot haste to condemn me for keeping aloof from Hawaiian lepers, for knowing nothing of Father Damien, and for being ignorant of the geography of Molokai. I beg your indulgence for a brief statement of facts, personal to myself, yet pertinent to the question at issue." Hyde then mentions his own work with the Hawaiian lepers, and concludes his direct response: "In regard to Mr. Stevenson's brilliant invective, I have only to say that, so far as I am concerned, it lacks the essential elements of truthfulness." He actually had been to Molokai, actually had met Damien, he writes.

Hyde continues with a long discussion of the work being carried on by Protestant missionaries and the Hawaiian government in the care of lepers in Hawaii, insisting that the Catholics, and Father Damien, have in no sense been alone in this work. He defends his "modest house which the generosity of friends in Honolulu has furnished for my occupancy" on the grounds that "in lift[ing] up a people out of their superstitious degradation . . . the Christian home life of the missionary is an important factor." In a "spirit of detraction" Stevenson has lauded Damien by contrast, "as if there were superior sanctity in dirt" (*The Congregationalist*, p.282; *The British Weekly*, p. 262). For all that has been written on the subject, Hyde continues, "no proof is given that Damien was other than I have represented him to be." Indeed Stevenson's own harsh description of Damien only confirms what he himself had said of the same matters and "is presumptive proof that I had equally good reason for saying what else I said of him" (*Ibid.*). "No one in this world can know with what stress of pain I have taken the stand I have maintained as a witness for the truth," Hyde ends his reply by saying, "assailed on the one hand by the arrogant pretentiousness of the Catholic hierarchy, and betrayed on the other by the fanciful falsities of a sentimental humanitarianism" (*The Congregationalist,* p. 282, not rptd.). Further on Hyde and his reply see Gavan Daws, *Holy Man*, pp. 227-32, and Harold Winfield Kent, *Dr. Hyde and Mr. Stevenson: The Life of the Rev. Dr. Charles McEwen Hyde* (1973).

A copy of Hyde's reply as it appeared in *The British Weekly* is pasted into one of Stevenson's mother's scrapbooks, Monterey State Historical Monument Stevenson House Collection, California, vol. 3, pp. 124-27 (xerox, Yale). Before he received it, Stevenson wrote to Mrs. Charles Fairchild in September 1890: "On the whole, it was virtuous to defend Damien; but it was harsh to strike so hard at Dr. Hyde. When I wrote the letter, I believed he would bring an action, in which case I knew I could be beggared. As yet there has come no action; the injured Doctor has contented himself up to now with the (truly innocuous) vengeance of calling me a 'Bohemian Crank,' and I have deeply wounded one of his colleagues whom I esteemed and like" (*Letters, 3*, 314). When Hyde's reply did reach him, Stevenson wrote to Andrew Chatto that he wished it printed along with *Father Damien*, the title page to state "in considerable characters" that Stevenson's work appeared "*With Dr. Hyde's Reply*." Chatto was also to include the following note: "It was my single end to defend the character of Damien. I conceive the end best served if I give all publicity in my power to Dr. Hyde's reply, a conclusion to a controversy not more gratifying than it is unusual. I do myself the pleasure to append an eloquent letter from Mr. Hastings. R.L.S." Henry F. Poor was to send this additional material from Honolulu, Stevenson was to bear all expenses of publication, and Chatto was to send twelve copies of the augmented pamphlet to Poor. But this augmented edition of *Father Damien* never appeared. (Stevenson to Andrew Chatto, 2 December 1890; text from slip letters, galley proofs made by Sidney Colvin in preparing his biography of Stevenson, abandoned in 1899, and *Letters . . . to his Family and Friends*; Lloyd Osbourne's copy, Silverado Museum, St. Helena, California, galley 42.)

[Navigation by the South Sea Islanders.] February or March 1890, possibly later. MS untraced if written. Unpublished. The only surviving record of this projected work is in Robert Scot-Skirving's "Trifling Memories of R.L.S." in Masson, ed., *I Can Remember Robert Louis Stevenson* (1922), pp. 228-30. During one of his visits to Sydney, Scot-Skirving recalled, Stevenson "came to my house, and I spent various evenings with him. He was very full of writing an account of the navigational knowledge of the South Sea Islanders as explanatory of the populating of islands so widely separated from each other. He never carried out this work. I talked with him much on this subject and on sea-things" (p. 229). Probably the conversations took place during Stevenson's first visit to Sydney, in February and March 1890, when he was just beginning *The South Seas.*

CANNONMILLS. August-September 1890. MS, Lloyd Osbourne, 1914, 577: 1½ pages, folio. Vailima Edition, 25 (1923), 377-79. Tusitala 16. Stevenson's one reference to this work appears in a letter to Adelaide Boodle, 1 September 1890: "I have a projected, entirely planned love-story—everybody will think it dreadfully improper—called *Cannonmills*" (*Letters, 3*, 313). He does not appear to have carried the work itself beyond the first few paragraphs, however.

THE RISING SUN. August-September 1890. MS untraced if written. Unpublished. Stevenson's one reference to this work appears in a letter to Adelaide Boodle, 1 September 1890: "I've a vague, rosy haze before me—a love story, too, but not improper—called *The Rising Sun*." He outlines the story briefly but seems never actually to have begun it. See *Letters, 3*, 313.

THE BEACH OF FALESÁ. Begun November 1890, resumed April 1891, and chiefly written September 1891. MS, Huntington HM 2391. Draft table of contents, copyright issue, Princeton University Library. Copyright issue, trial issue, galley proofs of serial version, Yale. Copyright issue: *The Beach of Falesá* (London: Cassell and Company, 1892). Twenty-five copies printed and bound, July 1892. Charles Baxter's copy, now at Princeton, is inscribed by him: "C. Baxter Recd. 23 July 1892. From Publishers. One of 'expurgated' set printed to secure English Copyright. C. B. on p. 16 Marriage Certificate is deleted v. 95 99." Trial issue: *The Beach of Falesá . . . and The Bottle Imp* (London: Cassell and Company, 1892). Printed from type of the copyright issue and sent to Stevenson for his consideration as a possible format for book-form publication. Beinecke 564, Yale, is Stevenson's copy of this trial issue, heavily corrected by him. "Uma; or The Beach of Falesa. (Being the Narrative of a South-Sea Trader)," *Illustrated London News*, six weekly installments, 2 July-6 August 1892; each installment signed Robert Louis Stevenson. *Island Nights' Entertainments* (1893). Tusitala 13. Many differences exist between the manuscript, the trial and copyright issues, and the versions eventually published. See the discussion of items 562-65 in the Beinecke Collection catalogue, *A Stevenson Library . . .*, pp. 249-52; and W. M. Hill *Unique or a Descriptoin of Proof Copy of The Beach of Falesa containing over 100 Manuscript Changes* (Chicago, 1914), a description of the trial issue, Beinecke 564. A complete critical edition of the manuscript, now in the Huntington Library, is in preparation by Professor Barry Menikoff, University of Hawaii.

Stevenson's first mention of this story is in a letter to Sidney Colvin, 6 November 1890, commenting on the powerful effect which clearing forest on his land in Samoa has made upon his imagination: "I have taken refuge in a new story, which just shot through me like a bullet in one of my moments of awe, alone in that tragic jungle;—*The High Woods of Ulufanua*." Stevenson lists seven chapter titles and characterizes the story as "very strange, very extravagant . . . varied, and picturesque . . . [it] has a pretty love affair, and ends well" (*Letters, 4*, 20). After writing the first chapter, however, Stevenson abandoned the story—"as a deception of the devil's," he wrote on 25 November 1890—and did not return to it until the following April

(*Letters, 4*, 25, 75). Again he seems to have abandoned it, only resuming and finishing it, under its present title, in September and early October 1891. On 14 October he sent the manuscript to Charles Baxter with lengthy instructions about terms to ask for publication (*Letters, 4*, 95, 99-101; *Baxter Letters*, pp. 286-87).

Stevenson had offered the story to S. S. McClure, and on 19 December 1891 Robert McClure entered into an agreement with Charles Baxter, acting for Stevenson, for serialization of the story. The McClures obtained serial rights in all countries for £500, £150 to be paid on or before 10 January 1892, £175 on publication of the first installment, and £175 on publication of the last installment (Society of Authors Archive, British Museum, MS. Add. 56638, f. 64). These amounts were paid into Stevenson's account with Mitchell and Baxter on 7 January, 2 July, and 5 October 1892 (Beinecke 7268). By the end of January 1892 Stevenson had proofs from the *Illustrated London News* and what he characterized as the editor Clement Shorter's "plaintive request" to alter the story so that Uma and John Wiltshire were "married properly before 'that night.'" Stevenson refused: "You see what would be left of the yarn had I consented" (*Letters, 2*, 149). He wished the marriage contract given as it stood in his manuscript: Uma is there "illegally married to *Mr. John Wiltshire* for one night, and *Mr. John Wiltshire* is at liberty to send her to hell next morning." Nevertheless, apparently without further consulting Stevenson, Shorter omitted the contract altogether in publishing the story in the *Illustrated London News*, remarking later that Stevenson "bore it very well—this ruthless vandalism. He doubtless uttered many curses in letters to intimate friends . . . but there it was. Some of the greatest things in literature cannot be published in journals for general family reading, and no editor who knows his business would worry himself about the feelings of an author, however great, when he had such a point for decision" (*Letters to an Editor*, 1914, p. iv). As "The Beach of Falesá" appeared in the *Illustrated London News*, 2 July 1892, the paragraph in which the marriage contract is mentioned ends simply: "when she got her certificate I was tempted to throw up the bargain and confess. What a document it was! It was Case that wrote it, signatures and all, in a leaf out of the ledger." The next paragraph begins: "A nice paper to put in a girl's hand and see her hide away like gold!" (p. 11).

In a letter to J. M. Barrie, 1 November 1892, Stevenson commented on another suppression in the story. Barrie had written to him about the changes made in Hardy's *Tess of the d'Urbervilles*, chap. 23, for serial publication in *The Graphic*. "Yon was an exquisite story about the barrow," Stevenson wrote, "but I think I can beat it. In a little tale of mine, the slashed and gaping ruins of which appeared recently in the *Illustrated London News*, a perfect synod of appalled editors and apologetic friends had sat and wrangled over the thing in private with astonishing results. The flower of their cuts was this. Two little native children were described [chap. 2, para. 4] as wriggling out of their clothes and running away mother-naked. The celestial idiots cut it out. I wish we could afford to do without serial publication altogether. It is odd that Hardy's adventure with the barrow and mine of the little children should happen in the same year with the publication and success of *Tess*. Surely these editor people are wrong." (Passage omitted at ellipsis, *Letters, 4*, 257; text from slip letters, galley proofs made by Sidney Colvin in preparing his biography of Stevenson, abandoned in 1899, and *Letters . . . to his Family and Friends*; Lloyd Osbourne's copy, Silverado Museum, St. Helena, California, galleys 12-13.)

Stevenson evidently saw the first installment of the *Illustrated London News* version of the story after it was published, in a copy of the magazine which Lady Jersey happened to bring with her to Samoa in mid-August 1892. (He had returned the proofs earlier in the year.) By then Stevenson was chiefly concerned with the text as it would appear in book form, and he was very distressed over the many misreadings of his manuscript which had been introduced. On 29 August he wrote to Sidney Colvin that he was sending him a wire about the matter, to be despatched by Lady Jersey when she returned to Sydney: "I will not allow it [the story] to be called *Uma* in book form, that is not the logical name of the story. Nor can I have the marriage contract omitted; and the thing is full of misprints abominable. In the picture, Uma is rot; so is the old man and the negro; but Wiltshire is splendid, and Case will do. It seems badly illuminated, but this may be printing" (*Letters, 4*, 229; on the illustrations, which Stevenson came to like better in later installments, see also *4*, 246-47).

Even from the time he sent the manuscript to Charles Baxter, Stevenson was hoping that the story could be published in book form by itself, "as a small volume through Cassell's and Scribner's" selling for half a crown or perhaps two shillings (*Baxter Letters*, p. 287). He also seems to have considered making up a volume entirely of realistic South Seas stories, to be called *Beach de Mar*, in which would appear "The Beach of Falesá" and at least one other story,—probably "The Labour Slave" which, as it happened, became unavailable for the volume when it was assimilated into the novel "Sophia Scarlet." On 9 December 1891 it was agreed with Cassell and Company that they would publish a volume of short stories approximating the length of *Kidnapped* or *The Master of Ballantrae*. This would be called *Beach de Mar* "or some such title" and would include "The Beach of Falesá" and other unspecified stories. Copy was to be delivered on or before 31 August 1892 and Stevenson was to receive a royalty of 15 percent on the retail price reckoning 13 copies as 12, £150 to be paid against royalties when the proofs were passed for the press. (Society of Authors Archive, British Museum, MS. Add. 56638, f. 13.) See also *Letters, 4*, 182, and the entries of "The Labour Slave" (September 1891) and "Sophia Scarlet" (January 1892). But on 25 February 1892 E. L. Burlingame of Charles Scribner's Sons advised Stevenson against publishing "The Beach of Falesá" separately (Beinecke 4148), and at the end of March 1892 he agreed to wait until he had more stories ready before seeing "The Beach of Falesá" published in book form (*Baxter Letters*, p. 295; see also p. 293).

Cassell and Company also objected to the marriage contract, and Clement Shorter recalls having been given "a very humorous description of a number of bearded gentlemen [at Cassell and Company] solemnly engaged in solving the problem how they were to pacify an author some thousands of miles away who had told his agents and representatives that not one word of the certificate was to be omitted from the story in book form" *(Letters to an Editor*, p. 5). By late April or early May 1891 the bearded gentlemen had evidently come to a conclusion, conveyed to Stevenson by Sidney Colvin; and on 17 May Stevenson replied. "Yesterday came yours," he wrote to Colvin. "Well, well, if the dears prefer a week, why I'll give them ten days, but the real document, from which I have scarcely varied, ran for one night" (*Letters, 4*, 182). In the marriage contract as it was finally published in *Island Nights' Entertainments* (1893) the proposed compromise was evidently followed. Uma is there "illegally married to Mr. John Wiltshire for one week, and Mr. John Wiltshire is at liberty to send her to hell when he pleases" (p. 18).

This matter having been settled, the next question was what else to include with "The Beach of Falesá" in volume form. Copyright was protected by printing the *Illustrated London News* version of the story in volume form in July; and one proposal for the eventual volume itself was to publish "The Beach of Falesá" and "The Bottle Imp" together. Sidney Colvin actually had made up and sent to Stevenson a trial issue with these contents. But Stevenson would have none of it, as he wrote to Charles Baxter before he had even seen this trial issue: "*The B. of F.* is *simply not* to appear along with *The Bottle Imp*, a story of a totally different scope and intention, to which I have already made one fellow, and which I design for a substantive volume" (11 August 1892, *Baxter Letters*, p. 302). Nevertheless, it eventually was with "The Bottle Imp" and "The Isle of Voices" that the story appeared in book form; see the entry of *Island Nights' Entertainments* below under date of autumn 1892.

AN ONLOOKER IN HELL. Late 1890 or early 1891, possibly later, MS, NLS. Four pages comprising personal reminiscences of the gambling casino at Hamburg and a list of chapter titles for a work to be called "An Onlooker in Hell." Typewritten copy, Silverado Museum, St. Helena, California. Unpublished. This fragment represents a start Stevenson made on a series of essays of reminiscence for *Scribner's Magazine*, on which see *Letters, 3*, 287, 298-99, and especially *4*, 33. "I was on the whole rather relieved you did not vote for regular papers, as I feared the traces," Stevenson wrote to E. L. Burlingame in December 1890. "It is my design [instead] from time to time to write a paper of a reminiscential (beastly word) description; some of them I could scarcely publish from different considerations; but some of them—for instance, my long experience of gambling-places—Homburg, Wiesbaden, Baden-Baden, old Monaco, and new Monte Carlo—would make good magazine padding, if I got the stuff handled the right way" (*Letters, 4*, 33). Stevenson may have begun this particular essay immediately, perhaps before the end of 1890 or early in 1891. On 22 May 1894, reminding him of their correspondence on the matter in 1890, Burlingame asked Stevenson whether he might now like to write such a series for *Scribner's Magazine* in 1895. On

8 July Stevenson replied that he was not at all interested, in fact quite the opposite: "I doubt if I could write essays now; I doubt . . . whether I should find I wanted to." Nevertheless, on 14 September Burlingame offered him $350 each for four to six essays, and on 9 October 1894, having refused again in the letter itself, Stevenson added in postscript: "Second thoughts. I'll have a try, if I bust. I'll send one article and you shall say if you like it." See their correspondence, Beinecke 2966-67, 4155-56. Probably the essay was "Early Memories," entered under date of October 1894, below. See also the next entry.

[Water of Leith.] Late 1890 or early 1891, possibly later. MS, Yale. Unpublished. Stevenson's untitled manuscript, slightly more than a page with many deletions and revisions, may represent another start he made on a second series of essays for *Scribner's Magazine*. See the previous entry. "It is not possible to exaggerate the hold that is taken on the mind of men by a familiar river," Stevenson writes in the first sentence, elaborating on this idea for a paragraph. In the second paragraph he names the Water of Leith and describes it, especially in comparison with other rivers. "Every child has his own adopted river, that he was born on or has played beside, and whose ancient voice returns to the ear of memory. . . . [The] stream my childhood boasted of was neither great nor very beautiful. . . . [It] ran from some not very memorable hills down a not very noticeable glen; skirted the outposts, vacant lots, and half-rural slums of a great city, and at last, running between the repose of a graveyard and the clatter of [an] engine factory, lapsed between dark gates and groves of masts and a long alley of weedy piers into an islanded salt estuary. . . . Such as it was, however, it was the river whose streams made glad my childhood and for that reason ever memorable to me. Often and often . . . " (Beinecke 6506). Here the manuscript breaks off.

1891

THE SHOVELS OF NEWTON FRENCH. Early 1891-late 1892. MS, Anderson 1914, I, 352. Vailima Edition, 25 (1923), 309-57. Tusitala 16. Listing works which were then partly finished, Stevenson mentioned on 1 September 1890 "five or six [chapters] of *Memoirs of Henry Shovel*" (*Letters, 3,* 312-13). Such a work, according to Sidney Colvin, "had been sketched out and a few chapters written as long ago as the seventies" (*Letters, 4,* 55n.). In May 1886 Stevenson wrote to Thomas Galpin of Cassell and Company: "I am glad you liked Kidnapped. My next story of that class will be 'Henry Shovel,' and will take a lad to the Peninsular War; he will not be as good a fellow as David. The trouble is that I cannot engage beforehand when a book shall be ready; as my Muse is wayward, and often goes from home" (Sotheby sale, 12 March 1968, lot 722). But not until early 1891 does Stevenson seem to have begun revising the earlier work, as *The Shovels of Newton French.* As he wrote to Sidney Colvin in February 1891: "I have a strange kind of novel under construction; it begins about 1660 and ends 1830, or perhaps I may continue it to 1875 or so, with another life. One, two, three, four, five, six generations, perhaps seven, figure therein; two of my old stories, *Delafield* and *Shovel*, are incorporated; it is to be told in the third person, with some of the brevity of history, some of the detail of romance." The idea had come to him, Stevenson adds, when a friend had read some of his *Memoir of Fleeming Jenkin* (1887), and, thinking it was fiction, remarked that it was strange but enjoyable (*Letters, 4*, 54-55). "The Adventures of John Delafield" was "largely planned" by February 1882 but is otherwise unknown; see *Letters, 2*, 185, 195, and the entry of this work above. On 19 May 1891 Stevenson asked Charles Baxter to send him various source books, sketched the story, and gave its title in expanded form: *The Shovels of Newton French: including Memoirs of Henry Shovel, a Private in the Peninsular War (Letters, 4*, 81). A year later, on 25 March 1892, Stevenson listed *The Shovels of Newton French* and two other works as "quite planned" although not yet written: "O, Shovel—Shovel waits his turn, he and his ancestors. I would have tackled him before, but my *State Trials* have never come" (*Letters, 4*, 168). Stevenson never again referred to this work. Probably he turned to the actual writing—in revised form the draft consists of three chapters—sometime after sending the finished manuscript of *David Balfour* to Charles Baxter on 12 October 1892.

THE BLOODY WEDDING. Projected March 1891 but never written. Apart from a passing reference to this work later as among several which he hoped to set, like "The Beach of Falesá," on an imaginary island called Ulufanua (*Letters, 4*, 94), Stevenson's only reference to this work appears in a letter to Sidney Colvin from Pago Pago, 24 March 1891. Hopeful that he will also gather in Pago Pago more material for his book on the South Seas, Stevenson writes: "In the meanwhile, I am seized quite *mal-à-propos* with desire to write a story, *The Bloody Wedding*, founded on fact—very possibly true, being an attempt to read a murder case—not yet months old, in this very place and house where I now write. The indiscretion is what stops me; but if I keep on feeling as I feel now it will have to be written. Three Star Nettison, Kit Nettison, Field the Sailor, these are the main characters: old Nettison, and the captain of the man of war, the secondary. Possible scenario. Chapter I. . . ." (*Letters, 4*, 64).

TALOFA, TOGAREWA! Summer 1891 (uncertain). MS, Yale: four pages cut into printers' takes, mounted after 1900 on stationery of the London Missionary Society bearing the name of the Rev. Arthur E. Claxton. At the end of the MS there is a note by Stevenson telling Claxton to "please yourself about whether it should be signed or not." The MS itself, which is written in English, is signed Robert Louis Stevenson. Details of publication unknown. In the Beinecke Collection catalogue, *A Stevenson Library . . .*, p. 2001, G. L. McKay suggests that the story "may have been published in *O Le*

Sulu Samoa," the monthly in which Claxton's translation of "The Bottle Imp" appeared, May-December 1891. "Talofa, Togarewa!" might be translated as "Hail, Penrhyn!" and in it Stevenson tells the "true story of an island" whose inhabitants came deeply to regret harboring lepers: "If this trouble come upon Samoa, God help us to do right" (Beinecke 6958). Stevenson's concern with the rapid spread of leprosy on Penrhyn, which he visited 9-10 May 1890 during the cruise of the *Janet Nichol*, is also evident in his essay on that island in the New York *Sun*, 24 May 1891, "A Pearl Island: Penrhyn" (Tusitala, *21*, 307-16). Politics divided Stevenson irrevocably from Claxton early in 1892. Probably, therefore, he wrote this essay and gave it to Claxton for publication, with or without translation, sometime in 1891.

PRAYERS. Summer 1891-December 1894. MSS chiefly Yale, on which see the descriptions in the Beinecke Collection catalogue, *A Stevenson Library . . .*, pp. 1938–39, 2597–98. MSS of some of the prayers first published in the 1920s remain untraced. Fourteen of Stevenson's prayers were first published, after his death, under the collective title, "Prayers written for Family Use at Vailima," Edinburgh Edition, 21 (1896), 379-88. These were reprinted from this source under the collective title "Vailima Prayers" in Balfour, *Life, 2*, 196-200. Two more prayers first appeared, as "Prayers at Vailima" but without individual titles, in the Bibliophile Society volume, *Hitherto Unpublished Prose Writings* (1921), pp. 193-95. Both are reproduced in facsimile in the volume; both MSS are now at Yale, Beinecke 8348, 6738; and both were reprinted from the Bibliophile Society volume in the Vailima Edition. Two more prayers were published in W. H. Arnold, "My Stevensons," *Scribner's Magazine*, 71 (January 1922), 60. Another MS of these two prayers is at Yale (Beinecke 6736, 8349). Arnold's MS, part of which is given in facsimile in the text, comes from Stevenson's notebook for *Travels with a Donkey* now in the Huntington Library (HM 2408). Twenty prayers appeared collectively under the title "Prayers Written at Vailima" in the Vailima Edition, 26 (1923), 138-63. These were, in order of their appearance in this volume: the fourteen prayers first published in the Edinburgh Edition; four prayers published here for the first time; and the two prayers first published in the Bibliophile Society volume. Three of the four prayers published here for the first time—"For Continued Favours," "For Fellowship," and "For Home"—derive from untraced MSS. The fourth, which begins "Give us peace of mind in our day" and is here titled "For Mind and Body," exists in MS at Yale (Beinecke 8349) and was published from another MS by W. H. Arnold. (The other prayer published by W. H. Arnold, which begins "God who has created our honourable [?] selves," does not appear in the Vailima Edition.) Tusitala 21, which reprints the material in the Vailima Edition.

"In every Samoan household the day is closed with prayer and the singing of hymns," Stevenson's wife wrote; and once they were settled at Vailima, and probably by the summer of 1891, Stevenson and his wife adopted this custom themselves. "After all work and meals were finished," Fanny

Stevenson wrote, the conch shell was sounded, and "the white members of the family took their usual places, in one end of the large hall, while the Samoans—men, women, and children—trooped in through all the open doors . . . moving quietly and dropping with Samoan decorum in a wide semicircle on the floor." She continued: "The service began by my son [Lloyd Osbourne] reading a chapter from the Samoan Bible, Tusitala [Stevenson] following with a prayer in English, sometimes impromptu, but more often from [the MS of his prayers], interpolating, or changing with the circumstances of the day. Then came the singing of one or more hymns in the native tongue, and the recitation in concert of the Lord's Prayer, also in Samoan" (Tusitala, *21*, 1-2). She adds that the prayer "Sunday," which Stevenson wrote and offered on Sunday evening, 2 December 1894, the night before he died, was written with Graham Balfour in mind, Balfour then being away "on a perilous cruise" (*21*, 3). It was offered at Stevenson's own burial service two days later. Further on Stevenson's prayers, which he seems to have written at intervals from 1891 to 1894, see *Letters, 4*, 161, and *5*, 75, 188, and Balfour, *Life, 1*, 60, and *2*, 122.

RECORDS OF A FAMILY OF ENGINEERS. August 1891; June-August 1893 and afterwards; conceived as early as 1887-88. MSS and three galley sheets (Beinecke 695, 7627) of the 1893 setting of this work, *Northern Lights.* Huntington HM 20536 is one leaf of the MS of this work, missing from Beinecke 7663. Source materials: Silverado Museum, St. Helena, California; Monterey State Historical Monument Stevenson House Collection, California. *Records of a Family of Engineers*, Edinburgh Edition, 18 (1896), 187-389. Edited by Sidney Colvin from Stevenson's MS of the introduction and first three chapters of this work. *The Manuscripts of Robert Louis Stevenson's Records of a Family of Engineers: The Unfinished Chapters*, ed. J. Christian Bay (Chicago: Walter M. Hill, 1929). See the commentary on the MSS used for both of these editions in the Beinecke Collection catalogue, *A Stevenson Library* . . ., pp. 1942-52. Tusitala 19, which contains only the material edited by Sidney Colvin.

As early as the winter of 1887-88 Stevenson was looking forward to writing, "if ever I can find time and opportunity," a work to be called *Memorials of a Scottish Family*, and to this end he was then asking various older friends of the family to send him any letters or personal reminiscences they might have "about my grandfather, my father, and my uncles" (*Letters, 3*, 181,184, and *Baxter Letters*, p. 188). Not until August 1891, however, does he seem to have written anything himself. In early September 1891, to Sidney Colvin, Stevenson writes that "for the last month" he has been immersed in his grandfather Robert Stevenson's letters and diaries and now has "one chapter and a part drafted" of a work which he outlines in seven chapters. Uncertain just what to call it, he offers Colvin four titles, soliciting his advice: *A Scottish Family; A Family of Engineers; Northern Lights*; and *The Engineers of the Northern Lights: A Family History (Letters, 4*, 92-93). Stevenson continued research and writing for his family history at intervals during the next two years, in the summer of 1893 especially. By mid-June 1893 he had three chapters "as good as done," the work as a whole was now titled *Northern Lights: Memorials of a Family of Engineers*, and eight chapters and an introduction were planned (*Letters, 5*, 37, 41, 44). In August, having gone on to the fourth chapter, Stevenson had Graham Balfour carry the manuscript of the first three chapters of *Northern Lights* with him to London, there to have them set in type for revision and for reading by Colvin and by his father's lifelong friend Professor William Swan (1818-94) of St. Andrews University (*Letters, 5*, 70, 79; *Baxter Letters*, p. 339; galley sheets of this printing, Yale). During the winter of 1893-94 Stevenson continued work on this project, making inquiries and soliciting Colvin's views (*Letters, 5*, 87-88, 115; Beinecke 2964, 4264, 4396-97). During the summer of 1894, and even up to 1 December 1894, two days before he died, Stevenson continued his research (*Letters, 5*, 164-66, 169, 181). Surviving manuscripts indicate that he at least began actually writing chapters 4, 5, and 6, although the work remains unfinished, unrevised, and incomplete.

THE LABOUR SLAVE. Projected September 1891, apparently for a volume of realistic South Sea stories to be called *Beach de Mar*, and eventually assimilated into the novel "Sophia Scarlet" (January 1892). Chapter 4 of that novel, in Stevenson's outline, is called "The Labour Wench." See the entry of "Sophia Scarlet" below. MS untraced. Unpublished. Stevenson's only reference to this story by title is in a letter to Sidney Colvin written in early September 1891: "You will shortly make the acquaintance of the island Ulufanua, on which I mean to lay several stories; the *Bloody Wedding*, possibly the *High Woods* [i. e. "The Beach of Falesá"] . . . a political story, the *Labour Slave*, etc." (*Letters, 4*, 94). But it seems clear that it was to this story he referred in writing to Colvin on 17 May 1892 that he took up the idea of publishing "The Beach of Falesá" by itself "only . . . when the proposed volume, *Beach de Mar*, petered out. It petered out thus: the chief of the short stories got sucked into *Sophia Scarlet*—and *Sophia* is a book I am much taken with" (*Letters, 4*, 182). "The Bloody Wedding" may also have been intended for this volume; it is entered above under date of March 1891. See also the entry of "The Beach of Falesá" under date of November 1890.

Letter to THE TIMES: SAMOA. 12 and 14 October 1891. See the combined entry of all of Stevenson's letters on Samoan affairs under date of 10 February 1889, above.

[History of Scotland.] Projected November 1891 but not written. MS Huntington HM 2393, 1 leaf, folio, may be connected with this project. The text consists of three paragraphs and the beginning of a fourth and progresses quickly from the idea that tribes, civilizations, and races are everywhere "coming and going like the tides of the sea" to the observation that today "almost one half of the men now living, and rather more than one third of the whole surface of the globe, [is] under the rule of those who speak the English language." Unpublished. On 18 November 1891, discussing what he may do now that *The Wrecker* is finished, Stevenson says that he may write a history for children, in particular a history of Scotland: "Scotch is the only history I know; it is the only history reasonably represented in my library; it is a very good one for my [general] purpose, owing to two civilisations having been face to face throughout. . . . [Scott's] *Tales of a Grandfather* stand in my way . . . and yet, so far as regards teaching History, how he has missed his chances! . . . Gad, I think I'll have a flutter" (*Letters, 4*, 114; see also *4*, 117). But Stevenson soon turned to *A Footnote to History* instead. "He preferred writing a book, for boys, of Scotch history," Fanny Stevenson wrote in her journal at about this time, "but, as he has great quantities of material for the Samoan book and as it may be a help to an understanding of the situation and may save Mataafa, I begged him to do it first, though he will get much less money for it than for the other" (*Our Samoan Adventure*, ed. Neider, 1955, p. 119). Stevenson does not appear to have carried this work beyond the first few paragraphs mentioned above, if indeed these are to be associated with it.

A FOOTNOTE TO HISTORY. November 1891-May 1892; begun but laid aside, early 1890. During the cruise of the *Janet Nichol*, as he wrote in the spring of 1890, Stevenson was busy "getting events co-ordinated and the narrative distributed" for this work (*Letters, 3*, 397) but he did not turn to the actual writing until more than a year later. MS notes, chronology, lists of contents, Yale. Beinecke 6224, fifty-seven pages of notes headed "Samoa," is a continuation of Stevenson's day-to-day record of events during the cruise of the *Equator*, Huntington HM 2412, and is described above in the entry of the manuscripts of *The South Seas* (October 1889). Beinecke 2622 is a galley sheet, corrected by Stevenson, of a portion of *A Footnote to History*. Parts of other galley proofs are reproduced in facsimile in H. J. Moors, *With Stevenson in Samoa* (1910), facing p. 26. "The Hurricane: March 1889," *National Observer*, 21 May 1892, pp. 12-15; signed Robert Louis Stevenson. This separate advance publication of chap. 10 of *A Footnote to History* was set from Scribner's proofs; see *Letters, 4*, 149, *Baxter Letters*, p. 296, and Beinecke 4632. *A Footnote to History: Eight Years of Trouble in Samoa* (New York: Charles Scribner's Sons, 1892); published 8 August 1892. English edition (London: Cassell and Company, 1892) published simultaneously but apparently from Scribner's sheets. On the edition printed for Tauchnitz and Company but suppressed by the German government see the discussion in the Beinecke Collection catalogue, *A Stevenson Library . . .*, pp. 254-55. Tusitala 21.

Stevenson's original plan for *The South Seas* was to include a number of chapters on Samoa among the rest (*Letters, 3*, 273-75), but he soon found that he had enough material on Samoa for a separate book. "I shall begin, I think, with a separate opuscule on the Samoan Trouble," he wrote to Charles Baxter on 28 December 1889 (*Letters, 3,* 279). And in February 1890, less than three months after he had first arrived in Samoa, Stevenson announced to E. L. Burlingame of Charles Scribner's Sons his intention "to write almost at once and publish shortly a small volume called I know not what" on recent Samoan affairs. He hoped it could be sold, but even if not Stevenson was willing to publish it at his own expense (*Letters, 3,* 288). Stevenson drafted three chapters in 1890, but other projects intervened and he laid the work aside for more than a year, until November 1891, when *The Wrecker* was finished. As has been detailed in the previous entry, Stevenson's first inclination was to write a history of Scotland for boys, but at his wife's urging he turned to Samoan affairs instead. By 7 December, as he wrote to Sidney Colvin, Stevenson had finished the first five chapters, "fifty-nine pages in one month; which (you will allow me to say) is a devil of a large order" (*Letters, 4,* 123). By 2 January 1892 he had finished three more chapters, ninety-one pages, and was hoping to finish the whole, adding four chapters to the eight already written, by the end of the month (*Letters, 4,* 136-37, 143). Chapters 9 and 10 were finished by the end of March, proofs of the earlier chapters having been sent to Stevenson in the meantime; chapter 11, the last, was chiefly written during the second and third weeks in May and finished on 26 May. Fanny Stevenson wrote in her journal on 17 May: "Louis . . . [has] just finished his Samoan history" (*Our Samoan Adventure*, ed. Neider, 1955, p. 163). The work itself is dated at the end 25 May 1892. And on 27 May Stevenson wrote to Sidney Colvin: "I was all forenoon yesterday down in Apia, dictating, and Lloyd typewriting, the conclusion of *Samoa*; then at home correcting till the dinner bell; and then in the evening again till eleven of the clock" (*Letters, 4,* 187).

Charles Scribner acknowledged as received on 16 June 1892 "the entire Samoa book, both corrected proofs and additional manuscript" (Beinecke 5455; see also *Letters, 4,* 168-69, 181, 187, and Beinecke 4147-49); and on 8 August the book was published. Meanwhile, on 27 July 1892 Cassell and Company wrote to Charles Baxter confirming their agreement with him on 23 July that they would have sole British Empire rights to *A Footnote to History* for a royalty to Stevenson of 15 percent on the retail price (Society of Authors Archive, British Museum, MS. Add. 56638, f. 16).

"Speed was essential," Stevenson wrote in the preface of *A Footnote to History*, "or it might come too late to be of any service to a distracted country" (*21*, 69; see also *Letters, 4,* 125-26). So he was understandably upset when copies had still not arrived in Samoa even two months after publication. According to H. J. Moors, *With Stevenson in Samoa* (1910), pp. 136-37, the first copy of *A Footnote to History* to arrive in Samoa was, ironically, the Rev. Arthur E. Claxton's—brought back from England in October, Claxton having had to appear there before his superiors in the London Missionary Society. Stevenson wrote to Lady Jersey on 8 October 1892 that Claxton had returned, "and I am sorry to say that he has returned in a belligerent humour and has begun proceedings against me for libel" (NLS typescript 9891, f. 29). When copies of *A Footnote to History* finally did arrive for Stevenson in late November, he was amused that they had been delivered by mistake to the German consulate, and disappointed that, to judge by the notices he had seen, it was being taken "as a pamphlet against Germany" (Stevenson to Lady Jersey, 1 December 1892; NLS typescript 9891, f. 35). Further on the despatch of copies to Samoa see *Letters, 4*, 275-76, and Beinecke 2952-54, 5385, and 6231. Henry Bellyse Baildon, who was then living in Germany, comments on the book's initial reception there in his *Robert Louis Stevenson: A Life Study in Criticism* (1901), pp. 4-5.

[Preface for Burns exhibition catalogue.] In prospect November 1891 but never written. See *Letters, 4*, 67-69, 85-86, 114-15, and Beinecke 3903. W. Crabie Angus, who was then organizing an exhibition of works by Robert Burns in Glasgow, wrote to Stevenson in the spring of 1891 asking that he autograph a copy of *The Jolly Beggars* for the exhibition. Stevenson's interest proved keener than had been anticipated, and by November he was "expecting the sheets of your catalogue, so that I may attack the preface" (*Letters, 4*, 115). Angus seems to have sent these on 20 October 1891 (Beinecke 3903), but Stevenson does not seem ever to have written the intended preface. Sold as Anderson 1914, I, 197, was a copy of R. B. Burns, *Isobel Burns (Mrs. Begg): A Memoir by her Grandson* (Glasgow: privately printed, 1891), inscribed to Stevenson by Angus on 22 June 1891.

ACROSS THE PLAINS. Collected late 1891; published 6 April 1892. Corrected page proof, Yale. Twelve essays, all but three published in *Scribner's Magazine* in 1888 and the others—"Across the Plains," "The Old Pacific Capital," and "Fontainebleau"—published elsewhere during the early 1880s. *Across the Plains With Other Memories and Essays* (London: Chatto and Windus, 1892); published 6 April 1892. American edition (New York: Charles Scribner's Sons, 1892) published simultaneously but from Chatto and Windus sheets. Tusitala 18, 25, 28, 30.

Sidney Colvin originated the idea of publishing another collection of Stevenson's essays and proposed it to him during the late summer of 1891. "I do not feel inclined to make a volume of Essays," Stevenson replied in September, "but if I did, and perhaps the idea is good . . . here would be my choice of the *Scribner* articles: *Dreams, Beggars, Lantern-Bearers, Random Memories*." He also suggests including the three essays published elsewhere, but not "Pulvis et Umbra." That essay, he writes, "is in a different key, and wouldn't hang on the rest" (*Letters, 4*, 95). In late November, having received Colvin's proposed table of contents, Stevenson wrote at some length about the collection. "I must say I like your order," he remarked, presumably referring to Colvin's presentation of travel, reminiscence, and then philosophic reflection; and he asked Colvin to take entire charge of production. "I shall return . . . the sheets corrected as far as I have them; the rest I will leave, if you will, to you entirely; let it be your book, and disclaim what you like in the preface" (*Letters, 4*, 120).

On 19 January 1892 Charles Baxter, acting for Stevenson, executed a contract with Chatto and Windus for *Across the Plains*, providing Stevenson royalties of one-sixth of the retail price of both the six-shilling and large-paper editions. On 27 February 1892, it was further agreed with the firm of Tauchnitz that Stevenson would receive forty pounds for the Continental reprint rights to each of his books as it appeared, beginning with *Across the Plains*. Until then, each volume had been sold individually for twenty pounds. (Society of Authors Archive, British Museum, MS. Add. 56638, ff. 36, 55.) On 11 April 1892, forty pounds was paid to Stevenson's account with Mitchell and Baxter by the firm of Tauchnitz in fulfillment of this agreement for *Across the Plains* (Beinecke 7268).

Sidney Colvin had finished reading the proofs of *Across the Plains* on 12 February 1892 (Beinecke 4214), and on 8 March Chatto and Windus sent 1,250 of the 4,000 copies printed for binding. The book was published on 6 April 1892, and in June Stevenson wrote to Colvin expressing his pleasure with it. "I don't know if I remembered to say how pleased I was with *Across the Plains* in every way, inside and out, and you and me," he wrote. "The critics seem to taste it, too, as well as could be hoped, and I believe it will continue to bring me a few shillings a year for awhile" (*Letters, 4*, 202).

1892

SOPHIA SCARLET. Planned January 1892. MS outline, Free Library of Philadelphia. Unpublished. On 1 February 1892 Stevenson wrote to Sidney Colvin that he had a new novel, *Sophia Scarlet*, "entirely planned." It was to be set in the present day, divided into two parts called "The Vanilla Planter" and "The Overseers," and (Stevenson wrote) was to be, "I blush to own it . . . a *regular novel;* heroine and hero, and false accusation, and love, and marriage, and all the rest of it—all planted in a big South Sea plantation run by ex-English officers" (*Letters, 4*, 149-50; see also *4*, 168, 182, and Beinecke 8311). Stevenson does not seem to have carried this novel much beyond the planning stage, although he does seem to have planned to take it up again in late 1894. His wife wrote: "He told me, shortly before his death, that he meant to rest from both [*St. Ives* and *Weir of Hermiston*] very soon, and begin something entirely different. The new book was to be called *Sophia Scarlet*, with all the principal characters women. The most important male character, an invalid with whom Sophia Scarlet fell in love, would die in an early chapter. 'There was a time,' he said, 'when I didn't dare to really draw a woman; but I have no fear now. I shall show a little of what I can do in the two Kirstys; but in *Sophia Scarlet* the main interest shall be centred in the women.' He did not tell me the plan of the story any further than that it was to be laid in Tahiti, Sophia Scarlet owning a large plantation, which she managed herself!" (Tusitala, *15*, xi-xii).

Stevenson's outline, fifteen folio pages chiefly in the hand of Isobel Strong to whom it was dictated, appears to be all that survives of "Sophia Scarlet." It contains a fairly detailed summary of each of the first ten chapters of the first part of this work and is headed "The Plantation," this apparently then being Stevenson's title of the first part. (It is not identified as an outline of "Sophia Scarlet," this obviously being assumed.) The tenth chapter is untitled. The others are: I. The Labour Ship; II. Dan Scarlett; III. The Three Miss Scarletts; IV. The Labour Wench; V. The Vanilla Planter; VI. An Adventure in the Bush; VII. The Over-seer's Table; VIII. The Verandah and the Garden; IX. Opinions of Major Rainsforth (MS pp. 1-14). The fourth chapter, "The Labour Wench," probably derives from the story Stevenson began as "The Labour Slave" and intended for a volume to be called *Beach de Mar*. See the entry for "The Labour Slave" above under date of September 1891.

The last page of the outline is in Stevenson's hand and contains slightly more than one hundred words of actual text for the novel and then breaks off. It is headed "Part I.—The Vanilla Planter" and begins straightaway with the text: "Dan Scarlet [*sic*], formerly of the dragoons, and perhaps the most popular white man in the South Pacific, had three daughters what is (I believe) called finishing in England" (MS p. 15).

TWO TAHITIAN LEGENDS. Early 1892, published March. MS untraced. "Two Tahitian Legends. I. Of the Making of Pai's Spear. . . . II. Honoura and the Weird Women." *Longman's Magazine*, 19 (March 1892), 568-72; signed Robert Louis Stevenson. Unpublished since its original appearance. Stevenson took an active interest in Andrew Lang's speculations on folklore, especially as pursued in the "Sign of the Ship" section of *Longman's Magazine*. This is one contribution he made himself. See also Lang to Stevenson, Beinecke 5102-4, and *Letters, 3*, 310-11.

DAVID BALFOUR. 13 February-30 September 1892. MSS: Yale (intermediate version; parts of earlier and later versions, including several versions of a number of passages); Widener Collection, Harvard University (final MS version); Huntington HM 2461, 2415 (fragment of chap. 13, draft outline of contents). Lloyd Osbourne, 1914, 568, 579-81 (twelve pages early or intermediate draft of chaps. 22-23, other fragments and outlines): probably some or all of these materials have been absorbed into the MS holdings already listed. Stevenson's intermediate MS (Yale) corresponds in pagination to his reports of progress in March 1892 and later; his final MS (Harvard) is the version he began copying from the intermediate MS in June 1892 and corresponds to the reports of the material he sent to Charles Baxter for publication, August-October 1892. Both are titled *David Balfour*, both have the text of whole novel except for some gaps where pages are missing; the novel was further revised in proof, April-June 1893. "David Balfour: Memoirs of his Adventures at Home and Abroad," *Atalanta*, 6, ten monthly installments, December 1892-September 1893; each installment signed Robert Louis Stevenson. Serialized also in *News of the World* and the *Weekly Telegraph*, and possibly other newspapers, in 1893. *Catriona: A*

Sequel to "Kidnapped" Being Memoirs of the Further Adventures of David Balfour at Home and Abroad . . . (London: Cassell and Company, 1893); published 1 September 1893. See the discussion below on this change of title for the English book-form edition. American edition (New York: Charles Scribner's Sons, 1893) published simultaneously but from Cassell's sheets; titled *David Balfour: Being Memoirs of his Adventures at Home and Abroad* . . . . Tusitala 7.

Writing *Kidnapped* in 1886, Stevenson realized that he wished to and could carry David Balfour's adventures well beyond David's return to Edinburgh; and by late May 1886 he had accepted Sidney Colvin's suggestion to conclude the novel in Edinburgh but leave room for a sequel. On 23 May 1887 Stevenson agreed with Cassell and Company to write and deliver to them "as early as possible" a volume of about the same length as *Kidnapped*, to be called *David Balfour*, "or some similar title." Cassell would have sole volume rights in the United Kingdom and agreed to pay a royalty of 15 percent on the retail price reckoning thirteen copies as twelve, against which £150 was to be paid when the proofs were passed for the press. Stevenson retained the American rights and was to receive half the proceeds of translation. (Society of Authors Archive, British Museum, MS. Add. 56638, f. 7.) On 1 November 1887, Stevenson promised the serial rights to S. S. McClure, a promise which resulted in fairly acrimonious negotiations during the summer of 1892 when the novel was at last ready. See the discussion below.

In September 1890 Stevenson remarked that he had "one chapter of *David Balfour* written" and that the manuscript was surely somewhere, "likely New York" (*Letters, 3*, 312). When he again took up the idea of writing a sequel to *Kidnapped* more than a year later, in October 1891, he may have found this manuscript or had it sent to him. But there is no evidence that he did, or that, except to outline it, Stevenson worked on the novel at all between finishing *The Wrecker* in October 1891—when he wrote to Henry James that *"David Balfour*, second part of *Kidnapped*, is on the stocks at last" (*Letters, 4*, 105)—and when he actually began writing *David Balfour* on 13 February 1892. Stevenson was chiefly busy writing *A Footnote to History* during late 1891 and early 1892; and as he wrote to Sidney Colvin afterwards, he simply "slid off into *David Balfour*" in February when he found the history hard to continue (*Letters, 4*, 154).

Once begun, the first half of *David Balfour* was written quickly. "I began it on the 13th of last month," Stevenson wrote on 9 March 1892 having completed twelve chapters, and on 12 March he added: "I have this day triumphantly completed 15 chapters, 100 pages—being exactly one-half (as nearly as anybody can guess) of *David Balfour*" (*Letters, 4*, 162-63). Proofs of the opening chapters of *A Footnote to History* arrived in mid-March, however, and Stevenson left *David Balfour* aside to write two more chapters of the history and correct the proofs. He did work on the novel at intervals during April and May, but not until the very end of May, when he wrote and sent off the last chapter of *A Footnote to History*, was Stevenson again able to give *David Balfour* much concentrated attention.

In late June, having added during that month five or six chapters to the 15 already written, Stevenson started recopying *David Balfour* for publication, revising as he went; and after another month he was hoping to send Charles Baxter "the whole first part (a good deal more than half) of *David Balfour* ready for the press"—as he did on 12 August 1892 (*Letters, 4*, 195-96, 205, 218, 220; *Baxter Letters*, p. 301). In late August, Lady Jersey's visit delayed Stevenson's progress again; but he was able to send Baxter six more chapters on 12 September and, with considerable effort, to finish the novel on 30 September and send copy for the printers to Baxter on 12 October (*Baxter Letters*, pp. 310, 304-5, 316, and 308n.8). As Graham Balfour writes: "In spite of endless interruptions it was actually finished by the end of September. It was the first of his works that was completed while I was at Vailima, and I well remember the agitation and stress with which it was brought to a close" (*Life, 2*, 140). "*David Balfour* done," Stevenson himself wrote on 30 September, "and its author along with it, or nearly so" (*Letters, 4*, 244). Altogether the writing had taken a little more than seven and one-half months.

On 15 November 1892 Charles Baxter wrote to Stevenson that "the whole of *David Balfour* is safely in Cassell's hands" and that after much trouble he had obtained £1,600 from Robert McClure in London for the serial rights (*Baxter Letters,* p. 308n.8). In this arrangement Stevenson was honoring a promise he had made to S. S. McClure in New York five years before, on 1 November 1887: "The next story I finish of the same character as Kidnapped, I shall place in your hands" (Beinecke 3186). And the McClures were honoring S. S. McClure's original offer of $8,000 (£1,600). Cassell and Company was already setting the early chapters in type for book-form publication when, on 5 October 1892, Baxter finally reached agreement with Robert McClure on the serial rights. For these rights in all countries McClure agreed to pay £1,600 altogether: £700 on or before 10 October 1892; £450 on 28 February 1893; and £450 on 30 May 1893. McClure was to provide security for the £900 balance due and Baxter was to send him the manuscript forthwith. (Society of Authors Archive, British Museum, MS. Add. 56638, f. 67; see also Beinecke 5178 and 5204.) Although £2,000 is listed as income on *David Balfour* in the general summary in the Mitchell and Baxter account books, only £1,535 of this is listed as paid to Stevenson's account by the McClures: £700 on 11 October 1892, £400 on 2 March, and £435 on 27 March 1893 (Beinecke 7268). Charles Scribner's Sons offered £600 for the American book-form rights and eventually agreed to pay £1,200 (Beinecke 3499, 5457).

On 11 October 1892, Robert McClure complained that the printed copy he was receiving from Cassell and Company was full of errors. So on 18 October Charles Baxter replied that he had instructed Cassell and Company to send the manuscript along with the proofs in future (Beinecke 5173, 3981). Production difficulties continued, however. Sidney Colvin remarked on 13 February 1893 that "flagrant disfigurements" were appearing in the text then being serialized in *Atalanta* from copy supplied by Robert McClure (Beinecke 4235). And in May and June 1893 Cassell and Company protested that the newspaper syndications arranged by McClure would surely harm their sales (see Beinecke 4500, 5175, 4501, 4498).

Stevenson's own proofs did not reach him until April 1893, and, busy then with *The Ebb-Tide*, he did not finish with them until mid-June (*Letters, 5*, 17-21, 38). Even at that, Stevenson had not been able to revise as much as he had wanted; and Sidney Colvin, who in May had refused Cassell and Company's request to correct the remaining proofs himself to expedite publication before the serial versions came to an end, found himself equally disappointed that there were not more revisions when he received the proofs from Stevenson on 21 July (Beinecke 4256, 4247). Despite all this, however, Stevenson seems never to have varied from the high estimate of the work he offered to Sidney Colvin the day he finished it. *David Balfour* and "The Beach of Falesá," Stevenson wrote, "seem to me to be nearer what I mean than anything I have ever done: nearer what I mean by fiction; the nearest thing before was *Kidnapped*." "I am sometimes tempted to think it my best work," he wrote to George Meredith a year later. "I shall never do a better book," he wrote to Mrs. Sitwell in April 1894, calling it "my high-water mark" (*Letters, 4*, 244, *5*, 75, 125; see also Mrs. Sitwell's reply, Beinecke 5529, and Stevenson to Ethel Storrs, 26 February 1894, Beinecke 3572).

Throughout its composition Stevenson referred to this work as *David Balfour*, the title which it bears in the manuscript and serial versions and in the American editions. But in England, as Stevenson's wife remarked, during the serial publication of the novel "it was found that many English people were confused . . . thinking that, as *Kidnapped* was the story of *David Balfour*, there must be only one book with a double title" (Tusitala, *7*, xv). Therefore Cassell and Company proposed that the book appear in volume form initially under the title *Catriona*, without illustrations, and that a two-volume illustrated edition of both *Kidnapped* and its sequel appear some time later as *The Adventures of David Balfour*. Stevenson accepted this proposal in January 1893, "as an amendent to one of mine" he wrote to Sidney Colvin; and after *David Balfour* was published he sent a corrected copy of *Kidnapped* back to England for this purpose (*Letters, 5*, 4, 95-96). This edition did not appear until after Stevenson's death. In his outline of contents for the Edinburgh Edition, Stevenson listed as the last two volumes of "Romances" *David Balfour*, vols. I and II (*Baxter Letters*, p. 343); and although not so presented on the title pages, *Kidnapped* and its sequel were designated on the spines of the volumes of the Edinburgh Edition which contained them as being the two parts of "The Adventures of David Balfour." Meanwhile, Cassell and Company in 1895 brought out a two-volume edition called on the title pages and half-titles (although not on the spines) "THE ADVENTURES OF DAVID BALFOUR," of which *Kidnapped* was "PART ONE" and *Catriona* was "PART TWO." For this edition *Kidnapped* was reset; earlier Cassell and Company editions of *Kidnapped* have 311 pp. of text, the 1895 edition has 319 pp. *Catriona* was not reset, copies of that novel in this two-volume edition being simply reprinted from the first edition of 1893. Both volumes have new title pages, however, both headed "THE ADVENTURES OF DAVID BALFOUR," followed by a rule, followed respectively by *Kidnapped* or *Catriona*, and ultimately by the date 1895. Beinecke 592 is a later printing of this edition of *Catriona*, dated 1898.

American editions of the sequel have always been called *David Balfour*, Stevenson's own title, because Charles Scribner preferred this original title and sought and gained permission to keep it in the American edition. See the correspondence, Beinecke 5457, 4249.

THE YOUNG CHEVALIER. Planned January-March 1892; begun May 1892. MSS: Yale (uncatalogued; 18 leaves, folio, sold originally as Anderson 1914, I, 322); untraced (13 leaves, quarto, Anderson 1914, I, 320). MS fragments, source materials, notes: Yale, Princeton University Library. Edinburgh Edition, 26 (1897), 63-83. Tusitala 16.

On the composition of "The Young Chevalier," intended as a full-length novel but completed only to the extent of the prologue and part of the first chapter, see especially Andrew Lang's comments quoted in Sidney Colvin's "Editorial Note" to this work (Tusitala, *16*, 184-86); Andrew Lang's letters to Stevenson about it (Beinecke 5084-5127); and *Letters, 4*, 137, 167-68, 184, 257. Late in 1891 Andrew Lang suggested to Stevenson that a story might be made from the tales of Prince Charles Edward Stewart's "secret adventures" in France and elsewhere after his official expulsion from France in December 1748. Lang had a copy made of the Jacobite pamphlet, *A Letter from H —— G ——, Esq.; One of the Gentlemen of the Bedchamber to the Young Chevalier* . . . (London, 1750), and sent this copy (Beinecke 7230; see also Beinecke 7385) to Stevenson with his own suggestions for the story. "My idea was to make the narrator a young Scottish Jacobite at Avignon," Lang wrote. "He was to be sent by Charles to seek an actual hidden treasure—the fatal gold of the hoard buried at Loch Arkaig a few days after Culloden. He was to be a lover of Miss Clementina Walkinshaw, who later played the part of Beatrix Esmond to the Prince" (Tusitala, *16*, 185-86). Stevenson found this, as he wrote to Sidney Colvin on 3 January 1892, a "most gallant suggestion," and by late March 1892 he had his own version of the story, then to be called *Dyce of Ythan*, "quite planned" (*Letters, 4*, 137, 167-68). In mid-May, taking a brief "holiday" from *A Footnote to History*, which he was then finishing, Stevenson wrote all that now survives of this work, remarking on 19 May 1892 that "the first prolingual episode is done" and outlining the whole story in detail (*Letters, 4*, 184-86). On 1 November 1892 Stevenson was still planning to continue this work, but as he noted on that date to J. M. Barrie he had just begun yet another Scottish story, the novel which became *Weir of Hermiston* (*Letters, 4*, 257). This novel and other projects soon engaged Stevenson's whole attention and he never again took up this work.

Letter to THE TIMES: THE LATEST DIFFICULTY IN SAMOA. 9 and 12 April 1892. See the combined entry for all of Stevenson's letters on Samoan affairs under date of 10 February 1889, above.

EATUINA. Summer 1892. MS, Yale (Beinecke 6662). 4 pages, folio, titled "O le Tala i a Eatuina o Teira." Unpublished. Written in Samoan as an exercise in learning the language, this story is mentioned briefly in Balfour, *Life, 2*, 130: "over the study of Samoan he [Stevenson] spent a good deal of pains, even taking lessons from the Rev. S. J. Whitmee of the London Mission, the best Samoan scholar in the islands. . . . Stevenson himself began as an exercise with his teacher to write in Samoan a story of Saxon times called *Eatuina* (Edwin), but only a few chapters were completed." Stevenson "wished to write a story in Samoan for the natives," Whitmee himself recalled, "and I suggested that he should bring a portion of his MS. for me to read aloud and criticise. This exactly suited him. Those points in grammar and idiom, also the appropriateness of words, about which he was almost fastidious, could be discussed. I found him to be a keen student; and the peculiarities and niceties of the language greatly interested him" (in Masson, ed., *I Can Remember Robert Louis Stevenson,* 1922, p. 232). Stevenson mentions his lessons with Whitmee, although not this story, in a letter to Sidney Colvin, 7 June 1892 (*Letters, 4,* 197). Various of Stevenson's exercises in learning Samoan are now held as Beinecke 6663, 6668 (4 notebook leaves), 6514, 6885, 5967, 6959, 6887, 6983 (1 folio folder), and 6485 (2 folio leaves, obviously once a folder identical with the preceding). All bear annotations and corrections in another hand than Stevenson's, probably Whitmee's. See also the entries of "The Bottle Imp" (December 1889) and "Talofa, Togarewa!" (summer 1891).

Letter to THE TIMES: SAMOA. 22 June 1892. See the combined entry for all of Stevenson's letters on Samoan affairs under date of 10 February 1889, above.

Letter to THE TIMES: MR. STEVENSON AND SAMOA. 19 July 1892. See the combined entry for all of Stevenson's letters on Samoan affairs under date of 10 February 1889, above.

SCOTT'S VOYAGE ON THE LIGHTHOUSE YACHT: NOTE. Dated 31 July 1892. MS untraced. *Scribner's Magazine*, 14 (October 1893), 492-94; signed Robert Louis Stevenson. Unpublished since its original appearance. On 11 September 1891 E. L. Burlingame accepted Stevenson's proposal, made in late summer, to publish his grandfather Robert Stevenson's reminiscences of Sir Walter Scott's tour of northern lighthouses in Scott's capacity as sheriff of Selkirk three weeks after the anonymous publication of *Waverley* in July 1814. "They are not remarkably good," Stevenson wrote, "but he [Robert Stevenson] was not a bad observer, and several touches seem to me speaking." Stevenson was then just beginning work on *Records of a Family of Engineers* but felt that this material might be "particularly suited for prior appearance in a magazine." He offers to condense his grandfather's manuscript and asks also: "Would you like me to introduce the old gentleman? I had something of the sort in my mind, and could fill a few columns rather *à propos*." Burlingame asked him to do so; Stevenson sent the finished manuscript with his "Note" on 1 August 1892; and Burlingame acknowledged receipt of it, remarking that it was "excellent," on 6 October 1892. See *Letters, 4,* 84-85, 107, and Beinecke 4414, 2950, and 4151. Stevenson's grandfather's essay is titled "Reminiscences of Sir Walter Scott, Baronet," and appears on pp. 494-502 following Stevenson's introductory note. Scott's own lengthy journal of the voyage appears in J. G. Lockhart, *Memoirs of Sir Walter Scott* (1837; London: Macmillan, 1900), *2*, 338-463.

AN OBJECT OF PITY. Late August 1892. MSS untraced. *An Object of Pity; or, The Man Haggard. A Romance. By Many Competent Hands.* "Imprinted at Amsterdam." Sydney, October 1892. Beinecke 853 is a copy of this edition inscribed by Lady Jersey with marginal annotations by Lloyd Osbourne identifying the six contributors and explaining their pseudonyms; see the Beinecke Collection catalogue, *A Stevenson Library* . . . , pp. 435-36. Another copy of this edition inscribed by Lady Jersey and more copiously annotated is in the Princeton University Library. Privately printed, Edinburgh, November 1898: an edition of 25 copies uniform with the Edinburgh Edition. Published in an edition of 110 copies (New York: Dodd, Mead and Company, 1900). Except in these limited editions and in vol. 7 of the variously titled edition, *The Works of Robert Louis Stevenson*, ed. C. C. Bigelow and Temple Scott, 10 vols. (New York: Lamb Publishing Company, 1906), this work is unpublished.

On the composition and printing of *An Object of Pity* see *Letters, 4*, 223, 229, Beinecke 5002, Lady Jersey's introductions in the 1898 and 1900 editions, and especially her *Fifty-One Years of Victorian Life* (1922), pp. 294-95, 313-16. Lord Jersey took up his duties as the governor of New South Wales in January 1891; and for three weeks at the end of August and in early September of the following year, 1892, his wife, her brother Rupert Leigh, and their daughter Margaret visited the British Land Commissioner at Samoa, Bazett M. Haggard. The evening after their arrival, Haggard held a dinner for them and the Stevensons, and it was at this dinner, 13 August 1892, that *An Object of Pity* was conceived. "At that dinner, which inaugurated our friendship," Lady Jersey wrote, "a very merry talk somehow turned on publishers and publishing." Shortly "it was suggested by someone, and carried unanimously, that we should form an 'Apia Publishing Company'; and later on in Haggard's absence the rest of us determined to write a story of which our host should be hero, and the name, suggested, I think, by Stevenson, was to be *An Object of Pity, or the Man Haggard*" (*Fifty-One Years of Victorian Life*, p. 295).

"The idea was that each author should describe his or her own character," Lady Jersey continued, "that Haggard should be the hero of a romance running through the whole, and that we should all imitate the style of Ouida, to whom the booklet was inscribed in a delightful dedication afterwards written by Stevenson" (pp. 313-14). The work was finished by the end of the month, the several authors being Stevenson, his wife, Isobel Strong, Graham Balfour, Lady Jersey, and her brother Rupert Leigh. The Stevensons gave a native banquet at Vailima on Sunday 28 August 1892; and when the banquet was over, wrote Lady Jersey, "a garland of flowers was hung round Haggard's neck, a tankard of ale was placed before him, and Stevenson read aloud the MSS. replete with allusions to, and jokes about, his various innocent idiosyncrasies. So far from being annoyed, the good-natured hero was quite delighted, and kept on saying, 'What a compliment all you people are paying me!' In the end we posed as a group, Mrs. Strong lying on the ground and holding up an apple while the rest of us knelt or bent in various attitudes of adoration round the erect form and smiling countenance of Haggard" (p. 315). Haggard returned the compliment in a volume of his own, *Objects of Pity; or, Self and Company. By a Gentleman of Quality.* "Imprinted at Amsterdam." Sydney, 1892. Haggard's own copy of this work, with a number of autograph corrections by him, and his copies of *An Object of Pity,* one with detailed annotations by him, were sold at Sotheby's, 16 December 1977, items 394-97.

Letter to THE TIMES: MR. STEVENSON AND SAMOA. 14 September 1892. See the combined entry for all of Stevenson's letters on Samoan affairs under date of 10 February 1889, above.

PLAIN JOHN WILTSHIRE ON THE SITUATION. Late summer or autumn 1892. MS, Anderson 1914, I, 518 (original), 519 (carbon copy): original untraced; carbon copy, Huntington HM 2409, 10-page typescript by Lloyd Osbourne marked by him as "By R.L.S. " at the top of the first page. Unpublished. This letter, written in the person and voice of the main character in "The Beach of Falesá" (1892), is addressed to the editor of the *National Observer* and is a point by point attack on *A Regulation . . . for the Maintenance of Peace and Good Order in the Pacific* (Suva, 1892) issued by the British High Commissioner for the Western Pacific, Sir John Bates Thurston, on 1 July 1892. "I used to be proud to be a British Subject," John Wiltshire writes. "Well, it's changed times now in Apia! A yellow dog would be ashamed to be a British subject here." Thurston's regulation, he writes, plainly has put an end to freedom of the press, made it dangerous for any British subject to open his mouth on any political subject in Samoa, and, most of all, seems expressly and simply aimed at a certain R. L. Stevenson. Thurston's regulation is quoted in H. J. Moors, *With Stevenson in Samoa* (1910), p. 117, together with much information about the reaction to it in Samoa and quotations from an interview with Stevenson in the New Zealand *Herald* early in 1893 (pp. 116-27).

[Definition of good literature.] Autumn 1892. MS, NLS 9892, f. 12. Unpublished. In a one-page outline to which Graham Balfour has given this title

Stevenson wrote a word or two under the several headings of order, material pattern, adornment of images, and manner of treating a subject. Below Stevenson's notes Balfour wrote: "These holograph notes were written down probably in the autumn of 92, and were brought home by me among some waste paper in Sept '93." Possibly Stevenson planned to write an essay on this subject.

WEIR OF HERMISTON. October 1892-December 1894. MSS: Pierpont Morgan Library (early version); Yale (published later version); MS fragments, source books, notes: Yale; Princeton University Library; Silverado Museum, St. Helena, California; Monterey State Historical Monument Stevenson House Collection, California. On these MSS see Vivian S. Jokl, "The Central Themes and Structure of Stevenson's *Weir of Hermiston*, Based on a Study of the Extant Manuscripts" (Ph.D. dissertation, Vanderbilt Univ., 1974; *DA, 35,* 1975, 7868A). *Cosmopolis,* 1, four monthly installments in the first four issues of this magazine, January-April 1896; each installment signed Robert Louis Stevenson. Sidney Colvin prepared the text for this publication from the later of Stevenson's two MSS (Yale), following it more or less completely and correctly. In the Edinburgh Edition, 26 (1897), 123-291, he corrected a few errors in the earlier version, but a few still remain. See the remarks by M.R. Ridley, *TLS*, 28 August 1959, p. 495, and by Ridley and others in continuation on 11 September (p. 519), 16 October (p. 593), and 23 October (p. 609). Copyright issue (Chicago: Stone and Kimball, 1896), three parts, received for American copyright on 4 January, 6 February, and 6 March 1896. Chicago *Tribune,* eight daily installments, 5-12 April 1896; each installment signed Robert Louis Stevenson. *Weir of Hermiston: An Unfinished Romance* (London: Chatto and Windus, 1896); published 20 May 1896. American edition (New York: Charles Scribner's Sons, 1896) published simultaneously. Three drafts of the very beginning of this novel (MSS, Princeton) are published together with the final version in Balfour, *Life, 2*, 207-10. Tusitala 16.

Stevenson began *Weir of Hermiston* in October 1892, on 28 October outlining the novel more or less fully in a letter to Sidney Colvin and proposing various titles for it (*Letters, 4*, 253-54). In January 1893 he wrote that "with incredible labour, I have rewritten the first Chapter of the *Justice-Clerk;* it took me about ten days, and requires another athletic dressing after all" (*Letters, 5*, 5). Other projects intervened, however, notably *St. Ives* and correcting proofs of *David Balfour*, and though he worked on the novel from time to time during the rest of 1893, and Colvin and Baxter were negotiating serial publication as early as March 1893, Stevenson did not return to *Weir of Hermiston* intensively until early the next year. See *Letters, 5*, 16, 28-29, 70, and Beinecke 4235-36, 4240, 4498-99.

On 6 February 1894 Isobel Strong recorded in her journal, "Louis and I spent a long and busy day over Hermiston; we've been working at it, already, several days" ("Vailima Table-Talk," *Memories of Vailima*, 1902, p. 67). But once more Stevenson left the novel aside, working on *St. Ives* instead during the spring and summer of 1894, and it was not until September 1894, when he felt that further progress on *St. Ives* was for the moment impossible, that Stevenson again took up *Weir of Hermiston.* (This was the title Sidney Colvin preferred. Stevenson usually called the novel *The Justice-Clerk*, although he did find Colvin's suggestion acceptable. See *Letters, 5*, 16.) On 24 September 1894 Isobel Strong wrote that "Louis and I have been writing, working away like steam-engines on *Hermiston*," and she describes the ease with which Stevenson was then dictating it, working from notes made each morning (pp. 96-98). On 30 November 1894, less than a week before Stevenson died, she remarked that they were "pegging away at *Hermiston* like one o'clock. I hardly drew breath, but flew over the paper; Louis thinks it is good himself; so we were in a very cheerful humour" (p. 99). "He wrote hard all that morning of the last day," Lloyd Osbourne wrote of the day Stevenson died, 3 December 1894; "his half-finished book, *Hermiston,* he judged the best he had ever written, and the sense of successful effort made him buoyant and happy as nothing else could" (*Letters, 5*, 185).

Charles Baxter, already on his way to visit Stevenson when news came of his death, brought the unfinished manuscript back to England with him in 1895. On 5 July 1895 Henry James, having read it, urged immediate publication (Beinecke 4910; quoted in E. V. Lucas, *The Colvins and Their Friends*, 1928, pp. 248-50). Colvin had a typescript ready by November 1895, sending it for comments to W. E. Henley and James M. Barrie among others (see their letters in Lucas, pp. 244-48), and the unfinished novel was published in the first four numbers of the new magazine *Cosmopolis*, January-April 1896.

In his "Editorial Note" to *Weir of Hermiston* (Tusitala, *16*, 124-36), besides providing a full account of the work's sources and compostiion, Sidney Colvin sketches the probable conclusion of the novel "so far as it was known at the time of the writer's death to his step-daughter and devoted amanuensis, Mrs. Strong." To this account should be added the Rev. Sidney R. Lysaght's recollection of visiting Stevenson and talking about the novel in Samoa in 1894, "A Visit to Robert Louis Stevenson," *TLS*, 4 December 1919, pp. 713-14 (rpt. in Masson, ed., *I Can Remember Robert Louis Stevenson*, 1922, pp. 257-67). Stevenson's plan differed somewhat from the plan recalled by Isobel Strong, Lysaght wrote: "The strongest scene in the book, he [Stevenson] said—the strongest scene he had ever conceived or would ever write—was one in which the younger Kirstie came to her lover when he was in prison and confessed to him that she was with child by the man he had murdered. His eyes flashed with emotion as he spoke about it, and I cannot think that he had abandoned this climax. It is a climax, too, which would seem to be much more in harmony with the genius and conception of the story and characters than the ending sketched in the notes, which was no doubt an alternative with which he coquetted" (p. 713).

THE ISLE OF VOICES. Autumn 1892, possibly earlier. MS, Anderson 1914, I, 377: 17 pages, folio. *National Observer*, four weekly installments, 4-25

February 1893; each installment signed Robert Louis Stevenson. *Island Nights' Entertainments* (1893). Tusitala 13.

Stevenson's only reference to this story by title is in a letter to Sidney Colvin, 3 December 1892, sending him this story and "The Waif Woman" to make up the contents of the *Island Nights' Entertainments* volume then in process of collection (*Letters, 4*, 268-69). But on 11 August 1892, commenting on the proposed contents of the forthcoming collection, Stevenson had remarked that under no circumstances did he want "The Beach of Falesá" published together with "The Bottle Imp." This latter story was, he wrote, "a story of a totally different scope and intention, to which I have already made one fellow, and which I design for a substantive volume" (*Baxter Letters*, p. 302). It is possible that "The Isle of Voices" is the "fellow" to which Stevenson referred.

Sidney Colvin received the manuscript of "The Isle of Voices" on 13 January 1893, and on 19 January he offered it to Thomas Heath Joyce, editor of *The Graphic* (letters, Princeton University Library). When Joyce could not find space for it immediately, Colvin sent the story to the *National Observer* instead, anticipating that it would bring about £120 (Beinecke 4231-36). On 24 January 1893 Charles Baxter, acting for Stevenson, contracted with Robert Fitzroy Bell of the *National Observer* fixing the price at £12 per 1,000 words for its appearance in that magazine. Bell agreed to publish the story within three weeks, to pay half the amount due on publication of the first installment, the rest when serialization was complete. On 13 February 1893, annotating the contract, Baxter noted that the story proved to be 8,293 words, the price therefore £96, and that half this sum had been paid on that date (Society of Authors Archive, British Museum, MS. Add. 56638, f. 70). On 1 February 1893 Stevenson's account with Mitchell and Baxter had been charged £1.9.2 for the typing of the manuscript; on 13 February £48.6.3 was paid into his account as the first payment from the *National Observer*; on 10 March the balance, £43.10.3, was paid in, Mitchell and Baxter having deducted their 5 percent commission (Beinecke 7268).

Stevenson did not see "The Isle of Voices" in print until he received copies of *Island Nights' Entertainments*, published in April, on 4 June 1893. He remarked then that some of the illustrations for this story by W. Hatherell were "very clever." But the illustration of the passage telling how Keola floated "in a wide shallow water, bright with ten thousand stars . . . " (p. 253 in the first English edition; the illustration faces p. 254) was mistaken. "I did say it was 'shallow,' but, O dear, not so shallow as that a man could stand up in it" (*Letters, 5*, 34). Arthur Johnstone, *Recollections of Robert Louis Stevenson in the Pacific* (1905), p. 103, quotes from the office diary of the editor of the *Pacific Commercial Advertiser* an interview with Stevenson in September 1893 in which Stevenson remarked that among his main concerns in his writings about the South Seas was to depict and analyze "the unjust (yet I can see the inevitable) extinction of the Polynesian Islanders by our shabby civilization." For this reason, Stevenson continued, "The Isle of Voices" was "not up to the mark—I left out too much of the civilized ingredient." Exactly when Stevenson wrote "The Isle of Voices" is unknown.

Probably it was during the autumn of 1892, after he sent the finished manuscript of *David Balfour* to Charles Baxter on 12 October. In her "Prefatory Note" to *Island Nights' Entertainments* (Tusitala, *13*, ix-x) Fanny Stevenson remarks that it was probably recollections of Fakarava in the Marquesas, visited aboard the *Casco* in September 1888, which inspired Stevenson in "The Isle of Voices."

THE WAIF WOMAN. Autumn 1892, possibly earlier. MS, Anderson 1914, II, 400-1: 14 pages, folio, and a typewritten copy of the MS, 25 pages, quarto. "The Waif Woman: A Cue—From a Saga," *Scribner's Magazine*, 56 (December 1914), 687-701; signed Robert Louis Stevenson. This publication includes a facsimile of the first page of the manuscript and color illustrations by N. C. Wyeth. *The Waif Woman* (London: Chatto and Windus, 1916); published 1 November 1916 in an edition of four thousand copies. Tusitala 5.

Stevenson's only reference to this story is in a letter to Sidney Colvin, 3 December 1892, where he remarks that he had hoped to publish "The Beach of Falesá" separately and make "The Bottle Imp" the *pièce de résistance* for my volume, *Island Nights' Entertainments*." Since it was now proposed to publish these two stories together, Stevenson goes on to say that he will enclose the manuscripts of two more stories, to be published along with "The Bottle Imp" in a section clearly separate from "The Beach of Falesá." These were "The Isle of Voices" and "The Waif Woman: a cue from a *saga*," and about them Stevenson remarked: "Of course these two others are not up to the mark of *The Bottle Imp*: but they each have a certain merit, and they fit in style." The next day he added, "my wife protests against *The Waif Woman* and I am instructed to report the same to you," and with his own letter he sent a letter from his wife to Sidney Colvin explaining her objections to the story (*Letters, 4*, 268-69, *5*, 5, and Beinecke 3677). Colvin, and perhaps others to whom he showed the story in London, shared Fanny Stevenson's low opinion of it; accordingly, when *Island Nights Entertainments* was published in April 1893, this story was not included.

Isobel Field, *This Life I've Loved* (1937), p. 326, recalls Stevenson's reading the story aloud at Vailima and says that "none of us cared for it very much." Of Fanny Stevenson's reaction she writes: "My mother said it showed the influence of a Swedish author Louis had been reading, and was not in his own clear, individual style." Fanny Stevenson's letter to Colvin also makes it clear that she found the story intrinsically poor and highly derivative, and as Stevenson himself noted it was not "up to the mark of *The Bottle Imp*" in any event. George S. Hellman's claims in *The True Stevenson: A Study in Clarification* (1925), pp. 217-20, are rightly dismissed in the light of all this evidence by J. C. Furnas, *Voyage to Windward* (1951), pp. 470-71, as a "masterpiece of fragile innuendo." Hellman argued that Fanny Stevenson wanted this story suppressed because in it Stevenson disclosed far too much about what Hellman believed was his extreme sense of oppression and exploitation by the womenfolk at Vailima.

"The Waif Woman," as Graham Balfour remarks, was immediately inspired by Stevenson's enthusiasm for the early volumes in *The Saga Library*, edited and translated by William Morris and Eiríkir Magnússon (5 vols., London: B. Quaritch, 1890-95); see Balfour, *Life, 2,* 144, and *Letters, 4,* 108, 158-59, 204, and *2*, 175, 177-78. But it is unknown exactly when Stevenson wrote this story. Probably it was during the autumn of 1892, after he sent the finished manuscript of *David Balfour* to Charles Baxter on 12 October. Stevenson had first asked E. L. Burlingame to send him individual volumes of *The Saga Library* a year earlier, in November 1891 (*Letters, 4,* 108).

ISLAND NIGHTS' ENTERTAINMENTS. Collected late 1892; published April 1893. Three stories, all previously published: "The Beach of Falesa" (July-August 1892), "The Bottle Imp" (February-March 1892), "The Isle of Voices" (February 1893). *Island Nights' Entertainments* (London: Cassell and Company, 1893); published 6 April 1893. American edition (New York: Charles Scribner's Sons, 1893) published 1 April 1893 but probably from uncorrected Cassell's sheets and the periodical versions. Tusitala 13.

Stevenson's original hope for republishing the stories eventually collected in *Island Nights' Entertainments* was that "The Beach of Falesá" might be published separately, "as a small volume through Cassell's and Scribner's," he wrote to Charles Baxter in October 1891 (*Baxter Letters*, p. 287). On 9 December 1891 it was agreed with Cassell and Company to publish a volume of realistic South Seas stories, including "The Beach of Falesá," under the title of *Beach de Mar*; see the entry for "The Beach of Falesá" above under date of November 1890 and Colvin to Baxter, 6 February 1892, Beinecke 4213. "The Bottle Imp," on the other hand, he intended as "the *pièce de résistance* for my volume, *Island Nights' Entertainments" (Letters, 4*, 268). It was to be "the centrepiece of a volume of *Märchen* which I was slowly to elaborate," Stevenson wrote to Sidney Colvin in January 1893, having earlier written emphatically to Charles Baxter on 17 August 1892: *"The B. of F.* is *simply not* to appear along with *The Bottle Imp*, a story of totally different scope and intention, to which I have already made one fellow [possibly "The Isle of Voices"], and which I design for a substantive volume" (*Letters, 5*, 5; *Baxter Letters*, p. 302). But on 25 February 1892 E. L. Burlingame of Charles Scribner's Sons wrote to Stevenson advising him against publishing "The Beach of Falesá" by itself (Beinecke 4148), and at the end of March he agreed to wait until he had more stories ready before seeing "The Beach of Falesá" published in book form *(Baxter Letters*, p. 295; see also p. 293).

Copyright in "The Beach of Falesá" was protected by printing the *Illustrated London News* version of the story as a separate volume in July 1892; and one proposal for the eventual volume itself was to publish that story and "The Bottle Imp" together. Even as Stevenson was expressing to Baxter his abhorrence of the idea of such a publication, Sidney Colvin was having printed and bound by Cassell and Company a volume containing these two stories, each with the original periodical illustrations by Gordon Browne and W. Hatherell respectively. This was sent to Stevenson, but even as late as 8 November 1892 Colvin was still uncertain whether Stevenson approved publication in this form (Beinecke 4225). Stevenson's copy of this trial issue is now held as Beinecke 564; a facsimile of its title page appears in the Beinecke Collection catalogue, *A Stevenson Library . . .* , facing p. 250.

On 3 December 1892 Stevenson approved publication of these two stories in the same volume, but he suggested nevertheless that "The Beach of Falesá" appear first. "Then a fresh false title," he wrote: "*Island Nights' Entertainments*; and then *The Bottle Imp*: a cue from an old melodrama. *The Isle of Voices. The Waif Woman*: a cue from a saga." With this letter he sent the manuscripts of these two latter stories and he added, anticipating the presentation of the stories eventually chosen: "Should you and Cassell's prefer, you can call the whole volume *I. N. E.*—though *The Beach of Falesá* is the child of a quite different inspiration" (*Letters, 4*, 269; see also *5*, 5). Colvin had Stevenson's letter of approval and the two additional manuscripts on 14 January 1892 and immediately began negotiations for serial publication of "The Isle of Voices" (Beinecke 4131-34). He shared Fanny Stevenson's estimate of "The Waif Woman" (see Beinecke 3677) and accordingly did not negotiate its publication or send it for the volume. Cassell and Company already had "The Beach of Falesá" and "The Bottle Imp" in type, and Colvin sent them Stevenson's corrected copy of the trial issue together with a sheet in his own handwriting giving the title page in the form it now has: "Island Nights' Entertainments / consisting of / The Beach of Falesa / The Bottle Imp / and / The Isle of Voices / by / Robert Louis Stevenson / Cassell & Co Limited / etc / " (Beinecke 564). The text of "The Isle of Voices" was probably set from sheets of the serial version published in the *National Observer* in February, eight illustrations by W. Hatherell being added, and the book itself was ready in early April. The American edition, although published on 1 April 1893 five days earlier than the English edition, was probably set from the copyright edition of "The Beach of Falesá" and the serial versions of "The Bottle Imp" and "The Isle of Voices," or from an uncorrected copy of the trial issue of the first two stories, rather than with the benefit of Stevenson's corrections to the first two stories in the trial issue he returned to Sidney Colvin; see Charles Scribner's Sons to Cassell and Company, 16 September 1892, Beinecke 5471.

"About *Island Nights' Entertainments* all you say is highly satisfactory," Stevenson had written to Colvin in the meantime, no doubt in response to Colvin's telling him that "The Waif Woman" was to be omitted and the three other stories published under the one general title. "Go in and win" (19 February 1893, *Letters, 5,* 13). Stevenson received copies of the volume on 4 June 1893, commenting only on Hatherell's illustrations for "The Isle of Voices," which he had not seen before (*Letters, 5*, 34; see the entry for "The Isle of Voices," above). And in November he told Colvin not to be disappointed with the sales of *Island Nights' Entertainments*. "Please note that 8000 is not bad for a volume of short stories," he wrote; *The Merry Men* did a good deal worse; the short story never sells" (*Letters, 5,* 83). On 1 February 1894 Charles Scribner's Sons reported to Stevenson royalty earnings on *Island Nights' Entertainments* of $496.50, being 18¾¢ per copy on 2,348 copies of the cloth edition and 3¾¢ per copy on 1,500 copies of the paper-covered edition (Beinecke 7285). Presumably these were on sales during the nine months from the date of publication through the end of 1893.

Letter to the SAMOA TIMES AND SOUTH SEA ADVERTISER. 18 November 1892. Original publication details not ascertained. Reprinted in H. J. Moors, *With Stevenson in Samoa* (1910), p. 173. Unpublished otherwise. According to H. J. Moors, Stevenson's only contribution to this paper appeared just before copies of *A Footnote to History* arrived in Samoa. In a letter dated Vailima, Nov. 18, 1892, Stevenson writes: "*Sir*: I have to ask you to find space for a correction. I have never in any of my letters to the *Times* or elsewhere, had occasion to criticise unfavourably the officers of the German Empire at this place. I am, etc., Robert Louis Stevenson."

THE GO-BETWEEN: A BOY'S ROMANCE. Begun late 1892 but never finished. MS drafts of opening two chapters, table of contents listing twelve chapters, Yale. Beinecke 5973, "Frances and Fred Archerfield," is also part of this work. Unpublished. Late in 1892, undaunted by the difficulties which had occurred over "The Beach of Falesá," Clement Shorter asked Stevenson whether he might have another story available for publication in the *Illustrated London News* the following summer. On 2 January 1893 Stevenson replied: "A story of mine of about the length of 30,000 words (my guesses are always rough) may possibly be ready, or partly ready, by next mail; it is called 'The Go-Between,' and might be lisped at a mothers' meeting" (*Letters to an Editor*, ed. Shorter, 1914, p. 3). Shorter was to apply to Charles Baxter for terms if he was interested, and about the same time Stevenson wrote to Baxter: "I am at work on a short tale, *The Go-Between*, which I estimate at 30,000 words. . . . 'Tis a prettyish tale—or should be: Haddington Coast, Whitekirk Parish, *temp* 182- , love story. As a bystander, I suggest not less than £500 for serial rights" (*Baxter Letters*, p. 292). Stevenson told Baxter that Shorter had written to him, and on 22 February 1893 Baxter wrote to Stevenson: "I have made a contract with the *London News* for *The Go-Between* at £500" (Beinecke 4041, in *Baxter Letters*, p. 327n.5). Stevenson's account with Mitchell and Baxter was charged £2.15 for the stamp on this contract on 14 February 1893 (Beinecke 7268), but the contract itself, having been canceled, does not appear to have survived.

On 14 February 1893 Sidney Colvin wrote to Baxter that he was anxious to have "the copy of the 'Go-Between' . . . in order that I may get it type-written" for the *Illustrated London News* (Beinecke 4236), and in March there appeared a note in the *Bookman*: "A short story from Mr. Stevenson's pen will commence publication in the *Illustrated London News* in July" (*Bookman*, London, *3*, March 1893, 175). But unfortunately all these transactions were in vain. As Stevenson wrote on 16 April 1893, replying to Baxter's news that he had sold the story: "I seem to have led you on the ice. . . . I have no short story ready, and I fear I am unable to prepare one for the mail. However, as I am in receipt of a letter from the editor, in which he says he will take my story, *whenever it comes*, I trust this will do no harm. I shall try to be more careful in the future" (*Baxter Letters*, p. 327). Stevenson refers to this story again on 6 June 1893 (*Letters, 5*, 36), but thereafter he seems to have abandoned it entirely.

1893

ST. IVES. January 1893-September 1894. MSS: Princeton University Library (early version, dictated to Isobel Strong at intervals 1893-94, chaps. 1-28 lacking chap. 15, 456 pp.; draft outline of contents); Yale (intermediate version, revised and copied by Stevenson from dictated MS, 1893, chaps. 1-13, 99 pp.; fragments of early and late versions; draft outlines of contents); Huntington HM 2388 (late version, revised by Stevenson from the earlier MSS, chaps. 1-19, 252 pp.): Widener Collection, Harvard University (fragment, 6 pp.); E. E. Chandler, 1925, 772 (fragment, 12 pp.; possibly absorbed into one or more of the MS holdings already listed). "St. Ives: The Adventures of a French Prisoner in England," *Pall Mall Magazine*, 10-13, thirteen monthly installments, November 1896-November 1897; all but the last three installments signed Robert Louis Stevenson, chaps. 31-36 being by Arthur T. Quiller-Couch and so signed. American serialization: *McClure's Magazine*, 8-10, nine monthly installments, March-November 1897. *St. Ives: Being The Adventures of a French Prisoner in England* (New York: Charles Scribner's Sons, 1897); published 2 October 1897. Stevenson is given as sole author on the title page; Quiller-Couch's writing of the last six chapters is explained by Sidney Colvin in an "Editorial Note," p. iii. *St. Ives: Being The Adventures of a French Prisoner in England* (London: William Heinemann, 1898); Colvin's "Editorial Note" faces the first page of the text in this edition. Tusitala 15.

"I got into *St. Ives*," Stevenson wrote to Sidney Colvin on 30 January 1893, "while going over the Annual Register for [*Weir of Hermiston*]. . . . Both [novels]. . . fall in that fated year [1814]" (*Letters, 5,* 8). This was during an attack of influenza he suffered in early January 1893, and, partly as a result of this illness, Stevenson began writing *St. Ives* by dictation to his stepdaughter Isobel Strong. "The relief is beyond description," he wrote to Colvin, "it is just like a school-treat to me and the Amanuensis bears up extraordinar'. . . . [I] really think it is an art I can manage to acquire" (*Letters, 5*, 6). According to Isobel Strong's journal entries, "Vailima Table-Talk," *Memories of Vailima* (1902), pp. 13-17, the dictation was underway by mid-January 1893, interrupted but resumed using the deaf alphabet on 16 and 18 January when Stevenson was forbidden to speak, and in progress again orally on 22 January. By the end of the month Stevenson was describing the novel as "one third drafted"—"Ten chapters are drafted and VIII recopied by me," as he wrote to Colvin—and asking Charles Baxter to have various source books sent to him promptly; to Colvin he also sent a sketch of the novel comprising twenty-nine chapters and more (*Baxter Letters*, pp. 320-21; *Letters, 5*, 8-9). Stevenson shortly left the novel aside to work on *The Ebb-Tide* and proofs of *David Balfour*; and on 19 July 1893 he described *St. Ives* as "postponed for a good few months, for I have come to one of my regular sticks in it" (*Baxter Letters,* p. 334). In fact, almost nothing was added to *St. Ives* from the end of January to late August; for when Isobel Strong again wrote of dictation, on 23 August 1893, it was with the end of chap. 11 and the beginning of chap. 12 that she and Stevenson were occupied (p. 62). Probably Stevenson dictated several more chapters, and finished his revised fair copy of the first thirteen chapters (intermediate MS, Yale), in the weeks before he left for Honolulu in mid-September 1893.

During his stay in Honolulu Stevenson seems not to have added much to the text; but he was energetic in ordering further source books for the novel, and this pattern seems to have continued after his return to Samoa in November 1893 and during the several months following (see Stevenson to Burlingame, Beinecke 2962-65, and *Letters, 5*, 112, 118, 123). By the end of January 1894 the books which he had ordered when he was in Honolulu had come—all save "the most important of all," Louis François Gille's *Les prisonniers de Cabrera: Mémoires d'un conscrit de 1808*, ed. Philippe Gille (Paris: Victor-Havard, 1892)—and by March Stevenson was again at work dictating.

"Yesterday and to-day we wrote steadily at *Anne*," Isobel Strong wrote in her journal on 10 March 1894, referring to *St. Ives* by the name of its hero (p. 73). "*St. Ives* is now well on its way into the second volume," Stevenson wrote to Charles Baxter a month later on 17 April. "There remains no mortal doubt that it will reach the three volume standard" (*Letters, 5*, 123). But in the same letter, and in another letter of about the same time to Sidney Colvin, Stevenson mentions suffering a setback as well. "I had miserable luck with *St. Ives,* " he wrote to Colvin; "being already half-way through it, a book I had ordered six months ago arrives at last, and I have to change the first half of it from top to bottom! How could I have dreamed the French prisoners were watched over like a female charity school, kept in a grotesque livery, and shaved twice a week? And I had made all my points on the idea that they were unshaved and clothed anyhow" (*Letters, 5*, 118, 124). By mid-May, remarking that *St. Ives* "still plods along: not at an alarming rate, but still so as probably to be in hand erelong," Stevenson notes that he has seventy thousand words dictated so far—some 350 pages in Isobel Strong's handwriting in the early manuscript version now at Princeton (*Baxter Letters*, p. 357).

Stevenson spent most of the summer of 1894 revising the earlier chapters, possibly then completing the revised fair copy of the first nineteen chapters now in the Huntington Library. For on 27 August 1894 Isobel Strong noted that the portion then being dictated was "the chapter about the claret-colored chaise" (p. 92), chap. 21, a point in the narrative not much later than that already reached in May. During September, Baxter having already agreed to terms of £22.11 per thousand words for publication of the novel in the *Pall Mall Gazette* (*Baxter Letters*, p. 361n.6), Stevenson continued dictating *St. Ives* but was again finding it difficult. "I'm sick of the thing as ever any one can be," he wrote to Sidney Colvin in early September, wishing he could simply lay it aside for a year and so "make something of it after all" (*Letters, 5,* 160; see also Colvin to Baxter, 13 October 1894, Beinecke 4312). And on 24 September Isobel Strong wrote in her journal: "Louis got a set-back with *Anne*, and he has put it aside for awhile. He worried terribly over it, but could not make it run smoothly. He read it aloud one evening and Lloyd [Osbourne] criticised the love-scene [chap. 28], so Louis threw the whole thing over for a time. Fortunately he picked up [*Weir of*] *Hermiston* all right, and is in better spirits at once" (pp. 96-97). *St. Ives* "ails damnably," Stevenson wrote to Baxter on 10 October; but even on 4 November, a month before he died, Stevenson was still "making a great effort to finish" *St. Ives* and hoped to send twenty-two chapters of "completed copy" soon (*Baxter Letters*, p. 370). On 26 November Stevenson acknowledged a cable from Baxter telling him that he need not hurry the completion of *St. Ives*, Baxter having arranged to delay the commencement of serial publication; accordingly Stevenson did not send the promised chapters, though he still hoped to finish the novel by year's end (*Baxter Letters*, p. 371). But on 3 December 1894 Stevenson died, leaving *St. Ives* in its present state of incompleteness and partial revision.

THE EBB TIDE. Final version written by Stevenson, February to early June 1893. Begun in Honolulu by Lloyd Osbourne, spring 1889; resumed by him in Sydney, March 1890, and taken up by Stevenson during the cruise of the *Janet Nichol*, April-July 1890, but again laid aside; resumed and completed by Stevenson alone in 1893. MS, Yale: written throughout by Stevenson and dated by him at the end 5 June 1893. Also at Yale are 3 pp. from an earlier typewritten version by Lloyd Osbourne and a duplicate of the final version of chap. 10 in his hand. "The Ebb-Tide. By Robert Louis Stevenson and Lloyd Osbourne." *To-day*, 1, thirteen weekly installments being the first thirteen issues of this magazine, 11 November 1893-3 February 1894. *The Ebb-Tide: A Trio and Quartette* (London: William Heinemann, 1894); published 21 September 1894. The subtitle appears in the MS, although not in the English serial version. Lloyd Osbourne is in all instances listed as joint author. American serialization: *McClure's Magazine*, six monthly installments, February-July 1894. *The Ebb Tide: A Trio & Quartette* (Chicago: Stone and Kimball, 1894); published 15 July 1894 probably from uncorrected *McClure's Magazine* sheets. Tusitala 14.

Stevenson and his stepson Lloyd Osbourne contracted in 1888 to supply the novel which—after five years, three separate periods of writing, and two intermediate titles—Stevenson finished alone, as *The Ebb-Tide*, from

February to June 1893. On 19 March 1888 S. S. McClure brought to Saranac Lake the proprietor of the New York *Ledger,* Robert Bonner, and before the end of the month a bargain had been struck. As Stevenson's mother wrote to Charles Baxter in late March: "Lloyd and Louis are engaged to write a story for the *New York Ledger*, a sort of American *London Journal* of a highly moral order. The proprietor is a very wealthy man, who wishes to raise the literary tone" (*Baxter Letters*, p. 325). The sum agreed upon was one thousand pounds, which Stevenson found it "rather handsome" of S. S. McClure to offer to pay five years later, when the story was finally ready but the *Ledger* no longer interested (*Baxter Letters*, p. 325; see also Beinecke 5206, 4220, 4046, 4258; McClure seems actually to have paid six hundred pounds for the serial rights). During the next two months in 1888 Stevenson and Osbourne tried out and abandoned at least two possible tales, "Fighting the Ring" and "The Gaol Bird," in pursuit of this commission. See the entries for those works above.

Not until after the cruise of the *Casco* in 1888-89, however, was the novel which became *The Ebb-Tide* actually begun—by Lloyd Osbourne at Honolulu, sometime during the spring of 1889. Osbourne wrote three chapters, Stevenson read them with great enthusiasm—"he fairly overflowed toward those early chapters," Osbourne told Graham Balfour (*Life, 2*, 33)—and, thus encouraged, Osbourne carried the first draft of the work, then called *The Pearl Fisher*, forward. By his own later account, *An Intimate Portrait of R.L.S.* (1924), p. 98, Osbourne "reached the end of the present book" in his draft, the intention then being to make this only the prologue to an even longer tale. "Then the commendation ceased," Osbourne continued: "try as I would I could not please RLS; I wrote and rewrote, and rewrote again, but always to have him shake his head. Finally at his suggestion and in utter hopelessness I laid the manuscript by, hoping to come back to it later but with greater success. But I never did" (p. 98).

Lloyd sent the unfinished manuscript with his sister Isobel Strong when she left Honolulu for Sydney in June 1889; and during the next eight or nine months—aboard the *Equator*, at Apemama, and at Samoa—the collaborators occupied themselves with *The Wrecker*. This was to be the first of three "South Sea Yarns" on which he and Lloyd Osbourne would collaborate, Stevenson wrote in October 1889, the other two being *The Pearl Fisher* (i.e., *The Ebb-Tide*) and a third work, *The Beachcombers,* which was never written. *The Pearl Fisher*, he added, "part done, lies at Sydney" (*Letters, 3*, 269). On his way to Sydney, in February 1890, Stevenson remarked that Lloyd's share of *The Pearl Fisher* was "half done," his own "not yet touched" (*Letters, 3*, 289). Once arrived, Lloyd seems to have taken up the draft again (see Beinecke 5812, Isobel Strong to Mrs. Thomas Stevenson, 7 March 1890). But Stevenson himself does not seem to have taken it up at all until the cruise of the *Janet Nichol*, April-July 1890.

"I have two huge novels on hand—*The Wrecker* and *The Pearl Fisher*, in collaboration with my stepson," he wrote from Sydney on 19 August 1890, a month after that cruise: "The latter I think highly of, for black, ugly, trampling, violent story, full of strange scenes and striking characters." And on 1 September he noted that he had "a good part of *The Pearl Fisher* (O, a great and grisly tale, that!) in MS." (*Letters, 3*, 309, 313). "This forced, violent, alembicated style is most abhorrent to me," Stevenson wrote in 1893 when he was writing the final draft; "it can't be helped; the note was struck years ago on the *Janet Nichol*, and has to be maintained somehow" (*Letters, 5*, 27). Exactly how much Stevenson wrote in 1890 is unclear. In November 1891 he referred to the novel as "about a quarter done" (*Letters, 4*, 177), but this was before the plan of making it a very long novel was abandoned. Graham Balfour says that the manuscript when Stevenson returned to it in 1893 consisted of "ten or eleven chapters" (*Life, 2*, 143), so perhaps Stevenson added as many as five chapters in 1890.

However much or little was actually written during the cruise of the *Janet Nichol*, obviously that cruise did contribute details to *The Ebb-Tide*. Attwater's accumulation of salvage, called "a whole curiosity-shop of sea-curios" in chap. 8, and the ship's figurehead incongruously set up on land, chap. 14, both existed in counterpart at the white trader's house on Penrhyn, where the *Janet Nichol* called, 9-10 May 1890; and Penrhyn itself, mentioned as the original home of one of Attwater's deceased workers (chap. 8), was a pearl island. See Fanny Stevenson's description in her diary, *The Cruise of the "Janet Nichol"* (1914), pp. 55-56; a striking photograph of the figurehead taken by Lloyd Osbourne faces p. 56. (Sidney Colvin suggest that Attwater is to some extent based on Stevenson's friend A. G. Dew-Smith; see Colvin's *Memories and Notes of Persons and Places*, 1921, pp. 125-27, 138.)

After the summer of 1890 Stevenson left the novel aside for almost two and a half years. Although he did refer to it twice during that interval (see *Letters, 4*, 117, 168), Stevenson did not work on the novel between 1890 and February 1893. On 4 October 1890, Robert McClure executed an agreement with Stevenson and Lloyd Osbourne to pay forty pounds each on the day of publication for *The Pearl Fisher* (ultimately published as *The Ebb-Tide*) and *The Wrecker*, and to divide equally with them the proceeds of serial publication (Society of Authors Archive, British Museum, MS. Add. 56638, ff. 61-62). Possibly this was for the Continental rights, a payment on *The Wrecker* of this kind having been made by the McClures; but in any event it was superseded by later arrangements.

Stevenson returned to *The Ebb-Tide* again in February 1893. "During the last week the Amanuensis was otherwise engaged," he wrote on 19 February 1893, having begun dictating *St. Ives*, "whereupon I took up, pitched into, and about half demolished another tale, once intended to be called *The Pearl Fisher*, but now razeed and called *The Schooner Farallone*" (*Letters, 5*, 13). As Graham Balfour writes: "Stevenson, talking to me one day, produced the unfinished draft of the story, which at this time included only the first ten or eleven chapters, and debated what course he should pursue. The fragment was originally intended as a prologue; Attwater was to be blinded with vitriol and then return to England. The remainder of the action of the book was to take place in England, and chiefly in Bloomsbury, where the Herricks lived. Stevenson now reconsidered the whole question, accepted a shorter ending, and grew more and more interested in the character of Attwater, as he worked it out" (*Life, 2,* 143). Stevenson may have had the manuscript with him at Sydney in March, and he may have worked on it upon his return to Samoa in early April; but probably he left the work aside entirely between his initial burst of writing and change of title and general plan, in February, and the last week of April 1893.

On 12 May 1893 Stevenson writes that he is "grinding singly at *The Ebb-Tide*, as we now call the *Farallone*," and he notes that in the last three weeks he has "only struggled from p. 58 to p. 82" (*Letters, 5,* 24). During the next three weeks Stevenson's letters contain almost a page-by-page commentary on his trials with the last three chapters of the novel (*Letters, 5,* 24-28, 32-38). Ten chapters were dispatched on 23 May, and by early June Stevenson was finished. "Well, it's done," he wrote on 5 June 1893, the same date as appears at the end of the manuscript. "Those tragic 16 pp. are at last finished, and I have put away thirty-two pages of chips, and have spent thirteen days about as nearly in Hell as a man could expect to live through" (*Letters, 5,* 35).

Sidney Colvin, disappointed with the first ten chapters when he received them on 22 June, received the last two chapters on 21 July and found them "done with astonishing genius" (Beinecke 4256; see also 4251-55). Nevertheless he continued to think the novel too grim to appear in book form except at some cost to Stevenson's reputation (Beinecke 4291, 4255, 4395-97), and in November Stevenson agreed to let book-form publication wait (*Letters, 5,* 84; see also *5,* 77-78). When he received sheets of the version serialized in *To-day*, 11 November 1893-3 February 1894, however, Stevenson found himself extremely pleased with it. "I did not dream it was near as good; I am afraid I think it excellent," he wrote to Colvin in February (*Letters, 5,* 114; see also Colvin to Baxter, 2 April 1894, Beinecke 4278). The book rights were sold in May, and Stevenson sent the corrected sheets back to England with the Rev. Sidney R. Lysaght; Sidney Colvin received them from him on 22 May 1894 (Beinecke 4057, 8270, 8251-55, 4292-93). Stone and Kimball, Chicago, published the American edition on 15 July 1894, probably from the version in *McClure's Magazine* although they may have had Stevenson's corrections during the last month before publication (see Beinecke 8253-55, 4303). William Heinemann and Company published the English edition on 21 September 1894, almost certainly from Stevenson's corrected sheets of the version published serially in *To-day*; Sidney Colvin would have read the proofs.

Two payments for the serial rights to *The Ebb-Tide* are listed in the Mitchell and Baxter account books, both received from S. S. McClure: £200 each paid on 1 November 1893 and 21 February 1894, both sums reduced to £190 in actual proceeds to Stevenson by Mitchell and Baxter's deduction of 5 percent. Presumably this was for English serialization in the magazine *To-day*, later payments for American serialization not being recorded: the surviving account books end at 11 July 1894. On 26 April 1894, McClure's office quoted to Stone and Kimball, Chicago, a price of £600 cash for the American book-form rights to *The Ebb-Tide*, and presumably this was accepted. Through 11 July 1894, total proceeds from the novel are listed at

£950, a figure consistent with assuming that £400 came from McClure and £600 from Stone and Kimball, Mitchell and Baxter deducting 5 percent from both sums. See the account books, Beinecke 7268, and the correspondence, Beinecke 8270 and 8251.

Although in *An Intimate Portrait of R.L.S.* (1924) he wrote that he carried the draft "to the end of the present book" (p. 98), Lloyd Osbourne's contribution to *The Ebb-Tide* actually extended only through the sixth chapter, and is significant only in the first four chapters. Surviving fragments of his typescript (Beinecke 6181) are from chaps. 5 and 6, and there is no evidence that he wrote any more than this, the MS of chap. 10 in his hand (bound in Beinecke 6179) being merely a transcription. As Stevenson wrote in August 1893: "He [Lloyd] has nothing to do with the last half. The first we wrote together, as the beginning of a long yarn. The second [chaps. 7-12] is entirely mine. . . . Up to the discovery of the champagne [chap. 5], the tale was all planned between us and drafted by Lloyd; from that moment he has nothing to do with it" (*Letters, 5*, 77, 79). Graham Balfour quoted Osbourne to similar effect: the first four chapters, said Lloyd, "remain, save for the text of Herrick's letter to his sweetheart, almost as I first wrote them. . . . [The] end of *The Ebb Tide* (as it stands) I never even touched" (*Life, 2*, 33-34).

FABLES. Final versions 1893-94; begun as early as 1874. MSS untraced except "The Clockmaker" (5 pp. numbered 15-19) and "The Scientific Ape" (4 pp. numbered 22-25), Yale. *Longman's Magazine*, 26 (August 1895), 362-79, and 26 (September 1895), 472-89; both installments signed Robert Louis Stevenson. "The Touchstone" was published separately in *McClure's Magazine*, 6 (February 1896), 300-3. *The Strange Case of Dr. Jekyll and Mr. Hyde With Other Fables* (London: Longmans, Green, and Company, 1896); published 16 March 1896. American edition, *Fables* (Charles Scribner's Sons, 1896), published 26 September 1896. Tusitala 5, 2. Stevenson worked on his *Fables* over the course of twenty years; see the entry under date of summer 1874. On 31 May 1888 he contracted with Longmans, Green, and Company for a collection of them, but other projects intervened and Stevenson's own contract was eventually superseded by one made after Stevenson's death by Charles Baxter on 4 February 1896; see Beinecke 6204, 7216, and Sidney Colvin's "Prefatory Note" (Tusitala, *5*, 77-78). Of Stevenson's work in early 1893 Graham Balfour writes: "The fables begun before he had left England [August 1887] and promised to Messrs. Longman [1888], he attacked again, and from time to time added to their number" (*Life, 2*, 143). Elsewhere Balfour lists the *Fables* as "begun" in 1887 (*Life, 2*, 220). Stevenson's fair copy of his *Fables*, of which the manuscripts listed above seem to be part, may have been made earlier, but he was at work on and probably further revised these twenty short pieces in 1893-94 as well. Further on the 1896 publication of them see Beinecke 3685-86, 7273, and 8182.

DEATH IN THE POT. Outlined early 1893 but apparently never written. MS outlines, Yale. Unpublished. Stevenson's only reference to this story by title is in a letter to Sidney Colvin, 6 June 1893. He remarks that among several stories he is likely to have ready soon is one called "Death in the Pot." He expects that it will be "a deal shorter" than half as long as *The Ebb-Tide* and remarks of its ending that it is "an ungodly massacre." In his note to this letter Sidney Colvin adds that it was to be "a tale of the Santa Lucia mountains in California." See *Letters, 5*, 36. This is clear also from Stevenson's outlines. One is headed "Death in the Pot" and is followed by notation of a prologue and six chapters, four of which have titles (Beinecke 6146). The other is headed "An Indian Brew" and then, beneath this, "Death in the Pot," and comprises a list of eleven chapter titles: The forest fire; The maid of the brook; Sandy Bairnsfather; The return of the adventurers; Mutiny at Point Pescado [Pescadero?]; The Señora's preparations; Father Mark till the yacht comes; The cavalcade; Bairnsfather in retirement; Barnisfather the drink and the antidote; Mark in the Palace Hotel [San Francisco] (Beinecke 6147). Probably it was to "Death in the Pot" that Stevenson referred in an interview published in the *Australian Star*, 4 March 1893. Among his current projects he mentioned "a short narrative of the California Coasts ten years ago" (quoted in George MacKaness, *Robert Louis Stevenson: His Associations with Australia*, 1935, p. 128).

Contributions to THE PRESBYTERIAN (SYDNEY). March 1893. MSS untraced. Publication details not ascertained. According to a clipping identified as from *The Presbyterian*, 1 April 1893, pasted in one of his mother's scrapbooks: "Mr. Stevenson has favoured the Presbyterian with five articles in all, each of which passed under his own eye and was corrected by his own hand before it was given to the public" (Monterey State Historical Monument Stevenson House Collection, California, vol. 5, p. 155; xerox, Yale). Only one of these articles, "Missions in the South Seas," has been reprinted; see the next entry. All were written during Stevenson's visit to Sydney in March 1893 and published there in *The Presbyterian* during March and April. J. C. Furnas, *Voyage to Windward* (1951), p. 537n.35, quotes five sentences from a luncheon speech which Stevenson gave to ministers attending the General Assembly of the Presbyterian Church of New South Wales in Sydney that month. Furnas cites *The Presbyterian Monthly*, 1 April 1893, but it is not clear whether this is a separate article or a reprint of one of the five articles originally published in *The Presbyterian*.

MISSIONS IN THE SOUTH SEAS. March 1893. MS untraced. *The Presybterian* (Sydney), 18 March 1893. Published from his own transcription of this article (NLS) by Graham Balfour, *Life, 2*, 193-95, but not otherwise reprinted. According to the prefatory note printed with this article in *The Presbyterian*, Stevenson's mother read this article to a meeting of the Women's Missionary Society and members of the General Assembly of the Presbyterian Church of New South Wales at Sydney in March 1893.

Stevenson was unable to read it himself due to illness. See the clipping of this article in Stevenson's mother's scrapbooks, Monterey State Historical Monument Stevenson House Collection, California, vol. 5, pp. 152-53; xerox, Yale. See also the previous entry.

ROSA QUO LOCORUM. March 1893. MS, Princeton University Library: "Random Memories. Rosa Quo Locorum." Written on the versos of eight leaves of stationery of the Union Club, Sydney. Edinburgh Edition, 21 (1896), 302-12. Tusitala 30. Stevenson probably began this essay during his stay in Sydney, March 1893, then left it aside when he returned to Samoa in April. He may have drawn upon it in late 1894 for the essay "Early Memories," begun with a view toward a second series of essays for *Scribner's Magazine*. But neither essay was ever finished. See the entry of "Early Memories" below under date of October-November 1894.

THE OWL. April 1893. MS untraced; a facsimile of the first page of the MS appears as the frontispiece of vol. 26 (1923) of the Vailima Edition. Vailima Edition, 25 (1923), 359-74. Tusitala 16. After his return from Sydney in April 1893, according to Graham Balfour, Stevenson began a story for the *Illustrated London News*. "He had lately been reading again Barbey d'Aurevilly, and his mind had turned to Brittany. The new tale dealt with the Chouans in 1793, and was to be called *The Owl*. But it did not prosper . . . and when one chapter had been written, he gave up the attempt and took up a half-finished piece of work [the final version of *The Ebb-Tide*]" (*Life, 2*, 142-43). In March 1892 Stevenson had asked to have *Le Chevalier des Touches* (1864) and *Les Diaboliques* (1874) sent to him; both in 1884 and in 1894 he writes of his great pleasure in these and other fantastic tales by Jules-Amédée Barbey d'Aurevilly (1808-89). See *Letters, 2*, 295, *4*, 170, and *5*, 35-36, 111. But his only reference to this story is in a letter to Sidney Colvin, 6 June 1893, where he mentions "The Owl" as one of several stories he may have ready soon. He expects it to be perhaps "half as long" as *The Ebb-Tide* and adds that it "only ends well in so far as some lovers come together, and nobody is killed at the moment, but you know they are all doomed, they are Chouan fellows" (*Letters, 5*, 36). After his work on it in April 1893, however, Stevenson seems never to have returned to this story.

MY FIRST BOOK: *TREASURE ISLAND*. Spring or early summer 1893. MS, Edith B. Tranter, 1952, 486: 8 pp. folio. *The Idler*, 6 (August 1894), 2-11; signed Robert Louis Stevenson. Also in the United States: *McClure's Magazine*, 3 (September 1894), 283-93. *My First Book* . . . , ed. Jerome K. Jerome (London: Chatto and Windus, 1894). Stevenson's contribution appears on pp. 297-309. Tusitala 2.

Stevenson seems to have to agreed to write this essay, which appeared last in the series of twenty-two such essays by noted authors of the day which

Jerome K. Jerome published monthly in his magazine *The Idler* from 1892 to 1894, sometime during the spring of 1893. Stevenson's account with Mitchell and Baxter shows charges for photographs taken at Pitlochry and Braemar for an article on *Treasure Island* on 31 March, 3 April, and 20 April 1894, the total charges being £2.17; and on 12 April £2.19 was paid in by S. S. McClure to clear these charges (Beinecke 7268). McClure was also in correspondence about terms for the article in May 1893 (Beinecke 5207). Stevenson probably wrote it during the spring or (most likely) the early summer, after finishing *The Ebb-Tide* in early June.

On 1 January 1894 Stevenson suggested to Charles Baxter that he might write prefaces for several volumes in the Edinburgh Edition then just proposed: "I have written a paper on *Treasure Island*, which is to appear shortly," Stevenson wrote, and he had another on *The Master of Ballantrae* "drafted" (*Letters, 5*, 108). But Sidney Colvin and Baxter both strongly opposed the idea, Colvin remarking in a letter to Baxter on 7 February 1894 which Baxter forwarded to Stevenson: "As to . . . explanatory prefaces, for God's sake let there be none of them. . . . The thing he has just written about *Treasure Island* would simply destroy the interest of the book, to any intelligent or imaginative reader, if it appeared by way of preface" (*Baxter Letters*, pp. 346-47). Accordingly Stevenson abandoned the idea, though not before revising his note on *The Master of Ballantrae* and beginning one on *Kidnapped*; see the entries of these two works below under date of early 1894. When the Edinburgh Edition was eventually published, after Stevenson's death, his various prefaces and notes, including this essay on *Treasure Island*, appeared in vols. 21 and 28, separate from the works to which they referred. M.R. Ridley, *TLS*, 28 August 1959, p. 495, points out that the misreading "a volume of logic stories" in the third paragraph of this essay—actually they were "bogie" stories—remained uncorrected until the Edinburgh Edition.

THE SLEEPER AWAKENED. June 1893. MS, Anderson 1914, I, 378: 4 pp., folio. "The manuscript starts off as a play, with a duet in the first scene, but on the last leaf is a list of chapter headings that would suggest a different treatment of the subject." Unpublished. Stevenson's only reference to this projected play or story is in a letter to Sidney Colvin, 6 June 1893, where he remarks that among several stories he is likely to have ready soon is one called "The Sleeper Awakened." He expects it to be perhaps "half as long" as *The Ebb-Tide*, but except for saying that it ends "reasonably well" Stevenson discloses nothing about it. Annotating this letter Sidney Colvin writes: "Of *The Sleeper Awakened* I know nothing." See *Letters, 5,* 36. Possibly this work is related to, or another version of, the untitled beginning of a play, Beinecke 6722, entered below under Additional Works.

HEATHERCAT. July 1893-summer 1894. MS, outlines of contents, notes, and source books, Yale. Edinburgh Edition, 26 (1897), 87-118. Tusitala 16.

Stevenson's first mention of this unfinished novel is in a letter to Charles Baxter, 19 July 1893. He lists three novels as in prospect: *The Killing Time, The Justice-Clerk* (i.e. *Weir of Hermiston*), and *The Young Chevalier*. But then he deletes the reference to the first of these to say only that he has "another" novel in prospect besides these two—lest saying more would only prepare "fresh disappointments for you" (*Baxter Letters*, p. 334 and n.). He asks Baxter to send him various source books on late seventeenth-century Scottish history, however, as he does again on 6 December 1893 when he also outlines the novel to Baxter and asks him to clear up several legal points. "This is for . . . *Heathercat*," he writes then, "whereof the First Volume will be called *The Killing Time* . . . [and] the Second Volume *Darien*" (*Letters, 5*, 91; see also Baxter's reply, 22 January 1894, Beinecke 4049, and G. P. Johnston to Baxter, 9 January 1894, Beinecke 5010). "All my weary reading as a boy, which you remember well enough, will come to bear on it," Stevenson wrote to his cousin Bob on 17 June 1894. *Heathercat* "is an attempt at a real historical novel, to present a whole field of time; the race—our own race—the west land and Clydesdale blue bonnets, under the influence of their last trial, when they got to a pitch of organisation in madness that no other peasantry has ever made an offer at." He would have called the whole novel *The Killing Time* had not S. R. Crockett just preempted the title (*Letters, 5*, 134). Another discarded title was *The Sweet Singer*, on which see *Baxter Letters*, p. 334n. Stevenson does not appear to have worked on *Heathercat*, however, after the summer of 1894, turning instead to *St. Ives* in late August and *Weir of Hermiston* again in late September.

Letter to THE PALL MALL GAZETTE: WAR IN SAMOA. 4 September 1893. See the combined entry for all of Stevenson's letters on Samoan affairs under the date of 10 February 1889, above.

Letter to the PACIFIC COMMERCIAL ADVERTISER. 6 October 1893. MS owned by Philip Spalding, Jr., in the collection of Hawaiiana left him by his mother. *Daily Pacific Commercial Advertiser* (Honolulu), 7 October 1893, p. 2. Reprinted with a facsimile of the original in: Arthur Johnstone, *Recollections of Robert Louis Stevenson in the Pacific* (1905), pp. 108–9; Eleanor Rivenburgh, "Stevenson in Hawaii—III," *Bookman,* New York, 46 (December 1917), 458; Honolulu *Advertiser,* 20 November 1970, p. A–17; and in Martha M. McGaw, *Stevenson in Hawaii* (1950), pp. 130–31.

On stationery of the Sans Souci Seaside Resort, Honolulu, Stevenson writes on 6 October 1893: "Will you allow a harmless sick man, who has just made out eight days of sickness here, to express his amazement and wholesale disapproval at the nickname recently tacked upon it in the papers: A Disorderly House?" The only thing disorderly at the Sans Souci, Stevenson writes, was the telephone which, two nights earlier, was "bleating like a deserted infant from the nigh dining room" when the ship *Adams* "was demanding her Chief Engineer." He has been entirely pleased during his stay.

SPEECH TO THE SCOTTISH THISTLE CLUB, HONOLULU. Delivered mid-October 1893. MS untraced. Original publication details not ascertained, but probably the report and partial text of Stevenson's speech which he corrected and expanded to make the text as published by Arthur Johnstone first appeared in the *Pacific Commercial Advertiser*, Honolulu, immediately after the speech itself was given in mid-October 1893. Published in full, from the newspaper version "personally revised and corrected" by Stevenson before he left Honolulu on 27 October 1893, in Arthur Johnstone, *Recollections of Robert Louis Stevenson in the Pacific* (1905), pp. 114-19; see also pp. 137-38. Otherwise unpublished. In his speech Stevenson informally reviewed "the long brawl which is Scottish history," especially during the eighteenth century. Scottish history offers little that is not "desperately cruel and brutal," he remarked in conclusion. "Yet there was something good, and this is the beautiful songs and ballads of Scotland," above all as these were summed up in the work of Sir Walter Scott.

Note to THE MASTER OF BALLANTRAE. Late 1893; revised early 1894. MSS: Silverado Museum, St. Helena, California (first draft; revised draft, pp. 1-6); Huntington HM 20535 (revised draft, pp. 7-8). Stevenson's first draft consists of three untitled leaves from a quarto notebook, slightly more than 4 pp. of text written in pencil; Graham Balfour has supplied the title "History of the Master of Ballantrae." Stevenson's revised draft consists of 4 folio leaves, 7½ pp. of text written in ink and titled by him "Note to 'The Master of Ballantrae.'" Both versions of the essay are unfinished. Stevenson's first draft was published from a transcription by Graham Balfour (NLS), Edinburgh Edition, 21 (1896), 297-302, where it was retitled "The Genesis of 'The Master of Ballantrae.'" Five paragraphs from Stevenson's revised draft were published in the Bibliophile Society volume, *Hitherto Unpublished Prose Writings* (1921), pp. 63-70, and from this source in the Vailima Edition, 26 (1923), 479-81. In both these publications, the material is titled as in the MS, "Note to 'The Master of Ballantrae,'" but the text consists only of those passages from pp. 1-6 of Stevenson's revised draft for which there is not some counterpart in the first draft. In the Vailima Edition no explanation is given of the location of the passages in the MS and the first two paragraphs, which are from two different places in the MS, are run on without marks of excision. The last two pages of Stevenson's revised draft were published in Elsie Noble Caldwell, *Last Witness for Robert Louis Stevenson* (1960), pp. 117-19. Tusitala 10, which includes only the material previously published in the Edinburgh and Vailima editions.

Stevenson's only reference to this short essay is in a letter to Charles Baxter, 1 January 1894, about the Edinburgh Edition then just proposed. He remarks that during the next six months he could spend some time in "revising the text [of his works] and (if it were thought desirable) writing prefaces." He has written an essay on *Treasure Island*, "which is to appear shortly," and he has one "drafted" on *The Master of Ballantrae* (*Letters, 5*, 108). Stevenson obviously refers here to his first draft of this essay, which therefore must have been written some time before the end of 1893, exactly when is unknown. His revised draft would have been written sometime early in 1894. For on 26 March 1894 Stevenson replied to a letter from Baxter, written the month before, in which Baxter concurred with and enclosed Sidney Colvin's emphatic condemnation of the idea of writing prefaces for the Edinburgh Edition. Stevenson said nothing about this matter in his reply, nor did he refer to it later: he seems simply to have abandoned the idea. See *Baxter Letters*, pp. 346-47. See also the next entry and the entry for "My First Book: *Treasure Island*" (summer 1893), above.

1894

Note to KIDNAPPED. Early 1894. MS, Huntington HM 2410: 1 leaf, written in ink, on paper identical with that used in the revised draft of the "Note to *The Master of Ballantrae*." The text breaks off abruptly in mid-sentence at the foot of the page; one or more additional leaves must therefore be missing. W. H. Arnold, "My Stevensons," *Scribner's Magazine*, 71 (January 1922), 65. Unpublished otherwise. Stevenson undoubtedly began this short essay on the genesis of *Kidnapped* early in 1894 at the same time as he was revising his similar essay on *The Master of Ballantrae*. See the previous entry.

Letter to THE TIMES: THE DEADLOCK IN SAMOA. 23 April 1894. See the combined entry for all of Stevenson's letters on Samoan affairs under date of 10 February 1889, above.

Letter to THE TIMES: MR. STEVENSON ON SAMOA. 22 May 1894. See the combined entry for all of Stevenson's letters on Samoan affairs under date of 10 February 1889, above.

[History of the Indian Mutiny.] Planned August 1894. MS untraced. Unpublished. The only surviving record of this composition appears in Graham Balfour's discussion of various uncompleted projects, *Life, 2*, 144: "In the August before he [Stevenson] died, he drew up with Mr. Osbourne the outline of a history, or of a series of the most striking episodes of the Indian Mutiny, to be written for boys, and he sent home for the books necessary for its execution." See also *Letters, 5*, 150, 153, and the entry of the novel on this subject which Stevenson and Lloyd Osbourne once planned, "The White Nigger" (April-May 1888).

[English grammar.] Planned ca. 1894. MS untraced if written. Unpublished. The only surviving record of this plan appears in Graham Balfour's discussion of various uncompleted projects, *Life, 2*, 144-45: "Another day he [Stevenson] sketched the plan of an English grammar, to be illustrated by examples from the English classics."

ADDRESS TO THE SAMOAN CHIEFS. October 1894. MSS, Yale. Published from a newspaper account Stevenson sent to Sidney Colvin, *Letters, 5*, 190-95, and earlier from the same source: partially in *Bookman*, 7 (London, February 1895), 136; complete as "Robert Louis Stevenson's Address to the Samoan Chiefs," *McClure's Magazine*, 5 (July 1895), 173-76. Unpublished otherwise except in editions of Stevenson's letters. Stevenson comments at length on this speech in a letter to Sidney Colvin, 6 October 1894 (*Letters, 5*, 171-72). As he wrote to Alison Cunningham on 8 October: "I helped the chiefs who were in prison; and when they were set free, what should they do but offer to make a part of my road for me out of gratitude? Well, I was ashamed to refuse, and the trumps dug my road for me, and put up [an] inscription on a board. . . . We had a great feast when it was done and I read them a kind of lecture" (*Letters, 5*, 174-75).

LETTER TO J. F. HOGAN ON SAMOAN AFFAIRS. 7 October 1894. See the combined entry for all of Stevenson's letters on Samoan affairs under date of 10 February 1889, above.

EARLY MEMORIES. October-November 1894. MS, Anderson 1914, I, 390; Blackwell's Catalogue 896 (Oxford, 1970), 229, untraced thereafter. Three leaves containing "reminiscences of childish days . . . small close writing, in ink, 2½ pages, each 11½ by 8½ ins." (Blackwell). Typewritten copy, Yale. Quoted in Balfour, *Life, 1*, 50-51, but otherwise unpublished. Probably this MS represents a start on the essay which on 9 October 1894 Stevenson agreed to write for a possible second series of essays in *Scribner's Magazine* to appear in 1895. See the exchange of letters with E. L. Burlingame, 22 May-9 October 1894 (Beinecke 2966-67, 4155-56), quoted above in the entry of "An Onlooker in Hell" (late 1890). See also the entry of "Rosa Quo Locorum," upon which Stevenson may have drawn for this essay, under date of March 1893.

ADDITIONAL WORKS

PROLOGUE: AT MONTE CARLO. MS, Beinecke 6588: 10 pp., folio. Unpublished. A facsimile of the first page of the manuscript appears in George S. Hellman, *The True Stevenson: A Study in Clarification* (1925), facing p. 156. Headed "Prologue: At Monte Carlo," the manuscript contains the beginning of a story about "John Carton . . . a young man (as they call it) of some promise" who "had shown aptitude for everything." But for want of any real guidance his life is now in disarray.

ARCHIBALD USHER. MS, Beinecke 7075: six lines of prose in ink, probably from a notebook. Unpublished. The text, apparently the beginning of a story, reads: "Upon a particular Monday morning in November of the year 1865, Mr Archibald Usher, Writer to the signet sat in his [pretty dreary; both words deleted] office, full of bitter thought. Mr Usher had justly [?] speculated of late days, and his speculations had been . . . "

ON TIME. MS, Lloyd Osbourne, 1914, 591: 1 p., folio. Vailima Edition, 24 (1923), 34-35. Tusitala 25. Possibly related to "Child's Play" (1878).

ON MORALITY. MSS, Beinecke 6677-78. Vailima Edition, 24 (1923), 36-37. Tusitala 26.

[The weak and the strong.] MS, Beinecke 7105: 3 double folio leaves, making a 12-page set, pages 12½ inches by 8 inches, watermarked "A Cowan & Sons / LOFT DRIED / Record Foolscap." Unpublished. Pages 5-9 are occupied with the headings for chaps. 1 and 2 of an untitled work. Chap. 1 is titled "The Weak and the strong." Chap. 2 is titled "The characters of men." Each title is followed by something over a dozen maxims, one of which from chap. 1 Graham Balfour quotes without mentioning its source, *Life, 1*, 160: "Acts may be forgiven; not even God can forgive the hanger-back." The first page of the manuscript contains a list of eighteen questions ("Shall I be rich?" etc.); the last page is headed "The Catspaw" and contains the outline of a novel, discussed in the next entry; also on the last page are eleven lines of verse beginning "The indefatigable Schiff." This material may be related to "Lay Morals" (1879, 1883).

THE CATSPAW. MS outline, Beinecke 6086. Unpublished. A list of twelve chapters, apparently for a novel, headed "The Catspaw." Eleven of the twelve chapters have titles, e. g. "The Shipwrecked Mariner." Written on the last page of the manuscript described in the previous entry.

[On the value of books and reading.] MS, Anderson 1914, II, 351: 1 p., quarto. Unpublished. As quoted in the catalogue of this sale, the MS reads in part: "So in reading books, a strong boy can learn something of what it is to be a weak boy, and a boy of what it is to be a girl, and a son of what it is to be a father or a mother, and the young of what it is to be old. Only a little, the more is the pity; but it is just by means of that little that we can be kind and good. Of these two things, the information and the moral that can be got out of books, the second is far the more important. Information is easily forgotten. . . . But the moral is of use all through." Possibly related to "The Morality of the Profession of Letters" (1881). See especially the middle part of that essay, Tusitala, *28*, 55-58.

DIOGENES IN LONDON. DIOGENES AT THE SAVILE CLUB. MSS sold as lots 151-52, David Gage Joyce collection, Hanzel Galleries, Chicago, 23 September 1973: "Diogenes in London" (incomplete), 7½ pp., octavo, numbered 28-35; "Diogenes at the Savile Club," 3½ pp., octavo. Photographs of 1 page of each MS are laid into copies of the printed versions, Beinecke 711, 715. A fragment of the MS of "Diogenes in London" containing the last 4 lines is tipped to the last text page in Beinecke 712. Beinecke 714 is a page proof of the printed version of "Diogenes at the Savile Club" giving December 1920 as the date of publication. *Diogenes in London* (San Francisco: Edwin and Robert Grabhorn for John Howell, 1920). *Diogenes at the Savile Club* (Chicago: Frank M. Morris, printed by Edwin and Robert Grabhorn, for David G. Joyce, June 1921). Published from these sources, Vailima Edition, 26 (1923), 7-15, 15-18. Tusitala 5. The satirical handling of such writers as Matthew Arnold, Mary Elizabeth Braddon, Besant and Rice, Gilbert and Sullivan, and Oscar Wilde suggests a date in the early 1880s.

THE BEACON BELL. MS outline, Gerhardt, 1915, 83: 2 pp. pencil list of chapter headings in a small quarto notebook. MS untraced if written. Unpublished. Graham Balfour lists "The Beacon Bell" in notebook RLS / D / 48, under date of 1883, in the notebook he kept while writing his biography of Stevenson (NLS 9903). But this work is otherwise unknown.

ROBIN RUN-THE-HEDGE. MS, Anderson 1914, II, 356: 8 pp. folio. MS outline of six chapters, Beinecke 7063. Both under the title of "Tribulations of one Mr Baskerfield of Singleton St Marys and his ward Robin Rutledge." Vailima Edition, 26 (1923), 9-11, being the first chapter of this work, probably the only chapter written. Tusitala 16. Stevenson referred twice to a work called *Robin Run-the-Hedge*, both times lamenting that he had to give it up when the title was preempted by another. In a letter to Adelaide Boodle, 1 September 1890, he mentioned among unfinished manuscripts "*Robin Run-the-Hedge*, given up when some nefarious person pre-empted the name" and said that it consisted then of (he thought) three chapters (*Letters, 3,* 312–13). Sixteen months before, on 27 April 1889, he asked Charles Baxter to register the name *The Pearlfisher*—for the novel ultimately published as *The Ebb-Tide*—lest it be preempted: "I have a dreadful fear someone will burk the name, as has happened to me once before with *Robin Run-the-Hedge*" (*Baxter Letters*, p. 246). Stevenson refers to Annette Lyster's *Robin-Run-the-Hedge* (1884), but more precise information as to when in the early 1880s Stevenson began this work is lacking.

[Civilization, law, public sentiment, etc.] MS, Beinecke 6098. Unpublished. Draft material, 46 lines of prose, attacking the recently expressed view that "to take the side of society even against dynamiters, is to be 'lacking in taste, lacking in heart, lacking in perception, lacking in magnanimity.'" Probably this material was written in the middle 1880s, possibly in response to the Fenian dynamite outrages of 1884. Compare the dedication of *The Dynamiter* (1885).

THE IDEAL HOUSE. MS, Anderson 1914, II, 369: 4 pp., folio. Edinburgh Edition, 28 (1898), 42-47. Tusitala 25. Graham Balfour, *Life, 2*, 218, lists this unfinished essay among works of 1884. George E. Brown, *A Book of R.L.S.* (1919), p. 125, says that it was written "at Davos in 1880 or 1881 (*aet.* 30)." Neither gives reasons for his choice of date, although Balfour's seems relatively the more probable.

[Imaginary dispatches.] MS, Beinecke 6516 and other numbers: 7 leaves, quarto, from a notebook. Unpublished. Stevenson's manuscript contains the text of five imaginary and satirical news reports. (1) In a letter dated "Leopoldville, May," Henry M. Stanley reports "the steady and increasing success of our 'Free State'"—chiefly, the letter implies, by the liberal use of bullets. Stevenson refers to the Congo Free State, brought into existence on 5 February 1885 by Leopold II of Belgium. (2) "The Supposed Death of Duke de Jenkins" consists of only eight lines of prose, contradicting rumors of Jenkins' death by citing an advertisement praising a certain tea in which one testimonial was his. (3) In a letter dated "Cannibal Islands, March 1885," Banzaboo, Prime Minister of His Majesty, requests advice. He and his people have eaten one lot of missionaries, who had converted them from drinking mint julep or punch to drinking morning cocktails. But now a second lot has arrived, condemning cannibalism and cocktails alike. Banzaboo wishes to know whether these new missionaries or the former ones are the impostors. (4) "American Pirates Trades Union" is the heading given a report of a meeting in New York at which it was said that British writers and publishers were now insisting that "if we want books we must pay for 'em (groans)." Stevenson may refer obliquely to the American Publishers' Copyright League, formed by the major American publishers including Charles Scribner's Sons in 1887. Stevenson supported its aims, especially the enactment of copyright laws protecting British authors in America, but many believed that it would only drive up the prices of books to the reader. (5) "Unconfirmed Rumors" is the heading given five short reports of recent events, including the meeting of American pirates and a report that the Mahdi has bought the Sudan railway "and intends running tourist trains in conjunction with T. P. Cooke [i.e. Thomas Cook]." Stevenson probably wrote these imaginary dispatches in the middle or late 1880s, but despite their topicality no more precise date than this can be assigned to them.

STORY OF A RECLUSE. MS, NLS. First sold as Anderson 1914, II, 387: 7 pp. originally in a small quarto notebook which also contained "The Enchantress" and an early outline of *The Master of Ballantrae. Hitherto Unpublished Prose Writings* (1921), pp. 102-8, and from this source, Vailima Edition, 25 (1923), 301-8. Tusitala 16. Probably this beginning of a story dates from the late 1880s, possibly from Stevenson's stay at Saranac Lake, New York, from October 1887 through April 1888.

THE GOLDENSON MYSTERY. MS photostats, Yale, Silverado Museum, St. Helena, California: typescript by Lloyd Osbourne, 6 pp., comprising the first chapter of a detective novel set in San Francisco. Original typescript untraced. Unpublished. Lloyd Osbourne was probably sole author of this work, on which he may have hoped to collaborate with Stevenson. It begins with the discovery of the strangled body of Charles George Goldenson, chief cashier of the National Securities Bank, in his apartment at 606 Jackson Street. Jim Clarke, the messenger boy who discovers the body, summons the police, and he and Sergeant Hogan discover that besides having been strangled, Goldenson has had his hand cut off, possibly in the fierce struggle which has obviously occurred. This work was no doubt begun at Saranac Lake sometime between October 1887 and April 1888.

THE LAST OF THE YEOMEN. MS photostats, Yale, Silverado Museum, St. Helena, California: typescript by Lloyd Osbourne, 9 pp., comprising three chapters of an unfinished, possibly comic, novel. Original typescript untraced. Unpublished. Lloyd Osbourne was probably sole author of this work, on which he may have hoped to collaborate with Stevenson. It begins with the young Sir Arthur deWinton's uncle Bobstock about to die, and Sir Arthur unfortunately pestered by the immensely friendly young pickle manufacturer John Hobbs, whom uncle Bobstock actually seems to prefer to his nephew. This work was no doubt begun at Saranac Lake sometime between October 1887 and April 1888.

THE ETHICS OF CRIME. MS, Beinecke 6199. Vailima Edition, 24 (1923), 274-78. Tusitala 26. References to Arthur Balfour as Irish Secretary date this essay as not earlier than 1887. Stevenson wrote at length on Irish affairs in "Confessions of a Unionist" (January 1888). Possibly this material is contemporary with that essay.

THE ENCHANTRESS. MS, Anderson 1914, II, 387: 27 pp. in a small quarto notebook which also contained "Story of a Recluse" and an early outline of *The Master of Ballantrae*. Sold as a separate MS, American Art Galleries, 18 April 1923, lot 885; a facsimile of the first page of the MS appears in the catalogue of this sale. Unpublished.

According to Lloyd Osbourne, this story "was written on a yacht when each of the whole party had to write a story and read it aloud to the whole company a la Boccacio. RLS never attached the slightest importance to it" (Osbourne to Benjamin H. Stern, photostat, Stevenson-Osbourne family papers, Bancroft Library, University of California). On a page originally in another notebook than the one which contained this story Stevenson wrote a list of four titles under the general heading "Strange Marriages" (MS, Silverado Museum, St. Helena, California). The first is "The Enchantress," the second "The Road to Gretna Green," a story otherwise unknown and subdivided into two parts, "My lord and his tutor" and "Unexpected guests." The third title, originally "Prince Amadeus," Stevenson altered simply to "Gotthold," the fourth is "The Doctor." It is unclear when this list was made, but after these four stories Stevenson then listed "Journal of a Cruise in Polynesia" and "Northern Lights," early titles of works better known as *The South Seas* and *Records of a Family of Engineers*. On the other side of the page on which this list is written begins Stevenson's pencil draft of his "Note to 'The Master of Ballantrae.'" Unfortunately, little more can be gathered about the date of "The Enchantress" from this information than that it was probably, though not certainly, written sometime between mid-1888 and the late summer of 1890, when Stevenson took up residence in Samoa.

As the first page of the manuscript shows, the story was at first titled "A Singular Marriage." This title was then deleted in favor of the present one. According to the 1923 auction catalogue, it tells "the adventures of a penniless man and a rich heiress in a foreign country" and seems to be "the first outline draft of this short story, which is full of action, with a brilliant denouement." It is written in the first person and opens with the protagonist, evidently a gambler, quite out of money and any further possessions to pawn, sitting on a bench in the casino grounds at Clermont considering his position "gravely." In subject-matter the story thus resembles the essay "An Onlooker in Hell," entered above under date of late 1890 or early 1891. George S. Hellman had the manuscript at one time, was refused permission to publish it, and seems to have kept a typescript of it, which he still had in the early 1950s (Hellman memorandum, Beinecke 7239).

THE CASTAWAYS OF SOLEDAD. MS, Anderson 1914, I, 381. *The Castaways of Soledad* (Buffalo, N. Y.: privately printed for Thomas B. Lockwood, 1928). Beinecke 6072 is a carbon copy of the typescript used in preparing this edition. Unpublished otherwise. Stevenson's manuscript consists of three complete chapters and one page of the fourth chapter of this story. The first three chapters are titled: I. In the launch; II. The Isle of Solitude; III. The Landing. The story was begun sometime before or during 1891 and then abandoned that year when H. Rider Haggard's *Eric Brighteyes* was published. In an undated letter to Haggard thanking him for sending him a copy of the novel, Stevenson remarked that Haggard and Hall Caine had both recently anticipated his ideas and so "the tale of the Castaways of Soledad lies forever castaway itself" (Sotheby sale, 29 May 1961, lot 213).

MATTHEW DAVENTRY. MS, Beinecke 6572. Unpublished. This manuscript comprises a first person narrative by Captain Daventry of events in 1721 and 1722, evidently the beginning of a novel. Chap. 1, "His Voyage With Captain Scott," is complete. Chap. 2, possibly titled "Fits out a sloop from Barbadoes," breaks off after a few paragraphs. After the first page Captain Scott's surname is always Blythe, and it is so corrected everywhere on p. 1 except in the chapter title. The handwriting suggests a date in the 1890s.

[Untitled play.] MS, Beinecke 6722. Eleven pages comprising Act I, scenes i-iv of an untitled play. It concerns, as G. L. McKay writes in the Beinecke Collection catalogue, *A Stevenson Library. . .* , p. 1934, "a young Englishman who was sent to Samoa by his rich uncle to find and bring back to England a girl whom the uncle had adopted many years before." Possibly this is a dramatic treatment of the story called "The Sleeper Awakened," entered above under date of June 1893. It may also be related to the scenario, "Less than Kith and More than Kind," Beinecke 7290, chiefly written by Fanny Stevenson but with two preliminary pages by Stevenson.

STEVENSON'S COMPANION TO THE COOK BOOK: ADORNED WITH A CENTURY OF AUTHENTIC ANECDOTES. MS, Anderson 1914, II, 394: 24 pp. folio, the first 15 in Stevenson's hand, the rest typewritten, titled "Sham Anecdotes." Beinecke 6515-16 and 6949 are probably MSS derived from this collection of "Sham Anecdotes," the original collection having been broken up to sell the various parts separately. Graham Balfour's transcription, presumably of the whole "Sham Anecdotes" MS, is headed "'A Companion to the Cook Book,' written apparently on the 'Casco'" (NLS) and contains the whole text later published. Vailima Edition, 26 (1923), 177-201. Tusitala 5.

Graham Balfour may be correct that this series of anecdotes was begun during the cruise of the *Casco*, June 1888-January 1889. But Stevenson probably kept adding to the series throughout his time in the South Seas. On 26 March 1894 he wrote to Charles Baxter that S. S. McClure was publishing for Fanny Stevenson "a series of articles" which he and Fanny intended later to put out as a book. "It is really a cookery book," Stevenson wrote, and he wished McClure reprimanded for leaving out the recipes: "he has published the plums and left out the cookery" (*Baxter Letters*, pp. 348-49). Two books of recipes by Fanny Stevenson survive, one in the Silverado Museum, St. Helena, California, the other at Yale (Beinecke 7287). In addition, there survives a list of contents giving the titles of fourteen or fifteen chapters for a work to be called "Ramblings of a Housewife," originally "Ramblings of a Kitchenmaid," written in Stevenson's hand but clearly to be based on Fanny's experiences. The first draft of this list is in the Bancroft Library, University of California; the fair copy, written on the same notebook paper as the draft, is now held as Beinecke 7297. Possibly it was for this work that "Stevenson's Companion to the Cook Book" was intended.

Index